# THE MASSES ARE REVOLTING

## VICTORIAN CULTURE AND THE POLITICAL AESTHETICS OF DISGUST

### ZACHARY SAMALIN

CORNELL UNIVERSITY PRESS

*Ithaca and London*

First published 2021 by Cornell University Press

Library of Congress Cataloging-in-Publication Data

Names: Samalin, Zachary, author.
Title: The masses are revolting : Victorian culture and
   the political aesthetics of disgust / Zachary Samalin.
Description: Ithaca [New York] : Cornell University
   Press, 2021. | Includes bibliographical references and
   index.
Identifiers: LCCN 2021007667 (print) | LCCN 2021007668
   (ebook) | ISBN 9781501756467 (hardcover) |
   ISBN 9781501756474 (epub) | ISBN 9781501756481 (pdf)
Subjects: LCSH: Aversion—Great Britain—History—
   19th century. | Aversion—Social aspects—Great
   Britain—History—19th century. | Aversion—Political
   aspects—Great Britain—History—19th century. |
   Aversion in literature.
Classification: LCC BF575.A886 S26 2021 (print) |
   LCC BF575.A886 (ebook) | DDC 152.4—dc23
LC record available at https://lccn.loc.gov/2021007667
LC ebook record available at https://lccn.loc.gov/
   2021007668

*For Sonali*

# Contents

# ACKNOWLEDGMENTS

For nearly a decade I have been trying to get my friends, family, students, and colleagues to be excited by heinous, unspeakable things, and I am grateful to them all for their patience, their extraordinary generosity, and, more often than I would have dared to hope, their appetite for the disgusting. Thanks first and foremost are due to my colleagues and students at the University of Chicago, who have encouraged the development of this book over the last six years. Special thanks are due to Frances Ferguson for sharing her truly singular knowledge of the obscene with me, and to Maud Ellmann for her inimitable lessons on writing like a rat. I have been lucky to have Heather Keenleyside, Jo McDonagh, Benjamin Morgan, and Sianne Ngai as interlocutors right down the hall, and to have the opportunity to conduct my research alongside a group of inspiring graduate students—Amanda Shubert, Matt Boulette, Madison Chapman, Kevin King, Julia Rossi, and Rebeca Velasquez. I've also learned a great deal from the talented undergraduate students in my seminar The Literature of Disgust, and I'm especially grateful to Siri Lee and Sophie Hoyt. Thanks as well to the Franke Center for the Humanities for support during a year of research leave, and to Jim Chandler, Patrick Jagoda, and Salomé Aguilera Skvirsky for their feedback during that crucial year. It is hard to say just how much my thinking on affect has been changed and sustained by conversations with Lauren Berlant, for which I will remain extremely grateful long after I have put disgust behind me. Elaine Hadley helped me to transform this project into a book, offering guidance, wisdom, support, encouragement, vision, criticism, and friendship at every step of the way—a simple thank-you doesn't even begin to cut it.

This book was born in New York City, but it grew up in Chicago, where it fell in with a group of absurdly brilliant friends who have managed to keep both it and me alive and kicking since 2013. Life-sustaining thanks to Daniel Borzutzky, Kate Broitman, Adrienne Brown, Corey Byrnes, Alexis Chema, Pete Coviello, Harris Feinsod, Leah Feldman, Andy Ferguson, Na'ama Rokem, and Itamar, Alma, and Yasmin Francez; Rachel Galvin,

Edgar Garcia, Adom Getachew, Tim Harrison, Florian Klinger, Anna Korn-bluh, Jon Levy, Emily Licht, Kim O'Neil, Julie Orlemanski, Gerard Passan-nante, David C. Simon, Justin Steinberg, Sarah Pierce Taylor, and Tristram Wolff. I single out Nasser Mufti and Chris Taylor for helping me survive the nineteenth century no less than the twenty-first, often with assists from Alicia Christoff, Nathan Hensley, Grace Lavery, Ben Parker, and Emily Stein-light. As always, I have the deepest love and admiration for my friends back home, who guided me through those early years and have stuck with me since: Ariel Aberg-Riger, Sari Altschuler, Liakos Ariston, Inbal Austern, Gabe Boylan, Nathanael Brotherhood, Lindsay Caplan, Mike Frank, Lauren Hall, Julia Jarcho, Rowena Kennedy-Epstein, Zeke Reich, Jay Boss Rubin, Chris-tine Smallwood, Mark Sussman, Vasiliki Touhouliotis, Charlie Wittenberg, and especially Jonah Westerman. I've been lucky to have Ben McKay in my life on the long haul from Baltimore to Chicago. Jonathan Goldberg has been a friend, mentor, and inspiration since I first met him at Johns Hopkins in 2003, and in a very fundamental way this book would not have been possible were it not for him and his writing.

I remain grateful to the faculty and staff of the doctoral program in English at the City University of New York, Graduate Center, where I was a student when the ideas for the project first took root. Talia Schaffer has been an ardent supporter, a meticulous reader and interlocutor, and a source of inexhaustible knowledge. I hope the following pages speak to the ways in which Joshua Wilner's writings on internalization have continued to inform my own about expulsion. John Brenkman has been a friend, a mentor, and an invaluable interlocutor for over a decade; if there are moments of insight or clarity in this book he is most likely responsible for them.

I also thank Mahinder S. Kingra, Jennifer Savran Kelly, and Bethany Wasik at Cornell University Press for shepherding my manuscript through the pub-lishing process with such keen insight and attention, and for keeping things moving smoothly along even during these dark, turbulent times. Likewise the indefatigable librarians working in adverse conditions at the University of Chicago Library. I'm grateful to audiences at New York University, North-western University, the University of Michigan, and the University of Penn-sylvania for their incisive feedback. I thank the American Council of Learned Societies for material support, and the Humanities Division of the University of Chicago as well as the City University of New York, Graduate Center for making available publication subvention funds.

As I comb through my finished manuscript in 2020, it is startling to realize how many of the ideas in this book I can trace back to a handful of brief but intense conversations I had with Eve Kosofsky Sedgwick in the winter and spring of 2009, in the months just before her death. I had drawn up a list of texts about disgust and nineteenth-century literature for my orals based on our conversations, but Eve passed away before I ever took the exam. Even so, she has continued to influence my thinking—about emotion and affect, about sexuality, and about the enduring relevance of the nineteenth century to our own times—every step of the way, and there are whole sections of this book which appear at least to me as attempts to address questions that she initially helped me to pose.

Before that, it is not easy to pinpoint when an interest in disgust and the disgusting first began to consume me, though all indications point to early childhood, and so my extremely generous family—Joan Shulman, Alan Samalin, and Danielle Samalin—are responsible for the cultivation of this project in ways that are difficult to calculate and even harder to acknowledge. At the other end of things, my daughter Niloufer arrived very late to this party, but she has already more than made up for lost time.

Sonali Thakkar came into my life while I was wading knee-deep into Charles Darwin's vomit, and I know for certain I would have sunk back into the muck of my own doubts and remained submerged there among my half-digested ideas were it not for Sonali's clarity of vision and the precision of her thought. She has read and reread every page of this book, and I have not stopped being inspired by her brilliance and grateful for her companionship and love. Somehow there is almost a decade of our life in this book, and I dedicate the whole mess of it to her.

# THE MASSES ARE REVOLTING

# Introduction
## Of Origins and Orifices

Late in 1867, Charles Darwin sent out a questionnaire titled "Queries about Expression" to a group of scientific contacts and personal acquaintances scattered throughout the world. An important piece of preliminary research for Darwin's 1872 book, *The Expression of the Emotions in Man and Animals*, the document consisted of seventeen questions concerning the way that people around the world expressed their emotions. "Is astonishment expressed by the eyes and mouth being opened wide and by the eyebrows being raised?" it reads. "Does shame excite a blush, when the colour of the skin allows it to be visible? . . . Is extreme fear expressed in the same general manner as with Europeans?"[1] Darwin's hypothesis, which continues to influence and to organize the psychological study of the emotions today, was that certain emotions were biologically innate and universal and thus would be expressed in like manner by all human faces across the globe. "Observations on natives who have had little communication with Europeans would be of course the most valuable," the end of the questionnaire reads, "though those made on any natives would be of much interest to me" (fig. 1). Darwin wove the responses he received into the text of *The Expression of the Emotions in Man and Animals*, where he argued that their "remarkable uniformity" was "evidence of the close similarity in bodily structure and mental disposition of all the races of mankind," including those he deemed the "savage races of man."[2]

With this goal of demonstrating the universality of emotions in mind, the questionnaire urged respondents to try to stick to the observable facts of what they saw, and to avoid generalization. "General remarks on expression are of comparatively little value," it explains. "A definite description of the countenance under any emotion or frame of mind would possess much more value." However, many of the replies to "Queries" fell far short of Darwin's proposed empirical standard, and often reflected little more than the racial prejudice and violence of the colonial setting in which the observations were made. For example, the Scottish botanist John Scott, whom Darwin had helped to secure a post as curator of the Royal Botanic Garden in Calcutta, wrote to Darwin of the difficulty in distinguishing shame from fear among natives, since their behavior was motivated by "the brute-like dread of corporal punishment and not the susceptibilities of a moral nature." In "native faces," Scott goes on, "really there is very little expression at all . . . but there is sometimes slyness and vindictiveness very evidently indicated."[3]

Though Darwin used their responses as evidence of the universality of emotions, his respondents tended not to agree with his insistence on the fundamental physical and psychological similarity between all human beings. Writing from within the spaces of colonial domination, some argued that certain kinds of emotional behavior were too culturally complex for non-European people and so did not exist within allegedly primitive societies. "Indeed, I do not think such semi-civilised races as those on which I am making the observations are capable of manifesting such a calm pensive melancholy as that indicated in your query," Scott responds to Darwin's question about grief. "Though enthusiastically demonstrative within the range of animal passions," he elaborates, "they are in general lamentably wanting in the higher characteristics of our race." In this view, emotions are not innate or universal modes of response shared by all humans but rather acquired cultural protocols that are distributed unevenly, according to a measure of something called "civilization" that was related but not quite reducible to racial difference. The term is inherently ambiguous, but ubiquitous. "Whatever be the characteristics of what we call savage life," John Stuart Mill hedged in 1836, "the contrary of these, or the qualities which society puts on as it throws off these, constitute civilization."[4] Just as there were alleged to be civilized and savage peoples, there were deemed to be civilized and uncivilized emotions. These uncivilized emotions were universal, but according to the circular reasoning and race thinking inherent to this view, the mark of civilization—of modernity and progress as well as of sensibility and refinement—lay in the "higher" capacity to overcome or to resist such "animal passions," as Scott calls them.

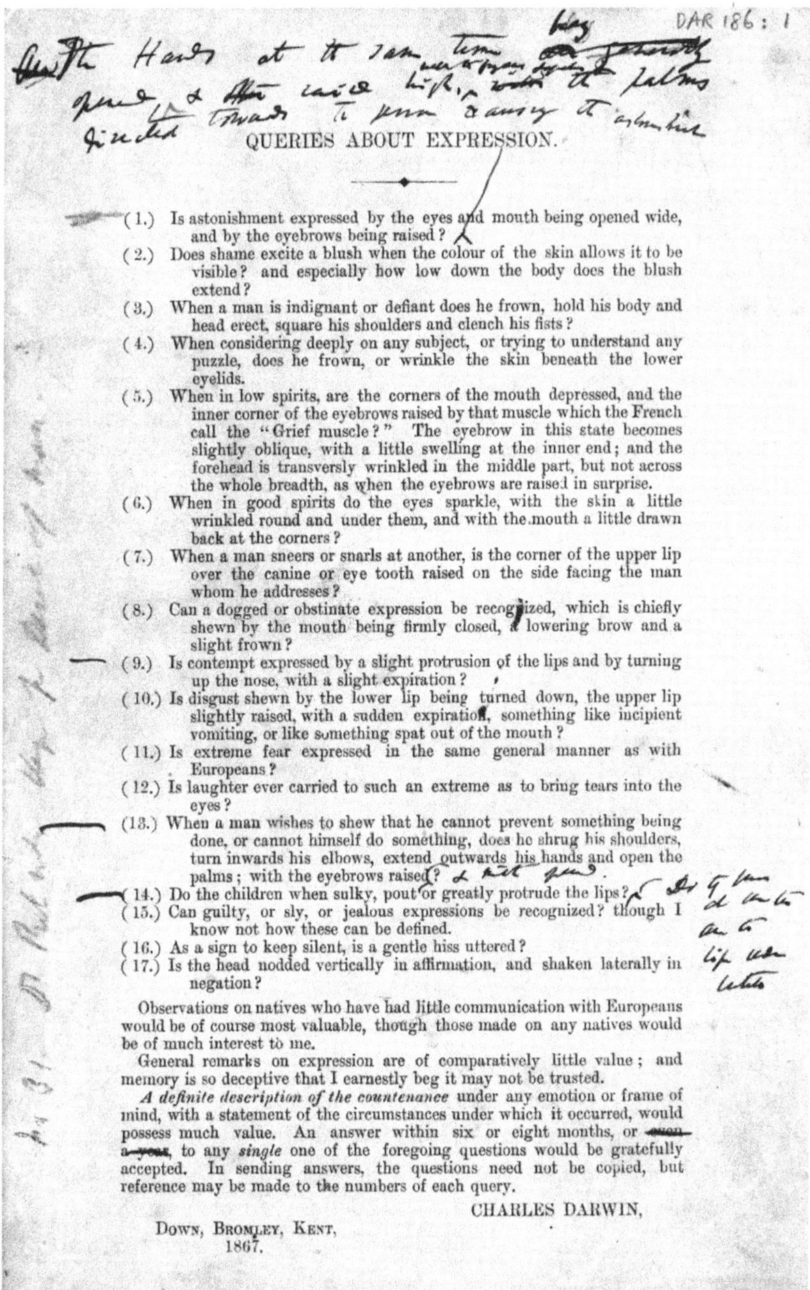

*[handwritten notes at top of page]*

# QUERIES ABOUT EXPRESSION.

(1.) Is astonishment expressed by the eyes and mouth being opened wide, and by the eyebrows being raised?

(2.) Does shame excite a blush when the colour of the skin allows it to be visible? and especially how low down the body does the blush extend?

(3.) When a man is indignant or defiant does he frown, hold his body and head erect, square his shoulders and clench his fists?

(4.) When considering deeply on any subject, or trying to understand any puzzle, does he frown, or wrinkle the skin beneath the lower eyelids.

(5.) When in low spirits, are the corners of the mouth depressed, and the inner corner of the eyebrows raised by that muscle which the French call the "Grief muscle?" The eyebrow in this state becomes slightly oblique, with a little swelling at the inner end; and the forehead is transversly wrinkled in the middle part, but not across the whole breadth, as when the eyebrows are raised in surprise.

(6.) When in good spirits do the eyes sparkle, with the skin a little wrinkled round and under them, and with the mouth a little drawn back at the corners?

(7.) When a man sneers or snarls at another, is the corner of the upper lip over the canine or eye tooth raised on the side facing the man whom he addresses?

(8.) Can a dogged or obstinate expression be recognized, which is chiefly shewn by the mouth being firmly closed, a lowering brow and a slight frown?

(9.) Is contempt expressed by a slight protrusion of the lips and by turning up the nose, with a slight expiration?

(10.) Is disgust shewn by the lower lip being turned down, the upper lip slightly raised, with a sudden expiration, something like incipient vomiting, or like something spat out of the mouth?

(11.) Is extreme fear expressed in the same general manner as with Europeans?

(12.) Is laughter ever carried to such an extreme as to bring tears into the eyes?

(13.) When a man wishes to shew that he cannot prevent something being done, or cannot himself do something, does he shrug his shoulders, turn inwards his elbows, extend outwards his hands and open the palms; with the eyebrows raised?

(14.) Do the children when sulky, pout or greatly protrude the lips?

(15.) Can guilty, or sly, or jealous expressions be recognized? though I know not how these can be defined.

(16.) As a sign to keep silent, is a gentle hiss uttered?

(17.) Is the head nodded vertically in affirmation, and shaken laterally in negation?

Observations on natives who have had little communication with Europeans would be of course most valuable, though those made on any natives would be of much interest to me.

General remarks on expression are of comparatively little value; and memory is so deceptive that I earnestly beg it may not be trusted.

*A definite description of the countenance* under any emotion or frame of mind, with a statement of the circumstances under which it occurred, would possess much value. An answer within six or eight months, or ~~even a year~~, to any *single* one of the foregoing questions would be gratefully accepted. In sending answers, the questions need not be copied, but reference may be made to the numbers of each query.

CHARLES DARWIN,

Down, Bromley, Kent,
1867.

**FIGURE 1.** Charles Darwin's questionnaire "Queries about Expression." Darwin wove the responses he received into the text of his 1872 book, *The Expression of the Emotions in Man and Animals*. Reproduced by kind permission of the Syndics of Cambridge University Library (DAR 186: 1).

It is easy to dismiss this civilizational ideology as an artifact of Victorian imperialism, with its plain basis in racism and self-serving pseudoscientific argument, but it is more difficult to measure its concrete effects on the formation of modern culture. This data was, after all, the foundation upon which the psychological theory of emotions was erected. How easily could the scientific substance of emotions be extracted from the civilizational ideology that was its raw material? What was left behind, and what carried forward, in the process of universalizing emotions? Such questions are not faced by historians of psychology alone. The apportionment and distribution of the alleged capacity for affective expression informed a far wider range of nineteenth-century social practices, from colonial policy to public works projects to the production of scientific knowledge across a variety of emerging disciplines. Not just psychology but all the new social sciences of the late nineteenth century—sociology, anthropology, and economics alike— shared in precisely this presupposition that the capacity for complex emotion expression was unevenly distributed throughout the world and could therefore be held up as a token of racialized civilizational difference. My point is not merely to critique Victorian culture's racial, sexual, and class prejudices but to think about how those prejudices—and more specifically the emotional discourses that underpinned them—came to organize knowledge and to structure social experience in unexpected and as yet unexamined ways. Tracking the entanglement of the discourse of emotion with the ideology of civilization therefore quickly opens up broader vistas of the rapidly transforming nineteenth-century lifeworld. And to the extent that the social world remains organized in pronounced ways by the concrete as well as the ideological structures of the nineteenth century, we remain saddled today with the baggage of Victorian civilizational thinking and its conflicted presumptions about the uneven distribution of the emotions.

This book reconstructs the singular, outsized role played by one particular emotion—disgust—within this wide-ranging and still-unfolding nineteenth-century drama of civilizational ideology, social transformation, and the universalization of emotion. Although it is often denigrated as a low emotion, disgust has had a tendency to turn up in unexpected places, connecting disparate areas of social life. Darwin's sources allow us to observe disgust's composition in particular. Unlike many of the other emotion expressions the survey asked about, in the case of disgust Darwin's informants concurred overwhelmingly with his characterization: "the lower lip being turned down, the upper lip slightly raised, with a sudden expiration, something like incipient vomiting, or like something spat out of the mouth."[5] In the reflexive recoiling of disgust, Darwin did seem to have identified a form of affective response whose universality was indisputable; it was in many respects the epitome of a low, animal passion. Yet even if disgust was deemed universal, it nonetheless sat in a contradictory relationship to the nineteenth century's civilizational ideology. For if disgust was an uncivilized emotion, it was also an important medium through which the claims of civilization were articulated. Indeed, where there is talk of civilization, or invocation of the tenuous attainments of culture, the appeal to disgust—with its churning stomach, gaping mouth, and pinched, recoiling nose—is never too far off.

In his response to the survey's question about disgust, Scott stages what Darwin describes in *Expression* as a "graphic scene" of coerced ingestion.[6] Though the scene raises more questions than it answers, it can nonetheless serve as an emblem of the discourse of disgust. "A servant of mine of rather delicate constitution and to whom I had thus frequently to prescribe . . . Castor-oil," Scott writes, "which he most cordially detested—used thus to express his disgust":

> The sight of the bottle indeed was quite enough to make him shudder and shrug his shoulders. When I handed it him he would open his mouth, with an eructation of wind and spasmodic backward with short rapid horizontal shakings of the head: then he would shudderingly put it to his lips, smell and withdraw with a shrug a few horizontal paralytic shakes of the head, firmly closed teeth with lips somewhat opened (or rather by the turning up and down of lips as you express it) and eyes obliquely upturned (avoiding the sight of oil) with a lowering brow and a disposition to vomit. I have seen disgust thus strongly pronounced frequently both in administering medicines to natives and in observing Hindoos of high caste coming contact in proximity [*sic*] to a defiling object &c.[7]

Scott describes a series of reflex actions, but those actions are so thoroughly embedded in the scene of colonial domination that it is difficult to know where one ends and the other begins. This indissolubility is central to the character of disgust. On the one hand, the expression of disgust appears here as a paradigmatic image of physiological mechanism—as a spasming, shuddering, paralytically quivering body that quasi-instinctively resists the incorporation of an unwanted object. On the other hand, these putatively reflexive behaviors are also described in unmistakably social terms that link the present scene to a matrix of presumptions about defilement and purification, and about caste status and cultural difference. Even while Scott describes disgust as a set of mechanistic reactions, he has preemptively yoked the emotion to structures of religious belief and scientific knowledge. Indeed, the emotion seems to offer a kind of ersatz knowledge, Scott suggests, as though your disgust *already knows* what it dislikes, what is pure and impure.

Not only is this confusion of physiological, moral, and cultural registers typical of descriptions of disgust in the middle of the nineteenth century, but it is in a sense one of the primary functions that has been assigned to the emotion historically—it is captured, for example, by a 1999 psychological study, which refers to disgust as "the body and soul emotion."[8] Disgust, on this account, is an emotion that collapses boundaries between body and soul, low and high, sweeping up bad smells, spiritual defilement, and moral infraction in a messy compound of repudiation and expulsion. But what Scott depicts is not merely the imbrication of the body's ordinary autonomous functioning with cultural categories, but rather an implicit judgment about that imbrication. We come to know the emotion's slippery character only within the frame of civilizational coercion and disapprobation. That is, Scott characterizes his servant as a person in thrall to a body that is crucially ignorant of the difference between poison and medicine, between superstition and knowledge, between individual preference and necessity, and at the most fundamental level, between what is to be resisted and what is to be taken in; hence he must be induced to take his medicine against his wishes. In this regard, we might say that Scott characterizes disgust as an emotion in need of discipline. It is, we are led to understand, an unruly affect, one that cannot be trusted to make sound judgments—and therefore one that needs to be excluded or overcome.

In the following pages, I place this nineteenth-century discourse of disgust within a wider historical and conceptual arc, one that reaches back into the eighteenth century as well as forward into the twentieth and toward the present. For the last three hundred years, modern European culture has been utterly fixated with its own disgust—the way you might pick fixatedly at a scab while reading a book. Although the experience of being disgusted might seem unambiguous in its capacity to pass forceful judgments about things felt to be too vile or too gross to stomach, the meaning of that experience has, by contrast, invited continuous rumination and provoked critical analysis from a range of different and often opposing perspectives. Zooming out from the Darwinian moment, we find that in the second half of the eighteenth century disgust was the focus of heated debate among German and British philosophers working in the new field of aesthetics, where the repulsive was taken to be the antithesis of the beautiful; now, in the first decades of the twenty-first century, the philosophers are joined by neuroscientists, who conduct brain scans of the insula, seeking to elucidate the primal nature of our revulsion. In between, both disgust and the disgusting have served as rich subject matter for artists and writers, psychoanalysts and evolutionary biologists, existentialists and Marxists; for sociologists, literary critics, legal theorists, and anthropologists alike. Disgust has been anatomized, anaesthetized, and operated on; theorized, dramatized, evoked, and regurgitated. For all the clarity we might feel in the revolted heat of the moment when, whatever else might be true, we are certain we are *not* going to eat *that*, the life of this emotion in modern discourse has been characterized by an anxious need to continually discover and rediscover its meaning that belies the unambiguousness the emotion arrogates to itself.

This book does not offer another theory about why people (and evidently only people) get disgusted, nor does it attempt to answer the well-worn question of whether the experience of disgust represents a kind of evolutionary hangover from the primordial past of the species. Neither does it provide an intellectual history of the different philosophical theories of disgust, repulsion, aversion, and nausea produced since the Enlightenment, though it certainly engages those theories. Instead, it starts from the premise that the meaning of our affective experiences is decided not in the illumination of the brain or the churning of the stomach, but in the grammar of our social existence. It asks what disgust has meant to particular people and a particular society at a certain cultural-historical moment, rather than what disgust means for the human being in some universal sense; and it looks to find answers to that question in concrete environments, such as sewers and courtrooms, novels and military bunkers, laboratories and alleyways. It takes it as a given that, however universal or evolutionarily hardwired our affective experiences may turn out to be, the meanings and values we assign to them are culturally and historically contingent, and can change, even drastically, over time. Unearthing a crucial moment in the history of disgust, it asks what role this emotion has played in the production of various aspects of modern culture.

However, precisely because it has been so heavily theorized for so long, disgust presents a special kind of problem for writing the history of emotions; its history in theory cannot be easily separated from its history in practice.[9] To list the intellectual figures who have produced major theoretical statements concerning the importance of disgust—Immanuel Kant, Charles Darwin, Sigmund Freud, Melanie Klein, Georg Simmel, Norbert Elias, Jean-Paul Sartre, Mary Douglas, Georges Bataille, and Julia Kristeva, among others—is simply to make a list of those thinkers who have, since the Enlightenment, taken a pronounced interest in the sensory and affective dimension of social life. That disgust appeared as a central feature of human experience to these thinkers is no less significant than the fact that they have helped to shape and produce its continued centrality.

Writing the history of disgust, perhaps more than some other emotions, requires attending to three relatively discrete discursive registers: first, the emotion's forceful *expression* by individual people, including its conventional articulation in cultural and literary artifacts; second, its *theorization* as a central aspect of human experience within a substantial body of philosophical and scientific inquiry; and third, the *deployment* and mobilization of knowledge about disgust as a technique of political control and administration. While the disciplinary field of the history of emotions has tended to focus on the history of expressions, and while various branches of intellectual and conceptual history have turned their attention to the development of philosophical conceptions of the passions and affects, my focus throughout falls, by contrast, on the dynamic relationship that inheres between the expression, theorization, and mobilization of disgust.[10] As with its more gregarious cousin, the history of sexuality, writing the history of disgust involves figuring out how various discourses—philosophical, psychoanalytic, psychological, literary, biological, political-economic, sociological—have intersected, been tangled up with, determined, and in turn been influenced by the expression of the emotion.

The problem of disgust for the history of emotions is not solved simply by taking into account the large body of philosophical reflection on the emotion and putting it into dialogue with some less speculative historical archive of "expressed" revulsion. To make matters more complicated, disgust already plays a historical role within the body of modern thought: the role of the so-called primitive or animal, holed up inside the human. It is as gag reflex, gut feeling, or bygone instinct that disgust has threaded its way through modern thought. Starting with the aesthetic theories of the eighteenth century and passing through psychoanalysis on to the psychology of the present, disgust has long been taken as an emblem of something primal, and so prior, that persists obtrusively within the modern person, like a vestigial organ or an extra appendage whose utility has been forgotten. That is, not just the canonical objects of disgust—rotten food, shit, vermin, corpses, and other usual suspects—but the emotion itself continues to be understood within the envelope of the allegedly primitive.

It is worth pausing to consider some of the ways that disgust has absorbed the discourse of the primitive in contemporary psychological and philosophical accounts that, working in the Darwinian tradition, seek to define the emotion and identify its universal features. In psychology, the most influential as well as the most innovative work is that of Paul Rozin. In Rozin's widely adopted view, disgust is a "food-related emotion [defined] as revulsion at the prospect of oral incorporation of offensive objects." This core disgust is distinguished by a specific facial expression—the so-called gape face, first identified by Darwin—as well as a host of other physiological responses, such as lowered blood pressure, nausea, and vomiting; it is one of few emotional experiences that can throw the digestive tract into reverse. Moreover, in Rozin's account, disgust possesses a characteristic form of reasoning, a logic of pollution and contamination that obeys primitive laws of "sympathetic magic." Along with this theory of contamination, Rozin has also helped to bring into focus the complex issues at stake in trying to determine whether disgust experienced toward food (and toward oral ingestion generally) is the basis for more socially and politically complex forms of the emotion—the question of the oral in the moral.[11]

These two features—magical thinking and the primacy of the oral—have come to define disgust's primitive or primal character, the sense that the emotion belongs or at least maintains an active connection to a different stage of human development. Silvan Tomkins, an important source for Rozin, had already suggested some bases for this primal quality in his seminal work of the 1960s, *Affect Imagery Consciousness*. There, Tomkins observed that disgust's close evolutionary association with the "intake drives" of ingestion and respiration "represents a more primitive type of affect-drive organization" than is found with other emotions. Disgust is, in Tomkins's account, quasi-instinctual; it is a kind of pseudodrive that resembles the affect systems found in other animals. "Disgust and nausea therefore have some of the characteristics of the other human affects," Tomkins writes, "but are more similar to the more specific linkages of affect and drive found in the lower animals."[12]

Other scientific accounts of the emotion join Tomkins in locating disgust in the primeval structures of what he calls the "older brain."[13] One neuroscientific study has traced our capacity for imaginative disgust—that is, our ability to be provoked to vomit or gag merely by the sight of something revolting, rather than its ingestion—to the anterior insula, which the authors describe as a "'primitive' mechanism" said to reflect "the evolutionarily oldest form of emotion understanding." (In her review of the neurological literature on disgust, the psychologist Rachel Herz describes the insula as "a raunchy, devilish brain region," asserting that "Freud would have dubbed the insula home to our id.") Another study by the philosopher Daniel Kelly suggests that modern disgust reflects the entanglement over the long term of two "evolutionarily ancient" mechanisms, one for pathogen avoidance and the other regulating food intake. This argument finds an epidemiological analogue in the work of Valerie Curtis, who has argued that disgust is human nature's primordial parasite-avoidance system, which persists as "a voice in our heads, the voice of our ancestors telling us to stay away from what might be bad for us." At bottom, these studies largely concur with more psychoanalytically and phenomenologically oriented accounts of the emotion from earlier in the twentieth century. "The analysis of disgust reveals the fact that the emotional life of civilized men," reads András Angyal's classic 1941 study, "still is largely determined by very primitive, archaic meanings."[14]

This internal consistency and widespread agreement about disgust's primitive nature stands out in a body of thought otherwise notable for its diversity of opinion; indeed, even when two thinkers have held incompatible or opposing views on the meaning of disgust, they have tended to agree over its primordial character. What this means is that to write about disgust is almost always to write about its perceived anachronism, its alleged obsolescence as a mode of behavior or mode of thought. The discourse of disgust comes freighted with an evolutionary vision of the long-surpassed past; put another way, within modern accounts of the emotion, disgust represents the unwanted persistence of an animal or primitive past as a feeling in the present.

This present into which disgust impinges is very specifically the present of European modernity: the modernity of rationality and rationalization, science and prejudice, disenchantment and nationalism, culture and imperialism. It is a present that, from the Enlightenment onward, increasingly defined its self-image in contrast to a fantasy of the primitive that derived from the imperialist encounter with other cultures, and from the scientific demystification of religious belief, myth, and received knowledge, especially about the origins of the human being. Within this fantasy, the role of disgust was to produce the present of civilizational modernity negatively, through its self-exclusion. As the historian of sensation Alain Corbin has detailed at length, disgust was deemed overemotional, animalistic, impulsive. If one followed one's gut or one's nose, then by definition one did not follow one's reason; disgust's quasi-instinctual nature threatened the fabled sovereignty of the self held up as one of the core ideals of Enlightenment subjectivity. Hence it had to go—though of course it didn't and couldn't go anywhere; for what would it mean to exclude an emotion, let alone one defined by its impulsive propensity to show up when least desired, hijacking the sensorium?[15] The story of disgust is woven into the philosophical discourse of modernity to a remarkable extent; the myth of its own primitive nature is part of the emotional baggage, so to speak, that the articulation of disgust brings into play.

When we turn to the social history of disgust with the norms of this philosophical inheritance in mind, it produces an unusual friction. Far from appearing as a surpassed or excluded mode of behavior, the appeal to disgust is one of the most enduring and commonplace of rhetorical moves. And this ubiquity was especially noteworthy during the nineteenth century, at just the turbulent historical moment when the ideology of progress was reaching its apogee, and in just the same years when the self-sovereign individual was being inaugurated as the political and philosophical ego ideal of the age. The following chapters explore the role of disgust in significant areas of social change in Britain, focusing in particular on a series of transformative events that took place in the years between 1857 and 1860, of which a study of London's sewage crisis in the hot summer of 1858 will serve as a prototype. This tight focus may at first glance seem to offset the zoomed-out picture of modernity with which I have prefaced it. Yet for all the density of disgust during these few years, the events I examine were uniquely connected in their shared reliance on a common discourse of disgust whose reverberations and ramifications extend well beyond both the period and the frame of this book.

The nineteenth century placed an inordinately strong faith in the power of its disgust. Especially in France and Britain, the literature and the sociology of the period reflect not only a pronounced interest in the mammoth heaps of filth and waste accumulating in the rapidly growing cities, but also a deep, not-quite-articulated conviction that the language of visceral revulsion and moral grossness was the most appropriate as well as the most effective response to those conditions. Victorian disgust spoke with a condemning authority about the rotten world that had been produced by the processes of modernization. Indeed, the articulation of disgust in the period was fused to the fantasy of negating the world as it currently was, if not entirely to the fantasy of another, better world to come. In its negativity, this revolted *taedium vitae* took on a sub- or pseudoutopian function. Likewise, in the public and political discourse of the age disgust gave voice to an important new collective feeling of unwanted togetherness, a not-quite-fully-secular angst that people had come to be joined together by a shared experience of communal revulsion that called out for its own purgation. Almost everywhere one turns in the archive of Victorian culture, one sees a similar elevation of the discursive function of disgust, reflecting an underlying social agreement that it was an emotion whose articulation had a major claim to recognition in the public sphere—even if all it articulated was an outrage directed at its own bug-eyed and gagging outrage. It was a public passion, even if it was a proscribed and denigrated one.

Disgust, we might then say, was cast in two opposing roles over the course of the nineteenth century. On the one hand, it was called upon to shoulder the Enlightenment burden of unwanted animality, to represent the allegedly primitive and irrational forces against which modernity strove to define itself and which were therefore normatively excluded from the social domain. On the other hand, disgust gradually emerged as a leading force in the concrete realization of that exclusion. It is in this role as an affective mechanism of exclusion, for example, that Freud, writing at the close of the century, saw in disgust a prototype of repression, which he described as an inner, mental nose, recoiling in revulsion from the stench of an unpleasant, undesired memory. Disgust became both an object of exclusion and the means for its own removal—the affect to end unwanted affect. This book is devoted to exploring the highly productive nature of this seeming contradiction in the discursive function of Victorian disgust. For it was precisely this instability in the double role the emotion was called upon to play that lent the appeal to disgust the dynamic, even volatile, quality that we find in the cultural archives exhumed in this book. In literature, law and legislation, the social and the natural sciences, and national as well as imperial politics, the discourse of disgust was a driving force of social change, fueled by the call for its own repudiation. Like a broom made out of dust, the more it swept up after itself, the more of itself it left behind.

## The Victorian Structure of Unwanted Feeling

Now let us turn to a very different kind of episode in the drama of disgust's entanglement with the rhetoric of civilization. Rather than a quotidian scene of colonial violence and coerced ingestion, here we are revisiting a University of Oxford lecture hall, where in November 1883 William Morris first delivered his talk on anticapitalist aesthetics, "Art under Plutocracy" (later "Art under the Rule of Commerce"). "Not only are London and our other great commercial cities mere masses of sordidness, filth, and squalor, embroidered with patches of pompous and vulgar hideousness," Morris inveighs in the lecture, "not only have whole counties of England, and the heavens that hang over them, disappeared beneath a crust of unutterable grime, but the disease, to which a visitor coming from the times of art, reason, and order, would seem to be a love of dirt and ugliness for its own sake, spreads all over the country, and every little market-town seizes the opportunity to imitate, as far as it can, the majesty of the hell of London and Manchester," Morris continues, building to his main point:

> Even if a tree is cut down or blown down, a worse one, if any, is planted in its stead, and, in short, our civilization is passing like a blight, daily growing heavier and more poisonous, over the whole face of the country, so that every change is sure to be a change for the worse. . . . So then it comes to this, that not only are the minds of great artists narrowed and their sympathies frozen by their isolation, but the very food on which both the greater and the lesser art subsists is being destroyed; the well of art is poisoned at the spring.[16]

This book is devoted to the task of anatomizing the prevalent structure of unwanted feeling captured here by Morris's fulmination against nineteenth-century civilization. Certain elements of Morris's criticism will serve as the building blocks for the studies that follow. The principal observation is that Morris elaborately describes his present phase of modernity as "a blight"— that is, as an atmospheric pollution or disease—"daily growing heavier and more poisonous." While this figure of social blight will be familiar to nearly any reader of Victorian prose—from John Ruskin's epochal storm cloud to Charles Dickens's stifling *Bleak House* fog—I want to emphasize its complexity, which conjoins the atmospheric and thus respiratory metaphor of the industrial smoke cloud with the totalizing concept of civilization. The problems of modernity, Morris suggests in a register that is more than metaphorical, but not exactly literal, can be evidenced just like problems felt in the nose or the lungs. This yoking of the respiratory to the civilizational in turn splits itself in two, following along a fault line in the evolution of the civilization concept that Raymond Williams expressed as the critical distinction between "an achieved state and an achieved state of development." In the latter instance, Williams explains, civilization comes to refer to new active processes of cultural attainment and personal as well as social development that began to take shape during the Enlightenment, whereas in the former "civilization was the achieved state which these new developments were threatening to destroy." "Civilization as threat, civilization as threatened," as Jean Starobinski concisely puts it.[17]

We can see how Morris's figure is able to exploit this ambiguity while fusing it to a potent and emotionally laden rhetoric of sensory disgust that, like John Scott's letter to Darwin, also culminates with an image of coerced ingestion. "Civilization" comes to name both the poisonous blight of industrial capitalism that is passing "over the whole face of the country" and the valued processes of cultural production and achievement that are presumed to be uprooted and destroyed. The language of revulsion—of "a crust of unutterable grime," miasmatic clouds of "disease" and "blight," "sordidness, filth, and squalor," and above all of a poison that must be ingested, imbibed "at the spring"—not only lends a presumptive self-evidence and urgency to the diagnosis of the problem, but also structures it. For if civilization names both the disease and its victim, then the rhetoric of disgust provides an important template for organizing this condition of immanent corruption. Disgust comes to serve as a form of evidence of the problem, in which the blight of civilization is registered in the language of a quasimetaphorical sensory outrage; it also offers a pattern for the complex sense that the problem is already within, churning around on the inside, affecting social life and behavior, and so needs to be expelled. Hence Morris complains not merely that there is a cloud of ugliness hanging over England, but that it has gotten inside people, has changed their tastes and sensibilities, and has altered their sense of what is morally good and aesthetically valued and politically right, while distorting the highest forms of artistic and cultural expression. It is from this sense of the immanence of the pollution that disgust itself comes to look like both a form of emotion expression that can designate filth and defilement and something unclean in its own right.

Keeping this set of concerns about the immanent corruption of civilization in view, there are two more features of Morris's invective that I want to tease out and add to the preliminary mapping of the Victorian structure of unwanted feeling. The first is that Morris deliberately frames this hybrid affective-civilizational pollution in terms of what Max Weber would a few decades later call the rationalization of the structure of modern society: "every little market-town," Morris observes, "seizes the opportunity to imitate, as far as it can, the majesty of the hell of London and Manchester." Morris links the affective dimension of physical and moral corruption specifically to the sociological processes of urbanization and centralization, that is, to the changes in the shape and composition of social and political structures that for Morris were the consequence of the transition to plutocracy, or capitalism. The key insight is that the affective, which is to say emotional and sensory, life of the subject has a dynamic relationship to the structure of society— even those aspects that might seem least grounded in affect and most rational, in the Weberian sense of being calculable, rule-bound, and planned.

The force that drives this undesirable rationalization in Morris's sketch is not quite a rationality, but rather something that from the perspective of a "visitor coming from the times of art, reason, and order, would seem to be a love of dirt and ugliness for its own sake." That is, from a truly rational perspective, the processes of rationalization Morris describes would look like a prurient desire for willful self-abasement. In the first place, this means that the rationality of rationalization is motivated on an affective rather than on a purely cognitive or instrumental level. But things get even slipperier at this point. Put in slightly different terms, what Morris is saying is that modern society has in fact *lost* its sense of disgust, which has been usurped by this salacious love or pleasure taken in the pathological "for its own sake." This is a crucial feature of the Victorian structure of unwanted feeling. Rather than an unruly animal passion, disgust here begins to function as the token of a tenuous level of civilizational attainment; its expression is the sign that one has not succumbed to modern cultural prurience. Disgust is therefore placed in an inverse yet substitutable relationship to pleasure and desire: the failure to experience the outrage of disgust comes to look like the pursuit of a kind of morbid desire, whereas the articulation of disgust is, conversely, lauded as a form of cultivated restraint. Finally, this formulation also asks us, counterintuitively, to align "reason and order" with the articulation of disgust toward the blight of modern civilization. A contorted and ultimately incoherent analogical structure starts to come into focus, in which modern rationalization looks like emotional excess, and disgust like civilization's highest form of emotional restraint.

Morris was neither alone in viewing his phase of modernity as a poisonous blight nor unique in understanding the social consequences of the industrialization and rationalization of society to be intimately bound up with questions of cultural and artistic practice, as well as with aesthetic and sensory experience. Nor was he alone in his anxious observation that in modern Britain a prurient appetite for the rotten and grotesque had supplanted traditional patterns of consumption, a perspective he shared with a diverse set of critics of nineteenth-century culture, ranging from John Ruskin and Margaret Oliphant to Friedrich Engels and George Gissing. Thus when we read of "the mephitic breath of plague given off by civilization," and are told that for the modern person "*dirt*—this stagnation and putrefaction of man—the *sewage* of civilization (speaking quite literally)—comes to be the *element of life*," we do not necessarily know, ideologically speaking, whether we are hearing from Thomas Carlyle or Karl Marx.[18] The entanglement of the discourse of disgust with the ideology of civilization cut a deep groove across the entire political spectrum of the nineteenth century, attesting to the prevalence as well as the stereotyped character of the Victorian structure of unwanted feeling.

Most significantly for this book, however, Morris joins a chorus of countless other voices in the period who likewise derived the terms and the force of their words from the language of disgust and the disgusting, while also seeking to organize their social world through the example of their revulsion. At the most fundamental level, the following pages are devoted to understanding the rise of this implicit belief in the availability of the language of disgust, its capacity to function specifically as a shared and public language that carried its own kind of self-evidentiary charge. In this regard, I follow and hope to extend Lauren Berlant's work on the political potency of appeals to "true feeling" in the nineteenth-century American public sphere. "Around 1830," Berlant argues, "a shift in emphasis with respect to the ethics of Enlightenment subjectivity emerged in the elite sectors of the United States, which challenged rationality as the core activity distinguishing the human being . . . supplanting [it with] an image of the person as a subject with moral feeling, and especially with a capacity for feeling and responding to the suffering of less fortunate others who could be described not as individuals but as members of a subordinated population."[19] This discourse of true feeling bears a strong family resemblance to the structure of unwanted feeling, though the peculiarly recursive negativity of disgust precludes its being identified entirely with pain and therefore keeps it from functioning simply as the flipside of sympathy. For what is unique about the rhetoric of disgust, in this context, is precisely the fraught self-consciousness of its own inadmissibility. Disgust proved to be highly effective as a form of social and political appeal, but for all that its efficacy remained uncelebrated, was deemed inappropriate, and was more often than not disavowed. Disgust was a true feeling, but it was also an unwanted one. It is a central claim of this book that to listen to the nineteenth century talk about itself is to immerse oneself in this revolted rhetoric of gag reflex and gut reaction—of an "unutterable grime" that was nonetheless uttered everywhere and all the time.

Berlant's work can also help to make sense of the disparity between the portrait I will be painting of Victorian culture as a culture of revolted outrage and a more familiar picture of a midcentury moment that prioritized rationality over emotion, promoted a disinterested and self-sovereign subject over an impulsive and instinctual one, and above all pursued liberal and utilitarian aims in its social and political endeavors rather than merely sensuous aesthetic ones. Part of my project in this book is to complicate the oft-told stories of nineteenth-century liberal subjectivity and rationalization by shedding light on the affective underpinnings of both of those concepts. In this regard, I join scholars such as Mary Poovey and Elaine Hadley, who have sought to add conceptual depth and archival complexity to the liberal and disciplinary conceptions of the subject that have anchored our broader understandings of nineteenth-century cultural formation. As Hadley has put it in her study of the liberal form of "embodied abstraction," although "the thoughts and sensations of liberalism are themselves always expressed through an abstracted body . . . it would be a mistake to assume as a result that midcentury liberalism had no feeling."[20] A principal task of this book is to analyze one of the most prevalent yet also most disavowed of those forms of feeling, as the outraged disgust amid the protracted civilizational crises of the late 1850s gave way to more muted years of liberal progress in the 1860s. In this sense, it is possible to see the discursive activity of disgust at play within the most disinterested of historical processes.

Writing of the sanitary crises of late nineteenth-century Paris, the historian of science and medicine David S. Barnes has argued that "disgust represents a promising and underexplored category of historical analysis," suggesting that scholars ought to attend to "the multiple ways this seemingly straightforward emotion . . . acts as both a *signpost* and an *engine* of historical change."[21] Building on Barnes's observations, I argue in this book that over the course of the nineteenth century disgust emerged as a prominent social and political passion, one that played a productive role in various areas of social change. In terms of the history of the emotion, the closing years of the 1850s in particular represent a period of unusually concentrated intensity. Between 1857 and 1859, in fact, the emotion figured centrally in the transformation of British society. Consider the density of the following events. Most notably, in the summer of 1858, there was London's Great Stink. A prolonged sewage crisis brought about by a six-week heatwave, the stink not only marked the culmination of a decades-long public debate over sanitation, but enabled a far-reaching reorganization of the infrastructure and social space of the world's largest metropolis. Only a year before, Parliament had passed the Obscene Publications Act of 1857, the first statutory obscenity law. Remarkably, the act sought to regulate the circulation of sexually illicit texts as though they were, in the eyes of the law, public nuisances—akin to chemical poisons, airborne pollutions, and contagious diseases—thus inscribing a sensory discourse of disgust into the juridical as well as the sanitary domain.

Bookended by the obscenity law and the sanitary crisis, the very same months also bore witness to one of the first truly global financial crises, commonly referred to as the Revulsion of 1857, which began when the Ohio State Life and Trust Company collapsed, and which quickly spread around the world. The specific conception of the financial crisis as a "revulsion" allowed critics and commentators to attribute obscure powers of contagion and contamination to socioeconomic phenomena, which left a lasting influence on Marx's social theory in the years to come. The eighteen months spanning from the spring of 1857 to the autumn of 1858 also witnessed the long and bloody anticolonial struggle of the Indian Rebellion, which was ignited when Hindu and Muslim soldiers in the East India Company's army revolted in response to rumors that newly introduced rifle cartridges, which had to be bitten open, were greased with lard and tallow and so threatened them with contamination and defilement. As another scene of forced ingestion, the rebellion epitomizes the ways in which the incoherent yet nonetheless powerful compound of disgust and civilizational thinking was mobilized in the context of British imperialism and exported as a technology of domination. Finally, these busy, splanchnic years also saw the publication of Darwin's *On the Origin of Species* in 1859, a text that brought about the most significant alteration in the medical, philosophical, literary, and of course scientific discourses of human animality and instinct of the period. Set against this visceral landscape of disgust, the Darwinian conception of the human animal might be said to characterize the historical moment more accurately than the influential but comparatively gutless liberal subject, who was nonetheless ushered into being by John Stuart Mill in the same year.

Focusing on this condensed era of revolt, revulsion, stink, and obscenity, each of the following six chapters studies a particular domain whose transformation during the second half of the nineteenth century hinged on the allocation of a new set of meanings and values to the emotion of disgust. The arc of the argument develops across three parts. In the first, "The Rationalization of Revulsion," I provide a detailed account of the way that the Victorian structure of unwanted feeling derived from a conception of disgust that was first elaborated within Enlightenment aesthetic theory. In chapter 1, "The Odor of Things," I show how this specifically aesthetic disgust was integral to the collective revulsion catalyzed by the Great Stink of 1858. Analyzing hundreds of newspaper articles, parliamentary speeches, and other documents of this shared olfactory panic, I ask what it means for an experience of collective emotion to have played such a pivotal role in the rationalization of modern society—a process traditionally understood to involve the exclusion of emotion and subjectivity from public affairs.

The second chapter, "Realism and Repulsion," shows how literary production in the period responded to the new centrality of disgust to Victorian social life. Attending to literary works such as Charlotte Brontë's *Jane Eyre* and Charles Dickens's *Little Dorrit*, I argue, affords the clearest view of the Victorian structure of unwanted feeling, and allows us to observe the new roles and functions that were being ascribed to disgust over the second half of the century. The chapter also offers a critical genealogy of the role of disgust in seminal theories of the realist novel, from György Lukács and

Eric Auerbach to Fredric Jameson and Eve Kosofsky Sedgwick. The opening chapters thus offer a complex and nuanced view of the aesthetic conception of disgust, with its presumptions about how the emotion worked, what rules and rationalities it followed, what its articulation meant, and crucially, when it should and shouldn't be provoked. Taken together, they show how this discourse of disgust came to function beyond the confines of the specifically aesthetic domain.

In the second part, "Primal Scenes, Human Sciences," I show how the extension of disgust beyond the aesthetic domain contributed to new forms of knowledge production in the natural and social sciences. Across a pair of closely linked chapters, I show how scientific discourse depended on the attribution of an unwanted primal character to disgust that was instrumental in attempts to distinguish the human from the animal, the natural from the cultural, and most significantly, modern from primitive civilization. Toggling between advances in gastric medicine, mechanistic physiology, and evolutionary biology, the third chapter, "Darwin's Vomit," turns to the Darwinian theory of disgust. Reading Darwin's earlier writings on instinct against his far more idiosyncratic evolutionary theory of vomiting in *The Expression of the Emotions in Man and Animals*, this chapter offers a comprehensive analysis of the allegedly primitive character of the emotion, while also showing how Darwin's account anticipates the characterization of disgust within psychoanalytic theory. The fourth chapter, "The Masses Are Revolting," shifts the focus from the natural to the social sciences. Against the economic backdrop of the financial Revulsion of 1857, I provide a genealogical account of the role of attraction-repulsion in early twentieth-century works of urban sociology and social theory through readings of mid-nineteenth-century texts by Friedrich Engels, Karl Marx, and Herbert Spencer. I show how a confusion between pleasure and disgust, which had been the de facto affective state for Victorian bourgeois social observers, was, for fin-de-siècle social theorists like Georg Simmel, Émile Durkheim, and Sigmund Freud, excluded from sociological method while simultaneously diagnosed as a fundamental precondition for all sociality.

The third and final part of the book, "The Disenchantment of Disgust," pursues disgust into the domains of law and empire, where it offered politicians, jurists, and colonial administrators a powerful vocabulary of pollution and contamination. Drawing on an archive of nineteenth-century legal materials, the fifth chapter, "The Age of Obscenity," examines the intersection of the aesthetic prohibition of the disgusting with the development of modern obscenity law and the regulation of sexuality. The conclusion, "Horizons of Expectoration," considers the function of disgust in the Indian Rebellion, as well as more broadly in the context of British imperialism and race thinking. If the opening treatment of the Great Stink demonstrates how disgust was a rationalizing emotion, whose affective volatility could be put to work in the reorganization and administration of public space, the final part of the book shows how disgust functioned as a technology for regulating sexuality and racial difference throughout the British Empire.

More than mere moral-aesthetic outrage in the face of the ugliness of industrialization, disgust was a generative and motivating force in the ongoing elaboration of these various forms of social control, knowledge production, and infrastructural development. In assembling this complicated argument with its many moving pieces, I have been aided by scholars who have noted the centrality of disgust and its eliciting objects to nineteenth-century European culture in general, and to the Victorians in particular.[22] Yet unlike most of their works, this book attempts to follow its slippery and often overflowing subject matter across the conventional disciplinary and thematic frames that have tended to corral studies of nineteenth-century disgust. My broadest contention is that what might otherwise appear as disparate and disconnected domains of society can and in fact should be grouped together and understood in light of their shared reliance on a common discourse of disgust. Thus when outraged Londoners appealed in the press to their overwhelming experience of collective revulsion during the dog days of 1858, they drew on a set of presuppositions and putatively commonsensical notions about the social meaning of their disgust that was also available to Engels, for instance, when he wrote of London that "the very turmoil of the streets has something repulsive, something against which human nature rebels."[23] Indeed, one of the most striking features of the nineteenth-century discourse of disgust is the anticipation of universal assent that was woven into its grammar; rather than seeing their disgust as an individuating and subjective experience, Victorians understood it to articulate something public and shared, a reflexive sense that a cultural or civilizational threshold had been transgressed.

It is in this sense of a set of underlying grammatical expectations that we can speak of Victorian disgust as discourse and as structure of feeling, as something that transcends the individuating rhetorical horizons of emotion expression and allows us to connect what might at first glance appear as remote areas of the social world. Yet to treat Victorian disgust as a discourse raises the further question of its origins, for sanitary reform, obscenity law, and urban sociology did not learn to speak the same language overnight. Disgust had been ascribed a destabilizing power in Enlightenment aesthetics, and this body of theoretical writing can be understood as a proximal point of origin for the discursive functions the negative emotion would take on throughout the nineteenth century.

## From the Aesthetics of Disgust to the Psychoanalysis of Repulsion

Midway through *Gulliver's Travels* (1726), Jonathan Swift's protagonist descends from the floating island of Laputa to visit the academy in the city of Lagado, describing the various scholarly undertakings of the faculty. The second person Gulliver meets there, "the most ancient Student of the Academy," is a scholar of shit, "his Face and Beard . . . a pale Yellow; his Hands and Clothes daubed over with Filth." Entering into this professor's office, Gulliver narrates, "[I] was ready to hasten back, being almost overcome with a horrible Stink," but his guide urges him on, "conjuring me in a Whisper to give no Offence, which would be highly resented; and therefore I durst not so much as stop my Nose": "When I was presented to him, he gave me a close embrace, a compliment I could well have excused. His employment, from his first coming into the academy, was an Operation to reduce human Excrement to its original Food, by separating the several Parts, removing the Tincture which it receives from the Gall, making the Odour exhale, and scumming off the Saliva. He had a weekly Allowance, from the Society, of a Vessel filled with human Ordure, about the Bigness of a Bristol Barrel."[24] Throughout this book, we will regularly encounter the actual descendants of Swift's wizened professor of the excremental and his coprophagic researches. We will listen to sanitary reformers who, in the middle decades of the nineteenth century, sought to capitalize on the sheer magnitude of London's daily effluence of human waste and use it as fertilizer, rather than continuing to import millions of tons of foreign guano. And we will meet gastric physiologists who, just like Gulliver's reeking academician, sought to analyze each step of the digestive process, charting the course of food through the stomach and the bowel and discovering what organic substances were added to and subtracted from it along the way.

In chapter 2, I will make the case that Swift's writings represent a turning point in the specifically literary history of disgust, a moment when the emotion itself fully takes center stage, rather than the grotesque objects and substances and bawdy actions associated with its provocation. What I want to draw out of Swift's parodic sketch at present, however, is simply its suggestion of a scholarly enterprise devoted to anatomizing systematically that which is grotesque and disgusting, and to overcoming its powers and cataloguing its effects. In Swift's century, this would become one of the foremost tasks of aesthetic theory, especially as it developed in Germany, and to a lesser but still significant extent in Britain as well. Whereas other emotions, affections, and passions were theorized in a variety of Enlightenment intellectual contexts, the formal task of analyzing disgust belonged almost exclusively to aesthetics. Holding up the disgusting as the antithesis of the beautiful, early philosophers of the aesthetic described disgust as a powerful, unwanted sensory disturbance that precluded the refined enjoyment deemed necessary to properly evaluate and reflectively appreciate works of art and literature. Although they were not interested in the physical properties of shit, these Enlightenment aestheticians nonetheless represent a plausible analogue to Swift's satirical vision of a science of the excremental and disgusting.

This book proposes that the discourse of disgust prevalent in mid-nineteenth-century British culture derived primarily from the privileged power to disturb the faculty of judgment that Enlightenment aesthetics granted to the emotion. In British aesthetic thought, disgust took shape specifically as a vulgar counterpart to the theory of taste found in works by David Hume, Edmund Burke, and Anthony Ashley Cooper (Lord Shaftesbury); in the German tradition, thinkers such as Gotthold Ephraim Lessing, Moses Mendelssohn, and Immanuel Kant sought instead to catalogue the precise effects and distinctive features of the disgusting, contrasting it to other negative aesthetic categories, such as the horrible, the terrible, the ugly, and the ridiculous. Lessing, for instance, devoted several chapters of his famous *Laocoön: An Essay upon the Limits of Painting and Poetry* (1766) to taxonomizing negative affects and aesthetic effects in relation to disgust, and to describing the conditions under which they can be produced. For example, he explains, in poetry "the ridiculous can be heightened by an element of disgust," whereas "what we call the horrible is nothing more than a mixture of the elements of terror and disgust"; "loathsome details," conversely, "make the terrible horrible"; and so on.[25] Like the psychology of the emotions that would emerge in the nineteenth century, much of eighteenth-century aesthetic theory was devoted to this task of mapping out these affective experiences and their modes of relationship in ever greater detail.

For Lessing and his contemporaries, disgust was of particular interest because it represented a kind of limit case within the formalist and taxonomical project of aesthetics. What both the British and the German traditions shared, as Winfried Menninghaus has shown, was a conviction that the visceral experience of disgust overwhelmed the senses, thereby blocking the subject from experiencing aesthetic pleasure and forming disinterested judgments.[26] "The more occult senses of taste, smell, and touch," Lessing writes, "cannot receive other impressions when in contact with the repulsive object."²⁷ According to this complex model of subjectivity, rising bile over-rides the refined palette; disgust commandeers the sensorium, in a kind of hostile takeover. As a strong feeling that nevertheless could make seemingly universal judgments, this compulsory character of disgust was understood to violate the basic distinction between fact and value upon which the edifices of Enlightenment thought were built. It was as though, in being disgusted, the difference between a fact and a feeling no longer mattered; in its unwantedness and negativity, the feeling became a fact all its own.²⁸ Disgust therefore tugged aesthetic theory in opposing but not-quite-incompatible directions. The emotion was increasingly understood to represent an irrefutable form of negative judgment, but it was also introduced into aesthetics only to be excluded from the repertory of responses that were acceptable to arouse in a spectator or reader.

We will return to this complex discourse of aesthetic disgust in the next chapter, taking a closer look at the mechanics according to which the emotion was said to disturb judgment and to interrupt the circuits of spectatorship and evaluation. Here I consider the methodological underpinnings of my assertion that aesthetic subjectivity can help to explain and to organize the areas of disconnected Victorian social transformation this book examines. There are two key pieces to this claim. The first is that, in the most general sense, the aesthetic theory of the eighteenth century sought to develop a new framework for analyzing how artworks elicited and provoked powerful sensations and singular forms of emotional response, and thus offered a distinctively affective theory of the subject.²⁹ As the aesthetic project grew more complex, it raised challenging questions about how to account for the powerful subjective experiences elicited in response to works of art as well as to the spectacle of the natural world. Such experiences seemed to be shared, but what could ground this commonality? What were the rules? Did aesthetic experience yield a kind of sensory knowledge—a "confused knowledge," as Alexander Baumgarten put it in the eighteenth century, and as Jacques Rancière has suggested more recently?³⁰ Pursuing these questions, aesthetics grew into a field of inquiry uniquely concerned with the philosophical analysis of affect as raised by the encounter with the work of art.

In this emerging domain of the aesthetic, affects and sensations, as well as the objects that provoked them, came to seem autonomous, in that they could be analyzed on their own terms, isolated from other activities and kinds of experience. And yet as the discourse of taste helps to make clear, this alleged autonomy of the aesthetic depended explicitly on forms of cultural access and social distinction to such an extent that it could hardly claim to be insulated from wider political contexts and economic frames of reference.

The second point to note about the relevance of the aesthetic to our historical study of disgust, then, is that through this claim to autonomy, aesthetics came into contact with an expanded field of social activity. For most latter-day commentators, it is Kant who first pushed the aesthetic beyond the restricted sense of the arts and letters, opening up into a broader critique of the faculty of judgment. With Kant, the ambition was no longer merely to produce a taxonomy of specifically aesthetic affects, but rather to question whether there were circumstances in which affective experiences could form the basis for shared and public activities, in the absence of rules or concepts that could provide objectivity.

There is a rich and varied tradition of theorizing the expanded field of the aesthetic domain, to which this book seeks to contribute. Hannah Arendt was the first to claim Kant's third *Critique* as a specifically "political philosophy," arguing that the judging spectator is a fundamentally political actor, and that the possibility of grounding judgments in the collective appeal to feeling would become especially important within pluralistic democratic societies. In Arendt's reading, that is, aesthetics offered a template for a politics in which subjective feeling could be converted into a public discursive activity of evaluative persuasion, which she memorably likened to wooing.[31] Following Arendt, this pair of insights into the affective basis of aesthetic judgment and the aesthetic basis of political action has led down a number of different avenues. Especially for those thinkers working in a Deleuzian tradition that shifts the focus away from emotion, the turn to aesthetics in political theory has seemed to offer a way of theorizing sensation as the radical disruption of a rational political order. For others, however, the turn to aesthetics foregrounds instead the complex interface where subjective experiences normally invalidated by political theory and in some senses excluded from official political discourse meet with and are converted into discursive activity.[32] In work related to both of these strains, Rancière writes of the rise of the "aesthetic regime" as having established a new "distribution of the sensible" (le partage du sensible), which he defines as "the system of self-evident facts of sense perception that simultaneously discloses the existence of something in common and the delimitations that define the respective parts and positions within it."[33] In this sense, for Rancière, certain forms of sensation and affect might sit outside or askew of a dominant social order, but the process according to which recognition is or is not allotted to sense experience is itself also a constitutive activity of that social order.

My overall approach to the entanglement of aesthetics and politics in this book is historical rather than prescriptive, but, like Rancière, I also see in the emergence of Enlightenment aesthetics a normative enterprise that sought to bring about a reapportionment of meaning and recognition to affective experience that would come to seem self-evident. Aesthetics, in this regard, offered a powerful means of policing the pivotal distinction between fact and value upon which the post-Enlightenment socio-epistemological order was established. Focusing specifically on the aesthetics of disgust makes this normative distributive function especially clear, since disgust was already theorized by and within aesthetics as a disruption that threatened to cause the whole apparatus of judgment to malfunction, and so needed to be excluded. But my broader point here is simply to emphasize the widened field and function of the aesthetic. Throughout this book, aesthetics will refer broadly to this social-grammatical process according to which meaning and value were distributed to affective experience, rather than to the more narrowly bounded sphere of the arts.

A final word about how aesthetics function in the expanded social field will help return us to the Victorian structure of unwanted feeling. As is especially apparent in the British discourse of taste, the aesthetic enterprise included a component focused on proper conduct that overlapped in important ways with a longer history of manners and self-cultivation. This aspect of the aesthetic has been more apparent to social rather than political theorists, with Pierre Bourdieu's *Distinction* representing the high-water mark in the sociological critique of the discourse of taste. Seen from this angle, the aesthetic domain offered an ascendant bourgeoisie the means of consolidating their class power through the construction of a code of conduct that was written in the language of affective expression and restraint; some forms of enjoyment would be excluded as vulgar, whereas other forms would betoken class belonging and exclusionary group identification. As a philosophical discourse, aesthetics, for Bourdieu, was merely the codification and reinforcement of an emergent bourgeois habitus, a structure of dispositions and sensibilities that determined how certain physical and perceptual experiences could come to be imbued with values that reflected class interests rather than merely individual identities. For Bourdieu, this process of forming the aesthetic habitus depended especially on the elevation of the social function of disgust as a means of denigrating and excluding the vulgar and lowly: "Kant's principle of pure taste," he writes, "is nothing other than a refusal, a disgust—a disgust for objects which impose enjoyment and a disgust for the crude, vulgar taste which revels in this imposed enjoyment."[34]

Here a recursive tension emerges in the status of disgust within aesthetics. Seen from the angle of political theories of *aisthesis*, disgust represents a form of normatively excluded disturbance that interrupts the circuits of sensory self-evidence. By contrast, from the perspective of the sociological critique of taste, disgust looks like the means for articulating and maintaining exclusions, but not like the thing that is itself meant to be excluded. Far from being a contradiction, this dynamic tension helps to explain how, from the right angle and under the right circumstances, bug-eyed disgust could come to look like a form of tight-lipped disinterestedness that would be able to serve in its own right as a powerful agent of transformation in the Victorian public sphere.

Before moving on, I want to offer a few remarks about the relationship of aesthetic disgust to the emotion's important role within psychoanalytic theory. Menninghaus has observed the important continuities between German aesthetic theory of the eighteenth century and Freud's writings on disgust throughout his career.[35] Part of this relationship can be explained as stemming from Freud's deep reading in the nineteenth-century German philosophical tradition, with Arthur Schopenhauer and Friedrich Nietzsche serving as the intellectual-historical dots connecting Kant's comments on disgust and judgment to Freud's theory of the oral roots of judgment in his 1925 essay "Negation."

However, this intellectual-historical argument only partially explains the continuities between aesthetic theory and the emergence of psychoanalysis. A more substantive and direct historical line connects the bourgeois culture of aesthetic taste, with its emphasis on manners, conduct, and proper judgment, to the theory of civilization that Freud developed out of his observations of the fin-de-siècle European bourgeois family and its stringent moral hygiene. Indeed, as we will see in the next chapter, Freud was himself keenly attuned to the transformations in the sanitary landscape that took place in his lifetime. Bearing this in mind, I regard the attribution of different psychoanalytic functions to disgust as the realization and also the mutation of certain aspects of the emotion's aesthetic conception that became increasingly apparent with the transformations in bourgeois culture over the course of the nineteenth century. Most significantly, the emphasis on disgust's role as an unwanted disturbance shifted substantially toward an understanding of its role as a mechanism for excluding unwanted disturbances. From the historical perspective of this book, then, psychoanalysis has a special double role: it appears, on the one hand, as a body of theoretical writings that are especially useful to the study of disgust, and on the other, as a discursive formation whose emergence at the close of the period we are interested in represents a historical horizon just out of reach of our articulators of nineteenth-century revulsion. This inversion—whereby theory comes to resemble rather than to explain historical phenomena—will be a theme that recurs throughout the book.[36]

Disgust plays multiple and at times incompatible roles within Freudian psychoanalysis that, taken all together, reflect a historical shift in the function of disgust over the course of the nineteenth century. Freud's first major engagement with disgust is in a letter to his friend Wilhelm Fliess from 1897, in which he formulates his initial theory of repression as a kind of inner disgust. "To put it crudely, the memory actually stinks just as in the present the object stinks," Freud writes in the letter, "and in the same manner as we turn away our sense organ (the head and nose) in disgust, the preconscious and the sense of consciousness turn away from the memory. This is repression."[37] I will return to this passage several times in the following chapters, but for now observe that Freud here describes disgust not as an admissible disturbance to the social or psychological order of things, but rather as the mechanism by which such disturbances are excluded from consciousness. As he went on to develop increasingly complex accounts of the psychology of disavowal and repudiation, Freud continued to rely on disgust as a model or template for other such mechanisms. In the 1909 *Five Lectures on Psychoanalysis*, for instance, Freud introduced the idea that shame and disgust were the "watchmen" who maintain repression over time—no longer the mechanisms of repression, but rather of resistance.[38]

What begins to emerge, as one works through Freud's oeuvre with an eye for disgust, is that the emotion comes to take on an ever more interwoven and dynamic set of psychic functions. This trend culminates in two distinct statements. The first is the important essay "Negation," mentioned above, where Freud describes the infant's spitting out of what tastes bad as the moment of primal subject formation as well as the origin of the faculty of judgment—an account of disgust that would influence Melanie Klein's development of object relations psychoanalysis as well as Julia Kristeva's concept of abjection and Jacques Lacan's writings on fetishistic disavowal. "Expressed in the language of the oldest—the oral—instinctual impulses," Freud writes, "the judgment is: 'I should like to eat this,' or 'I should like to spit it out.'"[39] Disgust on this account is what first allows the infant to distinguish inside from out, to become a subject who can judge good from bad and, crucially, reality from fantasy. Yet note how Freud has continued to increase disgust's psychic workload: it is the model for repression, the affect that maintains repression, and now a general form of negation or negativity that serves as the basis for a whole range of faculties and mechanisms of exclusion.

Finally, in *Civilization and Its Discontents* (1930), Freud draws on the 1897 letter to Fliess in order to extend his conception of disgust's primal function into a speculative anthropological theory of the origins of human culture. In a long, often-cited footnote to that text, Freud describes disgust not simply as the impetus for subject formation, but as the engine motivating humanity into its upright gait and, ultimately, into the neurotic constrictions of modern civilization. Thus, if aesthetic theory had tried to maintain a sharp contrast between revolted feeling and disinterested judgment, by the close of the nineteenth century Freud had picked up instead on the ways that emotions like disgust and contempt could lurk beneath the smooth surfaces of the disinterested civilized habitus. If anything, Freud's scattered theoretical remarks suggest that modern society was becoming more easily revolted, readier than ever to give voice to its disgust, putting increasing pressure on the emotion to do the work of civilization.

## The Gag Reflex in the Age of Equipoise

The nineteenth century casts a long shadow on twentieth- and twenty-first-century theories of disgust. Even the most universalizing, transhistorical accounts of the emotion derive, almost without fail, from the period—often in uncritical or unacknowledged ways. Indeed, while researching this book, the more deeply I read in the philosophical, scientific, and critical-theoretical scholarship on disgust, the more convinced I grew that there was a special historical relationship that bound theories of the emotion not merely to the Darwinian psychological tradition but to the distinct cultural historical terrain of the Victorian era. We can see in Rozin's important body of research on the emotion, for instance, the imprint of Victorian anthropology when he argues that disgust follows the "laws of sympathetic magic" that James Frazer described in his 1890 study, *The Golden Bough*, a work that also had an important influence on Freud's descriptions of primitive thinking in *Totem and Taboo* (1913).[40] According to Frazer's principle of contagion, objects that come into contact with disgusting things become disgusting, while according to that of resemblance, objects that look like disgusting things will also provoke revulsion. In a crucial sense, the logic of contamination and pollution that has come to define the emotion received its precise formulation first within the context of the Victorian civilizational ideology of primitive thought and the savage mind.

Rozin does not explore this historical relationship, which of course sits outside the purview of his research as a psychologist. Yet this tacit dependency on nineteenth-century thought has introduced complications into the study of the emotion across disciplinary boundaries, in part because of the powerful influence of Rozin's compelling body of work. Take, as another brief example, Martha Nussbaum's complex legal-philosophical study of disgust, *Hiding from Humanity: Disgust, Shame, and the Law* (2004).[41] Nussbaum accepts Rozin's characterization of the emotion as a source of pollution thinking, asserting in turn that the logic of contamination represents a form of subrational thought that places disgust outside the bounds of what she calls public reason, and which therefore ought to invalidate it as a basis for legal judgment. In a lucid critique of the misogyny of obscenity law, Nussbaum winds up arguing that even though the appeal to disgust would seem to register the existence of something offensive, it does not therefore adequately register a harm. Instead Nussbaum asserts that disgust articulates a kind of ersatz, irrational claim to injury. Yet here too Nussbaum returns us to the Victorian lifeworld, grounding her description of the rational public order in her adaptation of John Stuart Mill's account of harm, as he presented it in *On Liberty* (1859). I consider Nussbaum's reliance on Mill as well as her argument about obscenity at greater length in chapters 2 and 5, respectively. Here I simply observe that Nussbaum's argument about disgust is structured in significant ways by Victorian accounts of the emotion and of the harm it might pose to the social world.

These examples raise important questions about the embeddedness of contemporary, universalizing theories of disgust in particular, and emotion in general, within the conceptual framework of the civilizational ideology of the nineteenth century. One of the central aims of this book is to shed light on this ongoing historical relationship, according to which the Victorian discourse of the primitive survives in the interdisciplinary study of disgust. Norbert Elias's sociological study, *The Civilizing Process* (1939), which sought to synthesize Weber's rationalization thesis with Freud's theory of civilization, offers an important final lesson for the argument I have been making about the embeddedness of theories of disgust within the cultural terrain of the nineteenth century. Taking a long view of modern European social formation, Elias argued that the gradual centralization of state power from the Middle Ages through the early modern period, as well as the resultant monopoly on the use of force and violence, was responsible for wide-ranging changes in the affective life of subjects far removed from the seats of power. There was a connection between state formation, or sociogenesis, he insisted, and subject formation, or psychogenesis; if the former could be said to follow an unplanned path of rationalization at the institutional level of bureaucratic organization or the structures of law and taxation, the same could be said of the latter at the level of what Elias called the civilizing habitus, characterized by "the muting of drives" and other forms of "affective molding." There was in this sense a long-term "social constraint towards self-constraint," as Elias memorably put it in a chapter of the same title, for which he found abundant evidence in the documentation of changes in the history of manners and etiquette.[42]

*Civilization* was Elias's name for the long unfolding of this interplay between the social processes of state formation and the psychological processes of self-restraint that resulted in the formation of the modern habitus. This has often been dismissed as Elias's psychoanalytically inflected infantilization of the Middle Ages as an era of impulsiveness and unrepressed emotionality, contrasted with the alleged emotional maturity of modernity.[43] It is true that the range of affects that Elias imagined necessary to have at the ready in a society where violence was not meant to be the sole prerogative of a centralized state was greater than in a modern, centralized, and functionally differentiated society, where even basic social tasks, such as driving down the street, require intensive affective regulation and restraint. In an important sense, modernity and rationalization for Elias did involve increasing emotional restraint. As I will discuss at length in chapter 4, this put Elias's theory squarely within a nineteenth-century tradition of racialized civilizational discourse, which deemed "premodern" and non-European people as infantile and overly emotional, and which also gave rise to the modern sociological method. Yet Elias also pointed the way toward the eventual dismantling of this prejudice, insofar as he argued that the medium through which the civilizing process made its demands for affective restraint was what he called "advances in the threshold of repugnance and the frontier of shame."[44]

This small detail in Elias's sweeping argument has far-reaching consequences for the way we judge the plausibility of his synthesis as well as for our understanding of the social functions of disgust in the nineteenth century. Elias adapted the emphasis on shame and disgust from Freud, who theorized the emotions as "watchmen" who maintain repression, as well as a model for repression itself. What starts to become clear in the more historically grounded world of Elias's study (clearer than in the mythic anthropology of its close contemporary, *Civilization and Its Discontents*) is that there is not ultimately a basis for distinguishing in any conceptually meaningful way between the affects that are restrained in the civilizing process and the affects that do the restraining. That is, if civilizational training is effected by making *more* experiences feel *more* disgusting and *more* shameful at a prereflective emotional level, then it becomes difficult to see how the psychological analogue to the rationalization of state power is a process of emotional restraint rather than one of emotional augmentation and amplification. Even if one accepts that the range of different affects called into play by the civilizing process is more restricted—a very different argument, it seems to me—we might just as well argue that moderns had become more impulsive, more emotional than their "uncivilized" forebears, albeit more affectively homoge-nized and predictable. But even that argument has the ring of absurdity to it. In a world where disgust is the medium through which affectivity is policed and pressured into new organizations, allegations of emotional histrionics and impulsivity are foundationless, and ultimately collapse in on themselves. "It is difficult to see," Elias writes, "whether the radical contraposition of 'civilization' and 'nature' is more than an expression of the tensions of the 'civilized' psyche itself, of a specific imbalance within psychic life produced in the recent stage of Western civilization."[45]

Read this way—against its own terms, to a degree—Elias's civilizing pro-cess more closely resembles Michel Foucault's account of the biopolitical optimization of the disciplinary subject than Freud's story of the unbearable constrictions of modern alienation.[46] For Foucault as for Elias, rationaliza-tion depended on the malleability of aspects of one's psycho-physiological constitution that seem as though they should be least likely to change. In *Discipline and Punish* as well as in *The History of Sexuality*, Foucault showed that the historical transformation of discursive and social structures such as took place in the late eighteenth and nineteenth centuries could hardly transpire without a concomitant transformation of the habitus and affective organization of the individual. "We believe that feelings are immutable," Foucault observes, "but every sentiment, particularly the noblest and most disinterested, has a history. We believe in the dull constancy of instinctual life, and imagine that it continues to exert its force indiscriminately as it did in the past. But a knowledge of history easily disintegrates this unity, depicts its wavering course, locates its moments of strength and weakness, and defines its oscillating reign."[47]

What both thinkers help us to see is that the range of social meanings that can accrue to an emotion are subject to historical change, and that those changes themselves at once influence and are influenced by larger-scale pro-cesses of historical change in unexpected ways. "The formation of feelings of shame and revulsion and advances in the threshold of repugnance are both at once natural and historical processes," Elias writes. "These forms of feeling are manifestations of human nature under specific social condi-tions, and they react in their turn on the socio-historical process as one of its elements."[48] The following study draws its methodological inspiration from Foucault and Elias, seeking to track precisely such alterations and continuities in the social functions of disgust, against the already volatile backdrop of social transformation in Britain throughout the second half of the nineteenth century. Among the most significant of these changes was disgust's coming to prefigure a civilizational crisis in its own right, even as self-consciousness and theoretical knowledge about its central role in the civilizing process increased. That is, disgust came at once to function as a significant medium of affective restraint and regulation, as well as an emblem of the disruptive and primitive nature that needed to be restrained and regulated. In this regard, the emotion took on its unstable recursive structure, the contours of which we have already begun to trace.

One of the most historically recent sources Elias drew on was the 1859 etiquette manual *The Habits of Good Society*. With chapters including "The Teeth," "The Nails," and "The Hair," as well as a host of sections on social activities ranging from "Self-Defence" and "Dancing" to "Carving a Joint" and "Habits at Meals," the book is memorable for its presentation of an emphatically embodied Victorian person at precisely the historical moment when the abstractions of the liberal subject were being given their most sophisticated articulation. Yet as should by now be clear, I do not treat this as an antithesis. Although the book goes to great length to detail with extreme precision the best way to police and to regulate the human body, its ultimate object was to instruct Victorians on how to become "an agreeable member of good society" and "to give pleasure and happiness to others." The goal of all this corporeal training, that is, was to render the body inert or unreactive, undetectable to others—a well-groomed body that might excel at certain activities but could nonetheless belong to any member of its class. In the challenging case of one's mouth, this neutralization of the body meant attending not only to objects stuck in the teeth but also to one's breath, the odor of which extended beyond the immediate envelope of the self and threatened to negate all one's conscious striving to be sociable and articulate by provoking disgust in one's companions. "Let words be what they may," the book warns, "if they come with an impure odour, they cannot please."[49]

·   Civilization is the primary register in which *The Habits of Good Society* articulates this neutralization of the body in the service of social aspiration, and in the zero-sum game of Victorian manners, the provocation of disgust in others is at once the token of their cultivation and of one's own barbarism. Thus in a passage Elias quotes in his discussion of the evolution of the fork, the book cautions against eating with one's fingers, adding that "as we are not *cannibals*, I am inclined to think [forks] were a good [invention]." Moreover, this sense of disgust as the stamp of civilization allows the author of the manual to compare it to a religious treatise, arguing that a sermon is "the necessary appendix" to a book of etiquette, and vice versa: "the missionary of the South Sea Islands will tell you that it is useless to teach the savage religion without the addition of a few rules of courtesy."[50] One can see very clearly how the instruction of disgust, its installation at the level of habit and habitus, went hand in hand with the Victorian civilizing project; what was most savage was to have no disgust.

Yet if for Victorian manners bad breath and civilization sat in an inverse relationship to one another, we may return to William Morris's fulmination that "our civilization is passing like a blight, daily growing heavier and more poisonous, over the whole face of the country" in order to find instead the reverse. Rather than the mortified fear of provoking the disgust of the other, we find an anxious complaint that civilization itself had become the bad breath of the world, which as I have suggested was by the close of the century common enough to cut across the ideological spectrum in unpredictable ways. "And yet observe: that thin, scraggy, filthy, mangy, miserable cloud," Ruskin, for instance, writes of the modern blight in his famous lecture "The Storm-Cloud of the Nineteenth Century," adding, "by the plague-wind, every breath of air you draw is polluted."[51] The following pages ask how disgust came to be cast in this complex and often contradictory role: considered the calling card of civilization, it was nonetheless deemed a form of emotional disturbance that needed to be excluded in its own right; debarred in this manner as a disruptive form of excessive feeling, it alone seemed able to provide evidence that civilization itself had gone sour, had rotted from the inside out. What was it in disgust that offered such a rich palette for representing nineteenth-century culture? "They were dust," E. M. Forster would write of British society at the fin de siècle, looking back on the nineteenth century, "and a stink, and cosmopolitan chatter."[52]

# PART I

# The Rationalization of Revulsion

# CHAPTER 1

# The Odor of Things

A trailing robe of sludge and slime,
    Fell o'er his limbs of muddy green,
And now and then, a streak of lime
    Showed where the Board of Works had been;
From out his mouth's mephitic well,
    Poured fetid stench and sulphurous flames,
And—was it sight, or was it smell?—
    All there, somehow, knew Father Thames.

—"How Father Thames Appeared to the Cabinet,"
*Punch*, July 31, 1858

To put it crudely, the memory actually stinks just as in
the present the object stinks; and in the same manner
as we turn away . . . the head and nose . . . in disgust,
the preconscious and the sense of consciousness turn
away from the memory. This is repression.

—Freud to Fliess, November 14, 1897

In June 1858, a heat wave descended on London, leaving the Thames sitting slightly lower than usual and revealing to the nearly three million inhabitants of the metropolis that the river from which they drew their drinking water had become an open sewer visibly overflowing with their own semisolid excrement, which was washed up- and downstream with the tide twice daily in "thick, slushy waves" before coming to rest on the "muddy" shores. For anyone in the vicinity of the riverbanks, the stench was overpowering. No interior space was impregnable; doors and windows were shut tight, but to no avail, "a thick, warm steam, surcharged with odours from every imaginable abomination penetrating into the apartment, and into you," as one self-described "Sufferer in Thames Street" put it. Soon enough, Parliament was engulfed, its windows hung with lime and fresh air pumped in through vents in the Star Chamber as the stench made its way to the core of the state. The *Daily Telegraph* reported a "Panic in a Committee Room," as Benjamin Disraeli, "with a mass of papers in one hand, and with his pocket-handkerchief clutched in the other and applied closely to his nose, and body half-bent, hastened in dismay from the pestilential odours" in search of new quarters in which to debate the Bank Act; a proposal to relocate the whole of Parliament to the countryside was promptly put into circulation.[1] Meanwhile, the Dreadnought infirmary, a floating hospital for retired seamen, pulled up anchor and shipped itself downriver; a woman who had jumped off London Bridge in an attempted suicide was rescued alive but insensible, knocked out cold by the river's hot fumes; shore workers known for their strong stomachs were seen vomiting spontaneously off the docks. And crucially, after six weeks of olfactory crisis and unceasing communal revulsion, a colossal system of intercepting sewers and palatial pumping stations was commissioned, along with the embankment of the Thames—a vast public works project that had been stalled in bureaucratic limbo for more than a decade, and which radically transformed the sanitary, spatial, and administrative landscape of the metropolis.

In this chapter, I consider what it means for a social transformation of this magnitude not only to have been rooted in an experience of collective disgust but also to have been understood as such at the time. For London's Great Stink, as it came to be called, was just that: a moment in which an appeal to unwanted communal affect was generally acknowledged to have been taken as sufficient grounds for juridical intervention in the public sphere and for a major expansion and consolidation of government authority. "This has been a Sanitary Session," the *Times* editorialized. "The Parliamentary gorge has risen quick and high. The House of Commons has followed its nose, and nausea has become a principle of legislation."[2] Disgust had produced political consensus where before there had been none—but in so doing it had also produced a self-consciousness about the general role of sensory and affective experiences such as nausea and revulsion in steering and shaping public affairs. In this regard, the Great Stink was not only an instance of social agreement that came together around a particular understanding of the meaning of the subjective experience of disgust, but also a pivotal moment in the broader historical process of determining which features of the subject (or collectivity of subjects) count toward social agreement in the first place.

The usual name given to this broader historical process, according to which certain disinterested modes of judgment and deindividualized formal qualities of the subject have been given priority over others in the gradual reorganization of the social domain as a space dominated by collectively managed institutions, is *rationalization*. Indeed, one would be hard-pressed to find a better emblem of the rationalization of the city space and the consolidation of the bureaucratic institutions charged with administering it than

Sir Joseph Bazalgette's plan for the drainage of London and the embankment of the Thames, a proposal that threaded its way through parliamentary gridlock over the course of many years. Antiquated and haphazard methods of waste removal—the accumulated outcome of centuries of conflicting attitudes toward urban filth and municipal responsibility—gave way to a more effectual and systematic approach; concrete infrastructure paved over mud; ancient tunnels were modernized; and London's so-called *cloaca maxima* was buried out of sight, all but out of mind, with the goal of rooting out from the social domain unwanted and disruptive affective experiences and the public health dangers they were feared to pose. "In the large-scale transformation of the river and its human ecology," Jules Law has written, "politicians and public alike could find a model for the 'progressive' state management and regulation of entities straddling the boundary between public and private. The embankment thus symbolized and consolidated one of the most profound shifts in relations between bodies and public space in mid-Victorian Britain."[3]

Disgust was a significant motive force behind the specific rationalization processes that were catalyzed by the Great Stink. The peculiarity and difficulty of establishing this fact lies in claiming to find subjective emotion expression and the appeal to affective experience at the very heart of rationalization processes whose raison d'être has been understood precisely, in Weber's terms, as the elimination "from official business [of] love, hatred, and all purely personal, irrational, and emotional elements which escape calculation."[4] Yet time and again, and in various arenas of social change throughout the nineteenth century, disgust became the discursive-affective medium through which the exclusion of subjective and affective experience from putatively rational processes took place. Consequently, the discourse of disgust that was mobilized in the wake of the Great Stink complicates our received understanding of rationalization in a number of very specific ways. This chapter focuses particularly on the extent to which mid-nineteenth-century rationalizing appeals to disgust depended, contra Weberian accounts, on ascribing to the emotion a total irrationality nevertheless characterized by its utter calculability, a reflexive dependability that was often taken as a kind of ersatz or pseudo-objectivity. To experience disgust was understood as an intensely sensuous, highly subjective experience, unable by definition to transcend the realm of strong personal feeling—and yet for all that, it was also an experience whose alleged universal undesirability was implicitly acknowledged, without apparent contradiction, to provide a sufficiently predictable albeit unstable basis for a model of social agreement that prioritized disinterestedness and objectivity.

While the first section of this chapter paints a portrait of this structure of unwanted feeling, within which disgust was simultaneously invoked and disavowed as a foundation for social agreement, the second traces the underlying conception of revulsion as a negative sensus communis back to its proximal origin in debates in Enlightenment aesthetics, where the disgusting was excluded from artistic composition as the antithesis of the beautiful. Aesthetic theory offers the sole sustained theoretical investigation into the meaning of disgust prior to Darwin and after him Freud, and aesthetic subjectivity also offers the strongest explanatory model for understanding how disgust took on its specifically contradictory status as an emotional basis for the exclusion of emotion from the realm of social judgment. Yet while thinkers as diverse as Hannah Arendt, Pierre Bourdieu, and Jacques Rancière have for quite some time understood the relevance of aesthetic theory to lie in just such an expanded social and political context rather than in the restricted domains of art and literature, the specific pleasures and disgusts of the aesthetic subject have rarely been invoked in the context of nineteenth-century British culture, where the discourses of liberalism, sympathy, and utilitarianism have for various reasons held sway. Part of my endeavor in this chapter, then, is to show how the aesthetic discourse of disgust and the revolted subject it calls into being are better equipped than either the principle of utility or the self-sovereign individual to explain the public role that disgust came to play during the Great Stink.

I call the process by which strong, putatively excessive feeling was installed as an engine of the depersonalization and desubjectification of particular social domains *aesthetic rationalization*. Like Foucault's discussion of the sensory and affective dimensions of disciplinary power and Elias's historical account of the formation of the modern rationalized habitus through affective shaping and the molding and muting of drives, this account calls attention to the precise ways in which rationalization depended on alterations in the meanings afforded to aesthetic experience broadly construed. Disgust figures centrally in the unfolding of this long-term process for a number of reasons that bear directly on its active role in the public processes surrounding the cleansing of the metropolis. First, disgust came to be understood as a calculable, quasi-instinctual form of judgment, a compulsory voice bubbling up from within the body and demanding agreement about the need to be rid of its unwanted objects. On this account, the strength and reflexive automaticity of feeling constitute the grounds for judgment; the proof is in the puking. This compulsory attribute of disgust allowed it to integrate into a politico-juridical framework that placed an increasing emphasis on predictable, rule-governed processes that connected cause to effect. In the context of the Great Stink, disgust proved for this reason to be a highly effective administrative emotion.

Second, the rhetorical strength and pseudo-objectivity of disgust were complicated by a self-effacing activity that was not so much ascribed to the emotion as enacted by it, and that was connected to a constellation of phenomenological characteristics traditionally associated with the emotion's confusion of boundaries and its negative grammar. In articulating one's disgust, this account of the emotion goes, one confers recognition on an object through its seemingly instinctual repudiation—as in the simplest cases, by spitting it out or vomiting, or by turning away. In bestowing meaning on some object through its repudiation, the involuntary *act* of rejection thus also becomes a *performance* of rejection, a socially symbolic gesture that conveys its negative judgment to others, regardless of its success in eliminating the unwanted thing. Yet while the expression of disgust only sometimes overlaps with the actual rejection of a disgusting object, this distinction between gag reflex and communicative action or performance is rarely remarked; to the contrary, the confusion is part of what gives disgust its rhetorical force.

The play between symbolic or enacted repudiation and embodied or corporeal rejection can ramify in significant ways. In "Negation," for instance, Freud invoked and further developed this double-sided structure of disgust when he observed that the infantile ejection (or egestion) of objects from the body sits at the root of adult capacities for qualitative (i.e., good/bad) as well as existential (i.e., real/unreal) judgments about the external world. In this light, what is thrown outside the self in disgust is at once gone and bad or, more to the point, gone because bad, and in this sense the emotion depends on a particular affective mode of imagination or fantasy—specifically, the fantasy that one's deeply negative subjective experience will take effect as a kind of objective disappearing act.[5] It is through this fantasy that disgust serves as a complex grammatical pivot point between the qualitative and the existential, between fact and value, between the sensation of distaste and the desire for an absence.

That absence can be attributed to a particular object, but it can also be attributed to the sensation of distaste itself, and it is this latter formation that contributed so prominently to disgust's absorption into the sociopolitical affairs of the nineteenth century. In this case, the primary confusions between reflex and symbolic gesture and between qualitative and existential negativity are exacerbated by further confusions about the location of the objects that provoke one's disgust, and by anxiety regarding the transgression of boundaries. Sometimes the revolting object is something diffuse or ephemeral that threatens to enter the self through the body's openings, like a rotten smell or unavoidable atmosphere; sometimes it is something already internal, something that comes back up. Sometimes the object of disgust is neither wholly external nor exactly an object, but rather, as Darwin hypothesized, a disgusting idea or imagination or memory. Such boundary confusions reduplicate in theoretical accounts of disgust and tend toward a more fundamental ambiguity about whether what has to be rejected are the objects that cause feelings of disgust or the feelings themselves. For once the self's boundaries have been opened up and transgressed, object and feeling may be too closely enmeshed with each other to be fully distinguished. Rather than naming a subjective state belonging to a coherent self, then, we might say that disgust names the performed, aspirational repudiation of an unwanted collapsing of relations between a subject and an object.

With surprisingly little variation, this constellation of effects and relational features has accompanied the discourse of disgust from its initial aesthetic theorization through psychoanalysis and on to contemporary psychological and neuroscientific studies. There is, in a sense, a relatively stable set of meanings that can be attached to collective disgust, even if the meanings themselves appear explicitly as forms of fantasy or are defined as unstable in themselves. Consequently, the appeal to disgust has long claimed a special coherence and self-evidence in public discourse as a form of collective affective experience entitled to demand social recognition. It is in this regard that collective disgust is able to produce a powerful variant of the kind of politics of sentimentality and sympathetic identification that, according to thinkers such as Lauren Berlant, in large part organize national belonging in contrast to and alongside juridical forms of sociopolitical membership. The revolted subject is in many ways a version of what Berlant has called "the subject of true feeling," a wounded subject whose affective experiences can claim a "hard-wired truth, a core of common sense [that places it] beyond ideology, beyond mediation, beyond contestation." Pain, in particular, Berlant argues, has the status in the "dominant public sphere" of a "universal true feeling," which can galvanize collective identity around the desire for its eradication. Significantly, in discussing pain—that most utilitarian of aversive experiences—Berlant slips into an olfactory register. "Theoretically," she writes, "to eradicate the pain those with power will do whatever is necessary to return the nation once more to its legitimately utopian odor."[6]

What is singular about the role of disgust in this context is that it is an affect invoked specifically to demonstrate the self-evidence of the general need to delimit and police the role of affect in the public sphere. This introduces a recursive character to the collective appeal to disgust that makes it difficult to account for simply in terms of the utilitarian pleasure-pain calculus. That is, while an outcry of collective revulsion such as the Great Stink certainly called for the eradication of the particular, localized nuisance, it also sought to further the progressive disqualification of affective experience as a basis for social agreement. Unlike the sentimental politics Berlant describes, this project has in general tended to look forward, rather than backward, for its justification, toward a fantasy of a sanitary future rather than toward the restoration of the "utopian odor" of the past.[7] Through its own productive exclusion, disgust has been a passion of rationalization, modernity, and civilization.

Needless to say, the self-effacing activity of the discourse of disgust makes it difficult to determine what cultural materials form part of its history, since the language of disgust is itself constantly provoking disgust and so being repudiated or rejected in various ways. This difficulty has led some to doubt the very possibility of a history of disgust separate from its history in theory. "The ambition to write a history of 'actual' disgust . . . meets with almost insurmountable difficulties," writes Menninghaus. "The relevant data have made only a negligible entrance into the cultural archive. As a rule, it has not seemed worthwhile to record such data; what is more, their recording would have been rejected as unworthy, indecent, and abominable."[8] Yet this is an obvious overstatement. The cultural archive of disgust is not only out there but also voluminous—the Great Stink alone yielding "an epidemic diarrhea of speeches, motions, notices of questions," as the sober *Lancet* put it in the heat of the moment.[9] But to be sure, this archive does not yield a positive history. Rather, it provides a narrative of disgust that comes in and out of focus across a strikingly diverse body of texts and cultural artifacts— from the periodical record of the Great Stink to the concrete solidity of the Thames Embankment and the shimmering splendor of the Crossness and Abbey Mills sewage pumping stations. Such cultural artifacts show us the unstable centrality that "actual" disgust claimed throughout the Victorian period in producing its own rationalization and in performing its own erasure. All throughout the nineteenth century, one encounters such fantasies of successful elimination, radiating out from the strong sensations caused by disruptive objects to ever more diffuse and metaphysical cultural conditions. Not merely a matter of dredging the Thames, the Great Stink became the occasion for ridding civilization of its pollutant animality, of removing "the filth of the greatest city in the universe," as though London were a modern Thebes.[10] And this ever-increasing ephemerality, too, is part of the

A DROP OF LONDON WATER.

**FIGURE 2.**   *Punch*'s 1850 cartoon "The Wonders of a London Water Drop" prefigured the "Sanitary Session" of the summer of 1858. *Punch*, May 11, 1850. Courtesy of the University of Chicago Library.

self-sanitizing historical drift of the emotion. The archive of communal disgust that constitutes the record of the Great Stink of London is written in a language that is perpetually mopping up after itself, cleansing its own words of their reliance on the articulation of unwanted feeling—but for all that, it was documented ad nauseam.

## The Sanitary Session

In the two decades prior to the Great Stink, sewage, sewers, and public health were all integral to the gradual consolidation of Britain's state apparatuses and to major transformations in the way the social sphere was conceptualized and social space was regulated. Driving these changes was the sanitary commissioner Edwin Chadwick with his controversial "sanitary idea," an insidious utilitarian vision of a deodorized state, cleansed of its reeking lower classes and managed by a central government that would be empowered to wash the nation physically, morally, and socioeconomically all at once. Subtending the sanitary idea was Chadwick's adherence to the now benighted miasma theory, which held that diseases such as cholera were transmitted through respiratory and olfactory pollution. Consequently, miasma theorists placed an extreme importance on smell, nuisance, and the evidence of disgust, which even from the perspective of germ theory, developed only a few decades later, already appeared as a pseudoscientific superstition rooted in premodern beliefs about contagion. However, at the height of Chadwick's adherence to the miasma theory—when, for instance, he uttered his now-famous dictum that "*all* smell is disease"—the scientific disenchantment had yet to take place.[11] Instead, competing theories of disease transmission circulated and clashed alongside equally incommensurable political ideologies in the emergent domain of public health. It was the augmentation and transformation in the role of disgust that actually made it possible to overcome the miasma theory, rather than a straightforward narrative of scientific progress.

A former member of the Poor Law Commission in the 1830s, Chadwick brought the disciplinary and observational techniques that had been forged in the context of the workhouse to bear on questions of public health and domestic sanitary conditions across the nation. The result was his 1842 *Report on the Sanitary Condition of the Labouring Population of Great Britain*, which combined empirical testimony with statistical tabulation to produce an account of the dire living conditions of the British working class and to call for a major overhaul of government policies on drainage and waste removal. As Mary Poovey has persuasively argued, Chadwick's vision of a sanitary society was motivated at once by an anxious desire to regulate the working class and administer their domestic spaces so as to minimize their opportunities for political association, and a self-serving desire to promote his own class interests by arguing that only an elite group of technocratic administrators could properly undertake that task.[12]

Rationalization and centralization were the two great pillars of Chadwick's vision for the sanitary society. Where he saw a tangle of conflicting local ordinances, outdated nuisance laws, and antiquated, inefficient systems of drainage and sewage collection, he strove to erect a modern, uniform, and economically rational infrastructure that would work the same way in all towns and cities throughout Great Britain. "The advantages of uniformity in legislation and in the executive machinery, and of doing the same things in the same way (choosing the best), and calling the same officers, proceedings, and things by the same names," the 1842 report concludes, "will only be appreciated by those who have observed the extensive public loss occasioned by the legislation for towns which makes them independent of beneficent, as of what perhaps might have been deemed formerly aggressive legislation."[13] Animated in large part by Chadwick's disciplinary and rationalizing vision, the Public Health Act of 1848 created Britain's first national board of health and empowered local governments to create their own boards on the national model, reflecting the extent to which the kind of formal rationality and uniformity Chadwick had been assiduously promoting were taking root as common practice in the political sphere.

The sewer was the pièce de résistance in Chadwick's sanitary overhaul of society.[14] The overaccumulation of human feces in cesspools behind individual houses; the wafting clouds of miasmatic stench they emitted, believed to transmit deadly diseases, such as cholera, from house to house; the haphazard inefficiency and threatening contagion of the nightsoil men who came to cart off the excrement, tracking it across town—against the backdrop of precisely these conditions of anxiety-provoking seepage, of human waste and smell transgressing the boundaries of the city, Chadwick held up the sewer as the techno-rational answer to the filth of the modern metropolis. More than a simple improvement on already extant city infrastructure, the sewer for Chadwick was the principal weapon in a full-scale hydraulic war waged against the overflowing, leaking city. It was the perfect technology: out of sight, deodorizing, centralizable, and efficient—the only truly rational answer to the problem posed by the identification of smell with disease. Especially in the sanitary landscape of London, Chadwick and his supporters were relentless in their advocacy for drainage and reform. While it did not fully realize Chadwick's centralizing vision, the passage of the Metropolitan Sewers Act (1848), Michelle Allen writes, "marked an important step in standardizing London's drainage, from both an administrative and a technological perspective," and resulted in the eradication of the cesspool and its eventual replacement by the flush toilet and new sewer pipes.[15]

The results were devastating. Within a matter of years, nearly all of London's feces were being sluiced underground and dumped into the Thames, where they would sail around with the tides until they sank to the bottom, washed up on the muddy shore, or were pumped into a glass of drinking water. Meanwhile, water consumption spiked with the popularization of the flush toilet and strained the old sewer system past the point of rupture.

Infrastructurally, the city had hit its limit; it was bursting at the seams with its own excrement. Thus Chadwick's answer to the stagnant residential cesspool helped make the Thames into a single "great cesspool instead of each person having one of his own," as the prominent London builder and architect Thomas Cubitt put it.[16] This state of affairs had the effect, on the one hand, of gratifying opponents of drainage and, perhaps more importantly, opponents of government centralization, who saw in Chadwick's agenda a major overreach of state authority; on the other hand, it exacerbated what had already been an ideologically volatile public debate about how to meet the infrastructural needs of the city, how to avoid the next outbreak of cholera, and above all what to do with London's mountains of garbage and rivers of waste.

Within the context of this debate, Chadwick's statist and utilitarian ideology is remarkable for its faith in a comparatively simple logic of *removal*, a logic derived from Jeremy Bentham's hedonistic pleasure-pain calculus. Extending the principle of utility to the legal, medical-scientific, and sensory contexts of nuisance law and public health reform, Chadwick saw the sewer as a liberty-increasing and pain-removing technology. In tension with this focus on removal, however, one finds all throughout the period a vast discourse calling for the *reuse* of feces as manure that, while not opposed to the utilitarian view, nevertheless depended on an entirely different imagination of the social status of waste and placed less emphasis on the construction of new sewers as an end in itself. Indeed, even Chadwick himself saw the appeal of developing technologies for treating sewage that would allow Britain to "complete the circle," as he put it, "and realize the Egyptian type of eternity by bringing as it were the serpent's tail into the serpent's mouth."[17] Among the many voices leading this charge was the social investigator Henry Mayhew, who, bolstered by his calculations that 278,000 tons of sewage were being discharged into the Thames each day, argued that the failure to reuse London's homegrown sewage as fertilizer (instead of imported South American and Caribbean guano) meant that "we are positively wasting £4,000,000 of money each year; or rather," he caustically concluded, "*it costs us that amount to poison the waters about us.*"[18]

Like Chadwick's attachment to the sewer as a technological solution, Mayhew's fervent enthusiasm for the reuse of human manure produced a comparably ideological account of the modern metropolis. Mayhew's fantasy was homeostatic, a techno-utopian vision of the city as a self-regulating and self-calibrating machine that, if it followed proper scientific principles, could in fact be fed and nourished by its own excrement—a fantasy that largely depended on rationally overcoming or being free from disgust. "It has been mercifully ordained by a bountiful Providence that the excrements of men and animals returned to the soil should become the germ of all that is lovely in creation," a letter to the *Times* titled "Dirty Cleanliness" urged its readers to consider, going on to argue strenuously against wastefulness in the management of waste.[19] Later in the century, Émile Zola would fully elaborate this position in *La terre*, taking its inherent utopianism to a fever pitch through the voice of his character Hourdequin, whose "theory was that everything that came from the soil was a proper material to return to it":

> "The yearly refuse of Paris alone would be sufficient to fertilise some seventy thousand acres," said the farmer. "It has all been properly calculated. And yet this is all wasted. There is only just a small quantity of dried night-soil utilised. Just think of it; seventy thousand acres! Ah, if we could only have it here, it would cover all La Beauce, and then you would see the wheat grow!" He embraced the whole level extent of La Beauce in a sweeping gesture; and in his enthusiasm he mentally beheld all Paris pouring out its fertilising flood of human manure over the spreading tract. Streamlets were trickling along in all directions, overflowing the fields as the sea of sewage mounted higher and higher beneath the glowing sun, sped onward by a breeze which wafted the odour far and wide. The great city was restoring to the soil the life it had received from it. The earth slowly absorbed the fertilising tide, and from the glutted and fattened soil there burst forth great teeming harvests of white bread.[20]

A full history of this pervasive autocoprophagic fantasy about the productive, self-sustaining capacities of waste has yet to be written, but it extends far beyond Mayhew's imaginative tabulations about London's waste economy and Zola's reveries of an engorged Paris. On the one hand, this history would intersect with the long-term formation of what Peter Sloterdijk has called "merdocratic space," the necessarily atmospheric and olfactory nature of all cityscapes as they deal with their own waste; this way of understanding cities as the corporeal emanations and exhalations of their populations, Sloterdijk observes, is intrinsically territorial, even nationalist: "What one calls home is the place whose stench one views as a merit."[21] But on the other hand, this history would also take in the full extent of the "guano era," the international trade in avian fertilizer that emerged in the wake of the industrialization of European agriculture and the long reach of informal empire: a global history of the slow-moving boats, laden with shit, that, for a few decades in the middle of the nineteenth century, inched their way out from the Peruvian Islas Chincha, Oman's Khuriya Muriya Bay, and the Leeward bird isle of Redonda, steaming back to the docks at Rotherhithe and Saint Katharine alongside the heaps of oranges, tea, and ivory.

Set against both the utilitarian sanitary idea and this utopian vision of self-sufficiency, a deep current of antistatist and anticentralization political ideology, of which Herbert Spencer's *Social Statics* (1851) was one of the most significant statements, also shaped mid-nineteenth-century sanitary reform. As Allen has shown in some detail, Spencer's chapter "Sanitary Supervision" pushed back against Chadwick's rationalizing and centralizing plan. His argument was that allowing the government to take a public interest in "health" would lead down a slippery slope toward "the universal supervision of private conduct": "He who contaminates the atmosphere breathed by his neighbor, is infringing his neighbor's rights," Spencer admitted—but beyond mitigating such infringements, the law had no right to intervene.[22] Spencer pursued this line of thinking so far as to argue that neither the state nor even local and municipal governments possessed the right to collect garbage, to provide drainage, or generally to attend to public health. Instead, "houses might be readily drained on the same mercantile principle that they are now supplied with water. It is highly probable that in the hands of a private company the resulting manure would not only pay the cost of collection, but would yield a considerable profit."[23] In a sense, this position simply ran Chadwick's idea about drainage in reverse: where Chadwick had seen sewer pipes as a means of draining dangerous filth and moral-political transgression *from* working-class domestic spaces, Spencer saw the very same pipes as obtrusions that would transgress *into* the bourgeois home, and so represented an assault on domestic autonomy. Both ideologies worked in concert to protect bourgeois class interests, but where Chadwick saw an interventionist opportunity for an expansion of state power, Spencer saw an open field of free-market competition that he alleged was already solving all the age's public health problems. "One would have thought that less excuse for meddling existed now than ever," he writes, "now that spontaneous advance is being made at an unparalleled rate; now that the laws of health are beginning to be generally studied; now that people are reforming their habits of living"—and so on.[24]

Modern public health and sanitary reform were born at this knotty juncture of irreconcilable ideological positions and competing medical-scientific explanations. While Chadwick's influence on actual policy and legislation ebbed and flowed throughout the 1840s and 1850s, the trend toward the centralization of government authority and toward treating sanitation as a basic public service clearly reflects the general contours of his social vision, even if Britain's administrative state apparatus did not expand to the same degree as that in France.[25] Perhaps more than anything, Chadwick, along with Engels and Mayhew, left his individual mark on the history of social investigation and analysis, which is the closely related subject of a subsequent chapter in this book. What is significant for the present discussion is that in the spring of 1858, the possibility of authorizing the construction of a £6 million centralized sewer system was ensnared in so much red tape and bureaucratic chicanery that even its staunchest advocate would have laughed at the possibility of passing it through both houses of Parliament by the end of the summer. And yet this is exactly what happened. Within weeks of the Great Stink's first fumes the Local Government Act, which would supplant Chadwick's 1848 Public Health Act, was already making its way through various committees—not without resistance, but with a sense of forward momentum that seemed likely to cut the Gordian knot the sewage question had become.

This momentum was generated and maintained almost entirely through the public appeal to the collective experience of disgust during the five or six weeks when the stench of the river engulfed the city. "The stench of the Thames," the *Lancet* reported, "has fairly taken the public by the nose, and compelled them to entertain most seriously questions of sanitary reform. The subject can no longer be burked, for it literally forces itself down our throats."[26] This urgency was channeled principally along two discursive axes: first, in the periodical press, where hundreds of columns, letters to the editor, medical-scientific analyses, and transcripts of debates and board meetings transformed the appeal to collective disgust into a technology of sensory persuasion, a rhetorical tool for producing consensus as a foregone conclusion of the social body; and second, in Parliament, where the olfactory encroachment of the open sewer into the penetralia of the seat of government produced a crisis about the actual location of the state and introduced a newly volatilized civilizational dimension into what had previously been a much drier jurisdictional affair. Disgust in this respect took on an affective-rhetorical role in the press, at the same time that it provoked a cultural crisis in the discourse of politics. Neither of these interlocking ideological functions was entirely new—to the contrary, they appeared to come as it were naturally to the way that people understood the experience of their own revulsion. What was new, however, was that the discourse of this unwanted emotion was so readily available as a juridical and collective ideology. What did it mean that this society was so willing, eager even, to declare as its sensus communis the gagging, bug-eyed experience of shared disgust, and to allow nausea to become "a principle of legislation"? And in these months leading up to John Stuart Mill's public inauguration of the disinterested and self-sovereign individual as the public face and ego ideal of the Victorian era, what kind of subject could claim the reflexive churning of its stomach as the grounds for taking the plunge into a rationalized modernity that had been anxiously forestalled for decades?

One of the more insistent refrains in the periodical press throughout the stink was that the intensity of disgust reported by everyday Londoners needed to be felt by those who held political power in order for change to occur. As the stench lingered, there was a mounting conviction about the political efficacy of disgust in provoking action. "Sir,—Ten days' hot weather is likely to do more for the purification of the Thames than ten years of commissions, blue-books, and all the intricate machinery of proving 'officially' the existence of an evil of which every one is 'practically' cognizant," one such letter to the editor begins, adding, "without being hard-hearted, I sincerely hope that Monday will be a scorching day, that the river will be at dead low water, that the stench will be overpowering, and that . . . the chairman of the Committee will live in metropolitan history a prototype of Hercules in a classic stable."[27] "What a pity it is that the thermometer fell ten degrees yesterday!" another letter exclaims.

> Parliament was all but compelled to legislate upon the great London nuisance by the force of sheer stench. . . . It is right that our legislators should be made to feel in health and comfort the consequences of their own disregard for the public welfare. . . . Now that they are fairly driven from their libraries and committee-rooms—or better still, forced to remain in them, with a putrid atmosphere around them—they may, perhaps, spare a thought for the Londoners. . . . Let them be confined in a river steamer and compelled to ply between London and Vauxhall bridges until they have agreed upon a plan, or the last man of their number has been summoned away to regions where the stench which they have protected can trouble them no more.[28]

Or better yet, from the pages of the British Medical Journal:

> What is to become of us Londoners in the year of grace 1858? Are the terrible events of 1665 to be repeated? and is this vast metropolis to be devastated by plague? . . . We rejoice, however, that their lordships' library is nothing better than a stench-trap. If the Lord Chancellor would only have a mild diarrhœa, it would be of infinite service; and the fainting of a few cabinet ministers from a similar cause would

be indeed an invaluable occurrence to the nobodies of this vast town, who have so long suffered from the state of the Thames in silence.[29]

As the stink lingered on, then, there emerged a widely held sentiment that "conviction rose with the quicksilver in the thermometer."[30] Clearly this sentiment had the unchallenged and incontestable status of common sense—a common sense about the status of the senses, and about the capacity of unwanted sensation to persuade where reason or argument could not. One couldn't argue with disgust; it forced itself on you and you rejected it and that was all. In the following section, I will put this formulation into dialogue with its exact counterpart—*de gustibus non est disputandum*—the commonplace of aesthetic theory that one needn't bother arguing over mere tastes. For now, it is enough to observe that the Great Stink made it clear that arguing over *dis*taste was held to be useless not because it was subjective and therefore private, but because it was subjective and yet nevertheless public and reflexive; in fact, such evidence of the senses was the only standard for public action that would do. Where blue books and inquiries, medical science, and feats of engineering had failed, public discourse declared disgust the blue book of the nostril, a form of sensory pseudo-objectivity that no one could question. Let the lord chancellor have diarrhea, the papers all seemed to agree, then he will *feel* "'practically'" what he does not "'officially'" *know*.

In these outcries from the public sphere, the appeal to disgust was a rhetorical tool that sought not only to persuade the government to act but to persuade everybody about what ought to count as the grounds for persuasion in matters of social importance. Implicit in these acts of persuasion was the notion that disgust represented an unofficial discourse, a voice from below or within that the officially recognized discourses of science and politics had ignored or disavowed; against this ideological obfuscation, a chorus of revolted subjects demanded that the collective voice of disgust be heard in the highest levels of the public and political spheres. Yet the message that this collective voice would deliver was an urgent petition for its own removal. Listen to your nose and your gut, it said; one should never have to listen to one's nose and one's gut. The strong, reflexive sense experiences of the stink were the best evidence that strong sensation ought to be minimized and marginalized within the social domain—for who could argue with the story the body told about itself? Rhetorically, then, disgust was construed as both the means of removal (the only voice capable of speaking up for the public interest) and the object to be removed (an unwanted experience anathema to ordinary public life).

In the debates over the stink that took place in Parliament, this recursive conception of disgust came up against and ultimately merged with an acrimonious jurisdictional debate over who would be charged with the maintenance of the river: London's cash-strapped and administratively hamstrung Metropolitan Board of Works or a mostly unwilling Parliament made especially eager to head home for the summer. Even if one accepted the urgency of the appeal to collective revulsion, the matter of which agency and what level of government would pay for and oversee the construction of such a massive sewer still needed to be decided. While debating this question was treated in the press as the epitome of ineffectual parliamentary bureaucracy—"The two houses of Parliament have put their foot in it. They cannot move"[31]—it nevertheless led the way into a related set of complex questions about the role and the location of the state that could not be so easily dismissed. For even while the question of who would pay seemed merely to reignite the debate over centralization, the basis for this ideological dispute had real roots in a more fundamental lack of clarity about whether the unwanted mass excreta flowing through the heart of the nation's capital belonged to or even represented Britain at large. And so from this initial lack of jurisdictional clarity, a litany of increasingly anxious questions followed. Who *did* London's shit belong to? Was London merely a physical city, or was it a material symbol of the British nation and empire? And if the latter, what did it mean for Britain's imperial egotism and ambition to have an open sewer gurgling through the heart of town? The suggestion was that a nation unable to toilet train its own leaky capital would be equally incapable of exerting mastery over the rest of the world. What seemed at first a dry procedural affair quickly took on a more volatile character, as the stakes were raised and the stink seemed not only to threaten local operations but "to perpetuate indefinitely a state of things which is a disgrace to the Empire."[32]

As the river's stench transgressed deeper into parliamentary process, it trailed a disruptive sense of unwanted immanence along with it. Indeed, the task of producing the British state from the dead center of the stink began to feel both onerous and incongruous, if not outright impossible. Mr. Brady, MP, "wished to call attention to the House of the impracticability of carrying on the public business of the country . . . in the pestilential atmosphere of the Thames," urging Parliament to petition the queen for permission to relocate to the countryside;[33] whereas Mr. R. D. Mangles was adamant that action needed to be taken: "I wish to ask the noble Lord the Chief Commissioner of Works whether he intends to take any steps with regard to the present state of the River Thames," he asked the House, after which the transcript reads, "[Laughter and Cheers]." "My question, I perceive, excites the laugher of some hon. Gentlemen, but I can assure them that if they lived in the vicinity of the Thames they would not think my question one of little importance."[34] Soon the maintenance of the parliament building itself was in serious trouble. Charged with ventilating the government, the inventor Goldsworthy Gurney reported that he could "be no longer responsible for the health of the House; that the stench has made most rapid advance within two days; that up to Tuesday he got fresh air draughts from the Star Chamber Court; but that when night came the poisonous enemy took possession of the Court, and so beat him outright." Judicial proceedings were likewise stymied by the stink. "The stench of the river is most offensive," Sir Frederick Pollock reported from the Court of the Exchequer, over which he presided, "and I think it right to take public notice of this, that in trying this case we are really sitting in the midst of a stinking nuisance."[35] Lord Campbell reported similar disturbances at the Queen's Bench, which he had almost evacuated in the middle of a trial. "There were no powers," he observed, after suggesting proceedings be moved to Oxford, "which the Government could ask which he would not be prepared to grant them in order to enable them to get rid of so great an evil."[36]

The more urgent and immediate the smell, the more the anxiety it provoked was articulated in the distancing nationalist and imperialist language of civilizational failure and cultural vulnerability. "The question was really one of an imperial character," Mangles—recently appointed head of the East India Company and author of *How to Colonize* (1842)—continued to rail. "He felt persuaded that Parliament ought at once to . . . take the matter into its own hands. This metropolis was by far the most populous and wealthiest city in the world, and yet it appeared that its inhabitants were unable to relieve themselves from the pollution of their own filth."[37] Mr. H. Berkeley argued in a similar vein "that it was a great national question" and that "the proper plan was for the Government to act upon the centralizing principle and ask for dictatorial powers"—otherwise, "they were a weak Government."[38] Disraeli concurred that "the City of London is of a peculiar character." Though he opposed having Parliament pay outright for the sewers, and ultimately carried the day with a complex compromise in which Parliament guaranteed loans, which the municipal government borrowed against future revenues from a new local tax, Disraeli nonetheless agreed that London "is not merely a city in Her Majesty's dominions, but the Metropolis of Her Majesty's dominions . . . not only the most extensive [city] of modern times, but greater than any ancient cities of which we have authentic records." "The inconveniences experienced [in London]," he concluded, "are of a national character."[39] "Old Father Thames is now in his glory," the *Times* weighed in. "He is at once the glory and the shame of this great empire. No metropolis but London could make such a dirt, and foul so large a wash-pot."[40] Beyond the immediate nuisance and the perceived threat of plague and infection, the political rhetoric of disgust took the form of an anxious conviction that Britain could not lay claim to the greatness it had arrogated to itself if it could not administer its own waste; in fact, "the disgusting, disgraceful, and dangerous state of the River Thames—the Putrid River of modern times"—threatened to reverse Britain's civilizational progress and return it to a repulsive state of premodern animality: "Is this atrocious state of a semi-barbarous age to continue?"[41]

Through this shift from sensory urgency to civilizational anxiety, the political proceedings of the Great Stink reproduced in the language of cultural crisis the same self-effacing, recursive rhetoric of disgust as their journalistic counterparts. The characteristic movement is outward: away from the self, away from the subjective experience of revulsion that nevertheless anchors the whole response; and instead toward the assertion of boundaries, toward cultural self-definition and the designation of otherness, and eventually toward the administrative matters of mastery, dominance, and management through which Victorian culture tended to express its racial and imperial arrogance. This whole structure of unwanted feeling is exemplified by the following late-July editorial from the *Times*, in which one can see clearly how the experience of disgust catalyzed the response to the Great Stink and yet was nevertheless disavowed as a motive for action:

> Taken all together, the debate of Monday evening was a good expression of the actual conditions attending the great metropolitan drainage question. Most people can find objections to the measure proposed, nobody feels quite satisfied, in most quarters there are strong misgivings, and yet in the end the Bill is read a second time without so much as a division. The truth is, that this is a case where the fool's argument that "something must be done" is applicable. Something *must* be done. . . . That effluvium showed what the Thames had actually come to. That stink showed what might follow at any time from the filth of our own manufacture under the influence of a few days' sun. By and by, perhaps, the action of the sun may be hardly needed, and we may feel the nuisance every hour. The sewage of a mighty city lies in a broad stream under our very noses, churned up in its waters, putrefying on its banks, and steaming up from its surface. . . . Everybody sees that "something must be done"—a very simple something, so far as its

definition goes. The filth must be carried away, and our atmosphere relieved from pollution.

Now, since it was first thought expedient to do "something," we have passed through exactly ten years without doing anything. . . . It is a bad thing to go upon vicious principles in drainage as well as other matters; it is sad to sink money uselessly; and it will be lamentable if we find ourselves encumbered with a costly and insufficient system of sewerage after all our exertions; but it is, unhappily, beyond all question that if we wait for a concurrence of opinions on this subject, we shall never stick a spade in the ground or construct either a drain or a tunnel, or get, in fact, a single inch beyond the recent expedient of correcting Thames water with tons of lime. . . . The stench of June was only the last ounce of our burden, or rather it was an accidental flash of light which brought a great fact before our eyes. That hot fortnight did for the sanitary administration of the Metropolis what the Bengal mutinies did for the administration of India.[42]

The article begins by justifying its claim exclusively through the appeal to the sensory experience of the nuisance itself. The threat of danger and infection, the sense of frustration at bureaucracy, the imperialist flourish—all take second place, rhetorically, to the odor of things, the olfactory experience which the article presumes will supersede all possible reservations about the need for action. Alongside this battle cry is the anxious articulation of self-implication—"the filth of our own manufacture"—reminding readers that the Great Stink hovering over London was nothing more than the excrescence of their own bodies and adducing a blurring of boundaries and a correspondence between visceral interior and noxious exterior. Analysis published in the *Lancet* went as far as to detail the remnants of last night's dinner floating in the sewage-filled water (samples from beneath London Bridge contained especially noteworthy quantities of "muscular fibre stained with bile, cells of vegetables including potato, hairs, and husk of wheat, and living organic productions of all the classes of cryptogamia").[43]

This boundary confusion, however, enacts the complex rhetorical shift between sensory and cultural registers, making it unclear whether the actual problem is to be found in the river or in the way of life that polluted it. The need for swift repudiation of filth is now a matter of civilization overcoming its own barbarism and animality, of disgust for a total social condition: "The sewage of a mighty city lies in a broad stream under our very noses, churned up in its waters, putrefying on its banks, and steaming up from its surface." If this counts as raising the stakes, it is also a way of denying the initial sensory point of departure, as the stench is handily recast by the end of the editorial in distancing imperial terms: "That hot fortnight did for the sanitary administration of the Metropolis what the Bengal mutinies did for the administration of India." Bounding from the "drainage question" to the collapse of the Mughal Empire, the rhetoric of revulsion in fact sanitizes its own argument; no longer an olfactory crisis within "our very noses," the stink has been metaphorically visualized, "an accidental flash of light which brought a great fact before our eyes." Illuminating the need for deliberate action that is not merely a gut reaction, the article ends by targeting the very expressions of disgust with which it began.

The sense of disgust toward a total social condition formed part of a new structure of feeling that emerged over the course of the first half of the nineteenth century, in response to a heightened sense of moral and physical implication in the ever-increasing pollution of the world. At the center of this structure of feeling lay the physical transgression of the boundaries of the body, primarily through the mouth and the nostrils, and an attendant respiratory repulsion toward suffocating smells felt to enshroud and contaminate from without, even while they emanated from within. This meant that rather than directing disgust at specific objects that could be removed, the aspirations of Victorian social revulsion targeted a whole cultural atmosphere and climate; as the material instigators of revulsion increased by orders of magnitude, the particular shape of Victorian disgust became,

## OUR NASAL BENEFACTORS.

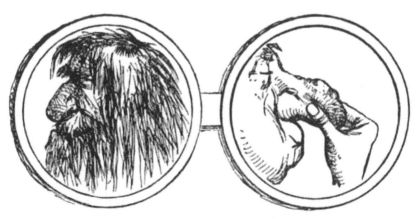

**FIGURE 3.** On July 10, 1858, at the height of the stink, *Punch* called on the government to send out "a Smelling Expedition, for which service none but the sharpest-nosed M.P.s were allowed to volunteer." Courtesy of the University of Chicago Library.

counterintuitively, less corporeal and more ephemeral. This ephemerality highlights a central feature of the rhetoric of Victorian disgust; namely, that it proceeds by repudiating the articulation of physical revulsion that initially anchors it. This form of self-censorship reproduces on a discursive level the corporeal boundary confusion between inside and outside induced in the first place by foul smells; instead, *expressions* of disgust are treated as though they were disgusting *things* themselves which needed to be done away with—a recursive confusion between revolting objects and revolted subjects typical to the Victorian discourse of disgust, but which needs to be understood in light of its proximal origins in eighteenth-century aesthetic theory.

## The Public Nostril

"I look on the question of diverting the sewage of London from the Thames rather as a question of taste than a sanitary question," John Snow declared in the months leading up to the Great Stink, "and I shall not attempt to decide whether the improvement in the appearance of the river would be worth the cost." An outspoken and pioneering critic of the miasma theory, Snow meant that the mere sight and smell of the filthy river posed no particular public health threat to Londoners; in fact, he wrote, "I consider that the river in London was never in a better state, regarding it from a sanitary point of view. Not a single water company now obtains a supply from it, hardly any of the inhabitants on the banks dip a pail into it, and I believe the water is much less used among the sailors . . . than formerly."[44]

Let us take seriously Snow's tongue-in-cheek assertion that in the spring of 1858 the putrid Thames had never been better off—"from a sanitary point of view"—and ask what it would therefore mean to follow him in understanding the great sewage crisis looming over London as a "question of taste." What business did the discourse of taste, first put forward a century earlier amid the well-appointed drawing rooms, philosophical treatises, and picturesque garden rows of the Age of Reason, have with the heaps of human sludge mounting up on the riverbanks, or with the proposed rationalization of the urban environment? What forms of specialized knowledge about the meaning of unwanted feeling did taste offer that could make a claim for consensus in the bourgeois public sphere that neither sanitary nor medical discourse could supply? What was the process by which the aesthetic was absorbed into its new domain? The historiographical implications are no less significant, if what we are tracking is not merely an incidental resemblance between the revulsion of Enlightenment aesthetic theory and the Victorian structure of unwanted feeling, but rather a discursive relationship that was itself to some degree constitutive of how those on the ground seized and made meaning of their own experiences.

Snow's remarks reflect his expectation that readers of the *Medical Times and Gazette* would be able to distinguish between properly sanitary and merely aesthetic justifications for public action. Yet this expectation needs to be understood in the first place within the context of Snow's own intervention, several years earlier, into the rise of public health reform, when he famously demonstrated that cholera was transmitted through contaminated drinking water, rather than through olfactory pollution, by removing the handle of the Broad Street pump during the outbreak of 1854. When Snow distinguishes between aesthetic and sanitary points of view, he therefore also engages an underlying epistemological tension between sanitary or public health concerns and the unstable status of medical-scientific knowledge throughout the 1850s, when the miasma theory still held sway despite Snow's controversial demonstration to the contrary. If concerns about public health were to keep people from contracting cholera, then from Snow's reasoned medical-scientific point of view, people needed to be kept from drinking water contaminated by human feces. However, since there was not yet scientific consensus about the status of the miasma theory, and since policy was still in large part organized around the avoidance of foul smells, Snow here adopts an instrumental attitude toward non-scientific justifications for public action that nonetheless led to reduced risk from Snow's medical-scientific perspective. If the ugliness and stench of the river rather than sound knowledge of disease kept people from drinking their own shit, Snow argued, all the better for London's public health, whereas the question of whether or not it was worth it to clean up that ugliness for its own sake fell outside his sanitary jurisdiction, so to speak.[45]

Where and how does the aesthetic discourse of taste fit into this complex matrix of historico-epistemological concerns? Snow anticipates that his readers will grasp the precise meaning of his suggestion that the cleansing of the river ought to be understood as an aesthetic concern, even if they were to disagree with his argument; it presumes a widespread capacity for understanding certain forms of action in the bourgeois public sphere to be rooted in justifications that appeal principally to matters of appearance and perception, as well as to affective and sensory experience, rather than to scientific or medical principles or to juridical precedents. As we shall see, aesthetic discourse offered just such an approach to dealing with matters of public concern for which no preexisting rule or law or moral precept could be called upon, and yet for which subjectivism was nevertheless felt to be insufficient. Scholars such as Eileen Cleere and Jules Law have given persuasive accounts of how the norms and ideological presuppositions of sanitary reform exerted influence on the aesthetic and cultural production of the middle decades of the nineteenth century; yet the present discussion makes clear the need for an understanding of the sanitary domain itself as drawing on the norms and ideological premises of aesthetic discourse for its justifications.[46]

Snow's comments can point us toward the historically concrete ways that aesthetic theory offered a discursive framework within which affective and sensory experience could be given a legitimate status within the world of public action and debate. Moreover, they suggest that this appropriation of the terms of aesthetic discourse was already by midcentury a self-conscious operation, since Snow's allegation presupposes that some key areas of social life not conventionally understood to be aesthetic (in the restricted sense of the arts) or to be governed by appeals to sensation (in the sense of *aisthesis*) could nevertheless be illuminated by being subsumed under the category of taste. Whereas disgust took on a highly mediated rhetorical function in both political discourse and in the press, this rhetorical function itself made use of and was inflected by a previously existing philosophical discourse of disgust. Indeed, we can glean from Snow a sense of how aesthetic theory came to impact the role that disgust played in the social transformations of the mid-nineteenth century, and to inform the way that people understood the social meaning of their own affective experiences.

Thus Snow sends us back to the Enlightenment discourse of taste in search of a plausible model for the kind of revolted public agreement provoked by the smell and sight of the polluted river. And indeed, his implicit assumption that matters of taste are defined by their exclusion from scientific and objective domains would have been at home in eighteenth-century philosophical debates regarding the nature of aesthetic judgment, which were largely animated by a desire to identify an autonomous faculty of decision-making that was neither purely sensual nor determined by rules or concepts. While the articulation of this mode of judgment may have taken shape in concert with the formal analysis of artworks and the experiences they provoke, the significance of philosophical aesthetics was never fully reducible to a theory of art. To the contrary, it was a field of inquiry that identified in the social grammar of aesthetic experience a much wider and more politically dynamic potential for achieving collective agreement, whether in the form of exclusive ideological communities of taste, such as Shaftesbury's notion of "the liberty of the Club, and of that sort of freedom which is taken among gentlemen and friends who know one another perfectly well," or in more universalizing conceptions of the sensus communis underwriting the validity of aesthetic judgments for culture at large.[47]

In this respect, the people who called upon their overwhelming sense experiences in order to evidence the need for social and political change during the Great Stink acted, broadly speaking, as aesthetic subjects. But this moment of transformation also aligns with aesthetic subjectivity in more particular, concrete ways, and the collective agreement over the public value of disgust that emerged during the hot months of 1858 represents an absorption of the specifically aesthetic disgust that had been forged in debates over the nature of taste in the previous century. Aesthetics, to recall, was the only branch of Enlightenment thought to produce a sustained analysis of the meaning and nature of human disgust. Thomas Hobbes had theorized in a related vein that all human action was at bottom motivated by appetite, aversion, or contempt; and René Descartes, Baruch Spinoza, David Hume, and Jean-Jacques Rousseau, among others, all wrote extensively on the topics of affect, affection, and the passions in general; but neither the philosophy of emotions nor the theory of human appetites and interests can fully explain with any degree of specificity the particular sociopolitical function that public appeals to a shared threshold of disgust came to acquire throughout the nineteenth century. It was first within the aesthetic context that disgust emerged as a fully differentiated philosophical object that needed to be understood in its own right, at once as the antithesis of the beautiful and as distinct from closely related negative affective states such as aversion, displeasure, lack, and pain.

German aesthetic theory, in particular, as Menninghaus has shown, overflows with accounts of disgust and the disgusting as an antiaesthetic category. Lessing's Laocoön devotes several chapters solely to differentiating the aesthetic effects of the disgusting from other kinds of ugliness; his discussion is in large part an extended reply to Moses Mendelssohn, who had already singled out disgust as "an altogether different case" from other forms of negative aesthetic response.[48] The treatment of disgust is rather different in the British context, where aesthetic discourse was in general less focused on effects and forms of response (Edmund Burke's sensuous reflections on the beautiful and the sublime notwithstanding) than it was on cultivating the principles of proper judgment and refined manners that were deemed necessary in order to fully comprehend one's encounter with a work of art. And yet even so, as Denise Gigante has argued, this emphasis on proper conduct was understood by writers like Shaftesbury and Joseph Addison in very corporeal terms as a process of evacuation, a purging of the body of the impurities that impair judgment.[49] The body needed to be calibrated and refined if one was to demonstrate cultivation and civilization through the exercise of taste, and this process of calibration bore a close family resemblance to the articulation of disgust.

It is therefore possible not only to track how the conception of the judging subject that developed within aesthetic theory was taken up in significant areas of post-Enlightenment social transformation, but also to see in detail how the specific disruptive value assigned to disgust by aesthetics worked within this larger process of absorption. The Great Stink of 1858 is exemplary in this respect, at once reflecting the difficulty of delineating the normative terms of public agreement in an arena that was variously political, scientific, protosociological, moral, and cultural without being reducible to any single one of those domains, while also reflecting how the appeal to collective revulsion seemed to volatilize but also to settle the matter. In order to grasp how and why this (or any other) historical event can be understood through the prism of aesthetic subjectivity, then, it is first necessary to identify the fault lines and ideological tensions within aesthetic theory that helped to propel it beyond the formal domains of art and literature.

The central task of early aesthetic philosophy was to determine whether aesthetic judgments were rooted primarily in sensory pleasure and displeasure, or whether it was rather necessary to cultivate a more rarified and intellectual form of appreciation in order to deem an object beautiful, and not merely the source of vulgar enjoyment. The need for this distinction was partly a reaction to the increased availability of popular, entertaining cultural forms, such as aesthetic theory's more democratically accessible contemporary, the novel, which continually threatened the division between high and low while making apparent the need for a thoroughly delineated public standard for critical evaluation. But, as Raymond Williams argued, aesthetics also developed as a response against the increasing instrumentalization and commodification of social life throughout the eighteenth century.[50] From the start there was a conflict between the legitimately felt need to identify a separate domain of experience and a category of objects that were protected from (or at least resistant to) the reduction of social life to an economically rational battlefield of utilitarian interests, on the one hand, and the exclusionary enactment of that separation, and its subsequent theoretical reduction to a fantasy of the autonomy of the high from the low, on the other.

This tension in the aesthetic domain developed in the opposing directions that to a great extent still describe the aesthetic field today. At one end lay the project of cultivating a class of subjects equipped with refined sensibilities, which culminated in the discourse of taste, while at the other end lay the formalist and phenomenological tasks of cataloging the range of aesthetic objects and enumerating their effects on a generic subject. In the former case, the endeavor was to find in the vocabulary of taste a means of overcoming the alleged vulgarity of mere sensory enjoyment; perhaps counterintuitively, this gustatory rhetoric was positioned as a blow against the conception of human behavior as determined by appetite and the pursuit of pleasure, rather than as a continuation of it. Unlike appetite, taste was supposed to be disinterested and social, not self-interested and monadic. "You must be alone in order to think," Arendt glosses Kant; "you need company to enjoy a meal."[51] Yet this sociality was in most instances less concerned with making connection or theorizing actual commonality than it was with the formation of a habitus that would reaffirm the sensibility of an emergent bourgeois class in the name of a presumptively universalized set of subjective faculties. According to Hume, for example, in "Of the Standard of Taste," the goal of aesthetic judgment is "to mingle some light of the understanding with the feelings of sentiment." The reason "why many feel not the proper sentiment of beauty," he goes on, "is the want of that *delicacy* of imagination, which is requisite to convey a sensibility of those finer emotions."[52] While all people high and low were presumably endowed with the capacities for understanding, sentiment, and imagination, qualities like delicacy and refinement of sensibility pertain less obviously to a common conception of subjectivity than to a dining class and its inherently exclusionary world of manners, conduct, training, and connoisseurship.

In a related vein, the formalist-phenomenological cataloging of aesthetic effects and responses only helped to complete the self-confirming circularity of the aesthetic habitus. Rather than opening up the world of things to the unpredictability of tastes (and vice versa), aesthetics instead sought to produce a normative account of how certain formal features in artworks would produce the desired blend of cognitive and sensory pleasure in those subjects whose faculties of judgment had already been properly tuned to receive it. Within the context of this presumed autonomy, disgust arose as a disruption of the familiar Aristotelian inquiry into the representation of pain and suffering and the provocation of negative affect. Unlike with the arousal of pity and fear, Mendelssohn held—as did Lessing, Kant, and others—that there were "concrete reasons for disgust being unconditionally excluded from the unpleasant sensations that please in imitation."[53] The experience of disgust was felt to short-circuit the cultivated palate, precluding the disinterestedness requisite for aesthetic experience; no matter whether the disgusting thing actually existed in nature or was merely a representation or imitation—an object that disgusts, it was argued, will disgust as much in the putrid flesh as it will splattered on a canvas or a cave wall. "The feeling of disgust," as Lessing puts it, "comes always from nature, never from imitation."[54] The disgusting thing is felt to be too real, the disgusted response too automatic, the revolted relation too unstable and overwhelming.

Taken on its own, the formalistic side of aesthetic theory was incapable of answering the more epistemologically complex cultural problem about the basis of aesthetic judgment that had been raised—but likewise not resolved—by the discourse of taste. This was the problem of how to judge—for oneself, for others—in a social context where the apparent insufficiency of sense experience and self-interest of appetite would not do, but over which no body of rules or laws held sway. Though he did not see his way through the problem, a skeptical thinker like Hume understood that taste, conceived as refinement and cultivation, could not answer to this more fundamental anxiety about the need for a shared ground for judgment in the domain of culture. For if, as Bourdieu conclusively demonstrated, the aesthetic habitus is working to reinforce and reinscribe already extant forms of social division (such as class formations and the division of labor), then it cannot also serve as a means of establishing commonality. Under the guise of taste, aesthetics tended overwhelmingly to posit forms of exclusion as the answer to Enlightenment anxieties about universalism and inclusivity—anxieties whose urgency only grew more difficult to ignore during the revolutionary decades of the late eighteenth century. The response was ideological but the anxiety was real, and the problem of establishing or at least identifying common patterns of judgment came to saturate an ever-wider swath of public life throughout the nineteenth century.

Kant's *Critique of Judgment* differed from the bulk of aesthetic theory contemporary to it insofar as it sought to analyze the distinctive grammar of aesthetic experience, rather than simply to enumerate the features of aesthetic objects or to propose a set of guidelines for producing proper aesthetic judgments. What Kant seems to have seen more clearly than many of his contemporaries was that the real innovation of aesthetics lay in its attempt to make universalizing claims about the nature of a subjectivity that was always *in relation* to some object. That is, the aesthetic innovation was to socialize epistemology, to give an account of human thought and feeling as they were entangled not only with each other but with external things and other people as well. This complex degree of involvement is on display in Kant's opening account in the third *Critique* of the basic mechanics of aesthetic judgments, which runs something like this: In striking someone as beautiful, an object provokes a feeling of pleasure, which in turn produces a verbal judgment; but this putting into language of one's feeling takes a distinctive form, since rather than expressing or describing an inner state of pleasure or satisfaction, one instead places or locates one's feeling in the quality of the object that one calls beautiful. One in this respect discovers in the object a part of oneself that can no longer be called private, but which nevertheless remains subjective and maintains disavowed roots in personal feeling. Even more peculiarly, Kant argues, this attribution of one's feeling to the object itself takes the discursive shape of a normative expectation that others—that is, *all* others—will agree with one's judgment, even though one knows it is rooted only in one's own affective experience, and even though we do not ordinarily make demands that other people will necessarily feel how and what we do. At that moment, Kant says, we claim to speak in a "universal voice" that, quite significantly, seeks to derive a general rule from our own particular case. Thus the discovery of the intimacy of connection between one's innermost self and the form of the beautiful object transpires through the medium of a dialogue or argument between people that counterintuitively insists on a universality that nonetheless cannot be guaranteed—what Kant calls a "subjective universality." Such a complex account, of course, needs to be broken down into its constituent moving pieces in order to be fully understood; but it also needs to be said that in undertaking to describe a grammar of sociality that weaves together all the different elements of aesthetic theory, Kant's third *Critique* manages to differ in kind from the previous iterations of the discourse of taste upon which it builds.[55]

At the heart of Kantian aesthetics lies the epistemological anxiety over the status of affect and sensation in those regions of social life where there is no rule or concept according to which one must act, but in which allowing one's conduct to be dictated by private interests and the experience of pleasure and displeasure is collectively felt or understood to be insufficient. Though this anxiety was common currency within aesthetics, Kant shows the stakes of the confrontation between the reflective, disinterested subject and the aesthetic object to be decidedly more wide-ranging and socially significant than previous accounts of the dyadic aesthetic encounter had allowed. This is why Hannah Arendt saw in Kant's critique of taste his only significant attempt at what she called a "political philosophy"—a theory of judgment that pertained not only to philosophically slippery run-ins with works of art but to even messier questions of political action and conduct in the public sphere as well. Aesthetic judgment for Kant models a middle way through the two Hobbesian alternatives of the rule of appetite and the rule of law, by showing how sensory pleasure incites a public discourse that transcends appetite without recourse to law. "There can be no rule according to which anyone is to be forced to recognize anything as beautiful," Kant writes. "We cannot press upon others by the aid of any reasons or fundamental propositions our judgment that a coat, a house, or a flower is beautiful. People wish to submit the Object to their own eyes, as if the satisfaction in it depended on sensation; and yet if we then call the object beautiful, we believe we speak with a universal voice, and we claim the assent of everyone, although on the contrary all private sensation can only decide for the observer himself and his satisfaction."[56] Normally, Kant claims, sensation carries necessary meaning only for oneself, but in aesthetic judgment, we not only refer our sensation of pleasure back to the object as an objective quality but also go on to demand that others interpret their private sensory experiences in the very same way. Aesthetic judgments invoke the "publicity" (to borrow Arendt's term) of otherwise private experiences in an unconventional manner that insists upon their "subjective universal validity" for reaching collective agreement: "In all judgments by which we describe anything as beautiful, we allow no one to be of another opinion," Kant elaborates, "without however grounding our judgment on concepts but only on our feeling, which we therefore place at its basis not as a private, but as a common feeling."[57]

Common feeling therefore becomes the basis of collective agreement, even though feeling, in this context, is by definition singular and valid only for one person. Kant's approach to this apparent contradiction is to argue that the common feeling, or sensus communis, is only posited by aesthetic judgments as a condition of possibility for arriving at collective agreement. "Common sense . . . does not say that everyone *will* agree with my judgment, but that he *ought*," an ought that Kant goes on to call a "mere ideal norm" that "only signifies the possibility of arriving at this accord [of any one person with every other]."[58] Rather than a top-down universalism in which the deviation of the individual is flattened out in order to conform with the general rule, Kant proposes a scenario in which universality only exists as a horizon derived from the specific case. The particular yields the possibility of the general. To be sure, the strength and ingenuity of this formulation are also what make it so tenuous as a model of collective agreement. Kant leaves aesthetic relations radically open to the hazards of contingency and failure; on one side, private interests—both personal and those of private communities of taste—threaten

THE ODOR OF THINGS

to masquerade as universal values, while on the other, appeals to custom and tradition attempt to smuggle in unexamined rules or concepts as the grounds for common feeling. Meanwhile, incapable of practically reaching the horizon of universality, each concrete instance of judgment must start anew the restless activity of persuasion and argument by which one's case will be tested. As Arendt memorably puts it, "one can only 'woo' or 'court' the agreement of everyone else. And in this persuasive activity one actually appeals to the 'community sense.'"[59]

At this point, it becomes clear that what is on offer in Kant's critique of aesthetic judgment is neither an exclusionary habitus nor a formalism elaborating what sorts of things can count as beautiful or ugly, but rather a set of grammatical premises concerning the different values that can be attached to affective subjectivity and the different uses to which those values can be put. Kantian aesthetics takes the contrived skeptical crisis of the late-night philosopher ruminating anxiously over the monadic privacy of his sensations and proposes to inject it into a set of ordinary social scenarios in which the public stakes of subjectivity are perpetually tested and contested. The fundamental concern is to establish *when, how,* and *in what contexts* feelings and sensations are and are not granted a form of socially shared significance; the whole notion of subjective universality depends on attributing this particular balance of meaning and meaninglessness to the capacity to feel, not on simply disqualifying or suppressing affect in opposition to rationality or reason. Indeed, Kant makes it possible to argue that the fact that our personal pleasures and displeasures do not carry with them any objective necessity for other people is a prerequisite for subjective universality; our consciousness of the inadequacy of our feelings to count toward social agreement is what produces the need to overcome the privative nature of subjectivity by attributing them to beautiful things as though they were formal properties of the object. But then it becomes hard to say whether, strictly speaking, it is our feelings of pleasure or their disavowal that form the basis of aesthetic judgment; the great provocation of the third *Critique* was perhaps to leave the tension generated by this ambiguity unresolved.

Disgust enters into and radically disturbs Kant's account of the distribution of recognition to affective life. If there is one thing that does not make sense within the model of subjective universality that Kant has outlined, it is the idea that one's feeling could offer a judgment about an object that would be objectively and therefore compulsorily valid for all other people, *without* renouncing its roots in feeling. And yet that is in a sense just what the provocation of disgust seems to entail for Kant, when he adapts Mendels-sohn's account to his own purposes:

> Beautiful art shows its superiority in this, that it describes as beautiful things which may be in nature ugly or displeasing. The Furies, diseases, the devastations of war, etc., may, even regarded as calamitous, be described as very beautiful, as they are represented in a picture. There is only one kind of ugliness which cannot be represented in accordance with nature, without destroying all aesthetical satisfaction and consequently artificial beauty; viz. that which excites disgust. For in this singular sensation, which rests on mere imagination, the object is represented as it were obtruding itself for our enjoyment while we strive against it with all our might. And the artistic representation of the object is no longer distinguished from the nature of the object itself in our sensation, and thus it is impossible that it can be regarded as beautiful.[60]

In this formulation, the picture of the disgusting overflows the representational frame that allows other ugly forms to be transformed into objects of aesthetic pleasure, and, as a consequence, we confound the repulsive object with its representation; the picture of the disgusting necessarily becomes a disgusting picture. Moreover, the object *obtrudes*, confounding not only representation and reality but also subject and object, as Kant ascribes a powerful agency to the inert artwork that sidesteps his dictum that art should be purposive without having a purpose. To the contrary, the disgusting artwork *insists* upon being enjoyed, even "while we strive against it with all our might," suggesting that disgusting works possess greater agency than disgusted subjects, and impose their own consumption regardless of one's cultivated tastes.

This triple blurring of relational terms—picture and thing, subject and object, pleasure and displeasure—is further compounded by the double connotation of *Genuss* in German of both "enjoyment" and "consumption." As Menninghaus has observed, Kant surpasses previous aestheticians by implying that the perception of the disgusting entails an unwanted taking in—inhaling, eating, or otherwise internalizing—either by, or as though by, smelling or tasting.[61] The intentionality of the disgusting, the way it *obtrudes* and *insists*, suggests that it has already entered inside the viewer, as a sort of aesthetic effluvia. The disgusting thing is inside the mind, the way the particles of a disgusting stench are inside the nose; there is no opportunity for cool, measured reflection when one is being forcefully reminded of the porosity and oozing viscosity of the human body. This emphasis on an internalization preceding expulsion produces a strongly felt self-implication—the sense that the unwanted thing is internal to and therefore part of the self—which precludes the disinterestedness Kant thought was necessary to produce the subjective universality of aesthetic judgments.

The density of these remarks reflects the degree to which disgust signaled a major disturbance in the sensory field of the new aesthetic domain. The problematic element is not sensation per se, since Kant understood all aesthetic judgments to be rooted in sensation. Rather, the problem with disgust in this context is that, in forcing itself upon one, subjective sensation commandeers the publicity of agreement normally reserved for objective phenomena; disgust speaks in the universal voice, but without thereby denying its sensory origins; it is subjectivity become obtrusive to the point of being incontrovertible. Disgust threatens the entire regulatory apparatus of taste because it takes what is supposed to be our innermost private experience and vomits it up as an outward thing; value regurgitates fact. And, almost paradoxically, what is irrational in this and has therefore to be excluded is that, by insisting on the universality of one's disgust and attributing it to some slimy thing, one at once brings about the objectification of the self and the authorization of the object. So we say, it is disgusting because I am disgusted: we blame the feeling on some object; we use the evidence of our senses to classify and order types of offensive things. And yet in this configuration, our feeling becomes an object; one's subjectivity is impossibly reduced to a no-longer-private property, to a public, evidentiary thing.[62]

Before turning back from the aesthetic theorization of disgust to its concrete historical articulation during the hot days of the Great Stink, two clarifications remain to be made. The first is to observe that while Kant singles out disgust as the one emotion to be prohibited tout court in the spectrum of aesthetic experience, in doing so he in fact makes available, for the first time, the particular conception of disgust that has passed through the modern aesthetic, psychological, and psychoanalytic traditions and remains with us today. This is the account of disgust as irrational and sensuous, as a remnant of the animal in the human, as something atavistic, primal, and animistic. Yet in insisting on understanding disgust as an emblem of human instinctivity, this account of the emotion also understands it to be calculable, reflexive, and pseudo-objective, to be the administrative emotion par excellence, whose self-referential appeals to its own unwanted feelings are taken for facts. Thus Kant makes available as well the uncritical fantasy that, somewhere out there, there is an immense Public Nostril, bearing to the disgusting and to disgust the same relationship that the sensus communis bears to the beautiful and to taste; a transcendental entity that can ensure mandatory agreement over objects of distaste, just as there is hoped to be universal consent over objects of aesthetic taste. But if the sensus communis is posited as a horizon of possibility legitimizing our demands for universal assent, the Public Nostril is, to the contrary, imagined only as a foreclosed certainty; our disgust must be excluded *because* it is thought to be so effective at producing itself as the grounds for consensus: we tend to agree about the disgusting, Kant rather surreptitiously implies, in the same way that we never do about the beautiful.

The second clarification then is that while Kant inaugurates the influential account of disgust as the compulsory negative judgment made by the body, this alleged truth of our subjectivity itself only appears under negation, that is, as a truth that has been or ought to have been surpassed, either in some imaginary phylogenetic fantasy of overcoming or through the imposition of norms regulating proper conduct. Seen from this angle, then, the exclusion of disgust within Enlightenment aesthetics can be said to play an important role in the promulgation of the Enlightenment concepts of culture and civilization. The very sense of civilization as a process, as something possessing momentum and direction, depends on the notion that certain aspects of human subjectivity have been held over from a more primal past and must therefore be repudiated.

This gesture of productive exclusion turns out to be extraordinarily unstable. Following Kant, we cannot be sure whether disgust is to be excluded from the domain of aesthetic experience because it represents a perceived descent from rational conduct to a reflexively negative mode of vestigial animal behavior—disgust as the performance of impulsive magical thinking or wrongheaded kettle logic; or whether disgust is excluded in the sense that it represents a logical or ontological impossibility, an eruption into everyday affairs of a nonsubjective mode of feeling that threatens the stability of culture or civilization by undermining the very principles of noncontradiction that separate the subjective from the objective, the inner from the outer, facts from feelings. It is not hard to see how this latter, more disruptive conception of disgust would, at the far end of the nineteenth century, help to make possible the psychoanalytic intuition of the unconscious. But for this to have been the case, the model of disgust that Kant detailed in the aesthetic domain needed to be absorbed into the general social fabric of nineteenth-century culture through that uneven process of aesthetic rationalization to which we will now return.

**FIGURE 4.** A distant view of the pumping station at Crossness, in the days before its opening ceremony. *Illustrated London News*, April 8, 1865. Courtesy of the University of Chicago Library.

## The Concretion of Fantasy

Over the course of the nineteenth century, aesthetic disgust became social disgust. First theorized in the context of Laocoön's grimace, the uses to which this emotion and its exclusion were put proliferated, gaining currency in the natural as well as social sciences, in public health and cultural policy, in politics as well as law. This is of course not to say that there had been no social role for disgust before Enlightenment aesthetics, but rather to assert that the specific collective meanings and values that people attached to their experiences of revulsion within the nineteenth-century bourgeois public sphere bore the imprint of the emotion's elaboration in the domain of aesthetic experience. One can certainly place the conceptions of contagion and pollution that helped to animate modern disgust in older traditions; Sloterdijk, for example, begins his consideration of the modern nuisance in the Holy Roman Empire of the thirteenth century. Likewise, there are strong reasons for understanding the aesthetic disturbances ascribed to disgust in terms of a *longue durée* secularization of notions of spiritual and moral pollution, of fallenness, and especially, following Paul Ricoeur, of evil or sin as a stain that overflows symbolization.[63] But aesthetic disgust is nevertheless the *proximal source* of a nineteenth-century structure of revolted feeling that traversed disciplinary boundaries and social domains; and the aesthetic exclusion of disgust inaugurates a modern conception of an affective subject whose particular instabilities and involutions are everywhere legible in the century that follows. Much as we have come to understand the rise of modern sexuality as the result of a series of unforeseeable transfers between previously distinct discursive practices and formations—from confessional to couch, candlelit *ars erotica* to drab clinical sexology, and so on—the birth of modern disgust involved a comparable set of displacements, ramifications, and mutations in the ways that people understood the meaning of their revulsion and pushed it beyond the aesthetic frame.

One significant form that aesthetic disgust took throughout the nineteenth century was that of the cultural or civilizational crisis—of which the Great Stink is a prime example—and such affectively motivated crises played a counterintuitively central and as-yet-unexplored role in the rationalization of British society. These crisis formations carried over into their various social contexts a number of features that were specific to the Enlightenment aesthetic debates over disgust, foremost among them the notions that the articulation of revulsion represented a reflexive or instinctual mode of negative judgment; that this mode of judgment was unwanted, obtrusive, and consequently represented a threat to proper conduct and the social order that needed to be surpassed or excluded; and that nonetheless disgust, understood to be a powerful form of rejection in its own right, in some sense provided a template for this exclusion, if not the very means by which it would take place. Irrational and calculable, obtrusive and effective, disgust was at once the eruption of the primitive into modern life and the go-to mechanism for addressing and regulating the crisis of that eruption. We now turn to this last, recursive feature of disgust.

The opening of the sewage pumping station at Crossness in April 1865, nearly seven years and more than £4 million after the hot summer of the Great Stink, can help to illustrate the complex ways that disgust functioned during the sewage crisis itself and in its resolution (fig. 4). Along with its sibling on the north bank of the Thames at Abbey Mills, Crossness was a central piece of Bazalgette's master plan for London's new drainage system. Rather than flowing into the river, the city's human waste was now intercepted by a vast network of sewer tunnels and conveyed on a downward slope roughly fifteen miles east of the city to Abbey Mills and Crossness. Once there, four massive beam engines (named after the royal family) pumped the city's millions of gallons of sludge back up to the surface, whereupon it was discharged into the river far enough downstream that it would not wash back up with the tide, flowing instead out to sea. Allowing for London's future growth, Bazalgette estimated the system could handle the sewage of a city of

3.5 million inhabitants without needing any additions—though as Stephen Halliday has observed, the metropolitan population had already reached 4,225,000 when Bazalgette died in 1891.[64] The whole gargantuan project, which encompassed the sewers and pumping stations as well as the Victoria and Chelsea Embankments that housed the intercepting tunnels, was one of the most elaborate and most ambitious public works projects undertaken anywhere in the nineteenth century. Bazalgette was celebrated in his own time, and a small bust and monument marking his accomplishment can be seen today along the Victoria Embankment, under the Latin motto *Flumini vincula posuit* (He placed the river in chains).

No less impressive than the magnitude and scope of the sewer system is the aesthetic splendor of the Crossness and Abbey Mills pumping stations, built and designed by Bazalgette and the architect Charles Henry Driver in an overwhelming hodgepodge of Orientalizing styles (figs. 5–7). Replete with luminous wrought-iron archways and ornate columns with floral-patterned decorative work painted in a bright color scheme, "Venetian" chimney towers, mansard roofs, and elaborate brick and tile floors, both buildings immediately summoned to the minds of Victorian visitors fantasies of Byzantine churches, Mughal mosques, and Chinese temples.[65] By turns bizarre and breathtaking to visit even today, these so-called "cathedrals to sewage," with their aesthetics, craftsmanship, and attention to minute detail, reflect the intense social-symbolic significance claimed by the sheer enormity of labor, mechanical and engineering expertise, and resources that went into the whole task of cleansing the Thames. Even with its engines offline, the shimmering octagonal atrium at the heart of Crossness still hums with the imaginative and creative energies that were invested in its walls.

Most striking for the present discussion, however, is the fantasy of civilizational triumph and glory that propelled these structures' creation, a fantasy that is hard not to see concreted in their elaborate aesthetic of secular salvation. To begin with, there was understandably a great deal of public pride expressed over the epic scale of the accomplishment. The opening of Crossness was itself "a spectacle exceptional in its occurrence, unprecedented in its magnitude, tremendous in its import, unexampled in its celebration."[66] Hundreds of invited guests, dignitaries, and members of the press were led on a tour of the pristine and sparkling premises—"there was nothing but neatness and elegance and brilliance to be seen. You might have eaten your dinner off that natty ridge-and-furrow flooring of brick"—and then down to the lower level, which had been specially decorated with lanterns, and then

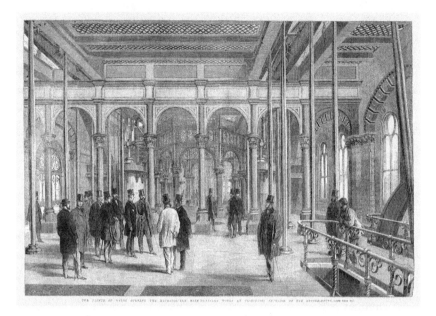

FIGURE 5.   Interior view of Crossness enginehouse. *Illustrated London News*, April 15, 1865. Courtesy of the University of Chicago Library.

FIGURE 6.   Exterior view of the pumping station at Abbey Mills. *Illustrated London News*, April 15, 1865. Courtesy of the University of Chicago Library.

**FIGURE 7.** Interior view of the pumping station at Abbey Mills. *Illustrated London News*, April 15, 1865. Courtesy of the University of Chicago Library.

**FIGURE 8.** The depths of Crossness, illuminated during the opening ceremony. *Illustrated London News*, April 15, 1865. Courtesy of the University of Chicago Library.

OPENING THE METROPOLITAN MAIN-DRAINAGE WORKS AT CROSSNESS: THE PRINCE OF WALES STARTING THE ENGINES.—SEE NEXT PAGE.

**FIGURE 9.** The Prince of Wales starting the engines during the opening ceremony at Crossness. *Illustrated London News*, April 15, 1865. Courtesy of the University of Chicago Library.

served a "splendid luncheon" in the workshop (fig. 8).[67] The guest of honor was the Prince of Wales, who inaugurated Britain's sanitary modernity with a ceremonious pulling of the crank to start the engines, inviting all to toast "the great national undertaking" (fig. 9).[68]

Yet this pride in the collective achievement represented by the opening of the "perfect shrine of machinery" quickly gave way to a more grandiose strain of rhetorical excess that raised the specter of the discourse of sensory overload and outrage that had burst forth during the stink.[69] "We have buried Dirt and Disease at Crossness Point, beneath the octagon of the engine-room," the *Daily Telegraph* weighed in, "and round about are the iron emblems of our victory—the beam, the piston and the cylinder, the mighty machines which are to go on pumping out the impure blood from the great heart-core of the metropolis of the world." And it is this latter sentiment, at once pervasive and paradigmatic, that captures the elements of fantasy and excess that haunted the opening of Crossness. The *Daily Telegraph* continues, in a quasiheroic vein whose commitment to parody is hard to pin down:

> It stands there, on the shore of the Thames, no mere architectural caprice—no mere engineering experiment—but a monument of work and labour done for a useful and beneficent end, *an enduring homage of civilisation to itself*. . . . The Prince of Wales lent yesterday his comely head to the great principle of usefulness. Let there be no beating around the bush. The place he came to inaugurate was a sewer . . . but *the mean, the vile, the repulsive in that which was around him were ennobled and sanctified by the purpose for which his aid was sought*. . . . The end justified, and justified most gloriously, the work.[70]

Here the strain of cultural shame and precariousness toward which the rhetoric of sensory outrage tended during the Great Stink reemerges in order to produce a progressive historical narrative of civilizational triumph, in which technology has literally banished animality to the lower regions. Not merely the disgusting, but disgust itself, has been buried, in a perfectly symmetrical inversion of values; what was vile and repulsive has been made noble and spiritual through its civilizing purpose; stench has been rendered visual, even resplendent, reminiscent of the description of the sanitary crisis as a "flash of light" years before: now "a factory becomes poetical, a furnace fairy-like."[71] What is lost in this techno-rational aestheticization of the story of London's sanitary evolution is the central, motivating role that had been played by negative sensory experience, and the widespread unanimity anticipated by the appeal to the automaticity of revulsion. The collective disgust sedimented in the construction of the sewer system and in the entire sanitizing process has been written out of the script; in its stead we are given a cultural feedback loop, according to which the actually uneven story of the development and implementation of modern sanitary norms can itself be sanitized and rendered "an enduring homage of civilization to itself."

At this point the instability of the relationship between disgust and civilizational crisis becomes clear in the fact of a certain constitutive duplicity in the role of disgust. In the first place, Crossness is the emblem of a civilization defined by its overcoming of the disgust provoked by modernity's repulsive excrescences—which is to say, the overcoming of its own intrinsic barbarism and animality, its lack of control over its bodies and their openings, its subrational instinctual expulsions and primal substances. Civilization on this account simply is the overcoming of disgust; disgust is the condensed sign of an immanent barbarism; the exclusion of disgust is the essence of the process of civilization. But almost immediately, the elaboration of this process of overcoming encounters a conceptual difficulty. Now civilization resembles not the overcoming of disgust, but its fulfillment; not the eradication of unwanted affect, but the increase in its potency, the proliferation of its functions, and the extension of its range. The moment of civilization is the moment of disgust; in a society without disgust, civilization would not be possible; disgust is the very means through which civilization produces its enduring homages to itself; in fact, Crossness is far more an homage to the centrality of disgust in the process of civilization than to civilization per se. Disgust does double duty, at once the means or medium of exclusion and a token of that which is excluded. The instability in this relationship stems from the duplicity of disgust, not only in the sense of its dual role but in the surreptitious way the discourse of disgust mops up after itself. The repudiation of disgust produces the rhetoric of civilizational progress at precisely those historical junctures that have been most intensely motivated by the superseded mechanisms of unwanted feeling.

These two sets of propositions about the function of disgust in producing nineteenth-century British culture in turn give way to two seemingly irreconcilable views on the broader history of European modernity, one characterized by its narratives of progress and supersession, the other by its genealogical emphasis on the inversion of values. In the first case, we bear witness to what Henry Jephson in 1907 termed the "sanitary evolution of London," as it emerges from the premodern quagmire of miasma theory and the sludge-filled river of the seeping plague years.[72] Even after historians of public health and sanitation like Allen, Tom Crook, and Christopher Hamlin have persuasively shown the political and administrative complexities and contingencies that both animated and hindered the long-term implementation of the sanitary idea, it has been nearly impossible to fully dispel the overwhelming sense of directionality and even purposive development in the rise of the modern hygienic regime. Yet while modern Euro-American sanitary norms may have developed in a particular "direction" and perhaps even in some respects according to a particular purpose, and while it is clear this development was coextensive with the rise of a modern, centralized state and its increasingly bureaucratized administration, the difficulty lies in seeing this total process as reflecting a rationalization in the precise sense of the disenchantment and supplanting of mythic or traditional values with modern, administrative ones. Sanitary historians can try to avoid participating in the triumphal narrative of modern progress itself by recovering the multivalent complexities that actually motivated the politics of public health, as Hamlin has done, but such accounts consequently cannot explain how and why the social transformations under scrutiny produced the ideological narratives of civilizational progress. In short, we are left with either a narrative that has been drained of its viscera and administratively mummified or one that conflates social transformation with progress and actively promotes the ideology of civilization.

From the perspective of an archaeology of modern disgust, this rationalizing narrative obfuscates the central role the emotion played in the processes they describe. Indeed, for some authors, the eradication of disgust is *the* story of modern sanitation; Steven Johnson's widely read *The Ghost Map*, for example, while not a work of academic scholarship like Hamlin's or Allen's books, narrates the supersession of the miasma theory by John Snow's rational-scientific hypothesis that cholera was waterborne as the story of the end of the hegemony of disgust and the beginning of the age of germ theory. "The scourge of cholera . . . seemed intractable . . . and superstition seemed destined to rule the day," Johnson writes of London during and after the 1854 cholera outbreak. "But in the end . . . the forces of reason won out. The pump handle was removed; the map was drawn; the miasma theory was put to rest; the sewers were built; the water ran clean."[73] We leap over the Great Stink here, and in so doing leap over what would constitute, by the terms of Johnson's own narrative, a regressive moment of progress, in which the elevation of superstition and irrationality are the means for rationalizing and purging their own function and significance.

We can also see the record of the Great Stink and its resolution in the civilizational aesthetics of Crossness as an example of a story in which nineteenth-century culture is constituted not by progress but by the inversion of values. Smell, the lowest sense, is transformed into sight, the highest; stench turns into splendor, disgust into beauty. In order for what has been buried so industriously to be allowed to return to the surface, it must first be translated into its opposite. In a more destabilizing register, the role of disgust in the burial of the disgusting must also be buried or effaced. The mechanism of producing civilization cannot be animality; it must be something in keeping with the inverted cultural signs that have been invested with value. The sense of progress, directionality, and rational development are in this regard simply effects of the effort it takes to spin shit into gold, a task countless Victorian manure enthusiasts strove to realize concretely. But while a structure like Crossness explicitly monumentalizes the conversion of waste into positive value, it only tacitly enacts the inversion of collective disgust into civilized rationality. The latter transformation, which is a transformation in the form of cultural agreement, remains out of sight, out of mind.

The spokespeople for this view are, of course, Nietzsche and after him Freud, specifically the Freud of *Civilization and Its Discontents*, where civilization is defined as the anxious sense of progress attending to the renunciation of human instincts in the name of collective social life. There, in an often-cited long footnote, Freud even goes so far as to revive one of his earliest ideas; namely, that the defining moment for the human species can be represented as a kind of primal disgust reaction, the moment of becoming upright when the smell and proximity of our fellow creatures' looming sex organs and anuses unaccountably become repulsive and are renounced in favor of an "erect posture" privileging the visual over the olfactory. This insight had in fact first emerged for Freud in his letter to Wilhelm Fliess of November 14, 1897, in which he describes repression as inner disgust. "To put it crudely," Freud writes, "the memory actually stinks, just as in the present the object stinks; and in the same manner as we turn away our sense organ (the head and nose) in disgust, the preconscious and the sense of consciousness turn away from the memory. This is repression." Freud also postulates in the letter that the phylogenetic origin of neurosis can be located in the transition to "upright walking, nose raised from the ground, at the same time a number of formerly interesting sensations attached to the earth becoming repulsive—by a process still unknown to me."[74] Even in Freud's penetrating comments, disgust serves at once as an emblem of the instinctivity that must be overcome in the civilizing process and as the means of its overcoming. Repression is inner disgust, the repudiation of unwanted imaginations and memory traces; disgust is externalized, object-oriented repression, betokening the prior repression of instincts that produce the values that require us to repudiate in disgust that which has been overcome. The origins of human civilization lie in primal repression, which is to say a disgust that propels us beyond our animal selves; and yet disgust is itself the embodiment of the instinctual mode of being, the very token of the animal that persists despite the constraints of civilization. To recall what Elias demonstrated in a much more historically specific frame, the affective constraint constitutive of the civilizing process is actually accomplished through advances in the threshold of shame and repugnance; *increasing* disgust is the paradoxical mechanism for *reducing* affective impulsiveness.

It is certainly possible to use Freud's theoretical statements regarding the interplay of civilization and disgust as a rubric for understanding the nineteenth-century historical phenomena discussed throughout this chapter. The whole aesthetic compound of the Crossness and Abbey Mills pumping stations, as well as the entire project of digging London's modern sewers, can be placed in productive dialogue with psychoanalytic insights about the slippery entwinement of repression, revulsion, and sublimation; indeed, once one has read through Freud or Norman O. Brown's ruminations on the alchemical psychic substitutions that can turn feces to gold and melt gold back into feces, it can be hard *not* to see the resplendent metalwork of Cross- ness, which rises up out of the deep trenches of excrement like brass trees, as an example of the conversion processes of sublimation and symptom for- mation (figs. 10–12). The question of which—symptom or sublimate, neu- rosis or cultural achievement—remains an unresolved problem at the end of *Civilization and Its Discontents*, which concludes by observing that there can be no diagnostic grounds for the psychoanalysis of culture; the sublimated products of civilization are no more than symptoms made collectively avail- able, social symptoms that are at once useful and yet constituted through repression. Any cultural-historical account of Britain's sanitary evolution must necessarily grapple with Freud's speculations and theories regarding sublimation and the inversion of cultural values.

Yet as should by now be clear, this chapter does not offer a psychoanalytic interpretation of nineteenth-century history grounded in the reportage of events during the Great Stink and its aftermath. On the contrary, it details a shift in the functions of disgust that can be identified in various areas of social transformation, rather than suggesting a transhistorical function of revulsion reaching back to the beginnings of human history. As we will see

**FIGURE 10.**    Crossness seen from outside in 2017. Courtesy of Trevor Yorke.

**Figure 11.** Interior of Crossness, 2017. Courtesy of Trevor Yorke.

**Figure 12.** Exterior of Abbey Mills, 2017. Courtesy of Trevor Yorke.

in the third and fourth chapters, such speculations on the primal role of disgust constitute the conceptual core of the emotion's modernity. And in this respect, it makes less sense to think of psychoanalytic theory as providing an explanation for nineteenth-century social transformation than it does to reverse the customary interpretive priority granted to our dominant theoretical paradigms and to see the development of psychoanalytic theory as one major cultural consequence among many of the aesthetic rationalization of the revolted subject that took place throughout the nineteenth century. The widespread distribution of new social functions to disgust during the period, and the way that this distribution affected how people understood the public meaning of their own subjective experiences, helped to produce the conditions of possibility for the emergence of psychoanalytic theory as a hermeneutic paradigm for explaining modern culture. But when we apply Freud's insights into the nature of disgust retrospectively, we are faced with a problem of backward compatibility. Phenomena that actually reflect the dynamic reorganization of the social world appear static, as though they instead reflected the transcendental stability of interpretive laws.[75]

It is in this light that we can read Freud's further observation in *Civilization and Its Discontents* that "a social factor is also unmistakably present in the cultural trend towards cleanliness, which has received *ex post facto* justification in hygienic considerations, but which manifested itself before their discovery."[76] Freud considered what he here calls the cultural trend toward cleanliness to be a key component in the broader process of civilization, a process he argued made immense demands on the individual psyche and had a profound effect on social organization. Yet this brief remark is striking for the divergence it suggests between the way that such cultural processes are actually motivated and the bodies of knowledge that are instrumentalized as rationales for justifying them. That is, Freud thought that the civilizing process was affectively and libidinally motivated (by desire, repression, disgust, shame, etc.), but that its component parts, such as the trend toward cleanliness, nevertheless attached themselves, even after the fact, to discursive fields that rely on radically different standards and criteria to establish their claims to legitimacy.

Placing Freud's remark alongside John Snow's comment that cleansing the Thames was an aesthetic matter, a just-barely-perceptible through-line emerges, tethering the "social factor" to which Freud alludes back to the "question of taste" that Snow believed was animating the desire to cleanse the Thames in the spring of 1858. And just as Freud drew attention to the way that the obscure motivations of such social processes might be papered over by ex post facto rationalizations, so too the debates over

London's sewage question sought to mobilize what was an aesthetically motivated problem in the name of public health and medical science. This continuity suggests our need for a fuller understanding of the crucial yet understudied role that the process of aesthetic rationalization played in the emergence of psychoanalytic theory and the model of historical time it presupposes, as well as in the triumphal narratives of progress deconstructed in Freud's writings on civilization and belied by the historical archives of nineteenth-century revulsion.

Walter Benjamin provided a useful image for thinking about precisely this set of historiographical problems when he wrote of the "Dream City" in the manuscripts now collected as the *Arcades Project*. Thinking of the Parisian arcades, Benjamin sought to develop the Swiss architectural theorist Sigfried Giedion's thesis that "in the nineteenth century, construction plays the role of the subconscious." "Wouldn't it be better," Benjamin asks, "to say 'the role of bodily processes'—around which 'artistic' architectures gather, like dreams around the framework of physiological processes?"[77] The distinction, while subtle, is especially apt in the case of architectural structures like Crossness and Abbey Mills, where the relationship between the need for construction and the aesthetic form that it takes can easily be grasped as the relationship between physiological process and unconscious or sublimated expression. Benjamin elaborates: "Just as the sleeper . . . sets out on the macrocosmic journey through his own body, and the noises and feelings of his insides, such as blood pressure and intestinal churn . . . generate, in the elaborately heightened inner awareness of the sleeper, illusion or dream imagery which translates and accounts for them, so likewise for the dreaming collective, which, through the arcades, communes with its own insides. We must follow in its wake so as to expound the nineteenth century."[78] As the arcades can provide insight into the structure of the nineteenth century's fantasy of its own consumption, so we might say that the sewers and pumping stations bear the same relationship to digestion and "intestinal churn." Yet while Benjamin's formulation gives a foundational role to bodily process and drive, his attention, unlike Freud's, is trained specifically on the particular historical forms through which the physiological process is expressed. Thus Benjamin also goes on to compare Marx's famous dictum that the economic base or infrastructure of a society determines or conditions its superstructure to the way that, "with a sleeper, an overfull stomach finds not its reflection but its expression in the contents of dreams, which, from a causal point of view, it may be said to 'condition.'"[79] At issue is not the fundamental nature of material base or bodily process, but rather the coordination of the fundamental process with its expression as dream or aesthetic artifact; not the fact of a reflex or an instinctual aversion underlying conscious or unconscious life, but the changes in the values and meanings attributed to instinct and other bodily processes. Indeed, it is in the nineteenth century, Benjamin suggests, that such processes take on their peculiar excluded centrality in the formalized domain of the unconscious. In this light, a structure such as Crossness helps us to see how the dynamic transformation in the values and meanings attributed to disgust in particular gave rise to the structural relationship between repression and sublimation ordinarily presented as an unvarying constant by the diagnostic discourse of psychoanalytic theory.

The following chapters of this book are committed to detailing the different ways in which the absorption of aesthetic disgust helped to transform the social texture and terrain of the nineteenth century, and to showing how these areas of transformation were integral in producing the theoretical innovations and disciplinary formations that are in many cases still with us today. If we skip over these historical disturbances, as Menninghaus suggests we do, or if we turn back upon the nineteenth century the very interpretive frameworks that it helped to produce, as has been far more common, we fail to see the immensely productive capacities to which disgust laid claim throughout the period. To get from aesthetic theory to the psychoanalysis of culture, we need to see how collective revulsion came to be installed and disavowed as the engine of social change and to understand what was at stake in the public wish that the lord chancellor of England would have a mild diarrhea. The highly volatile and unstable set of meanings and values that Londoners attached to their disgust throughout the Great Stink contributed to a wider process of reorganization and reconfiguration that took place throughout the period; this structure of feeling contributed to widespread instabilities, not only in the various social domains we will now go on to examine, such as obscenity law, but also in the theoretical systems that arose out of this altered social landscape. The archaeology of nineteenth-century disgust is the archaeology of modern theory; the theory, in this case, is quite literally in the groundwater.

# CHAPTER 2

# Realism and Repulsion

> For the way to perfection is through a series of disgusts.
>
> —Walter Pater, *The Renaissance*

Keeping in mind all we have come to know about the state of the Thames in the months and years leading up to the hot summer of 1858, let's now turn to an image of the river, culled from a novel of the very same moment: "And he thought—who has not thought for a moment, sometimes—that it might be better to flow away monotonously, like the river, and to compound for its insensibility to happiness with its insensibility to pain." The novel is *Little Dorrit*, the scene one in which its depressive protagonist Arthur Clennam gazes into the Thames from suburban Twickenham and fantasizes about dissolving himself into its "serene" currents and floating off a few murky miles downstream to the putrid waters of the city. The story is set thirty years earlier, in the 1820s, but as many have noted, the London it offers its readers is very much the teeming, overstuffed metropolis of the 1850s, when "through the heart of the town a deadly sewer ebbed and flowed, in the place of a fine fresh river."[1] To a Londoner following the novel during its serial publication from 1855 to 1857, or to one who purchased the whole volume the following winter, Clennam's reverie would have called to mind an image of willingly immersing oneself in the very same channel of excrement I have just been describing at length, as a means of escaping the ordeal of sexual, professional, societal, and familial obligation.

The brief scene raises important questions about the complex relationship between literary realism and the aesthetics of disgust, taking the latter term to encompass both the formal philosophical discourse of disgust and the midcentury social transformations that lent that discourse its widespread currency beyond the realm of arts and letters. For starters, we might ask how, at a moment when the whole city around him was crying out in collective revulsion over the state of the Thames, Dickens managed to see in its waters an image of respite from subjectivity, and of a solace provided by disintegration and insensibility. What kind of resonance would such an image have claimed? It is often asserted that Dickens developed an "excremental vision" that carried Jonathan Swift's project of satirical scatology forward into the nineteenth century. Yet while there is plenty of evidence to support some version of this claim, this particular image of reverie lacks precisely the mudslinging animus that has been attributed to the scatological at least since Swift's Yahoos.[2] In lieu of the defiling smear of the obscene, where filthy words collapse into unclean deeds, the description suggests a relation to the permeability of the body and to its primary substances that is not organized by the articulation of disgust but rather by some more positively valenced associations with the possibility of becoming "insensible" and "unfeeling," words that Dickens deploys within the ambit of the Thames throughout the novel. The dissolution of the body into its own muck, and the loss of conscious identity such a process would entail, are here offered as potential alternatives to life in a social world circumscribed by the utilitarian axis of pleasure seeking and the avoidance of pain.

This chapter addresses the complex relationship of realism and repulsion that is hinted at by Dickens's evocative image. Although Dickens here presents us with the dissolution of the self into its own primary substances in a manner that is free from disgust, nineteenth-century authors saw in the squeamish parameters and proscriptions of Enlightenment aesthetics an invitation for all varieties of exploration. From *Bleak House* (1853) with its "maggot numbers" and the festering carcass of "Une charogne" (1857), to the gastric spelunking of *The Belly of Paris* (1873) and the fine-tuned class gradations between gross, greasy, and grimy in *New Grub Street* (1891), realist literature very self-consciously flouted the aesthetic prohibition of disgust and the disgusting. This chapter thus presumes that the literature of the nineteenth century, and the realist novel in particular, knows a lot about disgust, and that the literary discourse of the period therefore stands out as a singularly useful resource for learning about what disgust meant during the historical moment when the emotion gained its widespread social and political currency.

At the same time, I want to propose that the entwinement of realism and repulsion is an underexplored and underrecognized recess of the theory of the novel more generally. How does arguing for the centrality of disgust to the literary endeavors of the nineteenth century disrupt or displace the pride of place that literary theory has at least since René Girard granted to desire and sympathetic identification as the forces animating and structuring the narrative impulse? Although this chapter is the first to situate the nineteenth-century literature of disgust in the context of transformations in the emotion's broader historical role, I am by no means the first to notice the importance of disgust, with its alleged reality effects and its antiaesthetic potential, to literary production in the period. Most immediately, this chapter builds on important criticism by literary scholars such as David Trotter and Eileen Cleere that has described authoritatively the important role that ideas of waste, mess, filth, and repulsion all played in the development of nineteenth-century arts and letters, and so, in the description of modern European culture. In particular, Trotter's invocation of Georges Bataille, and his postulation of a "poetics of mess, whose topic is the practice, in modernity's name, of a degree of 'formlessness,'" speaks directly to the questions I am raising here about Dickens's emphasis on bodily dissolution as an alternative to more conventional ideas about development and *Bildung*.[3]

However, if the matter of disgust has long been central to the way that major critical voices have sought to define the project of realism, the emotion itself has not always been sufficiently theorized. Mikhail Bakhtin's invaluable body of work represents the most robust as well as the most explicit engagement with the broad aesthetic matrix of disgust and the disgusting. "The entire field of realistic literature of the last three centuries," Bakhtin reminds us, "is strewn with the fragments of grotesque realism, which at times are not mere remnants of the past but manifest a renewed vitality."[4] But disgust crops up in unexpected places as well, where it has not been adequately interrogated; too often the emotion itself has been ascribed a transhistorical character that is left unanalyzed, even by the most historically nuanced critics. Eric Auerbach, for example, in his foundational chapters on realism in *Mimesis*, made the forceful case that the recognition of and experimentation with the aesthetic and affective potential of disgust and its eventual incorporation into the formal project of the novel proves to have been essential to the historical development of what Auerbach saw as a socially critical naturalist literature culminating with Zola. Lukács, by contrast, turned to Zola in "Narrate or Describe?" to argue that this same socioaesthetic fixation with the revolting represented a great denigration of and assault on literature. But while they disagreed vehemently about what naturalism heralded for modern culture, both critics shared the same underlying conception of disgust as an invariant, quasi-instinctual form of aesthetic response. Indeed, disgust was the clothes line on which both critics hung their arguments about the modern novel out to dry. Yet seen from the historical perspective of my book, it is perplexing that narratives focused so intensely on changes and transformations in the constitution of modern culture would nonetheless rely on a conception of disgust as itself something beyond transformation. With the important exception of Bakhtin, the theory of the novel has tended to treat disgust as a mode of aesthetic response exterior to the realm of historical change and flux, and in this regard disconnected from the social and political dramas of the nineteenth century, dramas in which seemingly all other aspects of social life were subject to change. In this sense, as we will see in the final section of this chapter, the aesthetics of disgust intersects with what Frederic Jameson has termed the "autonomization" of affect in the late nineteenth century, the evacuation of social and historical value from sensory and emotional experience.[5] To what extent, I ask, was this process of autonomization a consequence of the progressive imbrication, over the course of the nineteenth century, of realism with repulsion?

## Jane's Disdain

Before wading into these debates in the theory of the novel, let us first see what the Victorian novel knew about its own disgust. *Jane Eyre* (1847) will serve as our model, precisely because Brontë's text manages to present a remarkably consistent account of how disgust functions, even in the absence of a pronounced formal interest in the disgusting or grotesque. Jane's disgust encapsulates the broader structure of unwanted feeling I have been outlining, offering a compressed version of the discourse of disgust such as we found in the responses to the Great Stink, or as we will see in the parliamentary debates leading up to the 1857 Obscene Publications Act.

We begin in a fairly remote corner of the novel. Having left Rochester and Bertha Mason behind, Jane fortuitously arrives on the doorstep of her as-yet-unknown cousins. Things are looking up, and she manages to land a job as a teacher in the local school. Yet while Jane does ultimately find pleasure in the moral purpose of her new vocation, her first discovery in the classroom is that being among schoolchildren absolutely repulses her. Confronted with an "unmannered, rough, intractable, as well as ignorant . . . [group of] twenty scholars," whose heavy northern accents alone preclude mutual comprehension, Jane's first day of class prompts an evocative disgust reaction, couched in a complex meditation on the nature of her negative response:

> Was I very gleeful, settled, content during the hours I passed in yonder bare, humble school-room this morning and afternoon? Not to deceive

myself, I must reply—No. I felt desolate to a degree. I felt—yes, idiot that I am—I felt degraded. I doubted I had taken a step which sank instead of raising me in the scale of social existence. I was weakly dismayed at the ignorance, the poverty, the coarseness of all I heard and saw around me. But let me not hate and despise myself too much for these feelings: I know them to be wrong—that is a great step gained; I shall strive to overcome them. To-morrow, I trust, I shall get the better of them partially; and in a few weeks, perhaps, they will be quite subdued. In a few months, it is possible, the happiness of seeing progress and a change for the better in my scholars, may substitute gratification for disgust.[6]

Wavering between two strong negative judgments—of her students and of herself—Jane's account condenses into one knotty response a mixture of lacerating contempt and low-grade nausea, rounded off with a sharp spike of self-derogating shame. I want to look more closely at this passage, since, from her awareness that feelings of disgust are at once inevitable and wrong and so must be overcome, to her conviction that gratification and disgust sit in a substitutive relationship to each other, Jane's characterization of her emotion epitomizes many of the key features of Victorian disgust.

To begin with, there are two sides of Jane's account of her disgust that throw into relief the richness and internal contradiction that it claims as an emotion. The first side is captured by Jane's belief that she "had taken a step which sank instead of raising [her] in the scale of social existence," her sense of having been "degraded," as she puts it, and not merely frustrated or irritated, by her association with the uneducated, uncouth students. She feels that she will be lowered through coming into contact with the lowly. No matter, for now, that she "knows [her feelings] to be wrong," and never mind that she deems herself an "idiot" for having them; the point to grasp is the particular mode of thinking that Jane's disgusted feelings depend on, whereby simply coming into contact with a disgusting object threatens to transmit or transfer its vileness to the disgusted subject, as if the object were contagious and threatened the subject's autonomy.

Such belief in the pollutant powers of objects can produce a number of effects. On the one hand, it can lead to a kind of animistic belief that a disgusting object has agency of its own, a menacing capacity to get inside you: this animistic worldview was central to the rise of modern obscenity regulation, producing legal precedents for dealing with moral pollution that are very much still with us. Jane's reaction leans in the other direction, focusing less on the objects of disgust (her students) than on herself: it displays how disgust makes available a language of hierarchical judgment and imposes order on unruly things, shoring up the boundaries they threaten to transgress. In both cases, the crucial feature of this account of disgust remains its rootedness in negative affect. It is the strength of one's feelings that is taken to evidence the object's agency, and likewise it is feeling that produces the fantasy of disrupted hierarchy. Jane's feelings of degradation persist irrationally, which is to say, the feelings insist on their own validity regardless of Jane's assertion "I know them to be wrong." Disgust becomes the name of a forceful symbolic activity, which yields up a kind of ersatz objectivity and sits in a strained, even adversarial, relationship to knowledge.[7]

The second feature of Jane's account that I want to highlight is its anticipatory and self-condemnatory structure. The passage articulates her revulsion toward her students, but it also offers a pointed commentary on the social and moral value of that disgust which anticipates the reader's condemnation and presumes that such emotions will be met with widespread social disapprobation. Jane already knows her disgust is somehow beneath her, that the feelings themselves are unacceptable and loathsome, and above all, that one must strive to overcome and exclude them from the domain of public conduct. Indeed, within the reformatory ethos of work, renunciation, and self-discipline that Jane's post hoc reflections evince, it would seem that the expression of disgust is more unwanted, more degrading and potentially harmful to a presumptive set of egalitarian social ideals than the objects which might provoke the emotion in the first place. There is therefore a slippery, recursive dynamic at work here, by which Jane rejects her own initial rejection of her students, through an exclusionary gesture that itself very closely resembles disgust. We begin to see here how expressions of disgust can themselves do double duty as objects of disgust, which can in turn be rejected—a structure epitomized by vomit, itself at once an articulation and an object of disgust. Narratologically speaking, we only have access to Jane's affective experience of disgust in the first place through its subsequent repudiation; her revulsion for her students only exists within the narration of her disavowal of disgust as a dependable form of judgment. We get to know one rejection through another.

Far from an incidental structure, Jane's response to her students represents a fundamental conflict over the status of emotion and the exclusion of its alleged irrationality in a culture whose dominant self-definition was at the same historical moment beginning to peg itself—slowly, unevenly, and inconsistently— to liberal ideals of inclusivity and public reason. This seeming tension between rational liberal norms and the public function of disgust not only expresses the Victorian structure of unwanted feeling but also continues to exert pressure on contemporary debates about the status of affect in the public sphere. Martha Nussbaum's philosophical account of the role disgust ought to play in society and law epitomizes the persistence of this Victorian conflict into the present. Asserting along with Rozin that disgust "is usually based on magical thinking rather than on real danger," Nussbaum draws on Millian conceptions of harm and rational action in order to argue that the emotion itself is "problematic and irrational" and that its exclusionary judgments "cannot stand the scrutiny of public reason." Disgust, that is, rather than its objects, represents the actual social harm. Nussbaum recommends that we "go still farther: the really civilized nation must make a strenuous effort to counter the power of disgust, as a barrier to the full equality and mutual respect of all citizens," she insists, adding, "this will require a re-creation of our entire relationship to the bodily."[8]

Like Jane, Nussbaum invokes the rhetoric of the civilizing process in order to make an argument about the unacceptability of revulsion as a guide for rational social judgments in the context of the liberal-democratic nation state. For Jane as for Brontë, of course, this state did not yet exist even remotely to the extent that it does for Nussbaum. Yet Nussbaum grounds her argument explicitly in Mill's liberal-utilitarian philosophy of the late 1850s, and most concretely in his discussion of what social phenomena should be recognized as legitimate harms. Thus we can see that the sociopolitical framework in which disgust comes to seem a kind of social danger in its own right emerges in part as a product of Victorian liberalism's adaptation of Enlightenment universalism, but nevertheless continues to exert strong claims on the present. To the extent that it articulates a conflict between disgust and liberal rationality, Nussbaum's argument reflects the nonresolution of specific problems arising in nineteenth-century conceptions of the interface between the subject and the social world. And indeed, for Nussbaum no less than for Jane, the cornerstone of the argument about disgust involves a call for a "re-creation of our entire relationship to the bodily," which is to say, an alteration in the habitus of liberal modernity, another ambivalent advance in Elias's threshold of shame and repugnance. But the emergence of the modern habitus in the nineteenth century as a rational and liberal ideal of emotional restraint was itself bound up in forms of race thinking and prejudice that make it difficult to distinguish from the modes of thought it sought to exclude (see chapter 4). What Brontë makes clear is that the ideal of a "really civilized nation" invoked by Nussbaum, as well as the more complex idea of the civilizing process theorized by Elias, are not easily separated from the nineteenth-century imperialist project of the civilizing mission, which is the explicit context into which Jane's disgust reaction ultimately resolves.

The political stakes of this nested exclusion become evident in Jane's plan to confront her disgust, overcome it, and, in transforming her students from uncouth, illiterate peasants into industrious and relatively cultivated working-class Englishwomen, to thereby transform it into pleasure. It is a simple plan, which depends on Jane's reminding herself that "these coarsely-clad little peasants are of flesh and blood as good as the gentlest genealogy; and that the germs of native excellence, refinement, intelligence, kind feeling, are as likely to exist in their hearts as in those of the best born." Following Jane's reformed logic, disgust can be overcome by the imposition of a patriotic egalitarianism, through which both Jane's emotions and the very flesh and blood of her students are transformed: "Some time elapsed before . . . I could comprehend my scholars and their nature. Wholly untaught, with faculties quite torpid, they seemed to me hopelessly dull; and at first sight, all dull alike: but I soon found I was mistaken. There was difference among them as amongst the educated; and when I got to know them, and they me, this difference rapidly developed itself. . . . [And] I found some of these heavy-looking, gaping rustics wake up into sharp-witted girls enough."[9] By denouncing and overcoming her disgust, Jane changes her entire social perception. Differences emerge between individuals—or rather, individuals emerge—where before she had seen only the unwanted essential difference of one class from another. Yet what this individuation actually signals is that the feelings of degradation and repulsion according to which she had previously judged her students are not merely regulated, but—a chapter later, after Jane has inherited and divided her fortune, and is entertaining, under pressure from her cousin St. John, the possibility of taking up her higher calling as a missionary in India—entirely abolished: "I had long felt with pleasure that many of my rustic scholars liked me, and when we parted that consciousness was confirmed," she reports—but for how long could she possibly have felt that pleasure? "Deep was my gratification to find I had really a place in their unsophisticated hearts," we read—but how deep could it be? At the end of a month or so, Jane has substituted gratification and pleasure for contempt and disgust with such success, that it is as though her initial judgment had never occurred.

Jane's overcoming of her disgust produces the same effect of ordering social categories in a hierarchical structure that characterizes her gut reaction to the first day of class. She has merely widened the scope, according to a general pattern of externalization and expulsion. On the last day of class, it seems as though whatever egalitarian lessons about individual difference she has learned have only served to shore up a banal sense of nationalist identity, which mirrors her initial class prejudice on an international and imperial stage, rather than a local socioeconomic one: "I stood . . . exchanging a few words of special farewell with some half-dozen of my best scholars: as decent, respectable, modest and well-informed young women as could be found in the ranks of the British peasantry. And that is saying a good deal; for after all the British peasantry are the best taught, best mannered, most self-respecting of any in Europe: since those days I have seen paysannes and Bäuerinnen: and the best of them seems to me ignorant, coarse and besotted compared with my Morton girls."[10] While it has turned out that the British masses are not revolting, as Jane originally believed, the masses of everywhere else in Europe are; the unconverted inhabitants of India and snarling Bertha Mason in her attic represent the outermost limit of the moving wall of Jane's disgust, and return her to the external confrontation with a difference that she may or may not be able to civilize or subdue. Readers of the novel will recall that the book's final lines return us to precisely this question, with news reaching Jane from abroad of her cousin's "labour[ing] for his race" in India and of his impending death as a stranger in a strange land.[11] Her own disgust repudiated, the hierarchical fantasizing comes back, as though from without, from out in the world. The significance of this is not simply that certain forms of prejudice and bigoted fantasy cohabitate with Victorian liberal morality. Rather, Jane's nationalism helps us to see how, despite the explicit identification of disgust with a kind of fractured affective thinking that is not rooted in thought, the emotion continued to garner ever-wider public functions and to accrue new values, changing the way that people used and related to their revulsion in the context of a rapidly transforming social world.

## The Literature of Disgust: Dickensian Innovations

Brontë's treatment of Jane's disgust opens up two paths for our discussion. In the first place, by framing Jane's expression of disgust within the emotion's exclusion, Brontë provides a rubric for understanding how articulations of Victorian disgust constituted a broader structure of feeling whose meaning transcended and yet never quite left behind the individual subjective experience of repulsion. As we can see from the disavowed disgust lurking in the back of Jane's nationalism, revulsion worked like a ship's anchor in Victorian public discourse: once dropped out of sight, it nevertheless continued to set the limits for social perception and action alike. In particular, taken as the expression of a more pervasive modern habitus, Jane's disgust raises important questions about the relationship of this pattern of affective articulation and disavowal to the larger processes of rationalization, self-restraint, and discipline which have (since Weber, Elias, and Foucault, respectively) shaped our general understanding of nineteenth-century history.

Second, we can also now see how the literary text represents a special case within this larger historical framework. For while Jane disavows her disgust, Brontë examines it, lays bare its mechanics, and puts it to work. Unlike the other discourses this book examines—scientific, sociological, political, and so on—the novel can give us a second-order insight into what Victorian culture understood its disgust to mean, why it needed to be excluded, and how the consequences of that exclusion took shape. *Jane Eyre* epitomizes a tendency in the literature of the nineteenth century to be drawn toward the analysis of disgust as a discursive object. Whereas other social domains came to define themselves through the exclusion or repudiation of disgust as a subjective experience, a large cross-section of nineteenth-century literary texts cut their teeth on the explicit incorporation and anatomization of this prevalent structure of feeling, and can be read as a metadiscourse of revulsion.

This is why nineteenth-century realism was so often a literature of disgust, even when it was not or no longer appears to us today as a literature of the disgusting. It represents to the reader the mechanics of an emotional discourse, of the structure of unwanted feeling, rather than focusing more narrowly on the forbidden objects upon which the tradition of "grotesque realism" Bakhtin described had long relied to provoke outrage, hilarity, and discomfort: the body, its substances and the acts that produce them, its decomposition as carcass, the vermin that then eat it, and so on. To be sure, there is no opposition here. From Rabelais to Swift, the representation of the grotesque and disgusting had tended to be carefully fused to, not separated from, the exploration of the expressive powers of disgust and defecation. Especially in the satirical tradition, shitting, spitting, and speech, as well as vomiting and invective, go hand in hand.

The difference is that in the world depicted by the realist literature of the nineteenth century, disgust itself had come to play a new and outsized role in social life as both a force and a focus of exclusion. For Rabelais, this was not yet the case. The world must be outraged by the emetic nature of words—hence Gargantua names Paris by drowning it in a deluge of his own piss, "for a laugh [*per ris*]"—but the text has not itself become the locus for articulating revulsion or exploring its affective mechanics; although Rabelais courts and encourages his readers' outrage, it is not clear that disgust is the only or even the best name for their anticipated scandalization.[12] At the same time, and as Bakhtin has described at length, it is clear that bodily scandal in Rabelais is fused to his attack on the moral authority of the church, a connection that is progressively weakened throughout the early modern period. In Britain, if we follow Benedict Robinson's astute account, crucial transformations in the literary functions of disgust in the seventeenth century track this broader, secularizing shift in the values attached to sensory experience away from the religious domain and toward the new terrain of the aesthetic. "In order for disgust to become productive for the articulation of a socioaesthetics of taste," Robinson writes, "it had to be separated from a terrain in which aversive experience had long been made intelligible: the religious subject's visceral experience of sin and feeling repudiation of the body's pleasures."[13] This secularizing drift of disgust is most readily apparent in the legal-aesthetic category of the obscene, which can be understood as a condensation of the residual energies pertaining to sacred conceptions of pollution with more modern aesthetic concerns over unwanted sensation and negative affect.

When we turn to Swift, however, not only do we see that disgust can claim a prominent role in the world of a major literary imagination, but more importantly we are confronted with a new expectation that the emotion will be legible to readers according to a highly complex and largely implicit social grammar that nevertheless appears to be in a state of flux and transition. The Rabelaisian impulse is still there, but it is now also a citation, as with Gulliver's peeing on Lilliput to extinguish a city fire.[14] More significantly, however, in Swift the morally upright citizens of the outraged world are already a little too revolted for their own good—hence the awkward hilarity of the despondent Cassinus, who loses his wits when faced with the fact that his beloved "Celia shits."[15] The squeamish, too-easily-disgusted subject begins to emerge as the object of a ridicule that is premised on a presumptively shared sense of the emotion's overly constrictive social function but that is also fused to a misogynistic tendency to imagine the female body as the ultimate object of disgust. This is why Norman O. Brown was right to see in Swift a harbinger of Freud's later conceptual identification of disgust with repression, but wrong to therefore imagine that Swift had put his finger on the transhistorical pulse of psychoanalytic theory. Rather, Swift's excremental poems signal the dawning of a historical moment during which disgust would be mobilized as a new form of affective restraint, and heightened restraint would come to seem a social problem in its own right. There is now a satirical power in being able to call out revulsion, to expose its social dissimulations; at the same time, there is the intuition that the languages of satire and disgust, in preserving something of the excremental in their rhetorical and affective force, make possible a complex new recursive formation.

By the middle of the nineteenth century, disgust has begun to eclipse its provoking objects. Thus, while *Little Dorrit* has some notable scenes of London filth and human degradation, and Dickens is keen to remind us that "through the heart of the town a deadly sewer ebbed and flowed, in the place of a fine fresh river," it is above all a book concerned with narrating the refused confrontation with such unwanted facts of social life, in a world whose dominant ideology dictates, as one of its characters puts it, that "nothing disagreeable should ever be looked at."[16] Dickens for this reason represents the paradigmatic case for a midcentury realist literature of disgust. To be sure, the interest in the corporeal and the scatological, as well as in the embodied, emetic nature of invective, are alive and well in his work, but they now vie for pride of place with the diagnosis of disgust as a social disturbance in its own right. Or we might say that the social diagnostic function in Dickens itself has two sides. On the one hand, it made full use of Dickens's genius for satire and, in so doing, mobilized the Swiftian and Rabelaisian toolkit: the loping cadences of revulsion, the grotesque caricature, the gag reflexes of moral outrage. Yet on the other hand, in Dickens we also see the mid-nineteenth-century search for a systematic social criticism taking root. While this critical impulse grew out of the satirical tradition and continued to nourish itself on the latter's resources, it nevertheless represented a different order of literary project; and it is through this latter socially critical strain that Dickens came to focus on disgust as an object of critique, even while the emotion continued to provide the language for the activity of criticism.

Dickens, I am arguing, came to view the bourgeois refusal to grant recognition to unwanted or unpleasant aspects of everyday reality as a social pathology, one which he sought to understand and to critique with increasing precision and clarity in his major works of the late 1850s and 1860s.[17] Franco Moretti has argued a similar point when, pointing to Alfred Tennyson and Joseph Conrad, he names "disavowal" as "the underlying desire" of the bourgeois literature of the nineteenth century, asserting that "self-inflicted blindness is the foundation of Victorianism."[18] But this useful formulation nonetheless fails to grasp that the language of blindness and repudiation, and the configuration of disavowal, disgust, and hidden desire, are in fact the central innovations of the literature of this period—innovations that Dickens continued to push forward throughout his career. "The comfortable turn haughtily away," Raymond Williams once put it, "and from *Dombey and Son* onward we see a social system in which the turning away is as much a product of circumstances as the distress."[19] Whereas earlier novels such as *Hard Times* and *The Old Curiosity Shop* had pitted sympathetic feeling against callous, Gradgrindian rationalism, later works like *Little Dorrit* and *Our Mutual*

*Friend* reflect instead this heightened focus on the ways that disgust and dis-avowal coincided in Victorian culture. In other words, social antagonism, in the later works, is no longer generated by the conflict between sympathetic feeling and unfeeling economic rationality, but rather by the disavowal of a species of revolted feeling that masquerades as disinterestedness.

In *Little Dorrit*, Dickens pushes this play between disgust and disavowal to an almost farcical extreme in the character of Mrs. General, a schem-ing disciplinarian hired to oversee Amy Dorrit's socialization after her father inherits his fortune and is freed from debtor's prison. Under Mrs. General's regime, entrance into polite society depends on what she calls "the forma-tion of a surface"; this process turns out to be much less metaphorical than it sounds, and actually involves pursing one's lips in bilabial stoppage in order to prevent anything unwanted from entering into the self and anything unde-sirable from escaping it: "Papa, potatoes, poultry, prunes, and prism are all very good words for the lips: especially prunes and prism," Mrs. General tells Amy: "You will find it serviceable, in the formation of a demeanour, if you sometimes say to yourself in company—on entering a room, for instance— Papa, potatoes, poultry, prunes and prism, prunes and prism."[20]

This motif in *Little Dorrit* represents a thematic reversal of the Rabelaisian focus on the leaky, seeping body: puckering up and pronouncing one's plo-sives becomes a sociopolitically freighted act, at once a means of encasing the self—of plugging oneself up—as well as the precondition for entering into social and economic relations determined by the rules of proper con-duct. Rather than showing us a carnivalesque world of intermingled societal and corporeal disinhibition, Dickens presents a garish vision of modern life, in which the disavowal of the body's porosity and vulnerability corresponds directly with the disavowal of social reality. Yet it is essential to see that this disavowal remains tethered very deliberately to an embodied conception of disgust and its related negative affects, such as when we see the snobbish Mrs. Gowan "patting her contemptuous lips with her fan."[21] The affective compound of revulsion, contempt, scorn, and disdain is shown to be the medium through which affective life is disavowed; repulsion becomes a pri-mary means of disciplining the body.

In the previous section I described Jane Eyre's repudiation of her disgust as expressive of a modern habitus in which the experience of the emotion comes to feel like something out of step with the larger social structure. While Brontë allowed us to glimpse this interplay of structure and feeling, in *Little Dorrit* its ligaments and joints are much more fully articulated at a variety of levels. We are shown how the training and manipulation of the orifices—mouths, noses, eyes—can be used as a means of assimilating the self to an ideological social order that seeks to regulate the meanings that are ascribed to sensory and perceptual experiences. Beyond this, we are also asked to think about how this social order, which takes the body and its affects as a medium, also relates to concrete social institutions and processes, such as the novel's concatenation of carceral scenes: the first hundred pages, for instance, take place in a jail cell, a quarantine, a scene of home confinement, in the halls of the Circumlocution Office, and finally, on the main stage of the debtor's prison. It is against these various backdrops of institutional management and bureaucratic centralization that the novel stages its minute, local dramas of the orifice.

My point here is not so much to invoke Elias's civilizing process or the Foucauldian disciplinary and biopolitical paradigm, as it is to insist on Dickens's own dawning alertness to the particular role of disgust in the imbrication of the experience of affective regulation with the rise of modern social structures, on which both of those later theorists focused so intensely. This alertness, I will argue in the fourth chapter of this book, presages fin-de-siècle sociological attempts to theorize the very same nexus where rationalization, centralization, and the state monopolization of violence meet with the grammar of emotional life, even as it reflects the innovative potential that repulsion offered to the nineteenth-century literary imagination. Dickens thus helps us to see how disgust took on sociological as well as aesthetic functions in the broader development of nineteenth-century realism, showing not only how disgust claimed increasing centrality as a category for social criticism and analysis but also how the tools of the grotesque and satirical traditions could be repurposed in the production of a new literary form that would be characteristic of its age. It is for both of these tendencies that Bakhtin singled out *Little Dorrit* as the text that best exemplified his notion of novelistic "heteroglossia." On the one hand, heteroglossia was the technique by which the novel established its sociological vision and sociolinguistic breadth. On the other, it was the means through which the novel realized its distinctive aesthetic potential in light of the affective power of language and its rootedness in the bodily and even gustatory dimension of the orality of speech. "Each word tastes of the context and contexts in which it has lived its socially charged life," Bakhtin puts it, as though novelistic words were literally taken out from the mouths and bowels of others.[22]

Dickens was by no means alone in exhibiting these tendencies. The bearing of the analysis of disgust and its disavowal on both the sociological vision of modern life and the refinement of the aesthetic enterprise only becomes more apparent if we turn to *Les fleurs du mal* and *Madame Bovary*, each published within months of *Little Dorrit* and both tried for obscenity in 1857.

Especially in Baudelaire's poetry, the disgusting becomes a kind of alchemical fulcrum in the relationship between social reality and aesthetic idealism, a transfer point where the worthless filth of modernity could be converted to a new form of secular literary value: "I have extracted the essence from everything," Baudelaire wrote of his own poems. "You gave me your mud, and I made it into gold" (Car j'ai de chaque chose extrait la quintessence, / Tu m'as donné ta boue et j'en ai fait de l'or).[23] Likewise, if we look ahead to the developments in naturalism in the last decades of the century, one sees how authors like Gissing, Zola, and Thomas Hardy continued to explore the volatile points of contact between the social discourse of disgust and the aesthetic potential presented by the new centrality this discourse could claim.

Yet this development was contested every step of the way. Against such a literary-historical account of the socioaesthetic significance of disgust for the realist project, one finds a whole critical tradition insisting to the contrary on the intentional disgustingness and obtrusive prurience of the nineteenth-century novel. Starting with the scandalized critics of the Victorian period and reaching forward to the present, the exploration and examination of the meaning of disgust in the context of the nineteenth-century novel has been habitually taken as a disgusting thing in its own right. We see this in Moretti's oversimplifying comment that the Victorian novel was simply a literature of disavowal, rather than a literature which for the first time took the entwinement of disgust and disavowal to be a prevalent social phenomenon; and we see it in Morris's assertion, in the lecture "Art under Plutocracy," that "the disease" afflicting Victorian culture "would seem to be a love of dirt and ugliness for its own sake."[24] Above all else, we see precisely the same allegation in the history of obscenity, which from Baudelaire and Gustave Flaubert to Zola and D. H. Lawrence and beyond has remained stubbornly blind to the distinction between disgust and the disgusting.

This knee-jerk confusion of disgust for the disgusting is such a persistent feature of the history of literary realism that it cannot be written off as an aberration caused by Victorian prudery. Rather, it must be understood as the headlong collision of a reality effect already operating within the longer history of aesthetic disgust with the particular project of nineteenth-century realist literature. Enlightenment aesthetics specifically singled out this feature of disgust in mounting the case for its exclusion, arguing that the provocation of the emotion broke down the distinction between representation and reality. "Representations of fear, of sadness, horror, compassion, &c., arouse painful emotions only in so far as we believe the evil to be actual," Moses Mendelssohn writes, in a passage quoted at length in Lessing's influential *Laocoön* and ultimately picked up and adapted by Kant, whereas

"the consideration that it is but an illusion may resolve these disagreeable sensations into those of pleasure." By contrast, the provocation of "the disagreeable sensation of disgust" blows a fuse in this Aristotelian aesthetic paradigm: "No matter how apparent the art of imitation, our wounded sensibilities are not relieved [from the experience of disgust]," Mendelssohn goes on. "Our discomfort arose not from the belief that the evil was actual, but from the mere representation which is actually present." The point is not that the object being represented in the disgusting picture is somehow the "real" object, the referent, but rather that the force of the unwanted feeling of disgust that it provokes lends the representation a reality all its own, which nevertheless erodes the distinction between representation and thing. "The feeling of disgust, therefore," Mendelssohn concludes, "comes always from nature, never from imitation."[25] Disgust, in this formulation, sits right on the fault line of the fact/value distinction, destabilizing the delicate equilibrium of the aesthetic sphere. As we saw in *Jane Eyre*, the negative affective value attached to the disgusting thing produces an ersatz facticity, an unwanted feeling on parade as an unwanted fact.

To the extent that the discourse of literary criticism internalized the underlying premises of this influential aesthetic paradigm, we can begin to see why the literature of the middle of the nineteenth century posed such a special problem. For from the perspective opened up by the aesthetic exclusion of disgust, it could hardly matter whether an author was striving to reflect on or even to reject a set of social conditions, or rather seeking to produce a monstrous disruption of the social order. Their intentions were null; all that mattered was the obtrusive intentionality of the disgusting text, a realism that became reality as the reader registered its affective negativity. Thus the realist literature of disgust and its detractors found themselves in a slippery, recursive, and yet also dynamic relationship: the critics of realism wanted to disavow the very same revolting novels that quite often sought to represent the historical process whereby revulsion came to occupy its central role in social discourse as an affective mode of disavowal.

## Fiction—Fair and Foul

This recursive circuit of realism and repulsion is far more central to the history and theory of the nineteenth-century novel than is ordinarily acknowledged. While disgust has been alternately disavowed and celebrated as an antiaesthetic force running through the history of modern literature, there has nonetheless been widespread, often tacit, and largely uncritical agreement over the validity of the aesthetic conception of the emotion, which has persisted through various theoretical iterations. Even where dissent over what can or ought to constitute literary value is at its most intense, there tends to be consensus that disgust plays the part of a destabilizing force that reconfigures the hollowed-out space separating fact from value and reality from representation.

A page from the literary criticism of the nineteenth century can help to make clear the terms of this enduring problematic. Writing in *Fiction—Fair and Foul* (1880), John Ruskin decried the state of the modern novel, drawing his line in the sand with Walter Scott and rejecting outright most works of prose fiction printed in the intervening fifty years after 1830. Ruskin's chief objections have to do precisely with the relationship between "the forms of filth, and modes of ruin" of modern society, and a literary imagination that, nourished by this civilization gone sour, comes to express "incredulity of all sunshine outside the dunghill, or breeze beyond the wafting of its impurity." Targeting Balzac and Zola—but above all Dickens—Ruskin argues that the "pathologic labour of the modern novelist" is simply to reproduce with ever greater precision and detail the social pathologies of modern life:

> But for the children of to-day, accustomed, from the instant they are out of their cradles, to the sight of this infinite nastiness, prevailing as a fixed condition of the universe, over the face of nature, and accompanying all the operations of industrious man, what is to be the scholastic issue? . . . One result of such elementary education is . . . already certain; namely, that the pleasure which we may conceive taken by the children of the coming time, in the analysis of corruption, guides, into fields more dangerous and desolate, the expatiation of an imaginative literature: and that the reactions of moral disease upon itself, and the conditions of languidly monstrous character developed in an atmosphere of low vitality, have become the most valued material of modern fiction. . . . The resulting modes of mental ruin and distress are continually new; and in a certain sense, worth study in their monstrosity: they have accordingly developed a corresponding science of fiction, concerned mainly with the description of such forms of disease, like the botany of leaf-lichens. . . .
>
> But a much more profound feeling than this mere curiosity of science in morbid phenomena is concerned in the production of the carefullest forms of modern fiction. The disgrace and grief resulting from the mere trampling pressure and electric friction of town life, become to the sufferers peculiarly mysterious in their undeservedness, and frightful in their inevitableness. The power of all surroundings over

them for evil; the incapacity of their own minds to refuse the pollution, and of their own wills to oppose the weight, of the staggering
mass that chokes and crushes them into perdition, brings every law of
healthy existence into question with them, and every alleged method
of help and hope into doubt. Indignation, without any calming faith
in justice, and self-contempt, without any curative self-reproach, dull
the intelligence, and degrade the conscience, into sullen incredulity of
all sunshine outside the dung-hill, or breeze beyond the wafting of its
impurity; and at last a philosophy develops itself, partly satiric, partly
consolatory, concerned only with the regenerative vigor of manure,
and the necessary obscurities of fimetic Providence; showing how
everybody's fault is somebody else's, how infection has no law, digestion no will, and profitable dirt no dishonour.[26]

The tone is bombastic, but Ruskin's point is actually quite focused. Given the
fallen state of industrial society, he asks, how can the modern author fail to
produce a fallen literature? Morris would echo this lament a few years later,
writing that "the well of art is poisoned at the spring."[27] But Ruskin goes
further in his analysis than most other contemporary critics in describing the
modern novel specifically as a literature of disgust. There are two pieces to
his critique. The first is simply that modern social conditions have normal-
ized a state of urban degradation which has in turn produced a program-
matic and merely empirical "science of fiction," spurred on by a morbid and
nihilistic curiosity. This was a common enough critique of naturalism, and
of Zola and Gissing in particular, and in a sense it was not wholly untrue,
as essays such as Hardy's "The Science of Fiction" (1891) and Zola's "The
Experimental Novel" (1893) can evidence. More to the point, it is a critique
of literature as sociology (and by inference of sociology itself), in which the
chief concern is with the limitations of a purely reproductive or mimetic literary impulse to grapple with the inadmissibly disgusting fact of the world.

Second, in order to develop this critique, Ruskin details with precision
how the discourse of realism is produced through the corruption of the
modern subject by the disgusting. Invoking the language of revulsion, he
zeroes in specifically on a respiratory "pollution" that cannot be refused,
a "staggering mass that chokes and crushes." If we zoom out, the image
is of a society engulfed and overtaken by its own noxious excrescences, an
image that Ruskin would articulate even more fully and in a broader historical register in the lectures titled "The Storm-Cloud of the Nineteenth
Century" a few years later, and which we might now see as connected to
actual experiences of unwanted collective olfaction such as the Great Stink.

Here, however, we remain at the level of the subject, carefully focused on the formation of a habitus through the inverted experiences of morbid pleasure taken in the disgusting and corrupt, on the one hand, and disdainful "incredulity of all sunshine outside the dung-hill, or breeze beyond the wafting of its impurity," on the other. Consequently, this corrupted subject, caring only for the disgusting (but no longer disgusted by it), and experiencing only an indignant, self-reviling *contemptus mundi*, produces a reviling "philosophy," a discourse in which nothing beyond this restricted emotional range is even granted recognition. Hence, the world reproduced by the so-called "fimetic" literature of the modern novel reproduces only the disgusted modern habitus, which mirrors the corrupting social conditions that shaped it. Like its Enlightenment forebear, then, this Victorian aesthetics of disgust has a recursive structure. It is a feedback loop of revulsion, whose general form is that of an unwanted correspondence between container and contents, a rotten atmosphere, inhaled deep into rotting lungs, exhaled back into the rotten air.

There is much that is unique to Ruskin's diagnosis of modern literature, but let us instead focus on what in it is typical. In a less revolted tone and a more affectively neutral Marxist-philosophical idiom, for example, we can fast-forward half a century to find Lukács inveighing in "Narrate or Describe?" (1936) against Zola's descriptive method for a remarkably similar set of aesthetic infractions. "The dominance of capitalist prose over the inner poetry of human experience, the continuous dehumanization of social life, the general debasement of humanity," Lukács writes, "all these are objective facts of the development of capitalism": "The descriptive method is the product of this development. Once established this method is taken up by leading writers . . . and then it in turn affects the literary representation of reality. The poetic level of life decays—and literature intensifies the decay."[28] As with Ruskin's account of realism, Lukács focuses here on the mutually reinforcing relationship of corruption that pertains between naturalist literature and society, the latter now specified as capitalist rather than simply modern or industrial. Capitalist social relations debase the function of language; the author produces a merely descriptive, debased world in this debased language; the debased language debases the world; and so on. Written in the 1930s from a historical vantage point radically different from Ruskin's, Lukács's argument cannot be assimilated to the same set of aesthetic principles on display in "Fiction—Fair and Foul." My point is rather to emphasize the continuity in their thinking about the relationship between mimetic realism and fimetic repulsion, in spite of their significant differences in approach, historical worldview, and ideology. For both critics offer us a debased and diseased world, no longer capable of a cultural organicism, whose literature is presided over by a "science of fiction, concerned mainly with the description of such forms of disease."

As with Ruskin's ineluctable pollution, Lukács attributes to the naturalist's drive to describe the revolting conditions of modern social life a prurient intentionality and purposiveness that derives directly from the aesthetic conception of disgust: "We know that Zola's emphasis on man's bestiality was in protest against the bestiality of capitalism, a bestiality which he did not understand," Lukács continues. "But his irrational protest became transformed into an obsession with the bestial, with the animal-like. The method of observation and description developed as part of an attempt to make literature scientific, to transform it . . . into sociology. But investigation of social phenomena through observation and their representation in description bring such paltry and schematic results, that these modes of composition easily slip into their opposite—complete subjectivism."[29] It does not matter, Lukács writes, that Zola sought to critique "the bestiality of capitalism." The bestiality overtakes him, and his sociological protest reverts to "obsession" and "irrationality," as though the horror of the confrontation with capitalism were able to disorder an otherwise sober system of affective management. Lukács goes even further in this assault on naturalism, arguing that the "spurious objectivity" of the novelist seeking to catalog the effects of industrial capitalism reverts to a "complete subjectivism." Objectivity is revealed as stemming from feeling, science is revealed as growing out of irrational obsession, and both these inversions are condemned as perpetuating, rather than critiquing or transcending, the unwanted fact of the world. What is significant about this line of argument for our discussion is that for Lukács, as for Ruskin, the equation of the repulsive with the real remains intact. Disgust is that feeling capable of producing a "spurious objectivity," an objectivity that, in presenting itself as fact, masks its rootedness in affect. The result of this process is "decay" and "debasement," a process of social corruption that, significantly, the text enacts as an agent in the world, in much the same way that Mendelssohn insisted that the disgusting representation becomes its own kind of object. Finally, as with the Enlightenment paradigm, the cumulative effect of these features of the realist or the naturalist novel, for Lukács, is to justify a self-evidently negative aesthetic judgment rooted in the evidence of corruption, an exclusion of the descriptive method from the canon of what counts as politically or socially engaged high literature.

The realist impulse, Lukács implies but does not quite spell out, cannot be fully separated from the aesthetics of disgust. Disgust is a necessary piece of the puzzle, the affective medium through which the allegedly undistorted empiricism of literary observation lays claim to its mimetic objectivity. But

Lukács does not question his presuppositions about disgust with the same degree of scrutiny as he questions Zola's claim to literary value. To the contrary, he uncritically accepts the premises of a bourgeois Enlightenment aesthetics, only in order to condemn what he calls the "bourgeois sociology" of naturalism with the force of a self-evidence that is entirely typical of the appeal to disgust. It is this account of the self-evidence of disgust that is preserved and perpetuated by both Ruskin's and Lukács's exclusion of disgust from their otherwise distinct critiques of realism. Beneath the very different accounts of literary value, there is deep-seated agreement about the meaning that can be ascribed to disgust in particular, and affective experience in general. They share an underlying grammar of affect and sensation, derived from the aesthetics of disgust, which gives them license to police the borderline between fact and feeling.

A final example will help to drive home this point about the productive role the exclusion of disgust has played within the theory of the novel. In what can almost be read as a point-by-point rebuttal of Lukács's argument about Zola, Auerbach advances in *Mimesis* a strikingly complex historical account of the entwinement of realism and repulsion—although he too depends on an account of the reflexive nature of disgust, which he grants the unchallenged status of common sense about the senses. For Auerbach, Zola represents an important development of a prevalent midcentury structure of feeling, whose central element was "the aversion which precisely the most outstanding writers felt towards contemporary civilization and contemporary society," a society with which "they were themselves indissolubly connected" as representatives of the bourgeois class. It is this dynamic relationship between disgust or aversion and involvement or immanence that in Auerbach's view characterizes the literature of the middle decades of the nineteenth century, especially in its pursuit of pure style (Flaubert) and in the development of aestheticism (Baudelaire): "In this dilemma of instinctive aversion and necessary implication, yet at the same time amid an almost anarchic freedom in the realms of opinion, choice of possible subject matter, and development of idiosyncrasies in respect to forms of life and expression, those writers . . . were driven into an almost stubborn isolation in the domain of pure aesthetics and into renouncing any practical intervention in the problems of the age through their works."[30]

Fueled in equal parts by a bourgeois disgust for the world and a bourgeois aesthetic freedom, Auerbach writes, a literature developed that was fixated by the "aesthetic attraction of the ugly and the pathological." For the Goncourts or Baudelaire, that is, the interest in the underbelly of modern life was motivated by "an aesthetic and not a social impulse," an appetite for sensations rather than a desire for participation. It is not until Zola's generation, Auerbach argues, that the aesthetic interest in the disgusting was fused to "the core social problem of the age, the struggle between industrial capital and labor." Hence, he concludes, "it is surprising but undeniable that the inclusion of the fourth estate [i.e., the proletariat] in serious realism was decisively advanced by those, who in their quest for new aesthetic impressions, discovered the attraction of the ugly and pathological."[31] In Auerbach's nuanced history of nineteenth-century realism, disgust enters into the literary imagination first as an aesthetic category enabled by bourgeois ambivalence, and then as a sociopolitical category. Or to be even more precise, the development of the social function of the repulsive within realist literature depended on the prior rejection, on aesthetic grounds, of the exclusion of disgust from the repertory of affects and sensations deemed appropriate within the domain of aesthetic experience.

What I want to extract from this complex picture of the concatenation or nested structure of aesthetic and social aims is the overarching sense of the dynamism and volatility that Auerbach attributes to the functions of disgust during the very same years that we are concerned with in this book. In order to detail a major transformation in the way reality was represented in nineteenth-century literature, Auerbach was compelled to outline a related transformation in the meaning of repulsion. This latter change stemmed from the way that individual authors grappled with their "instinctual aversion" to the social world they inhabited, at a moment when freedom in choice of subject matter as well as more concrete political economic demands for social inclusion were rapidly transforming the nature of the literary text and the artwork. What is especially significant for us is the structure of involvement and disavowal that Auerbach situates at the heart of the midcentury upheavals in literary form. For now we can see clearly and in a less condemning light the same recursive dynamic that came to the fore in both Ruskin and Lukács but was obscured by their own strong repudiations of the realist embrace of repulsion. What Auerbach describes, almost as though describing the spirit of the age, is the prevalent feeling of unwanted identification with negative and destructive social processes that was given voice in so many Victorian cultural artifacts. Disgust was available as a means of expressing this structure of feeling in part because it was already a form of refusal, and in part because it was prohibited; it could express a rejection of the social order, but it could also, so to speak, put one outside the social order, or at least appear to gesture toward such an outside. For many novelists in the latter decades of the nineteenth century, disgust offered the lure of a highly productive negativity.

Yet in the midst of such historical dynamism and change—when the very terms by which reality and the real can be represented are seen to fluctuate and shift from decade to decade—how are we to understand this continued insistence on the instinctivity of even the most class-inflected experiences of disgust? Across a wide spectrum of incompatible positions, disgust's naturalized reflexivity remains constant. This conception of disgust as an automatic form of aesthetic response that cannot be refused has been extraordinarily productive, in these formative debates of literary theory no less than in the construction of London's sewer system. The next two chapters take a closer look at this conflation of disgust with instinct within the domains of both the natural and the social sciences; for disgust became available in new ways as a metonym for instinct and reflex during the same period of historical transformation in which realism was consolidating and reconfiguring its own resources.

Lukács and Auerbach both run the risk of losing sight of this variegated and multilayered history through their uncritical acceptance of the disgustingness of the oversimplified entity, "industrial capitalism." For it was not simply an allegedly reflexive horror at the conditions of capitalism that provoked this development within realism. Rather, as Marx himself was among the first to observe, it was the deeper sense that the emergence of the capitalist lifeworld was responsible for bringing about changes and restrictions in the distribution of meanings afforded to affective and sensory experiences. The ascription of an unwanted instinctive character to disgust might then be said to answer an ideological need endemic to nineteenth-century culture—in particular, the need to understand the seemingly unwilled character of affective and sensory experience as something primal and prehistoric, not only belonging to the past but also isolated from the action on history's main stage. Thus, the impulse to understand disgust as "instinctual aversion" can be seen as part of a broader process of coming to conceptualize affect more generally as autonomous, as a sphere of experience that sits outside or askew of social existence (understood variously as symbolic, everyday, historical, narratable, etc.). It is to this question of how the autonomy of affect relates to the aesthetics of disgust that we now turn.

## Autonomization or Deodorization?

Over the course of the nineteenth century, realism embraced repulsion. This would seem to be the consensus view offered by these three influential but otherwise incompatible accounts of the development of the nineteenth-century European novel, in particular in the British and French traditions.

Neither Lukács nor Auerbach presumes to offer the literary confrontation with disgust as a totalizing account of the narrative impulse, but for both the encounter is nevertheless constitutive of modern literature. For Lukács it is constitutive of the impoverishment of bourgeois literature as it inched toward modernist irrationalism and subjective fragmentation, whereas for Auerbach it was constitutive of modern literature's transcendence of bourgeois aesthetics and its incorporation of an anticapitalist politics. Nor is this view isolated to the three critics I have been discussing; rather, the general problem of disgust and the novel, as well as the more restricted interaction of realism and repulsion, is woven throughout the history of literary theory and criticism. Bakhtin presides over the question of the novel's corporeality in the form's development over the *longue durée*, but it would not be difficult to show how even less obviously visceral histories of the novel, especially those granting the coordination between epistemological fact and moral value a key role in the emergence of the genre, likewise confront or grapple with the socioaesthetic problem of disgust.[32]

However, this argument for realism and repulsion soon comes up against a major stumbling block. For at this point it is so thoroughly established in literary theory as to be taken as axiomatic that desire, and not disgust, is the motive force of realist narrative (if not of narrative in general), just as sympathy and identification, rather than revolted outrage and antipathy, are the ideologically appropriate aesthetic responses to the Victorian novel.[33] In making the case for a literature of disgust, and more specifically for the historical imbrication of realism and repulsion, I aim to loosen the totalizing conceptual grip that these more affirmative terms have exerted on the terrain of nineteenth-century literature. Indeed, sympathy and desire are not so much hypotheses about the narrative mechanics of nineteenth-century literature as they are premises of novel theory. And yet my hope so far is to have begun painting in the outlines of a rather different literary-historical picture: one in which not only the novels themselves but also some of our most canonical theoretical debates prove to have been animated by a set of preoccupations that focus on revolted rejection rather than positive wish fulfillment and on the production of aversive rather than identificatory reaction. In lieu of the demand for sympathetic identification, what we see when we look at this late-century terrain from the perspective of a literature of disgust is the presumption of a shared disidentification, a disavowed commonality rooted in negativity and refusal rather than positive affective connection or the capacity for fellow-feeling.[34]

In the context of this double tension between disgust and desire, on the one hand, and sympathy and antipathy, on the other, the question of disgust's reflexive character takes on a renewed significance. In the first case, this is because, taken as a form of primal and reflexive behavior, disgust starts to look as much like a kind of drive or instinct as desire; in the swirl of fin-de-siècle medical-scientific, literary, and philosophical discourses that Freud would organize into psychoanalytic theory, for example, disgust comes to be associated with repression and disavowal, desire with the pleasure principle—although we have already seen how disgust came to take on a more than merely repressive function within the nineteenth-century literature of disgust. What is harder to see is how this principle of instinctual aversion can be extended in order to account for collective or social experience, in the way that sympathetic identification can be said to account collectively for the individual subject. What does the collectivization of disgust look like in the context of the nineteenth-century novel? This question leads us back to Dickens's image of dissolution in the Thames.

In the British context, Gissing worked assiduously at developing an explicit aesthetic of disgust that would make it virtually impossible to sympathize with his novels. For example, Gissing's *The Nether World* (1889) takes as its epigram Ernest Renan's assertion that "a picture of a dung-heap could be justified provided a beautiful flower grew out of it; without the flower, the dung-heap is merely repulsive" (La peinture d'un fumier peut être justifiée pourvu qu'il y pousse une belle fleur; sans cela, le fumier n'est que repoussant). What follows from this opening salvo is an attempt to fulfill Renan's proscription of the disgusting, to paint the dunghill without the flower. Thus for Gissing, the novel became a space for experimenting with the recursive structures of disgust that we have been discussing throughout this chapter and for seeking out a form of unrecuperated socioaesthetic negativity; we see this experimentation in every discursive register of *The Nether World*, and not merely at the level of its aesthetic program. Thus, nearly all the characters in the novel are motivated by what Gissing repeatedly describes as an "impulse to revolt," a kind of psychosocial drive that encompasses the affective sense of revulsion; the political sense of revolution or uprising; and a more specific socioeconomic sense of "revolt against circumstances" and, in many cases, against the "wretched toilers whose swarming aroused . . . disgust"; finally, there is also a more nihilistic and existentialist sense of "revolt for revolt's sake."[35] It is a novel about the economic conditions of late Victorian England in which all the social and aesthetic dynamism that would conventionally be introduced by normative desire and the solicitation of sympathy instead derives from an antagonistic principle of sociality that Gissing identifies explicitly with disgust and that pervades his work on all levels. Indeed, more than any other English-language writer in the period, including Conrad and

Hardy, Gissing's style itself invited critical disapprobation in the language of disgust, which might be argued to bear some responsibility for all but three of his nearly two dozen novels having gone out of print. Even George Orwell, one of Gissing's few champions in the twentieth century, wrote of Gissing that "there is not much of what is usually called beauty, not much lyricism, in the situations and characters he chooses to imagine, and still less in the texture of his writing. His prose, indeed, is often disgusting."[36]

In Gissing, then, we see an author in search of an antiaesthetic, whose raw materials are fully saturated by a disgust whose satirical energies, moreover, have begun to dry up: characters who revolt against their social world; narrators who contemptuously reject their characters; an aesthetic paradigm which strives to substitute disgust for pleasure; and a critical reception that consequently cannot regard the final literary object with anything but revulsion. This nested, recursive structure of an exclusion that only becomes apparent through another exclusion is a prevalent form in nineteenth-century literature. In the fin-de-siècle literary imagination, however, it achieves a new preeminence.

All throughout Thomas Hardy's oeuvre, for example, one sees figures of precisely this same recursive disgust and negativity, albeit rendered in a more existentially rich language than in Gissing; hence in *Jude the Obscure* (1895), the young protagonist's belief that a "magic thread of fellow-feeling united his own life with" the crows he is employed to scare away from a curmudgeonly farmer's crops—a sense of common feeling rooted in the recognition that the birds "seemed, like himself, to be living in a world which did not want them." For Hardy, that is, the experience of being constituted as a subject is often one of perpetual expulsion. In the queasy *taedium vitae* that pervades Jude's Wessex, the feeling that puts one's insides in step with the obtrusive rotten atmospheres of the outside world is not a feeling of pleasure but of nausea or repulsion: "Jude went out, and, feeling more than ever his existence to be an undemanded one, he lay down upon his back in a heap of litter near the pig-sty. . . . As you got older, and felt yourself to be at the centre of your time, and not at a point in its circumference, as you had felt when you were little, you were seized with a sort of shuddering, he perceived."[37] What is striking about this structure of unwanted feeling is that it suggests an alignment of the revolted subject with its revolting environment, an attunement of self with world that proceeds by a principle of contagion or contamination that cannot be separated from its negativity. From *Jane Eyre* to *Jude the Obscure*, we come across this structure of exclusion nested within exclusion.

It is possible to see in these figures a pejorative, late Victorian antecedent to more outwardly affirmative modernist figurations of the self as subsumed by and indistinguishable from the atmosphere which contains it. Among such figures we might count Virginia Woolf's interest in the vertigo and elastic temporality of the microcosmic image: "Yet there are moments when the walls of the mind grow so thin," she writes in *The Waves*, "when nothing is unabsorbed, and I fancy we might blow so vast a bubble that the sun might set and rise in it."[38] But even more than Woolf, I have in mind Proust, as with, for example, the narrator's famous description of how he would

> amuse myself by watching the glass jars which the boys used to lower into the Vivonne, to catch minnows, and which, filled by the current of the stream, in which they themselves also were enclosed, at once "containers" whose transparent sides were like solidified water and "contents" plunged into a still larger container of liquid, flowing crystal, suggested an image of coolness more delicious and more provoking than the same water in the same jars would have done, standing upon a table laid for dinner, by shewing it as perpetually in flight between the impalpable water, in which my hands could not arrest it, and the insoluble glass, in which my palate could not enjoy it.[39]

For Eve Kosofsky Sedgwick, this figure emblematizes what she describes as a theme of permeability running throughout *À la recherche du temps perdu*, a breakdown of the boundaries normally cordoning off the subject from the outer world. This muted but insistent current of suffusive thematic material in Proust, Sedgwick argues, stands out against the sections of the novels organized more strictly around the circulation of desire and jealousy, "the closet melodramas of sexual privacy" that, as she rightly observes, tend to rigidify and consolidate the subject, policing boundaries rather than opening up the self and reveling in its inherent porosity. In her reading, however, these more clamorous sections, fueled by surges of Oedipal desire, are the exception. "More characteristically in Proust, though," she writes, "a creature is seen as plunging vitally into, navigating through, or resting in the midst of an element—water, air—that constitutes a minimal obstruction if any. In this more relaxed view, as [the psychoanalyst Michael] Balint says, 'It is difficult to say whether the air in our lungs or in our guts is us, or not us; and it does not even matter.'"[40]

Against the backdrop of Sedgwick's reading of Proust's atmospheres, I want to turn again to a scene in *Jude the Obscure*, in which the young Jude imagines he is breathing in the noxious air of the very culture and institutions whose promise of advancement will ultimately crush him. Beginning early on when he first sets his sights on the "bluer, moister atmosphere" of Christminster from afar, and "[draws] in the wind as if it were a sweet liquor," Jude's fantasy of educating himself and moving to the university town is described as a fantasy of inhaling it:

> He had heard that breezes traveled at the rate of ten miles an hour, and the fact now came into his mind. He parted his lips as he faced the north-east, and drew in the wind as if it were a sweet liquor.
>
> "You," he said, addressing the breeze caressingly, "were in Christminster city between one and two hours ago, floating along the streets, pulling round the weather-cocks, touching Mr. Phillotson's face, being breathed by him, and now you be here, breathed by me—you, the very same."
>
> Suddenly there came along this wind something towards him—a message from the place. . . . calling to him, "We are happy here!". . . . He had become entirely lost to his bodily situation during this mental leap.

The internalization of fantasy here involves physically breathing air thought to be exhaled by the cultural center; desire and existential drive become entangled, as interior and exterior merge in Jude's lungs. However ephemeral, this emphasis on the physical incorporation of culture lends Jude's reverie a materiality that persists upon his arrival in Christminster, when the damp "rottenness" of the stones "seemed to breathe his atmosphere," even while they suffocate his ambitions. This "oppressive atmosphere" pursues Jude all the way to the novel's end, to the "dreary, strange, flat scene, where boughs dripped, and coughs and consumption lurked," when Jude "is confined to his room by inflammation of the lungs, a fellow who only had two wishes left in the world, to see a particular woman, and then to die."[41] The libidinal desires for cultural acquisition and love, the ideological fantasy of socioeconomic advancement, and the existentially negative groping toward death—Jude's inspiration, aspiration, and expiration, respectively, we might say—all commingle in his overworked, overdetermined lungs.

I offer this contrast between the two novels and their respective scenes of submersion and permeability in order to suggest not only the versatility but also the historicity of this figure of alignment of container with contents, a figure that Alicia Mireles Christoff has described as "a controlling metaphor in literary and psychological writing" throughout the nineteenth and twentieth centuries.[42] Following Sedgwick's psychoanalytically inflected reading, Proust's glass jars would seem to hold out the possibility of an uncorked and diffuse subjectivity that serves in some manner to provide respite from the threatening rigidity of the novel's social and sexual drama. But what if we also saw this idealized image of suffusion as an externalization of the recursive structure of revolted feeling we have been pursuing throughout this chapter? The image from Proust, of course, would then appear to have been stripped of the negative affective valence that such a collapse of exterior into interior had in the examples from Gissing and Hardy. Indeed, for Sedgwick, the most fundamental form of this "x within x" structure is respiratory, as the contents of the lungs and the atmosphere outside the self commingle. But in the blighted air of the nineteenth century, of *Jude the Obscure*'s rotten atmospheres, Ruskin's storm cloud, and the Great Stink, this experience of the body's porosity was indissolubly linked to the affective experience of disgust and carried with it pollutant connotations. Nevertheless, can we still glimpse in Proust's reverie an offshoot of the entanglement of realism with repulsion?

One way to consider this progression from stench to revolt to existential negativity to the more positively open-ended sense of porosity would be along the lines of what Frederic Jameson has described as the autonomization of affect that takes place in the period, most emblematically for Jameson in Zola's work. In *The Antinomies of Realism*, Jameson proposes affect as one of the genre's "twin sources," the nonsemantic, nonpsychological, nonsubjective counterpart to the narrative impulse, according to which sequential action is produced and unfolds. For Jameson, that is, affect emerges in the second half of the nineteenth century as the focus of a broader tendency toward autonomy from the subject, action, and meaning. To exemplify this process, he contrasts the seemingly neutral description of the "boarding house smell" in *Le Père Goriot* (1835), which he insists is not an affect because "it *means* something" (that is, because it conveys an encoded judgment), to Zola's famous *symphonie des fromages* in *The Belly of Paris* (1873), the great parade of smells in which "the multiplicity comes before us not as things or visible objects but rather as names, it is the alien guts and insides of the words themselves that are overwhelmingly juxtaposed and arrayed against us in such catalogues, which are very far from expressing their original Whitmanian gusto." Thus in Zola, smell tends toward the depersonalized realm of affect as the "excess of the sensory becomes autonomous . . . [and] begins to have enough weight of its own to counterbalance the plot," while in Balzac smell remains stench, rooted in the social body and its semantically rich environments.[43]

For Jameson, then, affect represents the steady rationalization of emotion into something purely external to the self, ultimately finding expression in depersonalized descriptions of intensities that cannot be resolved into any particular register of sense experience: "unnamable sensations" that "no longer mean anything," affects rather are "states of the world" that "simply exist." Jacques Rancière has made a similar argument in a discussion of Auerbach, identifying "the temporality determined by the pure enjoyment of a sensible affect disconnected from any social plot of ends and means" as one of the principal axes running through nineteenth-century realism and leading toward modernist experimentation with temporality.[44] Crucially, both Jameson and Rancière want to see in the inner tendencies of nineteenth-century literature a movement away from the value-laden realms of epistemology and psychology into the ontological domain of affect, which each describes as a kind of stripped-down fact of the body subtending or prior to any nameable sensory or emotional experience. In the next chapter, the discussion of Darwin and his scientific milieu will show how this conception of depersonalized affect itself was first articulated in its modern form in those same decades in the second half of the nineteenth century that concern Jameson. Yet we will also see that disgust, guts, and especially vomit all figure centrally in the emergence of this category of nonsubjective experience.

The autonomization of affect that Jameson describes gives a new turn of the screw to the account of realism's relation to the aesthetics of disgust that I have advanced in this chapter. For if feeling and emotion were progressively externalized in the literature of the second half of the nineteenth century; if authors strove to find new and innovative ways to represent the nonsubjective element that seemed to inhere within all sense experience, without being reducible to any sensation; and if realism can be said to have served as the laboratory in which these experiments with the externalization and objectification of affective experience took place—then disgust not only provided a pattern for these aesthetic activities but also served as a motive force driving the process of autonomization itself. Indeed, there is a vantage point from which Jameson's description of autonomization as a process of objectification instead looks like a form of deodorization, which is to say an exclusion of negative affect (in the sense of emotion) that is in fact driven by negative affect. What if disgust, with its drive to cleanse the body of its humidity and smell, provides the template for the externalization of affect?

Our discussions of the autonomization of affect and of the relative permeability of the self can be reconnected to our discussion of disgust in a different manner, through a turn back to Elias. In Elias's theory one result of the long-term augmentation of shame and disgust as forces of restraint was the emergence of a "conception of the individual as *homo clausus*, a little world in himself who ultimately exists quite independently of the great world outside." Elias argued that this image of the individual as a sealed-off entity, protected by an outer shell and within which reside feeling, thought, and other "core" features of the self, was modernity's dominant ideological conception of the individual. That is, the outcome of the civilizing process was not only that individuals now viewed themselves each as a solitary *homo clausus*, but that all modern thought came to internalize this image as well: "Its derivatives include not only the traditional *homo philosophicus . . .* but also *homo oeconomicus, homo psychologicus, homo historicus,* and not least *homo sociologicus* in his present-day version." Needless to say, Elias was sharply critical of this conception of the walled-off self, which he thought reduced social processes to static states and downplayed or ignored the manifold interdependencies of individuals. "But the nature of this wall itself is hardly ever considered and never properly explained," Elias goes on. "Is the body the vessel which holds the true self locked within it? Is the skin the frontier between 'inside' and 'outside'? What in the human individual is the container, and what the contained? The experience of 'inside' and 'outside' seems so self-evident that such questions are scarcely ever posed."[45]

Elias's image of *homo clausus* points toward a bifurcation or structural ambiguity in the conceptualization of disgust we have been describing throughout this chapter. In Elias's account of the civilizing process, the closure of the self is the outcome of the intensification of disgust. Yet this already introduces a complication, for disgust is an emotion whose paradigmatic expressions can be seen either as an expulsive form of externalization (vomiting) or a corking up of the self (holding one's nose). The conceptualization of disgust might therefore be said to alternate between a characterization of the emotion as opening the body up, on the one hand, and a characterization of it as a form of enacted closure, on the other.[46] The incompatibility of these two characterizations in turn helps us to make sense of the unstable, recursive formulation according to which the articulation of disgust, of negative affect, provides a template for the exclusion of affect.

We can now return to the complex image with which this chapter opened. At a moment when the Thames was literally a vast open sewer, the smell of each Londoner's waste enfolding all Londoners in a cloud of their own emanation, what respite did Dickens imagine one could find in dissolving into the sewage, and allowing oneself to "flow away monotonously, like the river, and to compound for its insensibility to happiness with its insensibility to pain"? In its yearning for insensibility, the image captures something of the drive toward desubjectification that Jameson wants to anchor in the realism of the period. Yet as with Sedgwick's reading of Proust's glass jars, Dickens also suggests that the dissolution of the self can only offer a promise of relief to somebody in particular, to *homo clausus,* somebody stuck with or inside a self. Finally, in light of *Little Dorrit*'s investigation of disgust and disavowal, the image seems also to capture a motivation—something less than a desire, but perhaps not fully without disgust—to get over disgust, to have done with it in the most literal way, to plunge into the muck and find there instead an alternative set of meanings in the body and its primal substances.

# Part II

# *Primal Scenes, Human Sciences*

# CHAPTER 3

# Darwin's Vomit

I was at first as other Beasts that graze
The trodden Herb, of abject thoughts and low,
As was my food, nor aught but food discern'd
Or Sex, and apprehended nothing high;
Till on a day roaving the field, I chanc'd
A goodly Tree far distant to behold
Loaden with fruit of fairest colours mixt . . .

—Milton, *Paradise Lost*

What then is the relation between disgust and vomit?
It is indeed vomit that interests us rather than the
act or process of vomiting, which are less disgusting
than vomit in so far as they imply an activity, some
initiative whereby the subject can at least still mimic
mastery or dream it . . . believing that he *makes himself vomit*.

—Jacques Derrida, "Economimesis"

"I find the noodle and the stomach are antagonistic powers," Charles Darwin wrote his sister Caroline in May 1838, "and that it is a great deal more easy to think too much in a day than to think too little. What thought has to do with digesting roast beef, I cannot say," he concluded, "but they are brother faculties."[1] This was more than an idle observation. The relationship of brain to belly, and more generally of thought to involuntary bodily processes such as digestion, would remain in the decades to follow matters of vital interest to Darwin, intellectually as well as personally. Plagued throughout his adult life by long, painful cycles of vomiting and bilious indigestion that rendered him incapable of either working or socializing, Darwin turned his naturalist's eye for nuance and subtle alteration to the twists and turns of his own gastric illness, meticulously documenting in his "diary of health" the "acid vomiting," "excessive flatulence," and eruptive boils of his condition. Furnished with entries twice daily from the 1840s well into the 1850s, the diary places brief entries recording these emetic refluxes alongside descriptions of different states of nauseous feeling and malaise—"weak and languid," "heazish," "squashy, little oppressed"; it also offers a fragmentary but illuminating account of the sometimes desperate journey for relief that led Darwin to explore nearly every trend, gimmick, and advance that mid-Victorian gastric medicine had to offer.[2] As one reads through this strange, painful catalog, moreover, the major period of scientific and cultural realignment of the human and the animal that Darwin would usher into being at the close of the 1850s with the publication of *On the Origin of Species by Means of Natural Selection* begins to take on a new urgency and a heightened pathos. Questions of brain and belly, and of the distinctions between willed act, involuntary reflex, and physiological process, were not simply objects of study for Darwin; rather, they directly shaped his understanding of the lived experience of the human body at the moment of its most radical discursive transformation in modern history.

Continuing the discussion of the autonomization of affect where the previous chapter left off, this chapter delves into these intertwined matters of thought, digestion, and feeling, as they arise through Darwin's closely related writings on disgust and vomiting in his late book, *The Expression of the Emotions in Man and Animals* (1872). In a chapter devoted principally to what he considered a family of related emotions—contempt, scorn, disdain, and disgust—Darwin laid out a highly idiosyncratic theory about the evolution of the capacity for vomiting, which will be the primary focus of our discussion. But first, I return to Darwin's assertion to his sister that brain and belly are not only "antagonistic powers," but also "brother faculties," in order to ask what kind of relationship, precisely, is described by this beguiling pairing of terms—for the commonsensical tone of Darwin's letter belies an unstable complexity.

In the first place, "antagonistic powers" implies a binarism, a readily available mode of thinking about the mind and the stomach as incompatible, adversarial organs locked in a dualistic struggle over human motivation. This characterization of the stomach has a long history, stretching back into medieval and early modern medical notions that the gut could alter sense perception and so dangerously affect behavior, and which still had widespread currency in mid-nineteenth-century medical discourse and popular culture alike. Dickens's depiction in *A Christmas Carol* of Ebenezer Scrooge's frightened incredulity upon seeing the ghost of Jacob Marley provides a good example:

> "You don't believe in me," observed the Ghost.
>
> "I don't," said Scrooge.
>
> "What evidence would you have of my reality beyond that of your senses?"

"I don't know," said Scrooge.

"Why do you doubt your senses?"

"Because," said Scrooge, "a little thing affects them. A slight disorder of the stomach makes them cheats. You may be an undigested bit of beef, a blot of mustard, a crumb of cheese, a fragment of an underdone potato. There's more of gravy than of grave about you, whatever you are!"[3]

As in Darwin's letter to his sister, so we here see Scrooge give voice to the idea that the normal operations of consciousness can be disrupted and even deceived by "a slight disorder of the stomach," while also adducing a connection between the power of the stomach and the unknown, irrational realms of ghosts and hallucination. Epistemologically speaking, mind and gut are rivals or antagonists; the functioning of the one can interfere with or even override the other.

Yet as is clear from Darwin's letter to his own sister, this relationship is more specifically one of *sibling* rivalry, an antagonism between "brother faculties" whose competition and incompatibility are rooted in their shared origins. Thus, into the binary opposition of thought to digestion, Darwin introduces a genealogical complication. Now thought begins to look like any other crude bodily process—not a distinctly human achievement, but something confraternal with the mindless operations of the intestine and the bowels, its organ brothers. Even in this minor aside, one can already anticipate the force of Darwin's blow, dealt two decades later, to humankind's brittle conception of its own singularity, as thought and consciousness, along with language, soul, and morality, all came under the pressure of the evolutionary method. Cast as antagonistic powers, brain and belly were given opposing parts to play in a dualistic drama of the human subject torn between rational thought and gut instinct; when they are understood as brother faculties, however, the suggestion is rather that such dualism might prove untenable given the intimate relation of what have only come to appear as rivals. The alternating nature of Darwin's characterization of the relationship between digestion and cogitation can be grasped either as binary or as genealogy; it can be seen as a story of mutual entwinement over time, or as an unchanging structural opposition.

Much of Darwin's work on the human is organized by the conceptual duplicity suggested by this relationship of sibling rivalry. At stake for us is the question of how some of the most central binarisms of Enlightenment thought—man and animal, rational choice and reflexive instinct, and in the broadest register, culture and nature—could continue to be maintained in the face of Darwin's insights into the animal kingdom's web of shared origins and overlapping paths of evolutionary descent. What would be the fate of these deeply entrenched dualisms, now that the distinction of the human from other species was understood to be matter of gradation and chance mutation, accumulated through a new kind of historical time, rather than a matter of fixed metaphysical difference?[4]

Far from arbitrary starting points for thinking through these larger questions, the stomach, its refluxes and regurgitations, and the expression of disgust more generally, are all deeply enmeshed in the post-Enlightenment tradition of natural and social scientific thought concerning the place of the human and of human culture within nature, and the place of the animal or the allegedly primitive within the human. As we have already seen, this is a tradition that finds a significant proximal origin point in the aesthetic theory of the eighteenth century, where disgust was figured as an embodied form of quasi-instinctual judgment, whose allegedly universal undesirability was taken as evidence of a need to remove the disgusting object, as well as the need to be rid of the experience of disgust itself. Keeping the sociopolitical concerns raised by our consideration of the Great Stink in view, we will now be tracking how this conception of disgust was absorbed by the mid-nineteenth-century discourses of the life sciences, especially as they grappled with the Darwinian transformation of the timeline of human development.

This chapter argues that disgust played—and continues to play—a central role in the natural-scientific elaboration of what I will call the "primal scene" of European modernity. By primal scene, I mean to evoke a pervasive mode of cultural fantasy that draws on a storehouse of speculative evolutionary thought in order to establish a foundation for imagining humanity's entrance into the history of its own species. Unlike its social-theoretical analogue, the state of nature, which uses the unrecorded past as a medium for speculating about what forces impel human sociality into various forms of organization, humanity's primal scene serves instead to narrate the internal processes and external circumstances that propelled the human into its primitive humanity in the first place. The state of nature takes for granted the historical fact of human social life; the primal scene takes for granted the homogenous time of a primordial animality that preceded it. The role of the primal scene is to establish, for the modern person, the instinctivity that preceded rationality, the feeling anterior to the thought, the animal that came before the human, the natural before the social world. And in so doing, it grants an ambivalent priority to the biological domain, in the temporal sense of a prior state that has been superseded, built over, or developed to the point of transformation in the long-term institution of the human.

It is striking how consistently the emotion of disgust has been invoked in the elaboration of modernity's imagination of the primal scene. Although it is no more or less primal (in any meaningful way) than other emotions, disgust nonetheless seems to exert the greatest claim on the collective imagination of our primordial nature: its expression looks like something animalistic, its reflexiveness feels like something primitive, its unwantedness makes it easy to imagine its obsolescence. Hence there is a rich tradition of using disgust to envision humanity's evolutionary first steps, a tradition which, in its Judeo-Christian iterations, has focused rather unsurprisingly on the negative affective and sensory consequences of sex, orality, and consumption. For instance, in Kant's complex primal scene, humanity's entrance into historical time follows from Adam and Eve's choice of the wrong food (i.e., the apple), whereas for Freud, quadruped mankind's spontaneous disgust at the smell of its own reeking anuses and genitals is what inaugurates the bipedal ascent into civilization.

Evolutionary and neuroscientific studies of disgust revise or even dismiss these earlier, more openly speculative narratives, but in so doing they too have tended to leave unquestioned and even to reiterate the central role of disgust in the primal scene. In one contemporary evolutionary psychological account, disgust persists as "a voice in our heads, the voice of our ancestors telling us to stay away from what might be bad for us"; in another, neuroscientists trace our capacity to be provoked to vomit or gag merely by the sight or thought of something disgusting to the anterior insula, describing a "'primitive' mechanism" said to reflect "the evolutionarily oldest form of emotion understanding."[5] What remains constant among these distinct and otherwise incompatible paradigms for studying disgust is precisely the emotion's allegedly primal character, its presumed availability to serve as an unchanging baseline for differentiating humanity's present from its primordial past.[6] While the present chapter concerns disgust's function within this genre of natural-scientific thought, the following chapter pursues the emotion into the social sciences. Taken together, they represent a sustained inquiry into disgust's role as a token of the primitive and primal within the development of nineteenth- and twentieth-century scientific thought.

Darwin's observations on disgust's evolution exemplify the form of the cultural fantasy of the primal scene while also departing substantially from most other cases in crucial ways. Each part of the passage in question will be the focus of a section of this chapter:

[1] It is remarkable how readily and instantly retching or actual vomiting is induced in some persons by the mere idea of having partaken

of any unusual food, as of an animal which is not commonly eaten; although there is nothing in such food to cause the stomach to reject it. [2] When vomiting results, as a reflex action, for some real cause—as from too rich food, or tainted meat, or from an emetic—it does not ensue immediately, but generally after a considerable interval of time. [3] Therefore, to account for retching or vomiting being so quickly and easily excited by a mere idea, the suspicion arises that our progenitors must formerly have had the power (like that possessed by ruminants and some other animals) of voluntarily rejecting food that disagreed with them, or which they thought would disagree with them, and now, though this power has been lost, as far as the will is concerned, it is called into involuntary action, through the force of a formerly well-established habit, whenever the mind revolts at the idea of having partaken of any kind of food, or at anything disgusting. [4] This suspicion receives support from the fact, of which I am assured by Mr Sutton, that the monkeys in the Zoological Gardens often vomit whilst in perfect health, which looks as if the act were voluntary. [5] We can see that as a man is able to communicate to his children and others, the knowledge of the kinds of food to be avoided, he would have had little occasion to use the faculty of voluntary rejection; so that this power would tend to be lost through disuse.[7]

In this extraordinarily compressed passage, Darwin assembles most of the elements that have come to characterize nearly every study of disgust since the time of his writing: the centrality of oral consumption and of its reversal in vomiting; the opposition between voluntary and reflex action but also the undermining or rendering ambiguous of that opposition around the question of taste; and the imaginative or representational dimension of disgust, according to which thoughts themselves can trigger a powerful affective response. Most significantly, Darwin here answers the seemingly ineluctable call for disgust's genealogical elaboration, its substantiation through a narrative beginning in the prelapsarian past. Indeed, Darwin's text does not merely epitomize these conventions of writing about disgust; the whole chapter on disgust in many concrete ways helped to formalize the genre, just as *The Expression of the Emotions in Man and Animals* remains a foundational text in the psychological and biological study of the emotions more generally.

Placed under scrutiny, however, Darwin's brief speculation into the origins of vomiting is so distinctive and peculiar as to render it incompatible with other accounts of disgust. This is principally because, in lieu of an account of the emotion's primal character, Darwin gives us instead a strange narrative of its descent, its reverse evolutionary trajectory from voluntary capacity to habituated reflex. It is this inverted genealogy of revulsion's quasi-instinctivity—so different from the aesthetic conception of the emotion—that gives Darwin's theory a historical and conceptual purchase lacking in other theories of disgust. Following a preliminary section on Darwin's general ideas about emotion expression, each section of this chapter will focus on decompressing one aspect of Darwin's inverted evolutionary narrative. The second section shows how Darwin's assumptions (sentences 1 and 2) about the relation between vomiting, the stomach, and imagination drew heavily on Victorian theories of dyspepsia, which were in the process of being replaced by sweeping new developments in gastric physiology throughout the nineteenth century. In the third section, the discussion pursues Darwin's idiosyncratic notion of a lost capacity for voluntary food rejection (3 and 4), sketching the persistence in Darwin's late work of the Lamarckian theory of acquired characteristics. And in the final section, I take up Darwin's assertion that the development of a critical language would have gradually replaced the ability to vomit at will (5) in light of the Victorian theories about linguistic origins that Darwin adduces to make his case, none of which survived into the twentieth century. Hence, Darwin's positions on each of the three discourses subtending his theory of disgust—physiological, linguistic, and, ironically, evolutionary—have been subsequently discarded, or were in the process of being jettisoned in his day. And yet, these obsolete turns in Darwin's work take on a renewed salience when brought into contact with the far-reaching dualistic currents in post-Enlightenment thought that have determined disgust's role in modernity's primal scene.

## Disgust without Objects

Here is another episode of Darwin's disgust: the often-cited encounter between the naturalist and the native, sitting down to eat, eyeing each other with equal parts curious attraction and reflexive repulsion. "In Tierra del Fuego a native touched with his finger some cold preserved meat which I was eating at our bivouac, and plainly showed utter disgust at its softness," Darwin writes, "whilst I felt utter disgust at my food being touched by a naked savage, though his hands did not appear dirty" (236). Most immediately, Darwin uses the episode as evidence of the inherently gustatory yet highly contextual nature of disgust, remarking that "it is curious how readily this feeling is excited by anything unusual in the appearance, odour, or nature of our food." Objects of consumption are thus connected intimately to disgust, and yet Darwin's point here is closer to the culturally relativistic idea that dirt is "matter out of place" than it is interested in producing a taxonomy of the revolting. "A smear of soup on a man's beard looks disgusting," he continues in this vein, "though there is of course nothing disgusting in the soup itself" (236).

Dramatizing the experience of disgust as an encounter with the border between the "savage" and the "civilized," Darwin's scene of cross-cultural revulsion has attained paradigmatic status among recent theorists of disgust, and unlike the comparatively unexamined genealogy of vomiting that follows on its heels, citing it is practically *de rigueur* in studies of the emotion.[8] The very opening pages of William Ian Miller's influential study, for instance, turn to this passage in order to advance a claim about disgust's primitive affective logic: "Darwin fears ingesting some essence of savagery," Miller writes, "that has been magically imparted to his food by the finger of the naked savage." Building on Miller, the cultural theorist Sara Ahmed likewise uses the encounter as a springboard into her discussion of the "performativity of disgust," observing that for Darwin the native "is already seen as dirt," and so contaminating along a racialized vector that masks itself as hygienic concern.[9] In part because of the episodic way in which it folds together matters of race and culture alongside concerns with food and ingestion, the scene has come to be seen as an emblematic instance of disgust's associative logic of contamination, whereby, as Rozin and Fallon put it, "disgust is elicited by objects that have contacted [or that resemble] a disgusting item."[10]

Ahmed's analysis is suggestive, especially in light of the important concerns about the place of race thinking in Darwin's data with which I opened this book, but both her account and Miller's miss something central to Darwin's theory of disgust; namely, that it has no objects. Like Miller, Ahmed's principal goal is to unpack the inner mechanics of disgust, the way the emotion "thinks," and to explore what she terms its cultural politics. To do so, she turns to Sartre's evocative reflections on slime ("slime is the agony of water," Sartre writes), finding in his phenomenology of stickiness an important resource for understanding the metonymic logic of contamination according to which our revulsion selects its objects. "Disgust pulls us away from the object, a pulling that feels almost involuntary," Ahmed writes, "as if our bodies were thinking for us, on behalf of us," even while the objects of disgust "seem to have us 'in their grip,' and to be moving towards us."[11]

This notion that disgust is best understood through the analysis of its eliciting objects and their strong attractive-repulsive force is deeply entrenched in the theory of the emotion. From aesthetics and psychoanalysis to existentialism and present-day psychology, the study of revulsion has been motivated by a phenomenological impulse to describe the emotion principally through the medium of its objects. "The intention of disgust is much more markedly oriented outwards [than fear]," the Hungarian philosopher Aurel Kolnai wrote in his pioneering study, "Der Ekel," published in Edmund Husserl's *Jahrbuch* in 1929, adding elsewhere in the essay that "in the foreground of the phenomenon of disgust there remains the object with its specific features."[12] Kolnai attempted to further develop the obtrusive phenomenology that we have already seen at play in the aesthetic context, where the disgusting is described as overwhelming us, even as we struggle against it with all our might. For this tradition of thought, disgust enacts a form of negative judgment whose inherent grammatical purpose is to tell you something declarative about a particular thing or even a class of things. "Disgust reads the objects that are felt to be disgusting," Ahmed's analysis continues. "It is not just about bad objects that we are afraid to incorporate, but the very designation of 'badness' as a quality we assume is inherent in those objects."[13] Feeling, judgment, and object are fused to each other in this account of disgust's circularity, each in a sense presupposing the others as its logical antecedents.

The analytic road to disgust has by and large been routed through the terrain of the disgusting. There is in this regard not merely an empirical or commonsense rationale for approaching the emotion relationally, through the phenomenological description of its objects, but also a strong conceptual pressure to do so. It has proven difficult to think disgust beyond the collapsing dyad of subject and object, and while this tendency surely captures something about the unique experience of being disgusted, it has also functioned normatively, as a discursive limitation on the way that the emotion can be grasped and understood. This has meant that we really only get to know the emotion through its own account of the stinking, unwanted object world. Theorization of the meaning of the emotion has tended to be determined by observations about its dyadic morphology. Indeed, it is striking how regularly, by way of a slippage in registers, critical discourse about the emotion simply becomes description of the object from the perspective of the subject of disgust.[14] The historical perspective on disgust presented in this book suggests, however, that we ought to view this tacit collapse of registers with a degree of critical skepticism. Are we certain that the social significance of disgust is rooted in its structuration around the encounter between subject and object? Is it not plausible, rather, that this allegedly fundamental affect derives its value from some other less rigidly organized configuration of functions and positions?

Darwin's disgust, by contrast, has no objects. Lacking reference to the most familiar elicitors of revulsion, his chapter sits quite apart from the majority of luridly evocative pages devoted to the emotion over the last 250 years.

There are no oozing, slimy, chunky, or rotting things to be eaten; no worms or bugs picking their way through wounds; no splattering sexual fluids, no menstrual blood or reeking fecal matter; and relatively little mention of the dark crevices and orifices of our bodies, where who knows what might come in or get out. Instead, there is the schmear of soup in an unkempt beard, and the recollected meal with the "naked savage." Yet even these objects quite evidently do not have us in their grip; Darwin's interest consistently shies away from the agon of the reviled object, rerouting analysis around the dyadic encounter.[15] And, at the chapter's heart, there is the vomit—although significantly, there is nothing in it. ("I seldom throw food up, only acid and morbid secretion," he reported to Joseph Dalton Hooker in 1864. "Otherwise I should have been dead, for during more than a month I vomited after every meal."[16]) In the history of an emotion whose study has tended far too often to confuse its revolted subjects for its revolting objects, Darwin's chapter stands out for being about disgust, but not about the disgusting.

This distinction is in part a methodological consequence, with roots in the traditions of British empiricism and naturalist observation, and ramifications for twentieth-century basic emotions psychology, a field for which *Expression* is usually cited as a founding document. In order to bolster the case for a species-wide biological basis to the emotions, *Expression* emphasized the outward constants of disgust—facial movements, sounds, gestures—rather than the variables, the targets and elicitors of our revulsion, which Darwin believed were both culturally specific and contextually determined. As a result of privileging affective display, Darwin makes relatively few claims either about the objects we deem disgusting or about the inward experience of the emotion:

> I never saw disgust more plainly expressed than on the face of one of my infants at the age of five months, when, for the first time, some cold water, and again a month afterwards, when a piece of ripe cherry was put into his mouth. This was shown by the lips and the whole mouth assuming a shape which allowed the content to run or fall quickly out; the tongue being likewise protruded. These movements were accompanied by a little shudder. It was all the more comical, as I doubt whether the child felt real disgust—the eyes and forehead expressing much surprise and consideration. (239)

The description is precise, and Darwin is still credited with having here first identified what psychologists of emotion today refer to as the "gape face," the reflexive expression of disgust "by the mouth being widely opened, as if to let an offensive morsel drop out" (236). Darwin placed the gaping mouth at the core of a complex of negative emotions, which in his view grow increasingly oral as they intensify. "The term 'disgust,' in its simplest sense," he writes, "means something offensive to the taste" (236).

While there has been disagreement over different aspects of Darwin's definition of disgust, it remains by and large the paradigmatic account for contemporary psychologists. Indeed, Darwin's yoking together of disgust with food rejection has achieved a kind of commonsense status within emotion psychology that makes it difficult to dismiss, even when the shortcomings of orality as an explanatory basis for other forms of disgust unrelated to ingestion or oral incorporation have been made apparent. Yet considered in light of the passage above, Darwinian disgust offers a very unusual paradigm: the cherry itself is not meant to be understood as disgusting in the ordinary sense—we are certainly not meant to infer anything about the cherry, or about cherries in general—nor, we are told, does the infant even experience the "real" emotion, just as there was "nothing disgusting in the soup itself" in the previous example. The reflexive shudder and opening of the mouth alone are of interest. It was in pursuit of these interests, for example, that Darwin turned to the dramatically costumed set shots he commissioned from the pioneering Victorian photographer Oscar Reijlander, which were meant to render emotional experiences easily identifiable through a series of staged tableaux, as well as to Duchenne de Boulogne's electric-shock-induced portraits, made famous in his *Mécanisme de la physionomie humaine* (1862), which showed how the facial anatomy of emotion expression could be artificially stimulated (figs. 13–14). According to the terms of Darwin's project, writing about and analyzing disgust need not involve reference to the disgusting at all; indeed, it does not even need to involve "real disgust."[17]

Rather than being drawn ever deeper into the murky phenomenology of disgust, Darwin emphasizes the emotion's imaginative character, noting in particular "the strong association in our minds between the sight of food, however circumstanced, and the idea of eating it" (236). In pivoting away from the objects of disgust, in minimizing their claim over the experience of revulsion as well as its discursive elaboration, Darwin discovers in the emotion a unique capacity for fantasied or imaginative responsiveness: "It is remarkable how readily and instantly retching or actual vomiting is induced in some persons," the following episode begins, "by the mere idea of having partaken of any unusual food, as of an animal which is not commonly eaten; although there is nothing in such food to cause the stomach to reject it" (236–37). Thus what captures Darwin's interest in disgust is the way that it makes apparent the body's openness and porosity, both physically as well as psychologically. His emphasis falls as much on the gaping mouth and the

**FIGURE 13.** Expressions of disgust and disdain, as photographed by Oscar Gustave Reijlander. From Charles Darwin, *The Expression of the Emotions in Man and Animals* (1872). Courtesy of the Wellcome Collection.

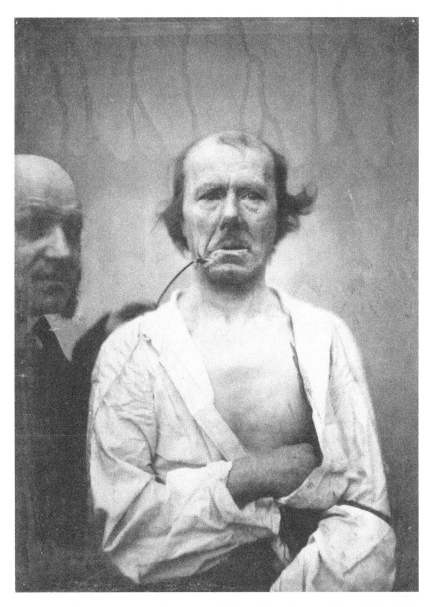

**FIGURE 14.** Expressions provoked by electric shock. In the first image, Duchenne induces "disgust" alongside a "relaxed expression." In the second, he stimulates "scornful laughter" and "scornful disgust." Both from Guillame-Benjamin-Amant Duchenne (de Boulougne), *Mécanisme de la physionomie* (1862). Courtesy of the National Gallery of Art, Washington, DC.

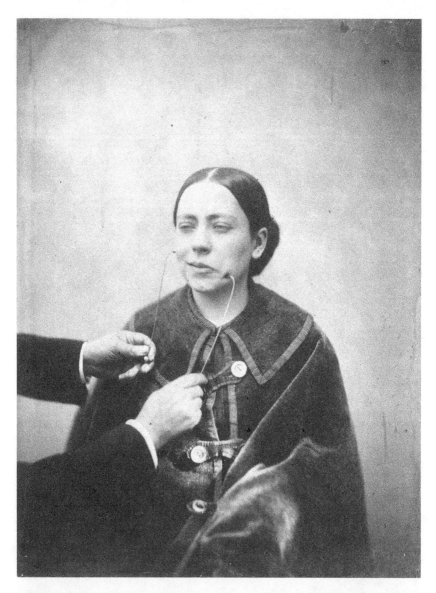

**FIGURE 14.** (continued)

extrusion of physical objects that have failed to be integrated into the self through digestion as it does on the human capacity, evident in the disgust reaction, to treat thoughts as objects within the body—on the responsiveness of the body to imagination, fantasy, and symbol. Just as Darwin had sought in *The Descent of Man* to trace the origins of language back to the capacity for song, here he is especially keen to discover in disgust an example of how the body's porous nature is involved in the production of more complex forms of symbolic meaning that are related but not identical to language.

Cast in this light, the repudiatory vehemence of disgust softens, as the unprotected openness and vulnerability expressed by the emotion come more fully into focus. This shift of emphasis allows Darwin to see in the seemingly involuntary but nevertheless not strictly physiological experience of imaginative vomiting the outlines of a provocative set of questions about human agency. Darwin observes that "when vomiting results, as a reflex action, for some real cause—as from too rich food, or tainted meat, or from an emetic—it does not ensue immediately, but generally after a considerable interval of time" (237). What is most striking to Darwin about vomiting from disgust is that it is *more* immediate, *more* apparently reflexive, than the vomiting that "results, as a reflex action, for some real cause." It transpires in a middle range of agency, somewhere between the "real cause" of the spoiled oyster, on the one hand, and artificiality of the stomach pump, on the other. Darwin's vomit leads us between the Scylla of the rational, picking and choosing what to take in and what to egest, and the Charybdis of the involuntary, sucking things down and spewing them out according to unknown motives and principles. It is in precisely this middle range that Darwin wants to locate what is distinctive to emotion expression, with its claims on a form of symbolic activity that seems to reside within the body, without being naturalized as the body's inner purpose. To explore this rich field of affective agency, we must now go down the hatch into the Victorian gut.

## The Dialectic of the Illuminated Stomach

"I have had a bad spell, vomiting every day for eleven days and some days many times after every meal," Darwin wrote to Hooker in December 1863, from the depths of his illness, remarking in another letter a few weeks later that "I sh$^d$. suppose few human beings had vomited so often during the last 5 months."[18] Darwin's idiosyncratic views about the agency of disgust and vomiting emerged out of the intensely positivistic body of nineteenth-century medico-scientific literature on the nature of the gut, which carried within it all the volatile tension between tradition and progress characteristic of the age. On the one hand, during the second half of the nineteenth century, the mechanistic functions of the living, secreting stomach were not only laid bare to the medical gaze but also, quite literally, illuminated. With the invention of instruments such as the gastrodiaphane and the œsophagoscope, the physical and epistemological darkness of the belly could be dispelled simply by inducing a patient to swallow a light bulb attached to the end of a rubber tube (figs. 15–18). On the other hand, alongside these positivistic and techno-rational advances, obscure and often superstitious ideas about the stomach's disruptive powers persisted. In the popular as well as the medical imagination of the period, the stomach could be invoked to demystify outright superstition at the same time that its own causal agency remained physiologically opaque; it could take on a rationalizing function within medical science while remaining tethered to fantasies about the body's autonomous operations that defied rational explanation. This synthesis of rationalizing and obscurantist conceptions of gastric causation also to a great degree influenced Darwin's understanding of the gut, shaping his theory of the agency of vomiting and disgust. As he once cautioned Hooker, "Do be careful of your stomach, within which, as I know full well, lie intellect, conscience, temper and the affections."[19]

The stomach has long seemed to modern thought a point where will and instinct collapse into each other, disturbing our understanding of how agency is distributed throughout the subject. More than other organs, the stomach seemed to possess an obscure will of its own, and in this respect the history of the stomach is interwoven with the history of the unconscious. In particular, gastric medical science in the nineteenth century raised questions about the body's capacity for intentional rather than merely reflexive agency that the Hungarian psychoanalytic theorist Sándor Ferenczi would in the early twentieth century organize under the heading of the biological unconscious. As Elizabeth A. Wilson has written, Ferenczi attributed "a nascent kind of psychic action (motivation, deliberation) . . . to biological substance" that allowed him to see in "the vicissitudes of ingestion and vomiting [a form of] complex thinking enacted organically."[20] Thus even as the churnings of the gut were illuminated and shown to be reflexive and involuntary, they came to seem over the course of the nineteenth century increasingly indistinguishable from the operations of thought. These counterintuitive ideas are not merely consonant with Darwin's writings on voluntary vomiting; they have a direct intellectual connection to Darwin and his milieu, and built on Victorian advances in the scientific knowledge of the body's mechanisms and presumed automaticity. "What a strange mechanism one's body is," Darwin again wrote Hooker during that same January of ceaseless vomiting, in a turn of phrase that captures both the rationalizing and the obscurantist currents running through the Victorian gut.[21]

The strangeness of the stomach's mechanism had for centuries troubled easy distinctions between voluntary and involuntary agency for thinkers of the body. Writing at what David Hillman has termed "a transitional moment

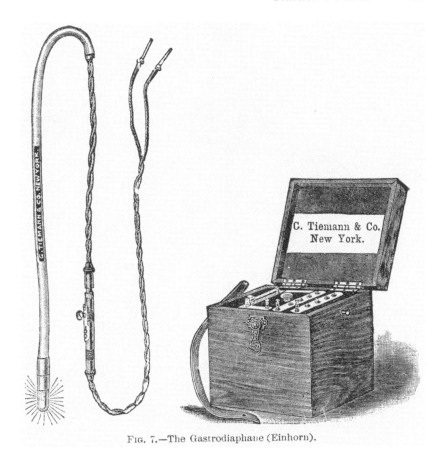

FIG. 7.—The Gastrodiaphane (Einhorn).

**FIGURE 15.**   The gastrodiaphane. From Max Einhorn, *Diseases of the Stomach: A Text-Book for Practitioners and Students* (1906). Courtesy of the University of Chicago Library.

in the history of the significance of viscerality in human affairs," early modern thinkers had turned to the organ's disruptive churnings in order to insist on the physiological rather than the supernatural basis of dreams and apparitions.[22] One can hear in Dickens's unruly blot of mustard a direct echo of Thomas Nashe's 1594 *The Terrors of the Night*, which asserted that "the fiery inflammations of our liver or stomach transform our imaginations to their analogy and likeness." "Our fluttering thoughts," Nashe continues, "when we are drowned in deadly sleep, take hold and co-essence themselves with any overboiling humour which sourceth highest in our stomachs."[23] For Nashe as for Dickens, the stomach was a powerful driver of behavior that could be invoked in order to explain otherwise inexplicable motivations and even magical phenomena; however, in performing this demystifying

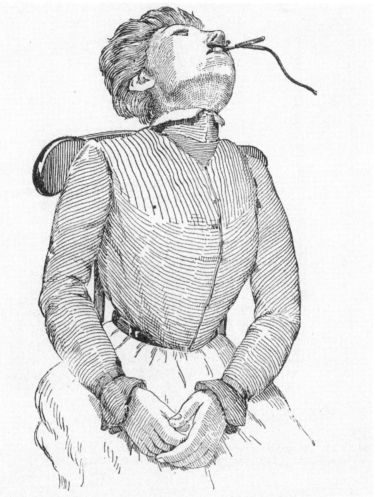

FIG. 6.--Showing Patient with Œsophagoscope inserted ready for Inspection.

**FIGURE 16.**    Patient with œsophagoscope. From Max Einhorn, *Diseases of the Stomach: A Text-Book for Practitioners and Students* (1906). Courtesy of the University of Chicago Library.

function, it consequently took on a role within early modern physiological discourse as a site of the unknown.[24]

That the stomach seemed to possess, for lack of a better term, a mind of its own, complicated the way some early modern thinkers understood agency to be distributed throughout the body. "There is a certain discriminating sense in the stomach," William Harvey's 1651 treatise *On Animal Generation* proclaims, "which distinguishes what is hurtful from what is useful,

FIG. 48.—A Patient Undergoing Examination with the Gastrograph.

**FIGURE 17.**    Examination by gastrograph. From Max Einhorn, *Diseases of the Stomach: A Text-Book for Practitioners and Students* (1906). Courtesy of the University of Chicago Library.

and by which vomiting is induced."[25] Harvey attributed a capacity for judgment to the stomach that was cut off from conscious sensory experiences, yet was nonetheless to some degree "aware" of changed circumstances within the body.[26] This gulf between the conscious and the sensate in turn gave rise to a peculiar language of unconscious gastric agency in treatises on the digestive process. Building on Harvey, Walter Charleton's *Natural History*

FIG. 51. —Leube-Rosenthal Apparatus for Gastric Lavage.

**FIGURE 18.** Washed on the inside with the gastric lavage. From Max Einhorn, *Diseases of the Stomach: A Text-Book for Practitioners and Students* (1906). Courtesy of the University of Chicago Library.

*of Nutrition* posited that "the stomach and guts . . . being oppressed and provoked by vicious humors, instantly rise in armes, and raise impetuous vom-
itings, nauseousness, convulsions, fluxes of the belly, and the like motions,
for the expulsion of their enemies: and as we have it not in our power, to
excite or suppress those commotions," Charleton concludes, "so have we no
particular cognizance of any such sense, which should extimulate those parts
to begin and continue them."[27] For Charleton, the activity of digestion fell
somewhere between willed action and outright mechanism; while it was a
kind of sensation or feeling, it nonetheless did not enter into consciousness.

Understanding the stomach therefore became a task of classifying this
unconscious experience. How could it be, Charleton asks, "that we have a
certain sense of Feeling, that is not . . . communicated to the Brain, and of
which we take no cognizance, but by various effects and commotions that
it causeth in our bodies"? "For, in this sense, we do not perceive that we
feel; but as it fares with men distracted, or otherwise agitated with any violent passion of the mind, who neither feel pain, nor take notice of objects
offered to their senses: so it is with us in this Sense, which operating without
our knowledge, is therefore to be distinguished from the Animal Sense, and
may properly enough be called a Sensation without Sense."[28] As Timothy M.
Harrison has observed, Charleton's idea of "sensation without sense" is a
distant forebear of more recent conceptions of affect that seek to theorize
the dimensions of sensory life that do not fall under the aegis of the cognitive or the conscious.[29] In keeping with Harrison's proposed genealogy,
I am suggesting here that the stomach in particular has served, and continues
to serve, as a discursive yet embodied locus for the historical development
of these ideas concerning the allocation of will and motivation (especially
unconscious motivation) throughout the subject.

These examples of early modern gastric discourse call attention to the
way that the rationalizing impulses that animated them served not so much
to demystify irrational superstitions about the subject's lack of agency as to
bury the problem of our unconscious heteronomy deep within the inflamed
bowels of the self. Over time, the stomach came to represent the unknown
and irrational aspects of the body in a more rationalized form. In the nineteenth century, rapid advances in physiological knowledge of the gut were
avidly chipping away at this darkness—both physical and epistemological—
in an effort to dispel the unscientific traditionalism felt to authorize older
views of physiological causation. Traditional beliefs about the body came
under extreme pressure in the second half of the century, as the extraordinary positivistic impulses of the Victorian will to knowledge intensified.
This enthusiasm for scientific progress into the body's interiors took many

disturbing shapes, most prevalent among them the vivisection of animals, but also including experimentation on enslaved people in the United States.[30] The paradigmatic and most influential case concerning the stomach, in particular, was that of the US Army physician William Beaumont and a young Canadian *voyageur* named Alexis St. Martin.

Stationed in Michigan in 1822, Beaumont came into contact with St. Martin, whose stomach had been blasted open by an accidental musket shot. Nursed back to health by Beaumont, St. Martin retained a hole in his belly that never sealed up, leaving behind a "perforation, resembling, in all but a sphincter, the natural anus," situated just below the nipple (fig. 19).[31] Housing St. Martin and contracting him to work as his manservant, Beaumont consequently enjoyed, in his own words, "opportunities for the examination of the interior of the stomach, and its secretions, which have never before been so fully offered to anyone . . . [under] circumstances which probably can never again occur."[32] During the many years in which the two men resided together, Beaumont conducted frequent experiments on St. Martin and his stomach, dangling pieces of food into the fistula and recording how long it took until the gastric juice had dissolved them; removing food at fixed intervals after ingestion to see how quickly digestion had proceeded; and removing vials full of the acid from St. Martin's stomach and dissolving different kinds of food in it in order to simulate the process externally. Until this point, knowledge of the chemical basis of digestion had been largely speculative; in particular, the precise composition and effects of the stomach acid, as well as the conditions under which it was produced, had long remained obscure. But with the publication of Beaumont's *Experiments and Observations*, which circulated widely throughout Europe in the 1830s, the stomach's chemical processes were brought into focus with an unprecedented degree of empirical clarity. "My opinions may be doubted, denied, or approved," Beaumont writes at the opening of his book, but "I submit a body of facts which cannot be invalidated."[33]

The case of Beaumont and St. Martin exemplifies the ways in which the exploration of the stomach could at once typify and problematize the body's mechanism. Much of the complexity stemmed from the confusion of orifices that characterized Beaumont's experimentation on St. Martin. While the wound itself was likened to an anus, it functioned more like a mouth, providing access to the stomach; conversely, the nature of St. Martin's wound and its connection to the mouth meant that, during his convalescence, he needed to be fed "through nutricious injections per anum."[34] This seemingly inherent reversibility of the digestive tract and the fungibility of its endpoints had a disruptive effect on the symbolic organization of the

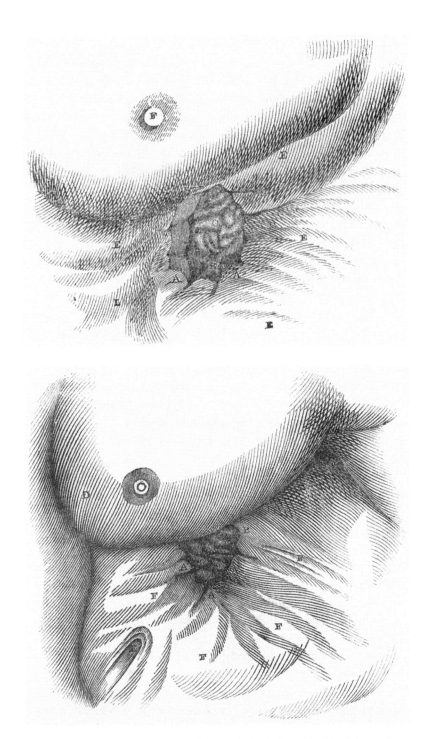

**Figure 19.** Beaumont's two renderings of the fistula in Alexis St. Martin's abdomen, "resembling, in all but a sphincter, the natural anus." From William Beaumont, *Experiments and Observations on the Gastric Juice and the Physiology of Digestion* (1838). Courtesy of the William Beaumont Collection, Special Collections Research Center, University of Chicago Library.

subject. With the introduction of a third orifice bizarrely positioned in the middle of the body, it suddenly became difficult to say which end was up.

Moreover, the interior discovered by Beaumont's gastric spelunking seemed less a space of intimate enclosure than a conduit of exteriority running through St. Martin's body, like a tunnel under a riverbed. This conception of gastric interiority also plays a central role within the psychology of disgust, especially as concerns the emotion's capacity to reverse the directionality of the gastrointestinal tract. Thus, Rozin and Fallon contrast a psychological understanding of interiority with "a biological perspective," according to which "the real self-outside border is the lining of the gut, because the gut can be viewed as a tube through the body, and hence the lumen of the gut [extending as far as the lips] is not part of the body": "Presumably, on this account, if one rammed a tube (pacem, human subject committees) through the navel and out the back (deftly exiting to the right or left of the spinal column) and then passed disgusting items through the tube, people should not be disgusted. On the other hand, the gut is psychologically as well as physically inside the body and is so viewed by children (Nagy, 1953) and, we are sure, by adults."[35] Rozin and Fallon's reflections on the difficulty of pinpointing the boundary between inside and out are themselves closely related to Jacques Lacan's notion of "extimacy" (itself an elaboration of Freud's *unheimlich*), according to which the intimate psychic spaces of subjectivity are seen to be conjoined with the alien surfaces of otherness and exteriority.[36] These concepts are especially helpful in understanding one of Beaumont's chief experimental goals, which was to replicate the action of the stomach *outside* St. Martin's body by extracting the acid, keeping it warm in a bath, and seeing how long it would take to "digest" different types of food into chyme. At the core of the body, the experiments seemed to confirm, lies an impersonal chemical process that has so little to do with the subjective sense of self that it can transpire in a manner that is completely external to the person; yet to arrive at this inner sanctum of the body was itself a deeply intimate and affect-laden affair, one that raised difficult questions about when and how human interiority could be rendered as knowledge.

Beaumont and St. Martin's "body of facts" helped to usher in a period of innovation and advance in nineteenth-century physiology that had a decidedly techno-rational character and was marked by a seemingly ineluctable tendency toward cruelty. Absent a freak accident like St. Martin's, was there an even remotely ethical way to open up the living body of *homo clausus* to scientific exploration?[37] The tools and techniques that were developed during the second half of the century with the purpose of illuminating the stomach would suggest not. The increased reliance on vivisection from the 1870s onward, in particular, which took the principle of mechanistic physiology to gruesome new heights, reinforced a mounting public perception that modern medical science had fully departed from its roots in traditional practices of caregiving and treatment.

One of the most brutal shapes taken by the Victorian will to gastric knowledge was the practice of sham feeding, which, as Ian Miller has described at length, was developed in Russia by Ivan Pavlov and honed in Britain by the eminent University College London physiologist Ernest Henry Starling. Researching the peristaltic process in laboratory dogs, Starling would methodically remove specific segments of the digestive system, in order to ascribe to each part a particular function.[38] In essence, the experiments sought to recreate with greater scientific precision and fewer ethical restrictions the same set of conditions that St. Martin's inadvertently opened gut had presented to Beaumont: holes would be bored into the dogs' stomachs in order to collect the gastric juice, as well as into their esophagi, so that they could be fed liquids through the artificial fistula. However, Starling soon realized that the stomach would only yield the high levels of acid needed for analysis if the dog were to actually grow hungry, see food, start salivating, and ingest the food through its mouth; another esophageal aperture was therefore required to prevent food swallowed from reaching the gut. This led in turn to the macabre spectacle of famished dogs tearing into morsels of food, which proceeded merely to fall back into the dish. "If the laboratory dog was provided with food when in a state of extreme hunger," Miller writes, "it might avidly attempt to eat in this futile manner for hours, without ever realizing that food would never reach its stomach."[39] The stomach, conversely, would continue to yield acid without "realizing" the food had never arrived.

Thus as knowledge of animal and human physiology became ever more precise, it only seemed further to confirm early modern mechanistic theories, such as Descartes's belief that living animals could not be distinguished from "machines having the organs and shape of . . . some other animal that lacked reason."[40] In an influential 1874 lecture, "Animal Automatism," for example, Thomas Huxley reaffirmed Descartes's mechanistic suspicion, insisting that "when we speak of the lower animals as guided by instinct and not reason, what we mean is that . . . they are machines, one part of which (the nervous system) . . . is provided with special apparatus, the function of which is the calling into existence of those states of consciousness which are termed sensations, emotions, ideas." Huxley goes so far as to compare animal behavior to the eighteenth-century French inventor

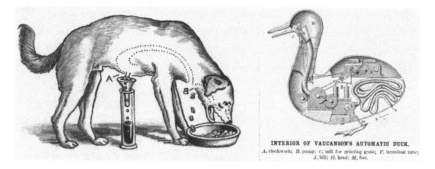

**FIGURE 20.** Two visions of the mechanism of digestion. *Left*, a depiction of sham feeding, based on an illustration of the technique circulating in turn-of-the-century Russian physiology texts. Drawing courtesy of Alan Samalin. *Right*, a hypothetical rendering of the interior mechanics of Jacques de Vaucanson's *Canard digérateur*. From *Scientific American*, January 21, 1899. Courtesy of the University of Chicago Library.

"[Jacques de] Vaucanson's automata—a senseless mechanism worked by molecular changes."[41] We might then see in Starling's dogs a lurid update on Vaucanson's *Canard digérateur*, the consuming and defecating duck, praised by Denis Diderot and Voltaire, whose simulation of the digestive process had invited rapt Enlightenment audiences to ponder the mechanical operations of the gut (fig. 20).

Moreover, Huxley surpassed his predecessor in asserting that humans too were a kind of "conscious automata," whose "mental conditions [such as thought and feeling] are simply the symbols in consciousness of the changes which take place automatically in the organism." Pushed to its logical extremity, Huxley insisted, mechanistic physiology would have to subsume not merely the self-evidently corporeal aspects of human behavior but also the psychological domain of emotions and the cognitive functions and conscious will. As he put it, "the feeling that we call volition is not the cause of a voluntary act, but the symbol of the state of the brain which is the immediate cause of that act."[42] This epiphenomenalism was controversial, but it nonetheless exerted so much pressure on the distinction between willed and reflexive behavior that the very concept of agency began to transform.

One significant direction that this line of thought would take would be determined by William James's still-influential theory of emotion, first put forward in 1884. James devoted a whole chapter to debunking Huxley's "automaton-theory" in his *Principles of Psychology* (1890), but his position that our emotions are the feelings of bodily changes excited in real time by perceptual experience surely depended on Huxley's prior observation that emotions are the symbols of physiological events.[43] At the same time, the mechanistic thought of the nineteenth century also led toward the systematic analysis of unconscious mental life. In the closing decades of the century, the mechanistic idea that consciousness was an aftereffect of physical experience would inch its way toward Freud's dictum that the ego was not master in its own house. Huxley's discussions of Hoffman's doppelgänger and of somnambulism already point up this major through-line, which connects the "physiological psychology" of the mid-nineteenth century to the fin-de-siècle psychoanalytic model of the dynamic unconscious.[44]

While the mechanistic conceptions of the self put into play by the illumination of the stomach had the effect of weakening the distinction between the voluntary and the involuntary within physiological, psychological, and philosophical discourse, the backlash against vivisection also raised the problem of will and willfulness in an important civilizational register. Perhaps unsurprisingly, Victorian critics of the gruesome practice came to see the pursuit of physiological knowledge as itself a gratuitous exercise of a perverted will to knowledge. Medical-scientific rationality, a chorus of prominent critics argued, had lost touch with its primary calling of alleviating pain and sickness, and had become more likely to cause suffering in the capricious drive to lay bare the body's functions. "The practice which is justifiable because implying laudable motives," Leslie Stephen wrote in an 1876 article, "graduates imperceptibly into the practice which is execrable because implying sheer brutality." "How brain secretes dog's soul," Robert Browning seethed more pointedly, "We'll see!"[45]

These concerns were both legitimate and necessary, but the critique of the barbaric flights of modern medical science also served to intensify a reactionary backlash, focused on the ostensibly widening gulf between physiological discourse and the prevalence of gastric illness in Victorian society. As Miller has persuasively argued, it was during this period that dyspepsia, understood as a catch-all for various digestive disorders, rose to such preeminence that it was heralded as "the national malady of Britain," and was said to "knock at the door of every gradation of society, from the monarch, in his splendid palace, down to the squalid inhabitant of St. Giles, whose exterior exhales the effluvium of filth."[46] Under pressure from the new physiology, a strain of Victorian gastric medicine backslid into an almost caricaturish refrain, which designated the emissions of the upset stomach as markers for the more general loss of traditional values. Pushed to its ideological limits, this backlash took the form of an incoherent gastric atavism originating in the hazy realm of dietetics. Faced with a whole era's indigestion, holistic physicians as well as outright quacks began to call for a return to simpler times, before modernity had soured the social body, and before modern physiology had ruined medicine. As Miller succinctly puts it, "The national mass of stomachs and nervous systems had yet to adjust to the problematic requirements imposed by the new conditions of modernity."[47]

Animating this reaction was a phylogenetic fantasy of restoring the spoiled stomachs of Victorian society to a premodern, preindustrial, and even prelapsarian state of gastric innocence, a primal scene set before the advent of anxiety-inducing dietary choices—or rather, before the advent of choice itself. "Savages, that have none of our stimulants," the Reverend Benjamin Parsons brazenly declared in his temperance polemic, *Anti-Bacchus*, "have scarcely more than one disease among them, and that disease is death—not sudden, or from apoplexy—but from the shaft of the warrior, or the gradual decay of nature."[48] The stomach could offer a species of primitive wisdom, a form of judgment that alone could put contemporary Britain back on its proper moral and digestive path. For the physician Thomas Lauder Brunton, this meant going back even before "the oldest diet table in the world . . . 'Of every tree in the garden thou mayest freely eat, but'—and here follows the one exception, of which Adam might not eat without injury," Brunton admonished his readers, an *et in Arcadia ego* for the dyspeptic 1880s. The sense that people had lost their way in a society that offered too many bad choices for consumption pervaded nineteenth-century dietary discourse; in order to regain its equilibrium, society's progress needed to be halted, and, in a kind of peristaltic exhumation, the stomachs of the past would be disinterred, revealing the hidden truth of humanity's digestive being without the violent incursions of the gastrodiaphane or the œsophagoscope. "We know that prehistoric man was fond of strawberries," Brunton goes on, offering what is perhaps the first "paleo diet," "because the seeds of some, which a man, ages and ages ago, had eaten and voided unchanged, still remain to inform us of the fact."[49]

The reactionary mythologizing of the savage stomach was both a rejoinder to the experimental brutalities of modern physiology and its dialectical complement in a matrix of questions and concerns about the scope and range of human agency that was undergoing a process of radical reconfiguration over the course of the nineteenth century. Whether modern medicine alone could find the cure for the churnings of the unruly stomach, or whether modernity itself and its perverted rationality formed the underlying condition, both responses worked together in the broader project of regulating and realigning the body's putatively unfailing, unthinking, and unchanging instinctivity in the period. The modern scientific will to master the stomach seemed less to answer to the desire to be free from bodily suffering, and more to express an anxious drive to be free from the newly confirmed automaticity of the body itself—that is, a desire for the freedom to choose, or for freedom per se, the disinterested yet brutal fantasy of autonomy that lies at the core of the rationalizing project of modernity. The reaction against modern physiology exhibited the very same fantasy of mastering the body, only it directed it against the onerous anxieties of autonomy, cooking up instead a fantasy of the primal scene, where the human is not merely led but also fully sated by instinctive mechanicity.

These broad historical questions of agency return us to those invoked by Darwin's meditation on the genealogical origins of vomiting. We can now see how Darwin's singular idea that disgust is a vestigial reflex derived from a bygone capacity for voluntary food rejection emerges out of the context of late Victorian mechanistic thought, even while it suggests a framework for thinking about human emotion radically different from that of his intellectual contemporary Huxley. For what Darwin asserts is that the digestive tract itself was at some point in human history the medium for a form of willed, rational judgment; the implied lines of evolutionary descent pass from voluntary to reflexive, from conscious to unconscious, and not the other way around. This lost capacity for vomiting at will exists in the present only in the behaviors of other species, and as a special condition of certain disordered human stomachs called rumination.

In *Expression*, the primary evidence that Darwin marshals on this point is that "the monkeys in the Zoological Gardens often vomit whilst in perfect health, which looks as if the act were voluntary" (257). Furthermore, in a footnote to this passage in the second edition of *Expression*, we are referred to two letters that Darwin received after the book's initial publication, each giving an account of voluntary regurgitation or rumination in humans. In the first, a man named James Dickson recalls to Darwin a young servant who would vomit at will, "for our amusement": "I have given him many a pocketful of fruit on the condition that he would 'throw up' a portion of it," Dickson writes. "It was always done with apparent ease, and he assured us it caused him no pain or uneasiness—his only objection being that of parting with the food."[50] This footnote would itself have a longer afterlife in the fin-de-siècle psychological and physiological literature on rumination disorder, including a significant essay by the French psychiatrists Jules Séglas and Désiré-Magloire Bourneville published across several issues of Jean-Martin Charcot's influential *Archives de neurologie* in 1883.[51] After Séglas and Bourneville's article, Darwin's footnote took on semicanonical status in the literature on rumination, where it would be cited alongside other cases of voluntary and selective regurgitation. The gastroenterologist and medical inventor Max Einhorn, for instance, refers in his *Rumination in Man* not only to Séglas and Bourneville's citation of Darwin but also to a case of "a boy of eleven years [who] was able, after having partaken of a meal composed of different food stuffs, to select one certain dish, which he liked most, for rumination; then only this favorite dish, without any admixture of other food-stuffs, was ejected into the mouth."[52]

For Darwin, rumination posed a special problem for thinking about how will, deliberation, and rational thought might turn out to be or formerly to have been distributed throughout the body in unexpected ways. For if it is possible under some circumstances for the mind and the digestive tract to become coordinated, then one question raised is why this is not always possible, or whether it in fact once was the case, as Darwin suggests, but is no longer. "The first mind we have is a stomach-mind," Wilson writes of Ferenczi's biological unconscious, though she might just as easily be describing Darwin's earlier position.[53] By the same token, however, the customary alignment of the reflexivity of the body with what is nonrational and primitive is also thrown into disarray. The primeval and the unreasoning are not coextensive in Darwin's theory of disgust. To the contrary, although we are provided with a speculative primal scene describing the originary nature of the gut, what is originary and primal is the organ's capacity for complex symbolic thinking, rather than the imagination of a prerational past in which we were not yet saddled with the burden of thought.

## Allegories of Instinct

We can now begin to flesh out the details of the singular primal scene Darwin imagines in his genealogy of disgust. To recall, what I mean here by *primal scene* is precisely the fantasy or speculation of humanity's entry into its own specieshood, a half beat before the state of nature, before the faculties and capacities of the ever-forming human have fully set. In the centuries prior to Darwin—as well as in the century and a half after him—the narration of this inaugural moment has overwhelmingly focused on the transition from the unlearned guidance of instinct to the anxiety-provoking but nonetheless superior exercise of reason; once there is reason, this narrative goes, social and political life, as well as culture and history, become possible. Yet in Darwin's gastric imagination, the primeval and the prerational are by no means coextensive, nor are the instinctual and the human mutually exclusive. The whole matrix of terms needs to be reorganized in order to set the stage for Darwin's primal scene.

The opening section of Rousseau's *Discourse on the Origin of Inequality* offers an instructive example of the genre. "How much you have changed from what you once were!" the philosopher exclaims to humankind, promising to narrate "the life of your species" and to enumerate "the changes that came about in the constitution of the body." Commenting on a diverse range of such transformations of human life throughout the first part of the *Discourse*, from the acquisition of language to the question of the species' bipedal nature, Rousseau's emphasis falls squarely and overwhelmingly on the underlying, tectonic movement from instinct to reason. "Left by nature to instinct alone," he writes, "or rather, compensated for the instincts he may lack by faculties capable first of replacing them and then of raising him far above nature, savage man will, therefore, begin with purely animal functions."[54] Note here Rousseau's equivocation over the matter of the instinctivity of "savage man," before the transition from purely animal to the fully human. On the one hand, Rousseau enacts his primal scene as the overcoming of instinct by the exercise of primitive, inchoate faculties, which are the exclusive possession of humankind, and whose development will place the species above and beyond the natural and instinctive; but on the other hand, following Darwin's more robust and nuanced treatment of the concept, we might ask, What is an instinct, if not precisely the kind of innate capacity for particular behaviors Rousseau has in mind?

The ambiguous meaning of instinct notwithstanding, this narrative of reason superseding and supplanting nature's built-in mechanisms of guidance can, with few notable exceptions, serve as a template for the broader genre of the primal scene. Another important dimension of this genre is the putatively emancipatory character of its narrative. Although Rousseau argued that the developmental trajectory he had traced out in fact led to the invention of private property and, with it, to the predomination of inequality as a social state of affairs, he still described reason's initial casting off of the strictures of instinctivity as a narrative of the human species' progress and deliverance from nature's bondage. Reflecting on this tension in Rousseau's *Discourse*, Kant too would soon after write his own account of "the development of freedom from its origins as a predisposition in human nature," observing that "while this course represents a *progression* from worse to better for the species as a whole, this is not so in the case of the individual," whom he suggests might have fared better in the primal state.[55] For Enlightenment thought, then, speculation about the origins of humanity *as humanity* raises the philosophical problem of human freedom and autonomy specifically as a tension between biological and social registers of explanation. These questions about the origins of human freedom arise out of concrete anxieties regarding the autonomy of subjectivity in the face of increased knowledge of physiological mechanism. Freedom, in this sense, is the freedom from the mechanism of the human body itself, and the primal scene is in this regard quite literally the issue of the body, projected onto a retrospective narrative form.

Breaking with his Enlightenment forebears, Darwin believed that spontaneous vomiting out of disgust, like most other forms of emotion expression, was an innate behavior that gestured back toward a primal exercise of the will—in this case, our progenitors' lost capacity for "voluntarily rejecting food which disagreed with them, or which they thought would disagree with them." It should be easy to grasp how and why this speculation cannot be squared with the narrative of instinct overcome, which I am suggesting epitomizes modernity's dominant imagination of the inauguration of the species. In Darwin's configuration, what is contemporary is the involuntary instinct, whereas what seems to be voluntary, the ability to judge freely, is already present in the primal moment.[56] In lieu of the narrative of the progressive and developmental acquisition of higher faculties and powers, such as free will, complex reasoning, and judgment, Darwin depicts instead a far more uneven, unpredictable process of descent into a complex and nonhierarchical web of learned, habituated, and innate behaviors. Thus, in order to understand the genealogical thrust of Darwin's remarks on vomiting and disgust, one has not only to understand what Darwin meant by the term *instinct* but also to grasp how and why he thought, along with Jean-Baptiste Lamarck and others before him, that instinctual behaviors could be acquired through habituation and evolutionary descent.

Darwin's reluctance to imagine disgust as the vestigial emblem of our nearly lost animal nature is of a piece with what, in the larger scheme of things, gives his thought its critical force: the notion that there is no instinctive animal nature to lose, or purely human nature to gain—nature, Darwin insists, is not bifurcated, and ought to be understood with ever more finely tuned gradations. Even Darwin's principal statement on the topic of instinct in *Origin* defies the enduring Enlightenment impulse to set the artificiality of human reason over and against the unreflective automaticity of primitive animal nature. From the earliest notebooks to the late publication of *Expression*, Darwin remained defiantly resistant to easy classifications of instinct as unerring or automatic, averring in *Origin* that "instincts are not always absolutely perfect and are liable to make mistakes."[57] Consequently, there is a wide gulf between Darwin's proposal that instincts are liable to lapse into error, on the one hand, and on the other, the long intellectual tradition holding that to err is human—which is to say, it is not animal, not instinctive, not corporeal—because errors of judgment are the product of rational thought gone astray, and are in the first place only errors from a rational standpoint.

Darwinian instincts are fundamentally at odds with this deeply entrenched and still-prevalent perspective, which takes the body to be mechanistically infallible, because sub- or nonrational.

Although Darwin insisted that the human-animal divide could not be maintained through an appeal to the outright isolation of reason from instinct, he of course did not discard the distinction formally. Instead, the opening passage outlining the subject in the chapter on instinct in *Origin* is marked by its ambivalence, at once expressing deep uncertainty that instinct could be entirely isolated, while acknowledging the implausibility of explaining animal behavior without doing so:

> I will not attempt any definition of instinct. It would be easy to show that several distinct mental actions are commonly embraced by this term; but everyone understands what is meant, when it is said that instinct impels the cuckoo to migrate and to lay her eggs in other birds' nests. An action, which we ourselves should require experience to perform, when performed by an animal, more especially by a very young one, without any experience, and when performed by many individuals in the same way, without their knowing for what purpose it is performed, is usually said to be instinctive. But I could show that none of these characters of instinct are universal. A little dose, as Pierre Huber expresses it, of judgment or reason, often comes into play, even in animals very low in the scale of nature.[58]

The bulk of Darwin's chapter is devoted to demonstrating this last insight, that instincts mingle with other forms of activity and judgment, thus nuancing strictly mechanistic accounts of behavior, and the dualistic outlook they imply. With the publication of *Origin*, it grew more and more difficult to say where the motivation of reason ended and instinct began, to the point that, as Darwin suggests, the concept itself came under pressure. Indeed, the decades after Darwin's intervention are characterized by a lack of consensus over the meaning of the concept, as well as a proliferation in its uses—a period, as Kathleen Frederickson has aptly put it, in "which instinct fails to become standardized."[59]

While Darwin's view of the entwinement of reason with instinct certainly met with opposition, the notion that animals were endowed with the same kind of rational faculties as man nevertheless had a notable lineage within British empiricist philosophy and naturalist thought. Unlike the rationalist tradition, empiricists held that sense data determined all experience, therefore providing a common material foundation for rational thought and instinct in man and other animals. Locke, for instance, had granted that "if they [beasts] have any *Ideas* at all, and are not bare Machins (as some [i.e., Descartes] would have them) we cannot deny them to have some Reason." In fact, Locke insisted, "the species of *Brutes* are discriminated from Man" principally by their inability to generalize their ideas. "This, I think, I may be positive in, that the power of *Abstracting* is not at all in them; and that the having of general *Ideas*, is that which puts a perfect distinction betwixt Man and Brutes."[60] Even though Locke believed this deficiency to be of divine origin and so insurmountable, such a higher-order distinction nonetheless afforded animals ideas in the first place, in a sense paving the road for the argument (which would nevertheless have seemed insupportable to Locke) that humans and animals differed in degree and not kind. In Locke's hands, the unbridgeable gap between man and animal shrank to the uppermost tip of the cognitive faculties, such as abstraction and the use of symbols. What looked from one angle like the assertion of the essential difference of humanity from other animals appears from a more historical perspective to be the slow erosion of that difference under the pressure of scientific obser-vation and materialist thought.

Empiricist philosophy continued to blur the line separating instinct from reason throughout the Enlightenment and well into Darwin's day. Half a century after Locke's *Essay*, Hume put the case forcefully in a section of his *Treatise* titled "Of the Reason of Animals": "No truth appears to me more evident, than that beasts are endow'd with thought and reason as well as men," Hume writes, adding caustically that "the arguments are in this case so obvious that they never escape the most stupid and ignorant." Asserting that animals possess both reason and instinct, Hume's polemic came with the added flourish of positing that reason itself "is nothing but a wonder-ful and unintelligible instinct in our souls, which carries us along a certain train of ideas, and endows them with particular qualities."[61] By the end of the eighteenth century and into the early years of the nineteenth, Hume's position on the nonoppositionality of reason and instinct had gained wider circulation among naturalists and philosophers of varying stripes, among them Darwin's grandfather Erasmus Darwin as well as Lamarck.[62]

The irreducible margin dividing man from animal continued to cede ground to the advances of an increasingly materialist and naturalizing body of scientific thought. This was true, as Robert J. Richards has shown, even within the context of the religiously motivated scientific thought of the early nineteenth century. As Richards has recounted in great detail, Darwin's own early ideas about instinct were heavily indebted to those of contemporary so-called natural theologians, such as the Reverend Algernon Wells, Lord Henry Brougham, and the Reverend William Kirby, each of whom managed to reconcile an attested devotion to God as the *primum movens* of all life with the empirical conviction that animals could exercise reason. "Though instinct is the chief guide of insects," Kirby wrote in his four-volume *Introduction to Entomology* (1815–26), "they are also endowed with no inconsiderable portion of knowledge."[63] Stemming from Hume's "instinct in our souls" and passing through the natural theology of the early nineteenth century, Darwin's eventual view that "a little dose . . . of judgment or reason often comes into play" in instinctive behavior emerged out of a well-established British intellectual tradition of antimechanistic materialist thought.

This same tradition was also a fertile source of inspiration for early nineteenth-century conceptions of heredity, such as Lamarck's, since it laid ample groundwork for thinking about how habituated behaviors could become inherited. Hume's argument that reason was a "wonderful and unintelligible instinct in our souls," for instance, had rested on the assertion that, although reason depended on habituated experience, "habit is nothing but one of the principles of nature, and derives all its force from that origin."[64] Thus, according to Hume, the unthinking automaticity of instincts could be derived from the gradual accumulation of learned and deliberate behaviors grown habitual and passed down over generations. Prior to Darwin's theory of natural selection, this view represented the foremost conception of how species could change and adapt their instincts through descent. Darwin himself forged his early position on instinct principally through such ideas about the heritability of acquired characteristics, including habits, though he failed to acknowledge his debt to Lamarck on this score, to whom he erroneously attributed the idea that species could adapt and even create parts of the body through the pseudomagical application of the will.[65] Dismissive of such unscientific reasoning, Darwin nevertheless held early on that instincts that were developed out of hereditary habits must operate on the substance of the brain independently of intention or will, constituting a form of unconscious or involuntary memory passed down through generations.[66] Thus Darwin never fully abandoned the Lamarckian model, even while championing his own theory of natural selection in *Origin*: "If we suppose any habitual action to become inherited—and I think it can be shown this does sometimes happen—then the resemblance between what was originally a habit and an instinct becomes so close as not to be distinguished."[67] Far from being superseded by the more robust mechanism of natural selection, as it has been in the history of evolutionary thought, the theory of habit-instinct adaptation came to play a significant role in Darwin's late work on the human, in particular as a constitutive part of his explanation of how the emotions had developed.

Not only did Darwin believe that voluntary behaviors could become habitual and ultimately be inherited as instincts, but also he considered instincts acquired in this manner, including all emotion expressions, "to be degraded in character, for they are no longer performed through reason or from experience."[68] Not bound by the principles of natural selection, and cut off from its original functional purposes, the expression of emotions through facial movements and other gestures was therefore deemed by Darwin to be a kind of defunctioned behavior. While he clearly acknowledged that emotions were still integral to human social life, Darwin nevertheless did not believe that the communicative nature of involuntary emotion expression would yield any necessary evolutionary advantage. In fact, he wrote, "there are no grounds, as far as I can discover, for believing that any muscle has been developed or even modified exclusively for the sake of expression."

> Nor can I discover grounds for believing that any inherited movement, which now serves as a means of expression, was at first voluntarily and consciously performed for this special purpose. . . . On the contrary, every true or inherited movement of expression seems to have had some natural and independent origin.
>
> . . . Although they [such instinctive actions] often reveal the state of the mind, this result was not at first either intended or expected. Even such words as that "certain movements serve as a means of expression" are apt to mislead, as they imply that this was their primary purpose or object. (325–26)

Automatic, stereotyped, and instinctual, and yet, from an evolutionary perspective, never ends in themselves, Darwinian emotion expressions are difficult to comprehend—not in the least because, thanks in large part to Darwin, we have become used to thinking about the evolution of animal behavior in the more pragmatic, functionalist terms of natural selection. Thus the elements Darwin assembles for his primal mise-en-scène have a strikingly un-Darwinian flavor: relying on a Lamarckian notion of the inheritance of acquired characteristics, and implying an antifunctionalist narrative of degradation and descent rather than fitness and selection, Darwin's voluntary vomiters find themselves on the wrong side of the philosophical as well as the scientific tracks.

Since the Enlightenment, disgust has been singled out, perhaps more than any other affect, for functionalist explanation within the context of the project of primal scenography. Because it obtrudes and feels unwanted, because it is reflexive, and because for these reasons it has come to be coded as irrational, it has taken on its vestigial and asynchronous character, which has in turn been put to work at producing the present of the human as the *telos* of the primeval past. What we are coming to see in this chapter is just how central the ascription of function to disgust has been to the philosophical discourse of modernity. So long as disgust remains available to the philosophical imagination as a referent for our supposedly unchanging primal instinctivity, its interpretation will continue to take shape as a story about our origins; in many ways, the production of such stories has been in the first place the point of the study of disgust over the last three centuries. Ongoing debate about whether or not we should listen to the ancient wisdom of our revulsion only persists in obscuring the far more significant fact that the interpretation of disgust serves the generative function of rendering the biology of the human species in a surreptitious narrative form: the animal before the man, the feeling before the thought, the taste before the judgment, the stomach before the noodle. And, at the same time, we are also coming to see how uneasily Darwin's vision of human evolution fits within a philosophical regime that imagines the present of the human species as a finished product or end. Consequently, Darwin makes it possible not only to see the limitations and the fault lines in the discourse of the primal scene but also to envision the human as something asynchronous and still in process.

In stark contrast to Darwin's work, contemporary evolutionary accounts of disgust depend almost entirely on the Enlightenment presumption of the emotion's primitive efficacy. For the epidemiologist Valerie Curtis, to take one recent example, discovering an evolutionary function for primal disgust is the only way to make sense of an emotion that "is so powerful and sometimes so apparently irrational that it can seem magical. To find it playing so many roles in so many spheres of life," she writes, "seems to defeat scientific explanation."[69] To counter disgust's promiscuity across domains, Curtis has advanced the strong unifying thesis that revulsion represents the body's very own built-in parasite-avoidance mechanism, adapted and refined over the *longue durée* of human evolution. Quasi-instinctive disease avoidance, in her view, comes to explain the eventual development of manners and morality as well as more seemingly visceral forms of aversive judgment. According to Curtis's imagination of disgust's role on the primal scene, "conversations around the late Pleistocene campfire probably went something like this": "'It stinks of poo around Og's house; I'm not going to visit him,' or 'Ig's kids are always filthy and covered in sores; I'm not letting my kids play with them,' or 'Did you see the lice crawling about in Ag's hair? I'm not sitting next to her.' And such gossip was of great interest, since humans are always hypersensitive to information that is salient to their survival and reproduction." While this scene might at first blush seem to resemble Darwin's quite closely, it is in fact directly opposed to it. Curtis takes recourse to language and volition in order to dramatize the motivation of disgust, but this is only a misleading shorthand she deploys in order to represent the neurobiological tendencies she wants to claim for disgust. "There is, of course," she reminds us, "no actual voice [of disgust] or direct impulsion." For Curtis, that is, the meaning of disgust is captured entirely by the selection advantage that the biological sensitivity to such hygienic matters would have conferred on early humans. Scientific knowledge about disease and contagion has today surpassed disgust in accuracy, and yet "we can never get rid of the ancestral voices in our heads that say, 'Don't touch! Don't eat!' and call out alarms whenever infection cues . . . are detected."[70] On this account, disgust is a residual aspect of human biology that has a sometimes adversarial, sometimes supplemental relationship to knowledge. It remains useful to social life to the extent that it coincides with and supplements rational scientific knowledge of how disease is transmitted; but it is also inimical to modern life, to the extent that some behavioral heuristics and mores that it has helped to promote, such as xenophobia, are putatively at odds with modern liberal values, which Curtis presumes to have a different genealogical story to tell.

At bottom, Curtis's scientifically informed account of disgust's primitive function remains tethered to the Enlightenment problem of thinking human freedom at the intersection of the social and biological domains. After three hundred years, it is striking to find that disgust's role in laying out and elaborating the primal scene has hardly changed within the evolutionary and psychological discourse of the present. This is not to say that the scientific methodologies deployed have not advanced, nor that the kinds of knowledge of the human that such methods have made available have not been radically transformed. What has not changed in such cases, however, are the rules of the game, the underlying principles that organize scientific knowledge of the human in advance. The basic elements setting the stage around Curtis's Pleistocene campfire can all be found in the primal scenography of the Age of Reason, and nowhere with more complexity than in Kant's "Conjectures on the Beginning of Human History."

A response to Rousseau in the form of a naturalized close reading of Genesis, Kant's essay reinterprets the Fall itself as an allegory in which the experiences of disgust and indigestion marked the painful and irreversible transition from the automated innocence of instinct to the anxiety of knowledge and volition. In this telling, "the newcomer must have been guided solely by instinct," which Kant surmises "could simply have been the sense of smell and its affinity with the organ of taste, along with that sympathy which is known to exist between the latter and the digestive process—in other words an ability, which is still in evidence today, to sense in advance whether a given food is suitable for consumption or not." Led by their noses and stomachs to all the delicacies on offer in this prerational Eden, Kant's primal couple are as yet unsullied by the burden of choice. Against this backdrop of mechanistic bliss, however, the overcoming of instinct through the initial use of reason constitutes the first, fateful transgression:

> So long as inexperienced man obeyed this call of nature, his lot was a happy one. But *reason* soon made its presence felt and sought to extend his knowledge of foodstuffs beyond the bounds of instinct; it did so by comparing his usual diet with anything which a sense other than that to which his instinct was tied—for example, the sense of sight—represented as similar in character. Even if instinct did not recommend it, this experiment had a chance of succeeding so long as instinct did not contradict it. But it is a peculiarity of reason that it is able, with the help of the imagination, to invent desires which not only *lack* any corresponding natural impulse, but which are even *at variance* with the latter.

Glimpsing a fruit that looks like one they have already consumed and relished, or a fruit which they had seen another animal eat with enjoyment, Adam and Eve choose to taste it, although it turns out to have "an opposite and harmful effect on human beings, whose natural instinct was consequently opposed to it."[71] Visual comparison, in conjunction with analogical thinking, supplant the innate guidance of smell—but as a result of this great leap forward, the couple grow sick to their stomachs. The first nausea, here understood as the instinctual outcome of the first denial of instinct, therefore becomes the symbol of the naturalized Fall, a solitary point of contact between the conscious human history that comes after, and the sensory prehistory that came before.

This Fall into rationality ushers in a state of perpetual anxiety, itself felt as a cognitive counterpart to the gut punch of corporeal repulsion which precedes and produces it: "He ["man"] discovered in himself an ability to choose his own way of life without being tied to any single one like the other animals," Kant writes, "but the momentary gratification which this realization of his superiority may have afforded him was inevitably followed at once by anxiety and fear." In this manner, "man" is at once encumbered and liberated by this newly minted autonomy; the first bout of dyspepsia in the garden was "enough to open [his] eyes." The primal pair now "stood, as it were, on the edge of an abyss": "For whereas instinct had hitherto directed him towards individual objects of his desire, an infinite range of objects now opened up, and he did not yet know how to choose between them. Yet now that he had tasted this state of freedom, it was impossible for him to return to a state of servitude under the rule of instinct."[72] Where to go, whom to blame, what to eat, how to choose? The first couple quickly begin to long for their prelapsarian menu—a prix fixe menu with no choices or substitutions—but, despite their anxious yearning, there is no returning to the unthinking wisdom of the instinct of smell, which has in a single fell swoop been marginalized and rendered vestigial by the initial misapplication of reason.

The first choice therefore inaugurates the permanent impossibility of not choosing, even if the anxieties of humanity's autonomy from its corporeality make regression to the bygone "state of servitude under the rule of instinct" seem desirable. It is not just that no one would, but that no one *can* choose to return to the guidance of instinct—because choice here represents the antithesis of instinct. In Kant's ingenious formulation, this impossibility constitutes original sin and reveals "the vacuity of [the] wish for a return to the past age of simplicity and innocence." According to Kant, we all must admit that, "in the same circumstances, [we] would have behaved in exactly the same way, in that [our] first act in using reason would have been to misuse it (even if nature advised [us] otherwise)."[73] To err becomes the defining feature of humanity, set against the receding horizon of an unrecoverable instinctual prehistory that nonetheless lurks inside each of us and rears its obtrusive head each time our bile rises in revulsion. From this moment on, disgust becomes the emblem of humankind's divided nature, its automaticity a remnant of our bygone instinctivity, its unwanted obtrusiveness a symptom of the irreversibility of the Fall into reason.

But now let us contrast Kant's powerful condensation of the primal scene with the assembled elements of Darwin's. In lieu of primordial instinct, Darwin gives us primal intention; we confront the matter of animal rationality rather than the conundrum of the rational animal, and discover a cryptic Lamarckian Darwin rather than a modern Darwinian one. Instead of evolved fitness and hard-won enlightened mastery over nature, we see a human deprived of former agency and driven by evolutionarily purposeless "degraded" behaviors. Darwin's genealogy of disgust describes the descent of man, but it does not trace out the rise of civilization or the beginnings of human history, and his voluntary vomiters fly in the face of received wisdom in the human sciences. Where the combined weight of the modern disciplines has given us an image of a disgust determined by its unerring functionality, the voluntary vomiters would by contrast see in *our* revulsion only a bizarre involuntary tic that was an echo of a lost volitional ability, as though they were to find that we used only seven of our fingers voluntarily. Moreover, the voluntary vomiters would be confused by our conviction that each flaring up of this unintentional tic had a necessary and fixed meaning, let alone one that philosophers insisted cut to the very core of our being. Perhaps above all else, they would find it strange and embarrassing that we had contrived stories about them—stories in which it was they who were ruled fully by unthinking instincts, and we who had leapt past them in a single bound with our abilities to reason and intend; important, self-congratulatory stories in which they served merely to help us comprehend our own allegedly divided nature; epic daydreams of development and progress, the protracted pillow talk of a long Enlightenment moment, with its proclivity for the impassioned disavowal of the passions and its overheated fantasies of cool rationality. As though the voluntary vomiters had simply been crawling around sniffing each other, stuck in some unchanging instinctual rut, just so that we could leap ahead to become the upright walkers, complex thinkers, and smooth talkers we are today. *"Natura non facit saltum*, cousins,"* they'd chide us, vomiting up some poorly seasoned cut of meat or unripe fruit. "You can make your disgust mean whatever you like," they'd say (assuming they could in fact speak), "only leave us out of it." But they would also see—as Darwin's strange theory helps us to see—how much we had *done* with our disgust, how much we had built with it and organized our knowledge around our presumptions about its meaning.

## Everybody's a Critic

Darwin's most radical assertion about the origins of disgust is that the advent of human language as the primary form of social communication would gradually have rendered obsolete the ability to vomit at will: "We can see that as a man is able to communicate by language to his children and others, the knowledge of the kinds of food to be avoided, he would have little occasion to use the faculty of voluntary rejection; so that this power would tend to be lost through disuse" (237). Now specifying an interpersonal, social function in his conception of early disgust, Darwin implies a period of continuity between some intentional physical behaviors, like vomiting, and certain complex uses of language—which in this case would best be described as a socially sophisticated form of judgment (involving a subject, an object, and a third party) along the lines of, "I wouldn't eat that if I were you." While Curtis's evolutionary theory implies a sharp break between the nonlinguistic behavior modifications of disgust and the consciously articulated manners and morals that eventually grow out of it, in

Darwin's theory, what is continuous between puking and speaking is precisely their communicative intentionality.

Proposing such a link between physical, even visceral faculties (for example, control over the directionality of the esophagus) and the putatively loftier linguistic powers was in keeping with Darwin's statements on the development of human language, the most significant of which he made in *The Descent of Man*. There, Darwin describes language in terms of its capacity to problematize overly stark distinctions between the innate and the acquired, since while language "is certainly not a true instinct, as every language has to be learnt . . . it differs, however, from all ordinary arts, for man has an instinctive tendency to speak, as we see in the babble of our children."[74] Language use, for Darwin, along with emotion expression and his definition of instinct more generally, occupied a liminal, mediating position with regard to the nature-culture binary; like the intentionally rejected food they supplanted, words would not fit neatly on either side of the divide.

Between the views he made explicit in *The Descent of Man* and those implied throughout *Expression* soon after, Darwin's position on the evolution of language represented a composite of a few closely related theories. Darwin held, first, that some features of language must have developed out of and supplanted certain forms of emotion expression, such as grunts and screams; second, that other features were derived from primitive forms of gestural communication; third, that the vocal cords of early humans had been shaped and strengthened through the innate tendency to imitate sounds made by other animals and in nature; and fourth, that driven by sexual selection, "some early progenitor of man, probably used his voice largely, as does one of the gibbon-apes at the present day, in producing true musical cadences, that is in singing."[75] Language, in Darwin's schema, was a fully embodied and evolutionarily ancient form of communication, unique in many respects to humankind, but it was not therefore the singularly prized possession that many of his contemporaries claimed it to be.

The intellectual milieu into which such unsettling statements on language entered was itself far from settled. As Foucault has shown at great length, along with Georges Cuvier's comparative anatomy and David Ricardo's labor theory of value, the first half of the nineteenth century saw the emergence of modern philology and, with it, a tumultuous shift toward conceiving of language as a fully objectified system of linguistic laws, rather than in terms of its representational capacity:

If the word is able to figure in a discourse in which it means something, it will no longer be by virtue of some immediate discursivity that it is thought to possess in itself, and by right of birth, but because, in its very form, in the sounds that compose it, in the changes it undergoes in accordance with the grammatical function it is performing, and finally in the modifications to which it finds itself subject in the course of time, it obeys a certain number of strict laws which regulate, in a similar way, all the other elements of the same language.[76]

Keeping pace with the leaps and bounds of European imperialism that had enabled its foundational comparison of Indian and European language families, the new linguistic science had by and large taken hold by the middle of the nineteenth century as the dominant method for the scholarly study of language.[77] Theories of the origins of language grounded in emotion expression or representational power gave way to a *Sprachwissenschaft*, epitomized by the work of Franz Bopp and the brothers Wilhelm and Jacob Grimm, and concerned primarily with the historical analysis of roots and particles within the Indo-European language system, as well as the typological standardization of phonetics. Detached from its expressive or emotive function, language at once became more concrete, as a formal object of study, and yet more ephemeral, isolated from its unsystematic and incidental occasions of actual use. As Foucault writes, it is because of these tectonic shifts in early and mid-nineteenth-century philology that "etymology will therefore cease to be an endless regress towards a primitive language entirely stocked with primal, natural cries; it becomes a definite, limited method of analysis."[78]

Darwin's remarks on linguistic origins tacked hard toward the very same expressive theories that Foucault describes as being on the wane. In particular, Darwin drew heavily and frequently from the writings of his cousin and brother-in-law, Hensleigh Wedgwood, an etymologist whose essay "The Origin of Language" (1866) argues that the complexities of human speech developed from more rudimentary forms of communication, such as gesture, imitation, and above all, onomatopoeic exclamations and interjections. In addition to Wedgwood, Darwin supported his linguistic views in *The Descent of Man* with references to F. W. Farrar and August Schleicher, a German philologist who had argued in his influential *Darwinism Tested by the Science of Language* (1863) that languages evolve like species. Invoking these three contemporaries, Darwin wrote in *The Descent of Man*, "I cannot doubt that language owes its origin to the imitation and modification, aided by signs and gestures, of various natural sounds, the voices of other animals, and man's own instinctive cries."[79] At precisely the intellectual-historical moment Foucault designates as when "there is no longer any attempt to refer [language] back to the cries from which it originated," Darwin allied himself with those theories that, about to be eclipsed, nevertheless sought out an origin to language in the sounds, gestures and expressions of the animal world.[80]

The chief proponent in England of the new linguistic science was Max Müller, a German-born Sanskritist who became the first professor of comparative philology at Oxford, and whose work Darwin explicitly distanced himself from in *Descent*, making sure to place the "celebrated lectures of Prof. Max Müller on the other side" of the increasingly central language question. In his popular *Lectures on the Science of Language* (1861), delivered almost a decade before *Descent*'s publication, Müller had already spoken out against what "I shall call the *Bow-wow theory* and the *Pooh-pooh theory*"—snide names for the imitative and interjectional linguistic theories subtending Darwin's own.[81] An especially complex figure, Müller has been credited with introducing the new philology into England, while he made use of its scientific rigor only in order to demonstrate the time-tested thesis that "the one great barrier between the brute and man is *Language*":

> Man speaks, and no brute has ever uttered a word. Language is our Rubicon, and no brute will dare to cross it. This is our matter of fact answer to those who speak of development, who think they discover the rudiments at least of all human faculties in apes, and who would fain keep open the possibility that man is only a more favored beast, the triumphant conqueror in the primeval struggle for life. Language is something more palpable than a fold of the brain, or an angle of the skull. It admits of no caviling, and no process of natural selection will ever distill significant words out of the notes of birds or the cries of beasts.[82]

Thus, while Müller's scientific apparatus was cutting-edge, his underlying motivations were at odds with the drift of contemporary evolutionary theory and harkened back to earlier attempts to reconcile scientific advance with religious convictions about the singularity of the human. In fact, he goes on to quote from Locke's assertion that the "perfect distinction betwixt Man and Brutes" lies in the specifically human capacity "to express their universal *Ideas* by signs." In Müller's hands, the very same passage from Locke that had cracked open the door to the further erosion of animal-human difference in Hume and, subsequently, Darwin, now became a final philosophical bulwark in the defense of humanity's insurmountable distinction. Only now, Müller had specified Locke's universal ideas using the well-defined rules of the new philology and its immutable linguistic roots and particles: "These roots," Müller proclaimed in one of his many broadsides against Darwin, "stand like barriers between the chaos and the kosmos of human speech."[83]

Language persisted as a significant battleground in Victorian debates over the definition of the human, and Darwin's take on linguistic matters reflected all the idiosyncratic force that characterized his larger views about human evolution. This meant that while Darwin explicitly opposed Müller's purportedly scientific linguistic exceptionalism and its religious implications, he also felt the need to distinguish his position from that of some of his allies, such as Schleicher, who argued that language had developed polygenically, after racial and geographical dispersion, and so held that allegedly inferior races could be identified by their apparently less sophisticated languages. As Stephen G. Alter has argued, despite the undeniable influence that polygenist thinkers such as Schleicher and Ernst Haeckel had on Darwin's late work, he could not reconcile their timeline with his own conviction that language must have arisen long before so-called racial characteristics had differentiated and distinct social groups had begun to settle in different parts of the world.[84] Such an early start was necessary to one of the most important tenets of Darwin's theory of language; namely, his belief that linguistic capacity and higher brain functioning had coevolved, since "the mental powers in some progenitor of man must have been more highly developed than in any existing ape, before even the most imperfect form of speech could have come into use."[85] With language as with other aspects of behavior, Darwin envisioned human history having begun far earlier than most of his contemporaries were prepared to entertain. The direct opposition to Müller's essentialist claims was therefore matched by a subtler distancing from polygenist racialist accounts, which wanted to see in the histories of particular languages evidence of European racial and cultural supremacy. To satisfy his underlying thesis that language and mind were coeval and extremely primitive, Darwin had to conceive of language as a necessary and constitutive feature of all human behavior, yet without thereby designating it as the essential and originary element of the human per se, set apart from all other kinds of activity.[86]

Weaving gesture, sound, and imitative learning into his speculations on vomiting, Darwin's notion that voluntary food rejection was rendered obsolete by verbal communication is in keeping with the broader position on language development I have just outlined. In a limited sense, then, Darwin designates the prototypical expression of disgust as one among the many potential templates for verbal communication available to the primitive ancestors of the human. As we have come to see, however, the picture of human evolution Darwin has in mind is atypical. We are not being given an Enlightenment picture of our species' progress from instinct to rationality, in which language emerges as the rational and so fallible harnessing of innate, unerring tendencies (here, to reject certain foods). Nor, however, is

Darwin's focus trained on the development of instinctive capacities for linguistic invention and grammatical or syntactic aptitude, as most efforts to understand the origins of human language would be after him and throughout the twentieth century. Instead, Darwin suggests that what language and voluntary vomiting have in common is their inherent intentionality and their functionality as mediums of social communication. In this regard, Darwin's theory of voluntary vomiting might be said to anticipate research being undertaken today into the origins of language that focus precisely on the evolution of primate capacities for intentional communication, rather than on the innateness of grammatical structures. At the forefront of this recent research, Michael Tomasello has observed the extent to which he has had to "turn the Chomskian proposal on its head, as the most fundamental aspects of human communication are seen as biological adaptations for cooperation and social interaction in general, whereas the more purely linguistic, including grammatical, dimensions of language are culturally constructed and passed along by individual linguistic communities."[87] In significant ways, Darwin's views on the early intersections of gesture, intentional behavior, emotion expression, and language are the forerunners to research like Tomasello's. Early speech may have arisen out of primitive cries, but those cries were not the expressions of magically authentic primeval instincts—to the contrary, the intentionality we ascribe to language is coeval in this case with the intentionality of primitive vomiting and other nonreflexive forms of primal communicative expression. As Sarah Winter has put it in a comparative study of Darwin and Ferdinand de Saussure, "Darwin imagined that language emerged gradually from expressions that were *already* semiotic in a biological sense."[88]

At the nexus of the linguistic and the emetic, Darwin once again refers us back to the body's inherent porosity and the unavoidable experience of the transgression of its boundaries. Whatever exits the mouth, whether it is words or regurgitated food, is recognized as social communication. This model of communication, moreover, requires that we reorient the fundamental rhetorical situation implied by the disgust reaction, so that the value of our disgust is located not in the dyadic relation between subject and object but in a more diffuse range of communal sociality. If we entertain Darwin's thesis of the early intentionality of food rejection, the rhetorical situation of disgust necessarily implies at least three parties: an eliciting disgust object, a regurgitating subject, and a person, family, or group to whom this reaction is significant.[89] Darwin thus places a strong value on the socially communicative function that the transgression of the body's boundaries can play, initially through voluntary food rejection and then through speech acts adjudicating what food is good or bad to eat. This function is best understood as a form of critical judgment, by which one person can intentionally transmit information about an object to a larger community of people; in this sense, for Darwin, while the origins of critical judgment pass through the mouth, as vomit, that vomit is most salient and significant to others.

These remarks about language allow us to see more clearly a dimension of Darwin's disgust that has played an animating part in each of the different sections of this chapter. For with the case of the regurgitating stomach no less than with the genealogical complication of instinct, Darwin's disgust has implicitly depended on thinking through the ways that the human being comes equipped with capacities for certain kinds of socially symbolic activity that are naturally embodied without being irrational, and intentional without the presumption of a sovereign faculty of consciousness.[90] Darwin's stubborn interest in the unsubstantiated onomatopoeic and interjectional theories of linguistic origins further makes explicit this interest in excavating an inherent capacity for symbolization. These even-then-benighted theories allowed him at once to ground an important evaluative function of language in the actual contours of the human body (the lips), while avoiding the temptation to attribute a natural or necessary meaning to a behavior simply for its being rooted in the body.

Darwin's disgust resides at this nexus, where symbolic activity intersects with and thus denaturalizes the natural, producing a primal scene in which the primal is the locus of alternative and obsolete modes of intentionality and volition, rather than automaticity and mechanism. Various strands of modern thought—from Ferenczi's (and Wilson's) idea of organ thinking to Tomasello's empirical work on primate communication—reflect significant continuations of these aspects of Darwin's work. But in alluding to these possible afterlives, my goal has not been to argue for the dominance of the Darwinian conception of disgust but rather to track the intellectual historical pressures that led to its obsolescence, to its being coded as itself benighted. "[Darwin's] narrative of disgust's evolution," Menninghaus writes, "has not found any followers to date; indeed, in psychology, it has been deemed hardly worth the effort of a commentary."[91] By digging in to Darwin's disgust, by charting the often obscure influences on which it drew and the no-less-bizarre doors that it opened, we have in turn been able to see that the Enlightenment conception of disgust and vomiting as shorthand for pure instinctivity was an integral component in the development of modernity's phylogenetic fantasies about the emergence of the human. Tellingly, each of the local ways in which Darwin sought to avoid participating in the theoretical isolation of the natural from the man-made, or the animal from the human, appears as a token of just how obsolete his thought is, when viewed from the broader perspective of modern intellectual history. Part of the theoretical currency and unsettling critical force of Darwin's genealogy of vomiting lies in this power to shine a light on the ways in which the discursive history of disgust has rendered certain possibilities and configurations of the human subject unthinkable.

With each of the discourses it engages, Darwin's vomit positions itself as a blow to what Bruno Latour has called the process of purification, according to which modern scientific culture came to isolate what was given and natural from what was culturally fantasied or socially constructed, so that "all the ideas of yesteryear—including those of certain pseudo-sciences—became inept or inappropriate."[92] Darwin's disgust, by contrast, cannot be explained through affiliation with either pole of the nature-culture binary; nor can it be explained away through accusations of obscurantism. This disgust is neither mystified nor techno-rational, neither wholly instinctive nor fully willed. We are left with a language of disgust that is neither disembodied nor originary, but nonetheless primeval and corporeal, a queasy verbal nausea that defies easy resolution into either noodle or stomach. If the afterlife of Darwin's statement on disgust has been a series of misreadings, misapprehensions, or simply missed opportunities for engagement—that is, if Darwin's genealogy has today come to look inept or inappropriate because of the polarizing processes that have guided each of its discursive bases into the twentieth and twenty-first centuries—then that only underscores the need for even closer examination of the resistant qualities in Darwin's work. Conceptions of disgust from Kant to the present day have again and again played a role in the very same processes that have left Darwin's vomit disfigured and partially unrecognizable from our vantage point. In pursuit of a prelapsarian past free from choice, and a rational future free from error, the interpretation of disgust keeps making the same mistakes, so that the emotion can appear genealogically static—as though disgust, and not history, were unalterable: "As a dog returneth to his vomit, so a fool returneth to his folly."[93]

# CHAPTER 4

# The Masses Are Revolting; or, The Birth of Social Theory from the Spirit of Disgust

as if the whole were one vast mill . . .
vomiting, receiving on all sides . . .

—Wordsworth, *The Prelude*

"Everything leads us to believe that early human beings were brought together by disgust and common terror," Georges Bataille proclaimed in "Attraction and Repulsion," the first of a pair of 1938 lectures delivered under the auspices of the short-lived Parisian Collège de Sociologie that he had helped to found the previous year. "The social nucleus is, in fact . . . untouchable and unspeakable"; it is "the object of a fundamental repulsion." Bataille claims in this short lecture to have uncovered a primal disgust motivating and organizing the enterprise of human sociality. "And even more," he elaborated two weeks later, in the second lecture, "I consider the act of recognizing what this heart of our existence really is to be a decisive act in human development. In other words, I believe that nothing is more important for us than that we recognize that we are bound and sworn to that which horrifies us most, that which provokes our most intense disgust." If repulsion can be deemed one of "the essential moving forces of human machinery," Bataille argues, then its recognition and perhaps even its affirmation take on a singularly important value for the sociologist or anthropologist.[1] At the broadest level, the implication is that disgust not only sits at the heart of social relations but is therefore inscribed at the heart of social science as well.

Bataille's work aspired to live up to this goal of confronting the rotten core of sociality with the tools of the social scientist. A penchant for sacred filth and defilement, an oozing drop of surrealism, a seething contempt for the hygienic abstractions of political economy, and a healthy dose of psychoanalysis on its most anthropologically excremental flights of fancy all combine to produce a visceral theory of the social in which that which we find most repulsive and most consistently devalued is installed at the center of human relations. Yet although Bataille is an idiosyncratic thinker—read his short essay "The Solar Anus" for a crash course in his idiosyncrasy—his notion that the emotion of disgust plays a primary and even originary role in the production of sociality was no outlier in the 1930s. On the contrary, the attribution of such a fundamental role to disgust played a pivotal role in the birth of modern social theory and urban sociology in the opening decades of the twentieth century. We have already seen how and why this would be true in the context of social theories influenced by the psychoanalytic tradition, like Bataille's and Elias's; in such cases, disgust figures as an emotional state closely connected with a constellation of negative mental phenomena involved in individual subject formation—such as repression, fetishistic disavowal, negation, projective identification, and so on—as well as more directly in adapting the Freudian civilizational story of humankind's collectively becoming upright. What is less predictable is that one encounters this insistence on the centrality of disgust to human sociality in the nonpsychoanalytically-inflected urban sociology and social theory of the fin de siècle and early twentieth century as well.

Georg Simmel, for instance, in his canonical 1903 essay "The Metropolis and Mental Life," posited "a slight aversion, a mutual strangeness and repulsion" as the "inner side" of his often-cited account of the "blasé attitude" of modern city dwellers as they go about their daily business of consumption and exchange (eine leise Aversion, eine gegenseitige Fremdheit und Abstoßung).[2] For Simmel, repulsion is the affective baseline that enables the coming together in exchange. As we will see, Simmel ultimately derived human sociality itself, in addition to social life in the metropolis, from this concept of a primary negative force operating beneath the veneer of interpersonal neutrality. Hence without "feelings of mutual strangeness and repulsion," he wrote in his long essay of 1908, "Conflict," "we could not imagine what form modern urban life . . . might possibly take."[3]

Even Max Weber's far drier historical analysis of the rise of the city as a form of collective dwelling organized around "the fusion of fortress and market," which is to say around politics and economy, has a slight hint of the attraction-repulsion framework that is more pronounced in sociological accounts of cities that are focused on urban subjectivity. In Weber's primarily nonsubjective account, economy and politics nevertheless resolve into consumption and defense, appetite and expulsion, which remain the anchors of the social; it is this Hobbesian tension generated by the fulfillment of basic but antithetical human needs that produces the social stasis or neutrality that Weber refers to as the "impersonality" of the city.[4] Moreover, Weber actually turns to the vocabulary of "attraction and repulsion" when writing about racial and ethnic groups in *Economy and Society*, where he suggests that repulsion in general and "ethnic repulsion" in particular play a powerful part in promoting the "monopolistic closure" of social groups to outsiders.[5] In this more anthropological register, attraction and repulsion represent the affective glue that allows people to come together in groups. However, Weber considers this affective binding a less fully rationalized principle of social formation than the principle of exchange, and so he ascribes to the force of repulsion a primitive character that is in keeping with Simmel's theorization. Weber's sober analysis of the exclusionary development that binds people together in cities and groups and Simmel's identification of the inward aversion that characterizes modern metropolitan consciousness both find a more bombastic analogue in Bataille's anthropological elevation of "disgust and common terror" to the organizing principles of social life at large. In all three cases, the apparent equilibrium of human sociality is attributed to the primary force of an attraction-repulsion.

This social-theoretical and urban-sociological focus on disgust in the early decades of the twentieth century also figures into the related body of literature on crowds and mass psychology that developed at the same historical moment. From Gustave Le Bon's 1895 *The Crowd* to William McDougall's 1920 *The Group Mind* and Freud's 1921 *Group Psychology and the Analysis of the Ego* and beyond, theories of the crowd depended on notions of regressive "primitive" psychological states and the contagion of affects and ideas that were themselves saturated with a rhetoric of disgust, and that in many ways derived from the Enlightenment aesthetic discourse explored in previous chapters. These theories of primitive psychology and of the contagiousness of allegedly subrational behavior can be traced back to late eighteenth- and nineteenth-century ideas about contamination and about the reality effects of the disgusting. Furthermore, for many theorists following in the wake of Le Bon, the crowd (or mass or mob or swarm) represented a degraded and animalistic deviation from normal social relations that, while it could be analyzed scientifically, also deserved to be met in practice with repugnance and disapprobation. In this sense, crowd psychology at once depended on a conception of disgust as a theoretical discourse and mobilized the negativity of disgust rhetorically as a means of identifying and setting apart its object in the first place. However, if we start out from the pervasive role of disgust within the general theory of sociality, then the exaggerated form of the crowd looks more like a special case of a broader social phenomenon than the luridly degraded aberration it was widely deemed to be.

Taken together, these disparate strains of sociological discourse—group or crowd psychology, urban sociology, and the general theory of human sociality—reflect the extent to which the particular aesthetic conception of disgust at issue in this book was, for a number of reasons and in a number of ways, installed at the heart of social-scientific thought over the course of the nineteenth century. More specifically, three aspects of aesthetic disgust bear directly on the emergence of modern social theory: the notion that repulsion binds people together in groups according to a principle of contagion and unwanted identification; the attribution of the status of a basic drive or primal instinct to disgust; and finally, the perception that disgust offers a kind of template or pattern for other socially significant forms of externalization and repudiation.

The first goal of this chapter is to trace a genealogy of this pervasive sociological dynamic of attraction-repulsion, as it transformed from the habitual attitude of bourgeois social observers throughout the nineteenth century to the conceptual premise of early twentieth-century theories of the underlying nature of social life. That is, I contend that the fin-de-siècle notion that attraction-repulsion sits at the core of all social relations cannot be understood in isolation from the fact that attraction-repulsion in various guises and iterations was a de facto affective posture for many of the major protosociological urban investigators of the preceding hundred years. The overall movement is thus one of conceptual incorporation and projection, whereby what was for Chadwick and Engels an articulation of their own subjective responses to particular social conditions was gradually absorbed into the theoretical definition of a generalized social scenario sitting outside or beyond any particular context or historical scene.

The main figures in this genealogy will be Engels, Marx, and Herbert Spencer, and the key concept we will track through their work is alienation, a concept that Marx in particular worked to transform decisively over the course of the century, and which relates to the aesthetic discourse of disgust in a number of complex ways. The close connection of disgust and alienation is already apparent in Simmel's diagnosis of "mutual strangeness and repulsion" as the baseline affective experience of modern life; in this formulation, the two are not merely related but almost identified with each other. In other cases, by contrast, we will see how the atavism represented by disgust complements the sense of alienation as a consequence of modernization; if disgust has been taken to represent the persistence of an unwanted and allegedly primitive mode of sociality into the modern present, alienation has, conversely, betokened the unwanted consequences of civilizational progress. There is a friction inherent in the relationship between disgust and alienation, having to do with these two not-quite-commensurable dynamics. This friction will come into sharper focus as we pursue both alienation and attraction-repulsion through three moments in the history of their relationship: Marx and Engels's early writings from the 1840s; the important shift in Marx's thinking at the close of the 1850s, which can be understood in large part as his response to the financial crisis of 1857; and Spencer's sociological writings of the 1870s and 1880s, as well as their bearing on the social theories of the turn of the century.[6]

The argument of this chapter also takes aim at a more fundamental historical transformation. More than just an important conceptual piece in the broad matrix of fin-de-siècle sociological thought, the uncritical appeal to and absorption of the discourse of disgust played a crucial role in the development of the social-scientific endeavor over the course of the long nineteenth century as an intellectual enterprise with its own distinct claims to objectivity. Indeed, for the protosociological discourse of the nineteenth century, the ersatz objectivity marshaled by disgust—whether experienced by the social analyst or diagnosed in the social body—seemed to occupy a singular territory on the border between natural-scientific and cultural-aesthetic modes of explanation. Thus in literary and cultural contexts the appeal to disgust was expected to lay claim to the authority of a natural or biological self-evidence, even while its status within the shifting terrain of Victorian medical-biological theories of instinct and the stomach remained thoroughly entangled with a cultural rhetoric of progress and the primitive. Neither purely literary nor fully scientific, then, the identification and articulation of disgust came to take on important rhetorical functions within the disaggregation of a separate domain that would not be adequately explained by either novelists or biologists. In other words, the conviction that the masses were revolting played a key role in the methodological delineation of the social domain and its particular brand of facts.

The second goal of this chapter, then, is to use the genealogy of attraction-repulsion to complicate the role that has customarily been attributed to emotion and affect in historical accounts of the rise of the social sciences. Although historians of sociology have offered diverse and in some respects competing accounts of the developments in nineteenth-century European intellectual culture that contributed to the burst of innovation around 1900, most agree that the elimination of emotional bias from sociological method was understood by its practitioners to be a crucial step toward fulfilling the scientific ambitions of the discipline.[7] Whether one stresses the positivism that animated advances in statistical analysis or the difficulty that early sociology encountered in differentiating itself from literary realism, the progressive repudiation of emotion as a solid basis for social analysis remains constant. Though individual thinkers differed substantially in the details of how they handled the question of emotion, maintaining and monitoring the fact/value distinction when dealing with social facts rather than physical ones was essential to the emergence of modern sociological thought in Britain, France, the United States, and Germany alike.

Émile Durkheim, for example, offered just such a strong repudiation of emotion when he argued in *The Rules of Sociological Method* (1895) that "feeling is an object for scientific study, not the criterion of scientific truth." Just as one's feelings toward natural phenomena ought not color or cloud scientific observation and analysis, so too, Durkheim argued, social facts must be separated from the feelings that imbue them with value so that sociological method can be properly differentiated from its objects of inquiry. Failure to disentangle fact from feeling, and object from method, Durkheim warned, would mean "the negation of all science." Moreover, Durkheim asserted that it was characteristic of his modern present that the emotional bonds people formed with the social world were necessarily stronger than those formed with natural facts, since the latter had long ago ceased to be constituted through sentimental attachments. "We enthuse over our political and religious beliefs and moral practices very differently from the way we do over the objects of the physical world." These uncritical, reflexive emotional bonds formed with the social are so potent, Durkheim writes, "they will not tolerate scientific examination. The mere fact of subjecting them . . . to cold, dry analysis is repugnant to certain minds." For Durkheim, emotion is at once a social thing that should be studied scientifically in its own right; an impediment to producing valid social-scientific knowledge; *and* the basis of a powerful resistance to removing that impediment. The overcoming of emotional attachments to social life and the overcoming of the repugnance or emotional prejudice that protects those attachments from analysis constitute methodological preconditions of a scientific sociology in which emotion and affect themselves can be studied as social phenomena that "have been shaped by history."[8]

Compared with some of his contemporaries' ideas, Durkheim's exclusion of emotion represented a polemical position. Weber, by contrast, was far less convinced that the social sciences were able to deal in scientifically empirical facts that were wholly isolated from evaluative presuppositions, since the significance of social phenomena derived in the first place from their culturally value-laden nature. Weber was also ambivalent about the form of progressive rationalization that Durkheim's scientific positivism represented. Nevertheless, Durkheim's strong stance captures something of the fin-de-siècle mood of residual Enlightenment enthusiasm over the possibility of producing a scientific knowledge of the social domain that had been freed from superstition and emotional prejudice; it is with precisely this idea of rooting out emotion in mind that Wolf Lepenies has characterized sociology's search for a method over the long nineteenth century as an "inner-disciplinary process of purification."[9] A fully disenchanted sociology, for Durkheim, represented the culmination of a type of progress that was inherent in the very notion of science. "There is no science," he writes, "which at its beginnings has not encountered similar resistances. There was a time when those feelings relating to the things of the physical world, since they also possessed a religious or moral character, opposed no less violently the establishment of the physical sciences. Thus one can believe that, rooted out from one science after another, this prejudice will finally disappear from sociology as well, its last refuge, and leave the field clear for the scientist."[10] While each different school of sociological thought negotiated the fact/value distinction in its own way, this goal of excluding subjective bias and emotional residue from the domain of social-scientific knowledge was held in common.

The role that disgust played in this process of "rooting out" emotional bias and superstition from social-scientific method cannot be explained straightforwardly in the terms of Durkheim's progressive narrative of disenchantment—although it may at first blush seem to do just that. As we will see, the genealogy of sociological attraction-repulsion hews closely to Durkheim's proposed trajectory, according to which an emotion that had been erroneously taken as a "criterion of scientific truth" by the innovative but prescientific fumblers of the mid-nineteenth century was gradually transformed into an "object for scientific study" that could be shown to "have been shaped through history" at the century's close. But this story raises more questions than it settles. For we have already seen how in the aesthetic context disgust was considered the emotion that most troubles the fact/value distinction—not because it mistakes or surreptitiously swaps value for fact, but because as a mode of evaluation it was claimed to override the underlying premise of separation that allows an object to appear as distinct from one's subjective experience of it in the first place. According to this view, an object that disgusts will never appear as anything other than a fact-value hybrid, will never be other than an *unwanted fact*. While from the perspective of Enlightenment rationality this might qualify as an irrational mode of thought, it was nevertheless the mode of thought out of which a series of fundamental sociological concepts emerged over the course of the nineteenth century, foremost among them the very idea of the modern city form itself, the rotten city with its stench clouds and its Malthusian hordes of alienated citizens. This need to be rid of the unwanted fact of the social was not merely a starting point for analysis; it was the affective logic according to which the basic objects of sociological discourse were carved out of the undifferentiated mass of social life, as well as the affective fuel motivating the engines of social-scientific disenchantment.

## Marx and Engels in the Vomiting Mill

"The very turmoil of the streets has something repulsive," Engels wrote of London in his 1845 survey, *The Condition of the Working Class in England*, "something against which human nature rebels" (Schon das Straßengewühl hat etwas Widerliches, etwas, wogegen sich die menschliche Natur empört). What follows this expression of disgust is one of the nineteenth century's most influential descriptions of urban alienation, a description of "the brutal indifference, the unfeeling isolation of each in his private interest" which culminates in Engels's indictment of "the social war, the war of each against all," and of capital, "the weapon with which this social warfare is carried on."[11] Engels's outraged excoriation signals the beginning of a complex transformation in the Victorian structure of unwanted feeling. There are two dimensions to this transformation. First, Engels's disgust has become closely and intimately entwined with the diagnosis of the apathetic self-interestedness of the urban mass. Held up as the token of a "human nature" in revolt against industrial capitalism, repulsion is specifically named as the unwanted affective response through which the alienation of the individual under the modern social system becomes recognizable and available for critique. And yet, this entanglement of excessive feeling and pathological unfeeling, of disgust and alienation, also points toward a methodological tension, characteristic of a mid-nineteenth-century moment in the development of the social sciences in which the evidence of the senses and of individual observation had begun to seem insufficient. Even in their early, subjectively oriented works, Engels and Marx made an immense effort to attribute the causes motivating social transformation to the political-economic register of capital, in which individual and affective experience cannot claim the centrality suggested by Engels's own rhetoric of disgust. Thus the method of social analysis and critique pulls Engels in two opposing directions, at once toward the burning evidence of unwanted feeling and the cold truths of inhumane structures and facts; or, put another way, the apathy pathologized in the diagnosis of alienation finds a strange reflection in the unfeelingness, the anesthesia of the emergent social-scientific method.

Within Marxist social theory, this tension is often understood as part of a decades-long shift in Marx's thought away from the early humanistic focus on the worker's alienated subjectivity in the works of the 1840s and toward the objective analysis of his or her exploitation and the extraction of surplus value in *Capital* (1867). More pointedly, this shift has been held up as an emblem of Marx's break with the bourgeois category of the individual, and his taking up the tools of scientific critique. But this alteration in the status of emotion and subjectivity was also representative of the overall development of the nascent and still-coalescing social sciences throughout the middle decades of the nineteenth century. More than just a turn away from his philosophical and humanistic roots, Marx's critique of political economy was enabled in its own right by major advances in statistical analysis by Adolphe Quetelet in France and Robert Jones, Charles Babbage, Thomas Robert Malthus, and others in the Statistical Society of London; this burgeoning field was itself developing out of an increasing sense that the subjectivity of individual perspectives rendered them incapable of accounting for changes in the social whole.[12] Indeed, the concept of the social whole or totality can be said in large part to have developed negatively, as a reaction against the affectivity, partiality, and undependability of the individual, even in contexts where the individual nevertheless remained enshrined as the primary unit of meaning. Similarly, Durkheim's own call in the 1890s to expunge affect from sociological method and to make it instead into an object of study explicitly built on Auguste Comte's midcentury positivism and Herbert Spencer's extensive racialized critiques of emotional bias as a form of "primitive" thinking. Between the 1830s and the 1870s, Paris and London were brimming over with social-scientific innovation, and the sense of progress that accompanied these developments in turn depended on furthering the Enlightenment civilizational project of excluding and overcoming unwanted emotionality.

These scientific ambitions extended as well to the protoethnographic domain of social observation and urban investigation, where subjective reporting laid claim to the status of objective fact despite its often striking resemblance to imaginative literary invention and its reliance on rhetorical appeals to its readers' emotions. Harriet Martineau, for example, argued in *Illustrations of Political Economy* that the "narrative picture" was not only the most useful but also the most rigorously systematic form for disseminating the social-scientific truths of political economy. Taking pains to distinguish such illustrations from merely didactic literary fiction, Martineau—who was also first to translate Comte's positivism into English—sought to ensure that her readers were "furnished with rich illustrations of every truth our science can furnish." Though it is difficult to grasp from a modern perspective, her point was not that narrative form is simply more engaging or better able to arouse sympathy or provoke emotional response, but that it is "the most faithful and most complete" form for representing economic truths having to do with production, consumption, and exchange.[13]

One also finds a comparable insistence on the scientific nature of narrated social observation in the far more chaotic urban surveys of Henry Mayhew, where reported speech and description of local color jockey for space on the page with wild statistical tabulations and moralizing social criticism. Despite the extraordinary literary qualities of his *Morning Chronicle* character sketches and interviews of the late 1840s, later compiled in the four-volume *London Labour and the London Poor*, Mayhew also understood his work to be further-ing the scientific spirit of the age. "I made up my mind to deal with human nature as a natural philosopher or a chemist deals with any material object," he reflected in 1850, adding that "as a man who had devoted some little of his time to physical and metaphysical science, I must say I did most heartily rejoice that it should have been left to me to apply the laws of the inductive philosophy for the first time, I believe, in the world to the abstract question of political economy."[14] Although Martineau's and Mayhew's works differ sharply in ideology and methodology, both nevertheless reflect the extent to which the scientific, rationalizing aspirations of mid-nineteenth-century social science had taken root, even in contexts where aesthetic or in any case subjective modes of presentation continued to predominate.

Caught up in this strong positivist current, disgust nonetheless played an outsized role in the formalization of sociological method in the mid-dle decades of the nineteenth century. This is true in the critical Marxist school as well as the more strictly positivist and especially Spencerian tradi-tion, though there are of course important differences between these two contexts. As I have already suggested, disgust features most prominently in Marx and Engels's midcentury writings in the slow transition from the humanistic focus on alienation in the early writings to the later objective focus on exploitation and surplus value that was best realized in *Capital*. Our discussion will focus first on Engels's survey and Marx's philosophi-cal writings, and then on the texts of the late 1850s, *A Contribution to the Critique of Political Economy* (1859) and the manuscripts of 1857–58 posthu-mously collected and published as the *Grundrisse* in particular. These lat-ter texts not only represent an important transitional moment in Marx's thinking about the nature of alienated subjectivity and estranged labor but also reflect the important impact of the Revulsion of 1857 on Marx's complex social theory. The "revulsion" (the term was used alongside *crisis* and *panic* at the time) was widely understood to have been the first truly global financial crisis, and Marx carefully tracked its impact, commenting on it in articles such as "The Bank Act of 1844 and the Monetary Crisis in England" (1857) and "The British Revulsion" (1857). Much about the status of disgust within the rapidly shifting terrain of the mid-nineteenth-century social sciences can be gleaned from thinking about the transformations in Marx's own thought as having taken shape within the larger context of this economic revulsion.

Let us return to Engels in the early 1840s. Detailing his entrance to the "colossal centralization, this heaping together of two and a half millions of human beings" called London, Engels's description represents one of the first as well as one of the most successful attempts to provide an ethnographic account of alienated life in which the immiseration of the urban population is understood as the systemic effect of capitalist economic organization on the working class.[15] In this sense it draws on but far exceeds other articulations of urban alienation in the period, such as Wordsworth's early description of the chaos and anonymity of London in *The Prelude* (1805), or the description of the metropolis Thomas Carlyle recorded in his notebooks during a visit in 1831: "How men are hurried here; how they are haunted and terrifically chased into double quick speed; so that in self-defence they *must not* stay to look at one another. . . . Each must button himself together, and take no thought (not even for *evil*) of his neighbor. There in their little cells divided by partitions of brick or board, they sit strangers, unknowing, unknown; like Passengers in some huge Ship, each within his own cabin: Alas! And the Ship is Life, and the voyage is from Eternity to Eternity!"[16] Carlyle here refers the fallen state of affairs he sees in London life to a higher existential register. The divisions between people are rooted in their way of life, which partitions each person into his or her own "cell." In only a few years, Carlyle himself would integrate this perspective with his more fully developed views on class struggle and the capitalistic form of social relations. But the significance of this social division here is first moral and spiritual, and only then economic. The social organization of the world puts the soul at risk.

With Engels, this same set of premises undergoes a decisive transformation. We see the same outsider's declared confusion amid the hubbub of city life; the same rejection of the atomization of social relations; the same sense of the rottenness and inhumanity of the modern way of life. But although the moral and affective urgency remains, the conditions are now grasped very concretely as pertaining to a state of political-economic conflict between two classes:

> After roaming the streets of the capital a day or two, making headway with difficulty through the human turmoil [*das Menschengewühl*] and the endless lines of vehicles, after visiting the slums of the metropolis, one realizes for the first time that these Londoners have been forced to sacrifice the best qualities of their human nature, to bring to pass all the marvels of civilization which crowd their city. . . . The very turmoil of the streets has something repulsive [*etwas Widerliches*], something against which human nature rebels. The hundreds of thousands of all classes and ranks crowding past each other, are they not all human beings with the same qualities and powers, and with the same interest in being happy? And have they not, in the end, to seek happiness in the same way, by the same means? And still they crowd by one another as though they had nothing in common, nothing to do with one another, and their only agreement is the tacit one, that each keep to his own side of the pavement . . . while it occurs to no man to honour another with so much as a glance. The brutal indifference, the unfeeling isolation of each in his private interest becomes the more repellent and offensive, the more these individuals are crowded together, within a limited space. And, however much one may be aware that this isolation of the individual, this narrow self-seeking is the fundamental principle of our society everywhere, it is nowhere so shamelessly barefaced, so self-conscious as just here in the crowding of the great city. The dissolution of man into monads, of which each one has a separate principle and a separate purpose, the world of atoms, is here carried out to its utmost extreme.
>
> Hence it comes, too, that the social war, the war of each against all, is here openly declared. Just as in Stirner's recent book, people regard each other only as useful objects; each exploits the other, and the end of it all is . . . that the powerful few, the capitalists, seize everything for themselves, while to the weak many, the poor, scarcely a bare existence remains.[17]

In this passage, Engels forcefully stresses both the subjective and the objectifying strains in his critique. It is written from a perspective in which the impulse to designate the individual, the self, as the locus of the effects of the social system is fused with a countervailing impulse to transcend the register of individual experience as the language of social critique. The account of

**FIGURE 21**   Like Engels's description of alienation in the London streets, the urban tumult in the foreground of Gustave Doré's "A City Thoroughfare" gradually fades into a faceless, impersonal mass in the engraving's background. From Blanchard Jerrold and Gustave Doré, *London: A Pilgrimage* (1872). Courtesy of the Special Collections Research Center, University of Chicago Library.

alienation is also the account of class war; the description of self-estrangement is pegged to the economic structure; the two are not isolable.

The disgust or repulsion that Engels explicitly describes in himself and ascribes to any observer is the fulcrum between these two registers, and through this appeal to disgust Engels lends both disapprobation and urgency to his call to arms. Engels's revulsion is the grounds for his social criticism, his revolt. But upon closer inspection, the affective reasoning of this passage is not so easy to follow. To begin with, the claim that "the very turmoil of the streets" (das Straßengewühl) causes the stomach to churn is not quite realized. In lieu of such an image of the metropolis as a bedlam of consumption, Engels describes a comparatively muted scene of flattened-out affectlessness, of the deadness, demoralization, and low-grade negativity of a mass of self-contained "monads," each lacking the positive charge requisite to come together as a collective (fig. 21). A half century before, Wordsworth, for example, had already seen in the alienated chaos of London a "huge fermenting mass of mankind," a "vast mill . . . vomiting, receiving on all sides"; Engels's far more sprawling and populous London is by contrast a depleted city, whose energetic "colossal centralization" is the flipside of the leeching and deformation of its inhabitants' productivity.

Yet if the chaos and turmoil of the streets is nothing more than the muted hum and downcast eyes of alienation, the latter is now seen to mask the deeper, more tectonic antagonism of the classes. Engels describes this antagonism in general, philosophical terms as a destructive social tendency, "the war of each against all," but his crucial innovation was to give this violence a particular socioeconomic and historical cast as the effect of capitalism, rather than of a state of nature or naturalized social scenario. Just as the turmoil of the streets is perceptible only in the neutral buzz of alienation, the violence of class antagonism transpires through the dispassionate discourse of exchange. Everything takes place between these two poles of neutrality and negativity, between the subjective blindness of alienation and the objective fact of antagonism. "Everywhere barbarous indifference, hard egotism on one hand, and nameless misery on the other, everywhere social warfare . . . and all so shameless, so openly avowed that one shrinks before the consequences of our social state as they manifest themselves here undisguised, and can only wonder that the whole crazy fabric still hangs together."[18]

Disgust, according to Engels, is the rebellion of human nature against the inhumanity of this historical state of "crude solitariness" that masks the violence of social warfare. The emotion rejects the inhuman social organization under capitalist political economy, the "discord of identical interests" that permits people to "regard each other only as useful objects," by opposing it to a collective morality grounded in a shared human nature.[19] Whereas life in the alienated city shuttles between the neutral and the negative, Engels here tacitly refers us to a full-throated wholeness or human essence that has not been drained of its vitality. Human nature is a revolt that cannot be put down or kept at bay but rather insists on repudiating the unwanted social conditions of the world. To be sure, there is nothing exceptional about Engels's invocation of disgust in the service of such a forceful moral critique of socioeconomic conditions. When Engels goes on to write of "those who have not yet sunk into the whirlpool of moral ruin which surrounds them, sinking daily deeper, losing daily more and more of their power to resist the demoralizing influence of want, filth, and evil surroundings," he very easily adopts the dominant moralizing voice of the period.[20] London as a whirlpool, as a sewer drain or toilet bowl, is a trope stretching back at least to Ben Jonson, passing through Wordsworth's "vast receptacle," on to Gissing's late novel *The Whirlpool* and beyond; without the unquestioned association of filth and immorality, the history of the nineteenth-century survey of urban conditions from Chadwick and Mayhew to Charles Booth would be unthinkable.

Engels's invocation of the disgusting nature of alienation at once borrows from and substantially departs from the Victorian rhetoric of filth and moral ruin he shares with his more conventional contemporaries. What he shares is the uncritical and implicit belief that the appeal to disgust can perform the rhetorical function of an appeal to human nature. The provocation of disgust is taken to be an indicator that the civilizational threshold has been crossed, and in that sense the emotion is cast as a primal defense of the core of the human being. Looking beyond the moralizing discourse of Victorian social observation, this is simply one of the basic roles that disgust has been called upon to play since the Enlightenment, whether in the aesthetic context, in the fin-de-siècle psychoanalytic domain, or in more recent formulations of disgust as a wisdom of the body that speaks out against the instrumentalism of modern society. And it is important to recall that there is no real basis for this hypothesis about disgust's primitive nature; it is no more primal or primary than other forms of affective response (whatever that would mean), and no wiser than other kinds of sympathetic or antipathetic connection. On the contrary, that which allows us to ascribe a primal character to our disgust is precisely its entanglement with the civilizational ideology of progress, a historically situated sense of somehow having, for better or worse, surpassed our gut reactions and left our gag reflexes behind, and not anything intrinsic to the emotion.

In any case, Engels is in good company in granting this compulsorily naturalizing role to disgust without remark. By contrast, what is unique to Engels's formulation is the implicit analogy he establishes between his own repulsion and the alienation it diagnoses. Disgust is not only the proper, the natural, and the automatic response to the ravages of industrial capitalism, but also in a sense a reflection, however distorted, of the affective state of alienated life under this new mode of social organization. If we fast-forward the fifty years to Simmel's analysis of metropolitan repulsion (*Abstoßung*), or a full century to Sartre's existentialist nausea, we see that this analogy progressively takes on the status of a commonplace. Alienation, *anomie*, *la noia*, and *angst* gradually become entangled, if not fully interchangeable, with *la nausée*, the *taedium vitae*, attraction-repulsion, primary repression, and other states of low-grade negativity that explicitly take disgust as their basis. This is not so for Engels, whose diagnosis of alienation depends on disgust without yet being fully identified with it. But the points of contact between the two states are already becoming clear. In the first place, they share a basic undesirability; they are both states to be overcome. Moreover, what needs to be overcome in each case is a certain form of deforming heteronomy, an unwanted lack of agency that produces a sense of the self as an object corrupted by unconscious or external forces. In this light, the principal distinction between disgust and alienation is that in the former, the forces shaping the individual are natural and instinctual, whereas in the latter they are political-economic and historical—the forces of social antagonism. Over time that distinction between the natural and the economic was in turn eroded. Thus what appears in Engels's writing as a conceptual opposition is, when seen instead from a historical perspective, a crucial moment of early contact, the beginning of what will prove to be a long romance between disgust and alienation.

Like Engels, Marx also at times wrote about the masses with disgust. In an infamous passage from "The Eighteenth Brumaire of Louis Bonaparte," for example, Marx describes the French lumpenproletariat—the unorganized and counterrevolutionary lower orders of society—as "the scum, offal, refuse of all classes."[21] But it is in Marx's philosophical writings on alienation (*Entäusserung*) and estrangement (*Entfremdung*) from the 1840s that we are able to see most clearly how and why these concepts would begin to inch toward the discourse of disgust in the coming decades, even as articulations of strong emotion, like Engels's, came to lose their rhetorical place in social-scientific analysis.

In these early manuscripts, Marx pursues the relationship between disgust and alienation along two lines. First, he develops the Hegelian theme that the alienation of labor is a process of externalization in which some object that is made by the human body is expropriated, seized, or renounced. In an important sense this process of producing and subsequently losing or forfeiting an object was, for Marx, already premised on other forms of embodied externalization and emission, and so bore a family resemblance to the articulation of disgust. But, especially at this stage in his intellectual career, Marx's thought also remained thoroughly enmeshed in the matrix of civilizational ideology that we have been tracking throughout this book. Thus while disgust and other kinds of bodily expulsion served as a template for his thinking about alienated labor, his excoriations of alienation under capitalism were quite often themselves articulations of disgust—articulations, that is, of the nineteenth-century structure of unwanted feeling.

Put in relatively simple terms, the central premise of Marx's reflections on alienation is that, under the capitalist social organization, workers own neither the objects they make nor their work itself. One's labor and its produce are expropriated, alienated in the legal sense of relinquished ownership. All the creative work that one has put into the object is lost as soon as the object is realized. Although Marx gestures in these early writings toward a positive conception of labor as a fundamental human activity that involves the whole person, the fundamental experience of being productive under capitalism is one of forced labor and loss: "External labor, labor in which man alienates himself," Marx writes, "is a labor of self-sacrifice, of mortification."[22]

Because labor is actually a process of extraction and expropriation, productive activity is denigrated and comes to feel alien or estranged. "The worker therefore only feels himself outside his work, and in his work feels outside himself," Marx writes. "He is at home when he is not working, and when he is working he is not at home."[23] Here and throughout, the emphasis falls squarely on feeling (fühlen): feeling oneself or feeling estranged, feeling content or discontent, the feeling of self-affirmation or of self-negation. Like Engels, Marx focuses here on the affective dimension of experience, in order to substantiate his broader critique of the capitalist system of exploitation. Although the systemic implications are acknowledged, at this stage in Marx's methodological development the injustices of living in capitalist society register first and foremost in one's affective life, in the individual degradations and deformations suffered by a whole class of people.

I stress this not in order to promote the early "humanistic Marx" over his later purportedly "scientific" works but rather to reemphasize and develop this chapter's overarching claim that, in the middle decades of the nineteenth century, we witness the progressive exclusion of affect from the social-scientific method, broadly construed. The transformation of Marx and Engels's conception of alienation represents the most illuminating and certainly the most complex case of this general trend in the period. For what Marx noticed that was lost on other social theorists of his day, such as Spencer, was that this progressive isolation of affect from the social-scientific method was itself yoked to the underlying social process of the alienation of labor and its objects from the worker. That is, Marx saw the need to renovate the methods of social analysis, not because he distrusted the categories of subjectivity and affective experience per se (as some strains of Marxist theory have held), but because he recognized that the wholesale reorganization of socioeconomic life he saw all around him was producing a no-less-radical redistribution and marginalization of the meaning and value of affective and sensory experience. The gradual methodological transformation followed what he perceived to be the actual reconfiguration of the affective life of the subject and its downgrading to a state of relative valuelessness.

I now turn to Marx's account of the feeling of estranged labor, specifically in light of our discussion of Engels's disgust. Marx's remarks on the dialectical distinction between human and animal productive activity are relevant here.[24] In addition to describing the experience of loss of ownership over both the produce of one's labor and one's labor itself, Marx argues that under the capitalist reorganization of social life, the fulfillment of one's basic animal functions comes to feel deeply personal (private, shame-laden, intimate, hedonic, guarded by strong repugnance, etc.), whereas the complex forms of productive activity that he considers more properly human (i.e., not immediately instrumental in fulfilling bodily needs) are debased, compulsory, and morally and physically degrading. "As a result, therefore, [of his alienation]," Marx writes, "man (the worker) no longer feels himself to be freely active in any but his animal functions—eating, drinking, procreating. . . . and in his human functions he no longer feels himself to be anything but an animal. What is animal becomes human and what is human becomes animal." Beneath the distinction between feeling at home and being at work, Marx points to a more fundamental transformation in the experience of the productivity of the body, whereby physiological functions come to be understood as subhuman and animal. "Certainly drinking, eating, procreating, etc., are also genuinely human functions," Marx continues, "but in the abstraction which separates them from the sphere of all other human activity and turns them into sole and ultimate ends, they are animal."[25] Eating and sex take on their status as "freely active" forms of gratification, while professionalized creativity and labor provide only for subsistence and survival.

Alienation, in Marx's account of it, is the process by which basic functions of the human body—digestion and waste production, consumption and reproduction—come to be understood as the center or core of human life, even as they are denigrated and remanded to the margins of a social world dominated by the imperatives of the commodification of labor and the accumulation of capital. This alone would be enough to establish digestion-excretion and even indigestion-vomiting as especially pertinent to the theory of alienation. For Marx is here talking about how the body's involuntary and physiological functions are made to take on the very same status as the inner but unwanted truth of human nature that Engels presumes in his articulation of repulsion at the sight of the alienated mass. This is the reason why disgust can seem like the proper or natural response to the violent artificiality of industrial capitalism. What was a dim identification of disgust with alienation in Engels becomes more pronounced in Marx. Indeed, we can push the identification even further. It is not just the case that for the alienated worker bodily functions take on a debased centrality in human life, but that the expropriation of his or her labor and its products are actually in themselves alienated bodily processes.

Marx's early reflections on alienated labor ultimately wind up in a revolted lament over the degradation of the human under capitalism that derives its force from an invocation of civilizational disgust. In the manuscript titled "The Meaning of Human Requirements Where There Is Private Property and under Socialism," Marx pushes the earlier discussion of the inversion of the human and the animal even further. On the one hand, he argues, under capitalism, human needs are reduced to the solitary need only for money. In an especially Carlylean passage, Marx describes how capital's monopolistic usurpation of the realms of desire and need leads in turn to the development of increasingly "inhuman, refined, unnatural and *imaginary* appetites. . . . Every product is a bait with which to seduce away the other's very being, his money," he writes, "every real and possible need is a weakness which will lead the fly to the gluepot." On the other hand, however, Marx goes on to insist that this "refinement of needs . . . merely resurrects itself in its opposite," which he characterizes as "a bestial barbarization, a complete, unrefined, abstract simplicity of need":

Even the need for fresh air ceases for the worker. Man returns to living in a cave, which is now, however, contaminated with the mephitic breath of plague [*Pesthauch*] given off by civilization, and which he continues to occupy only *precariously*, it being for him an alien habitation which can be withdrawn from him any day—a place from which, if he does not pay, he can be thrown out any day. . . . Light, air, etc.— the simplest *animal* cleanliness—ceases to be for man. *Dirt*—this stagnation and putrefaction of man—the *sewage* of civilization (speaking quite literally)—comes to be the *element of life* for him. Utter, *unnatural* neglect, putrefied nature, comes to be his *life-element*. None of his senses exist any longer, and not only in his human fashion, but in an *inhuman* fashion, and therefore not even an animal fashion. . . . It is not only that man has no human needs—even his *animal* needs are ceasing to exist.[26]

In this remarkable paragraph, Marx condenses all the constituent elements of the Victorian structure of unwanted feeling into a powerful critique of capitalist civilization. However, although this critique bears all the idiosyncrasies of Marx's particular blend of political insight and historical vision with Hegelian acrobatics, I want to emphasize its structured, even generic character. To return to the comparison I made in the opening pages of this book, if the *Economic and Philosophical Manuscripts* had not remained unpublished until the 1930s, one might easily imagine that William Morris was alluding to this very passage when he exclaimed that "our civilization is passing like a blight, daily growing heavier and more poisonous, over the whole face of the country."[27] Or here again is Ruskin, asserting in 1884 that "by the plague-wind, every breath of air you draw is polluted."[28] What is striking about these examples is their shared commitment to a critique of civilization that takes place entirely under the sign of civilization. Civilization has become the bad breath—the plague breath, the sewage—of the world, the token of savagery and barbarism; but the repudiation of barbarism in the language of disgust is itself the hallmark of civilizational ideology.

Marx's rhetoric in these early writings is impassioned and direct, but its forcefulness masks the extent to which he is struggling here to find a conceptual vantage point that is adequate to the argument he is making. Ultimately, the structure of unwanted feeling proved a limitation, a liability even, to the critical analysis of political economy and its structures of exploitation. For how could the appeal to disgust in the name of civilizational standards serve as the medium for a radical critique of civilization? Gradually, then, not just the focus on the subject, but the subjective emphasis of the analysis itself, faded from view, as Marx strove to detach his critical project from the matrix of nineteenth-century civilizational ideology. This detachment was never quite complete, however, and one still finds the appeal to civilization doing complex discursive work, even in Marx's later writing. In the chapter "The Working Day" in *Capital*, for instance, we are reminded that "the worker needs time in which to satisfy his intellectual and social requirements, and the extent and the number of these requirements is conditioned by the general level of civilization."[29] It is still not clear from what position exterior to civilization one is able to gauge "the general level of civilization" of the labor conditions of any given society. But here Marx is striving to fit the insights gleaned from his early bombastic analyses of alienated labor into a broader political-economic framework. Civilizational ideology becomes one of many moving parts in the complex machinery of Marx's argument, rather than the argument's source of imagined power and critical force.

If Marx's manner of argumentation became increasingly dispassionate as it developed, what became of his intuition that *"dirt*—this stagnation and putrefaction of man—the *sewage* of civilization (speaking quite literally)— comes to be the *element of life* for him"? It is not difficult to situate this assertion alongside other bursts of scatological energy from the period, such as Baudelaire's; nor is it a stretch to see it as a progenitor of the kind of psychosocial analysis of the inversion of values that Nietzsche and then Freud would undertake later in the century. But for Marx and Engels, the identification of such undesirable inversions seemed a set of novel, empirical insights into a newly arrived mode of organizing social life. What is this horrible new form of life, Marx asks, that is neither human nor animal in its relationship to filth—and how can we get rid of it? The registration of novelty through the medium of unwanted feeling carries with it the possibility of change, of a new social arrangement if not of a new humanity. We can see our way forward to Bataille's insistence that "nothing is more important for us than that we recognize that we are bound and sworn to that which horrifies us most, that which provokes our most intense disgust." Yet we also need to ask how what had been a historically situated unwanted social perception in Marx's early work took on the status of an anthropological truth across a variety of idioms and traditions of social and cultural analysis. The question concerns the changing status of feeling within the development of the social sciences: Was disgust being rooted out from the methods of social analysis, or buried within them as a fundamental premise?

## Between the Great Revulsion and the Antagonistic Tendency

If we follow Marx's thinking on alienation forward to the close of the 1850s, things look substantially different. Over the course of the intervening decade and a half, the methodological focus on the individual subject characteristic of Marx's earliest writings shifted decisively, and was largely displaced by the in-depth critical analysis of large-scale economic processes, such as production, circulation, distribution, and consumption. During the second half of the 1850s, Marx also undertook an analysis of the nature of financial crisis that reflects his increasing interest in the global dimensions of capitalism. This transition in Marx's thinking tracked what he increasingly saw as the saturation of social relationships by the material conditions of production, which meant that the former needed to be understood through the language of political economy. In this sense, the methodological shift remained anchored in the analysis of social life, even though it led away from trying to understand the effects of capitalism in terms of individual social actors and from conceptualizing particular social structures and domains as autonomous.

Two examples from the close of the 1850s exemplify this new methodological tension. During this period Marx proffered his now-famous formulation, in the preface to *A Contribution to the Critique of Political Economy* (1859), that the "mode of production of material life conditions [*bedingt*] the general process of social, political and intellectual life."[30] In this passage, Marx introduces the terms for what would become the more deterministic base-superstructure model of later Marxist analysis, in which there was little room for subject-centered concepts like alienation and estrangement. In its most reductive latter-day applications, this formulation has sometimes led to the dismissal of "social, political and intellectual life" as purely ideological domains that are derivative or secondary to the primary concerns of production. Yet for Marx this new form of analysis was crucially and explicitly derived from the initial focus on the social character of subjective life. Indeed, in terms of the development of his methodology, Marx arrived at his position regarding the economic conditioning of social life by increasing his focus on the centrality of social phenomena, rather than renouncing them. In the *Grundrisse*, for instance, he elaborates this process of conditioning, according to which social life is shaped by the specific features of the mode of production. "Hunger is hunger," he writes in an Eliasian vein, "but the hunger gratified by cooked meat eaten with a knife and fork is a different hunger from that which bolts down raw meat with the aid of hand, nail and tooth. Production thus produces not only the object but also the manner of consumption, not only objectively but subjectively. Production thus creates the consumer."[31] Conceptually, the emphasis in the work from this period falls on the organizing power of the production process; methodologically, however, the stress is reversed, and the primacy of production as a theoretical conclusion is still reached through the careful consideration and critique of social phenomena.

Perhaps most important for our discussion, Marx in this period also renovated his understanding of antagonism. Especially in the *Grundrisse*, Marx was at pains to theorize antagonism as a strictly social or socioeconomic phenomenon, rather than an interpersonal one, and to establish it as the motive force driving historical change.[32] This represents a significant transformation in his and Engels's thinking as they had articulated it in the earlier texts,

where the alienation of the subject occupied a pseudoevidentiary role in the diagnosis of social antagonism. Engels's own repulsion at the sight of the alienation of London's working class was the basis of his declaration of the social war in which capital is the principal "weapon." In that case, the analysis started from the subject's negative affect and moved outward, toward the state of generalized antagonism, ultimately coming to rest on the unjust political-economic scenario whose mechanisms explained it. Fifteen years later, however, the methodological emphasis had radically altered. "The bourgeois mode of production is the last antagonistic form of the social process of production—antagonistic not in the sense of individual antagonism, but of an antagonism that emanates from the individuals' social conditions of existence—but the productive forces developing within bourgeois society create also the material conditions for a solution of this antagonism."[33] Rather than showing how economic conditions produce antagonism on the interpersonal level, Marx here theorizes an antagonism without subjects. It "emanates from the individuals' social conditions of existence," rather than the individuals who are themselves shaped by those conditions. It is a subtle distinction, but a significant one, because it represents the extent to which the subject has been superseded in the development of a social-scientific critique of capitalism, even while certain categories of subjective experience, such as antagonism, remain necessary to Marx's understanding of the social world. It is this aspect of Marx's developing method that I now want to assess from the perspective of the broader rationalization of feeling within the emergence of social theory.

This period of transition and innovation in Marx's thought was precipitated by the Revulsion of 1857, a large-scale financial crisis that began in August, when the Ohio State Life and Trust Company collapsed. Generally understood to be the first truly global financial crisis, the revulsion saw panic spread from New York to the rest of the United States before crossing the Atlantic to Britain, then Hamburg and the rest of Europe, and finally reaching the Americas, Asia, and other parts of the world.[34] The revulsion is widely credited with prompting Marx to feverishly produce the notebooks of the *Grundrisse*, which contain significant sections theorizing the cyclical and predictable nature of economic crises. Marx also wrote a series of important articles analyzing the crisis for the *New-York Daily Tribune*, while together Marx and Engels assiduously tracked the progress of the revulsion, observing with excitement as the whole capitalist world system appeared to perch on the edge of the ultimate disaster.[35] Indeed, it was not only the economic mechanics of the crisis that captured Marx's attention, but the possibility for world revolution that such a global collapse promised to usher in, despite the lack of revolutionary political organization on the ground in Europe. The two men had eagerly anticipated the collapse, amid the rampant financial speculation of the preceding years. "When the CRASH comes, however," Engels wrote to Marx in October 1856, "there'll be a rude awakening for the English. . . . This time there'll be a *dies irae* such as has never been seen before; the whole of Europe's industry in ruins, all markets over-stocked (already nothing more is being shipped to India), all the propertied classes in the soup, complete bankruptcy of the bourgeoisie, war and profligacy to the nth degree. I, too, believe it will all come to pass in 1857, and when I heard that you were again buying furniture, I promptly declared the thing to be a dead certainty, and offered to take bets on it."[36]

Apart from Marx and Engels, the issue of the potentially calculable but putatively irrational nature of economic collapse was widely debated in the US and British public spheres, especially in the aftermath of the revulsion of the 1850s. Grappling with the fallout of yet another financial crisis, people came to question whether such events ought to be treated as permanent, recurrent features of modern life. As Charles P. Kindleberger, Ann Fabian, and others have shown, explanations for the 1857 crisis (as well as for financial crises more generally) tended to draw on either a moral-psychological rhetoric of euphoria, mania, hysteria, and panic, or on natural-meteorological metaphors of pressure, atmosphere, storm, and tornado. This rhetorical instability reflects an underlying ambivalence about the extent to which crises could be understood as natural or at least naturalizable phenomena, and about whether or not they should be regarded as having a positive or negative socioeconomic function.[37] Thus in the former case, a financial panic could be grasped as an aberration deriving from the moral fallibility and corruptibility of human agents, whereas in the latter, an economic disaster was to be understood as an unpredictable but also unavoidable and therefore to some degree necessary natural catastrophe—"as necessary as a thunderstorm in a mephitic and unhealthy tropical atmosphere," as the financial journalist David Morier Evans put it in the aftermath of the "extraordinary revulsion of 1857," adding that the collapse had "purified the commercial and financial elements, and tended to restore vitality and health."[38]

Across several articles written for the *Tribune* throughout the crisis, Marx offered a mordant critique of the mainstream understanding of the revulsion as a natural disaster or as the result of psychological miscalculation and hysteria. In general, the meteorological metaphor of the crisis as storm was meant to discourage anticipation, as Fabian argues; economic events were deemed to be as naturally unpredictable and unpreventable as changes in the weather. "After one of those storms in the commercial world which are known as 'commercial crises,'" the US philosopher Francis Bowen wrote in his *Principles of Political Economy*, "we may reasonably seek an explanation of the phenomenon, or the cause of its occurrence, though this knowledge should not enable us to tell when another or similar disturbance will happen."[39] By contrast, Marx insisted not only that he had anticipated the crisis (as many did), but that such crises could and should be dated precisely. In a *Tribune* article he argued that "it is evident that the crisis was already due in October 1855, that it was shifted off through a series of temporary convulsions, and that, consequently, its final explosion, as to the intensity of symptoms as well as the extent of contagion, will exceed every crisis ever before witnessed."[40] He reserved especially caustic remarks for Lord Palmerston's decision to temporarily suspend the 1844 Bank Charter Act, which had been written and passed with the stated intention of preventing another financial crisis but which had already been similarly suspended once before in the intervening years. What struck Marx as most corrupt and disingenuous was the posture of surprise and the rhetoric of exceptionality that characterized the response to the crisis in both the political and the financial sector. "If natural philosophers had proceeded by the same puerile method," he wrote in the aftermath of the revulsion, "the world would be taken by surprise on the reappearance even of a comet. In the attempt at laying bare the laws by which crises of the market of the world are governed, not only their periodical character, but the exact dates of that periodicity must be accounted for."[41]

While Marx believed that financial crises could be predicted, even down to the day, part of what captured his thinking about the subject was the extent to which crises appeared to have lives of their own as social rather than purely economic phenomena. This tension between social and economic registers is evident even in the journalism, where Marx puts the question to his readers quite directly: "What are the social circumstances reproducing, almost regularly, these seasons of self-delusion, of over-speculation and fictitious credit? If they were once traced out, we should arrive at a very plain alternative. Either they may be controlled by society, or they are inherent in the present system of production. In the first case, society may avert crises; in the second, so long as the system lasts, they must be borne with, like the natural changes of the seasons."[42] The immediate takeaway here is that financial crises are in fact produced by the mode of production, can therefore be anticipated precisely, and, most important, cannot be avoided or even controlled by changes in social policy. But it would nevertheless be too hasty to say that Marx here pits economy against society simply in order to show the deterministic primacy of the former over the latter. For the revulsion also

ushered Marx into a period of intense thought over the irreducible significance of the social or collective subject, which is to say, the class, in producing change within the apparently closed system of the economy. The case
of the revulsion therefore represented for Marx an important instance of an
antagonistic bourgeois subjectivity busily at work reproducing the ascendant
economic conditions of its own class. This was not, however, the individuating bourgeois subjectivity of the Victorian novel, with its asphyxiated interiority, throbbing passions, and regulatory rationality, but rather a collective
or class subjectivity that had spread by "contagion" from bank vault to bank
vault throughout the world, and was larger than any individual person or
self-interest. As Antonio Negri has put it with regard to Marx's thinking on
this topic in the *Grundrisse*, "*the antagonism between the collective worker and the
collective capitalist* . . . appears in the form of the crisis."[43]

What does it mean to assert that financial revulsion is the form taken by
social antagonism? We should be clear that, in this sense of the word, *revulsion* does not exactly mean disgust. It is on the contrary a financial term
adapted from an older medical usage that dates back at least to the early
sixteenth century. In this medical context, revulsion is the process by which
a disease localized in one part or region of the body is alleviated through
the treatment of an adjacent or in some way communicating region.[44] The
financial usage adapts the holistic emphasis on contagion and the sympathetic connections between the body's various zones, the sense of abrupt
reversal and change of direction, as well as the underlying sense of malady.
"A *Revulsion*, as applied in matters of finance," one commentator explained
in 1858, contrasting the term to "panic" and "crisis," "is not the act of throwing confusion or disturbance from one part of the system to another part,
previously healthy in its action, but the sudden and abrupt disarrangement
of one or many of the leading financial agents or interests; thus producing a jar in the machinery of an entire community or nation; and occasion-
ally, by sympathy, other countries, though far remote, are much shaken by
the revulsion, even as the wires of a charged battery may carry the electric
fluid round the globe."[45] Marx preserves this image of negative sympathetic
transmission or "contagion" in his writings on the financial revulsion, but he
upends the emphasis on mechanical chaos and "disarrangement" by arguing
that the crisis is the predictable and natural outcome of the economic system working precisely as intended. What Marx wants to demonstrate is that
the proper functioning of the system of production introduces conflict and
antagonism into the social domain, which is most emblematically manifested
through the event of the financial crisis. The goal is to show how this antagonism represents the openness and contingency of the putatively closed and

THE MASSES ARE REVOLTING     195

mechanistic economic system, as it produces a class struggle whose outcome cannot be predicted in purely economic terms, even though it is generated by economic contradictions.

If revulsion does not precisely mean disgust in this context, it is nonetheless not too far off. In the first place, we have already seen how financial crises were broadly understood by a variety of commentators to raise the problem of reconciling the irrationality of the social domain with the calculability of the economy. If the dominant discourse of the crisis tried to steer a course between the irrational, the natural, and the calculable, Marx instead saw in the principle of revulsion as contagion a way of theorizing the calculability of the irrational. At a theoretical level, then, these are the same questions about rationalization that in the other nineteenth-century contexts we have considered were addressed by the administrative emotion of disgust. But Marx's thinking through the 1857 revulsion intersects with the discourse of disgust in even more precise ways as well. It was during these years that Marx fleshed out his theory that the economic organization of society generates a fundamental negativity that is expressed through social rather than interpersonal relationships. This negativity, the social antagonism, is the baseline of sociality, over which the interpersonal life of exchange and commerce spreads its affectively neutral veneer.

Moreover, antagonism is contagious; like disgust, it follows obscure laws of contamination and sympathy as it shudders through the social body. And finally, this negativity holds the social domain together for Marx, even as it is also the antagonistic principle that breaks it up and introduces division and conflict. We need only recall the passage quoted above: "The bourgeois mode of production is the last antagonistic form of the social process of production . . . but the productive forces developing within bourgeois society create also the material conditions for a solution of this antagonism."[46] Antagonism is what presents the economic process of production as a unified and calibrated system in which panics and revulsions are chaotic blips in the otherwise smooth operation of a machine; and it is also what introduces change and contingency into that system, which take the form of crises and class conflict that have a material and social existence. In short, antagonism binds and divides. While this account may lack the visceral force of Engels's and Marx's disgust of the 1840s, it is nevertheless the dynamic formulation of antagonism closest to that which we see resurgent in the social theory of the fin de siècle, especially Simmel's. Indeed, Simmel's theorization of a fundamental social repulsion (*Abstoßung*) and later of conflict (*Streit*) drew on precisely this model of antagonism as a principle of social divisiveness and social binding. And, strikingly, Marx himself also defined this principle in several moments throughout the *Grundrisse* as a force of repulsion (*Abstoßung*). This is the aspect of Marx's social theory that I believe best accounts for the significance of disgust and attraction-repulsion in the sociological texts of the early decades of the twentieth century.[47]

Before moving on to those later developments, let us turn to a pair of related passages from the chapter on capital in the *Grundrisse*, in order to clarify how exactly Marx relied on a conception of repulsion to push his social analysis past the category of the individual subject. The first passage is an example of Marx's idea of alienation at this stage in his work. In the early manuscripts of the 1840s, alienation for Marx seemed closely connected to the disgust that Engels felt in the streets of London, insofar as Marx's ruminations on alienation seemed to point toward bodily functions as templates for the unwanted expropriation of the products of human labor. In the *Grundrisse*, however, Marx attempted to show more directly how the process of alienation relates the activity of labor to the larger social formation, rather than delving deeper into the individual subjective experience of estrangement. The new development was that Marx now understood the alienation of "living labor" to be one and the same process as the "objectification" of social relations as capital and the reproduction of the "relations of production." "The worker emerges not only not richer, but emerges rather poorer from the process that he entered. For not only has he produced the conditions of necessary labour as conditions belonging to capital; but also the value-creating possibility, the realization [*Verwertung*] which lies as a possibility within him, now likewise exists as a surplus value, surplus product, in a word as capital, as master over living labour capacity, as value endowed with its own might and will, confronting him in his abstract, objectless, purely subjective poverty."[48] Here Marx urges on the early concepts of alienation and estrangement toward their more objectified articulation in the concept of exploitation. As in the earlier formulations, alienated subjectivity is defined as a state of loss or poverty, bereft of its objects. But now it is also understood as "abstract," as opposed to what it has created, which is "realized" as concrete and objective. The object begins to take on that life of its own, which Marx will theorize most pointedly in the chapter in *Capital* on the fetishism of commodities: "The product of labour appears . . . as a mode of existence confronting living labour as independent . . . with a soul of its own."[49] The main focus in this passage, however, is less on the life of the object once it has been shipped off into the world than on the production of that life at the expense of its producer. This is an important innovation in Marx's thinking. Workers labor in order to create a social world in which they may be exploited, and in which their work has a more meaningful social existence than they do themselves.

Marx explicitly describes this series of actions, within which workers labor to produce a social world where the object of their labor becomes more socially valuable than they are, as a process of repulsion. While this was implicit in the earlier philosophical manuscripts, with their dual focus on bodily functions and externalization, Marx now goes out of his way to specify the act of self-expropriation through the language of disgust: "Living labour therefore now appears from its own standpoint as acting within the production process in such a way that, as it realizes itself in the objective conditions, it simultaneously repulses [abstößt] this realization from itself as an alien reality, and hence posits itself as insubstantial, as mere penurious labour capacity . . . belonging not to it but to others; that it posits its own reality not as a being for it, but merely as a being for others . . . or being of another opposite itself."[50] There are two things to note about this complex point. The first is that one labors to create not only an object external to oneself for some specific purpose, but an object whose value is realized objectively. In this context, counterintuitively, "objective" means as a commodity, or as surplus value; it refers to the social life of the object, specifically within the capitalist system of exchange. Within this social world, individual workers are made "insubstantial," their ability to work, "penurious." Second—and this is the key distinction for us—the object being repulsed in this formulation is not the same as the thing being created, but is rather the process by which "living labor . . . realizes itself in the objective conditions" and so "posits itself as insubstantial." It is this realization that is repulsive, spit out. Marx inherited from Hegel a whole framework in which all human productivity could be understood as objectification and externalization. But under the capitalist mode of production, this externalization is specifically like vomiting. It is involuntary and comes from within; it leaves the self drained and depleted, nauseous yet hungry; and it is antagonistic. This vomiting is antagonistic toward its object, the threatening, vomited object—in this case, not the thing being made, but its compulsory realization in the system of exchange. The realization itself is repulsive. Through their alienated work, workers spit up the social framework of their own exploitation, the world of their own "abstract, objectless, purely subjective poverty."

Repulsion, then, names not an individual affective state but rather the collective social process according to which the individual is constituted as a laboring subject and the object is produced as a commodity. One enters into the field of social relations by first repulsing them, producing them through exploitative work. Indeed, before one becomes a subject, one is first "living labor." But why does Marx retain this language of repulsion at all?[51] One might argue that repulsion—as opposed, for instance, to disgust—does not connote an affective state so much as a purely negative force or tendency, as in physics, where a "repulsive force" is understood to motivate the expansion of the universe.[52] But this merely sidesteps the problem. Marx arrived at this depersonalized understanding of repulsion as a social force through an extensive engagement with the affective discourse of disgust as it was articulated earlier on, for example in the important passage from Engels and to an extent in his own writings on alienation. Marx incorporated and transformed the negativity and the automaticity of repulsion that we saw so clearly in Engels's description of his disgust as the reflexive, knee-jerk revolt of human nature against capitalism. However, this incorporation took place within the broader context of what Negri has called "the displacement of the subject" in Marx's work, as well as within the depersonalizing tendency of social theory over the course of the nineteenth century.[53] Therefore, if repulsion seems to name an impersonal and collective force rather than an affective state, this is in large part because of the central role that the discourse of disgust and bodily expulsion played in mopping up after the subject in the development of an affectless sociological method.[54]

A final look at how repulsion works within Marx's account of capital as an economic totality will help make this point clear. Throughout the *Grundrisse*, Marx emphasizes how the capitalist model of production presents itself as a whole, as a closed system of exchange in which distinct economic processes, like circulation and distribution, production and consumption, come to appear as identical. From the standpoint of capital, "production is consumption, consumption is production," Marx argues early on, adding that if we mistakenly "regard society as one single subject . . . production and consumption appear as moments of a single act."[55] Against this reduction to the whole, Marx wants to understand the movement of capital as heterogeneous, to show how the totality actually depends on distinct functions and parts, while at the same time keeping his sights trained on the ways that even as an abstraction, the totality affects social relations in its own right. Taken as a political-economic whole, then, capitalism is a calibrated system of exchange, in which equivalence is the endpoint; taken as the sum of its pieces, it is a system of expropriation and exploitation, in which the production of surplus value is the endpoint. In the former conception, the system is closed; in the latter, it is open, and motivated by antagonism.

Once more, Marx makes use of the language of repulsion, now in order to analyze the process of differentiation that he believed at once enabled and disrupted the production of the economic totality. "The simultaneity of the process of capital in different phases of the process," Marx writes, "is possible only through its division and break-up [*Abstoßen*], each of which is capital, but capital in a different aspect."[56] Whereas in our previous example repulsion designated the process by which the subject constitutes itself through exploitation, here it names the process of differentiation, the fragmentation (translated as "break-up") of the whole into its parts, in this case the various "aspects" of capital. This is an instance of understanding repulsion precisely as an impersonal force of centrifugal negativity or socially binding antagonism, such as Simmel theorized in his account of the immanence of conflict to what he called "total group-synthesis"; for Simmel, the appearance of a repulsive force necessarily entails a larger social form, a group context within which antagonism can become socially meaningful.[57] However, just as Marx seems to be uncovering such an affectless or impersonal repulsive or differentiating force, he immediately proceeds to personify it in emphatically corporeal terms: "This change of form and matter is like that in the organic body. If one says e.g. the body reproduces itself in 24 hours, this does not mean it does it all at once, but rather the shedding [*das Abstoßen*] in one form and renewal in the other is distributed, takes place simultaneously. Incidentally, in the body the skeleton is the fixed capital; it does not renew itself in the same period of time as flesh, blood. There are different degrees of speed of consumption (self-consumption) and hence of reproduction."[58] In this remarkable extended metaphor, Marx now compares the force of repulsion that differentiates between the various aspects of capital to the sloughing off of dead skin or hair, or the production of waste or blood and the loss of bone mass—different aspects of the body's overall decay and self-regeneration. Although these various physiological processes may take place simultaneously, each transpires at its own rate, during distinct intervals, and it is this relationship of total simultaneity to differentiated decomposition within the body's constituents that actually produces the whole as an organic unit.

This strange image of capital personified as a body in perpetual decomposition and renewal captures an integral feature of what we might now call the birth of social theory from the spirit of disgust. Note that the image's organicism is not unique. Only a few years later, for example, Spencer's pseudoevolutionary sociology produced a far more fully realized vision of the "social organism," which he deemed "an aggregate constituted on the same general principle as is an individual organism."[59] The parallels between the two organic metaphors extend quite far, though there is no need to elaborate them here; my point is only that in mid-Victorian social thought, this organicism was very much in line with the methodological move beyond the frame of the subject. Marx's repulsive body is unique in that it is intended to disrupt rather than to fortify the concept of society as a unified whole. The body, which is a fundamentally open system, is decomposing, consuming on all sides; the hints of the grotesque are meant to pry open the closed, homeostatic organicism of the political-economic system, and to introduce the possibility of change and decay. Perhaps most significantly, our discussion has shown the extent to which Marx assigns to repulsion this function of introducing contingency into the economic system of relations: social relations construed as the outcome of a fundamental repulsion, society itself construed as an image of disgust. Yet the assignation of this role to disgust took place within the broader context of the Enlightenment project of overcoming affect and subjectivity in the rationalization of the social sciences, a project in which Marx participated, albeit with an ambivalence and complexity that set him apart from most contemporaries. Although this metaphor of the repulsive body is designed to resist the tug of the political-economic worldview, Marx's incorporation of the discourse of disgust makes possible a mode of disenchanted social analysis committed to distinguishing between unreliable individual affective states and objective social phenomena. It was not the disenchantment of the world that drove disgust from the observer to the observed, and from the analysis of the worker to that of capital; it was the disgust that drove the disenchantment.

## Restraining Orders

Disgust played a role in the emergence of the social sciences in two distinct but closely connected registers. First, the language of disgust was increasingly embroiled in the diagnosis of mass alienation, especially within the context of the modern city. As our readings of Marx and Engels have shown, this entanglement of repulsion and alienation shifted, over the course of the nineteenth century, from bourgeois social observers' vexed identification of their own affective state with that of the observed, to the description of a hybrid alienation-repulsion that is a social rather than subjective process. Disgust *toward* alienation gradually became disgust *as* alienation. Depending on the perspective one adopts, the basic movement was one of either projection onto the social field or incorporation into the sociological method. For example, when Elias attributes the development of the modern habitus in *The Civilizing Process* to "advance[s] in the threshold of repugnance and the frontier of shame," he incorporates the specific features of disgust into his understanding of a more pervasive field of rationalized, modern psychosocial relations.[60] Disgust has been brought into the social domain, and plays a key role in social analysis. Conversely, we might just as easily cast this incorporation as projection and say that, in the course of the development of classical social theory, the revolted attitude of the bourgeois observer was gradually attributed to the social phenomena to which it had originally arisen in response. When Simmel writes that without "feelings of mutual strangeness and repulsion . . . we could not imagine what form modern urban life . . . might possibly take," it would not be mistaken to say that he attributes what had been Engels's affective identification with the sight of industrial alienation to his own generalized definition of modern social relationships in the metropolis. In this respect, disgust has been projected onto the social domain.

The ambiguity surrounding the incorporation and projection of disgust into or onto the domain of social analysis is at bottom an iteration of the broader transformation of the distinction between fact and value that animated the social sciences in this stage of their development. Is disgust a fact of social relations, or a value attributed to them? Far from clarifying the matter, the simultaneous transition from the register of individual experience to that of non- or supra-subjective social relations makes it more difficult to answer this question. For now disgust appears to have played a signal role not only in the specification of the concept of alienation, but in the much more fundamental distinction of the social domain itself, as in Marx's later ruminations on repulsion. This, then, is the second register that has concerned our discussion. Disgust was incorporated into the methodology of social analysis within a general process of self-styled disenchantment and rationalization. It was installed at the heart of human relationality at a moment when a focus on individual experience was being subordinated to the examination of social and structural relations, and it became the bedrock of a variety of social theories at a moment when emotional bias and affective experience were being expunged from sociological method. In the remaining pages of this chapter, I examine some of the ways in which this process of aesthetic rationalization played out in the early years of the twentieth century, via the work of Herbert Spencer.

From the 1870s onward, Spencer contributed decisively to the developing field of sociology by combining Comte's positivist model of historical progress with a racialized theory of emotional restraint derived from Spencer's own research in biology and psychology. In short, Spencer thought that modern European societies could be differentiated from the so-called primitive ones they were colonizing around the globe because of the powerful self-restraint practiced by the modern individual, and alleged to be lacking in the "primitive mind." Self-restraint, Spencer argued, was what allowed Europeans to overcome their emotional impulses and attain the foresight necessary to create social structures whose development in turn led to the advanced stage achieved by modern European industrial societies. Blending pseudoscientific reflections on human evolution and psychology with the nineteenth-century arch-mythology of civilizational progress, Spencer's ideas about "primitive man" reflect the worst of the race thinking and cultural prejudice that legitimated the Victorian imperialist enterprise during the redoubled brutality of the "scramble for Africa." Thus despite Spencer's own antistatist and anti-imperialist politics, his sociological and psychological works lent purportedly scientific credence to the British imperial project. Indeed, it was with the contributions of precisely such nineteenth-century intellectual figures as Spencer in mind that Hannah Arendt wrote, in *The Origins of Totalitarianism*, that "imperialism would have necessitated the invention of racism as the only possible 'explanation' and excuse for its deeds, even if no race-thinking had ever existed in the civilized world."[61]

The very same constellation of intermingled ideas and prejudices regarding primitive emotionality and modern self-restraint was also at the heart of Spencer's search for a sociological method. The progress of Western society and the progress of sociology were intertwined with each other, in Spencer's estimation, because both depended on the overcoming of emotional and magical thinking and the deferral of affective gratification through self-restraint. Let us take two short examples. In a long section of *The Principles of Sociology* titled "The Primitive Man—Emotional," Spencer offers the view that "savage man" is at once more emotional and more antisocial than his "civilized" counterparts, positing an inverse correlation between emotionality and sociality whereby "ill-controlled passions" result in "comparatively little of the sentiment causing cohesion."[62] Society, on this account, necessitates affective self-regulation and self-discipline. Echoing this logic in a chapter in his methodological treatise *The Study of Sociology* titled "Subjective Difficulties—Emotional," Spencer exclaims, "How, then, with such perverting emotions, is it possible to take a rational view of sociological facts?"[63] In this case, sociology necessitates the overcoming of emotion, so that it can perceive its object, society. Thus emotional self-restraint is both a subjective prerequisite for an objective sociological method and a datum of sociological observation that distinguishes the racial and civilizational character of European societies and sets them above those of the so-called primitive world. To be even more precise about the circularity of this logic, the practiced methodological restraint of the sociologist takes place within the larger process of the rationalization of European society; however, this broader social development only becomes apparent through the methodological exclusion of emotion.

Spencer's self-confirming reasoning about emotional restraint can lead us back to our discussion of the role that disgust came to play in sociological discourse. At first blush, this might seem odd, since what Spencer is calling for is the disciplining or taming of emotion, not its incorporation into the core of social theory. The connection to disgust, though, lies in just this ambiguous idea of overcoming emotion. His logic here is thorny and full of gaps, but worth following. The social phenomenon Spencer refers to in the passage quoted above as "the sentiment causing cohesion" he elsewhere describes in terms of an interplay between "the attractive force" and "the repulsive force."[64] The attractive force is what binds people together in groups, whereas the repulsive force is what separates them out individually. Significantly, this repulsive force is for Spencer simply his account of unconstrained affectivity; not disgust or anger or any one particular emotion, but rather what he termed the "emotional variability" and "impulsiveness" of the "savage."[65] His idea is that people exhibiting little emotional self-restraint will be atomized rather than socialized, since the expression of strong emotions drives people apart and sets them against each other in what Spencer deemed the evolutionary struggle for existence. Conversely, the attractive force that binds groups together depends on overcoming such irrational, emotional behavior and supplanting it with rational action and foresight. But this now takes on a counterintuitive cast, since the restraint of emotionality and the muting and molding of one's affective motivations appear to be the same as the "sentiment causing cohesion." While primitive emotion is first contrasted to reason, the overcoming of emotion requisite for social cohesion is nevertheless itself a matter of sentiment. To address this confusion, Spencer makes an effort to differentiate between complex and simple emotions, reminiscent of the distinction between civilized and uncivilized emotions discussed in the opening pages of this book. But he does not pursue the distinction very far because it is ultimately rooted in racially prejudiced observations about "impulsiveness" that he simply accepts as given. The race thinking penetrates very deep into the empirical foundation of Spencer's thought, and provides the charge necessary to jumpstart the ideology of progress. Indeed, it is no overstatement to say that Spencer articulates the founding and most basic distinctions of his social theory in the language of racial prejudice, and that the fundamental instability of this race thinking inheres in the influential conception of the relation between psychic discipline and social structure that Spencer helped to make available.

This counterintuitive formulation, whereby emotion is the medium through which emotion is disciplined and overcome, would come to perform an important discursive function in the social theory of the coming decades. For it is, in a sense, a description of an unstable division that we are meant to take as characteristic of the structure of the modern habitus. Spencer, of course, did not recognize the instability of this psychosocial structure, which he understood in terms of the superiority of European culture over its impulsive neighbors. By the turn of the century, however, this understanding of the construction of a social form on the basis of emotional restraint had already begun to be widely conceived by social theorists as a disturbance or cultural pathology, rather than a civilizational feat to be celebrated; by the 1930s, Spencer's positivist cultural arrogance had been challenged substantially, as much by Weber's articulation of the toll of rationalization and of the modern individual's imprisonment in a "shell as hard as steel" as by Freud's suggestion that an entire "civilizational epoch—or possibly the whole of mankind—[might] have become neurotic."[66] The shift in attitude, of course, followed on the lurching historical events of the opening decades of the twentieth century. But the shift in the theoretical conception of the modern psychic structure and its relationship to the larger social formation had already begun in the last decades of the nineteenth century in the works of thinkers such as Durkheim and Simmel, as well as in Freud's early writings, for whom alienation rather than progress best described the overall drift of modern social life.

Through this resurgence of sociological interest in the theory of alienation at the fin de siècle, disgust comes back into the picture, now occupying the central role granted to it in the opening pages of this chapter. Even before Simmel described repulsion as the basic connective tissue of human sociality, Durkheim had already suggested in his study of suicide that the prevalence of *anomie* at the turn of the century could be understood as a widespread "hatred or disgust for what exists and . . . a similar need to destroy reality or to escape from it"; it was because this social revulsion had "reached an abnormal degree of intensity, because of some disturbance in the social organism," that it was now registering as a sociological phenomenon in French culture rather than a mere subjective aberration.[67] The decisive development, however, was not empirical but conceptual, as the theory of alienation merged with Spencer's theory of the interface between subject and social form or organism. The self-confirming developmental narrative of self-restraint and social integration now came to fasten onto disgust as precisely the strong emotion through which strong emotion could be constrained, repudiated, or overcome. Recall, for instance, Durkheim's ascription of a special function to the feelings of disgust that shield social phenomena from scientific analysis: "the mere fact of subjecting [our political and religious beliefs and moral practices] to cold, dry analysis is repugnant to certain minds." Repugnance here is meant to exemplify the benighted irrationality of emotion in general, a distortion of "cold, dry" rational judgment that demands the practiced restraint of the social scientist to be overcome. Yet this rather boilerplate dualism quickly gives way to a far more unstable conceptual structure, since what Durkheim here implies is that repugnance is a medium of restraint in its own right. It is an emotion, he suggests, whose articulation fends off the claims of reason. Hence feeling was to be resisted, but some feelings also exerted their own forms of resistance. How then could one distinguish between the disciplinary restraint of the sociologist and the affective resistance they were meant to overcome?

A keen reader of Spencer's psychological as well as sociological writings, Freud did more to develop this instability in the psychosocial conception of disgust as emotional restraint than any other thinker. As discussed in the introduction to this book, Freud ascribed a variety of interrelated functions to disgust throughout his career. Most significantly, he held the view early on that "mental forces such as shame, disgust and morality" function as "watchmen" that maintain fundamental repressions put into place in childhood—a view of disgust as one of a team of affective restraints disciplining the subject's mental life.[68] But we have already seen how Freud's first elaboration of repression was itself modeled on a conception of disgust. Within Freud's early and constantly shifting conception of the psyche, then, disgust was both a specific form of affective self-discipline that could keep repressions in place, and a template for the primal or originary repression necessary for humankind to overcome its animal nature.

Disgust thus came to be understood in turn-of-the-century social theory as a psychosocial force of restraint dividing the modern subject within a general state of alienation. This is precisely the opposite of Spencer's point about the divisive function of strong emotions and the flattening of affect in heavily differentiated modern societies. The strong emotion of disgust was now ascribed a generalized binding function—no longer in terms of a particular class or group formation, as in Marx, but in terms of social relations writ large. Note that in this context disgust is not an arbitrary emotion, but rather precisely the one to which had been ascribed all the allegedly primitive, irrational features (contagiousness, picture thinking, reflexive impulsiveness, and so on) that Spencer had sought to exclude from his account of the modern psyche. The fact that these aspects of disgust were understood in light of its more basic character as an affective medium for social exclusion made it available for the role of self-abnegation and restraint ascribed to it by Freud and, after him, Bataille, Elias, and others.

For Simmel, in particular, disgust took on an especially potent and central role in the description of the psychic life of the modern city dweller; to repeat his assertion quoted at the opening of this chapter, without "feelings of mutual strangeness and repulsion . . . we could not imagine what form modern urban life . . . might possibly take." City life, in Simmel's writings, stands as a powerful and complex counterpoint to the image of the modern lifeworld as a rationalized space of flattened affect and constrained impulses. While the calculating and instrumental nature of capitalist exchange does determine the "blasé outlook" of the urban individual, Simmel observes that "the entire inner organization of such a type of extended commercial life rests on an extremely varied structure of sympathies, indifferences and aversions of the briefest as well as the most enduring sort." Beneath the affectless veneer of capitalist relations characterized by instrumentality and indifference, Simmel saw a variegated emotional world that was moreover perpetually being excited by the fast-paced sensory bombardment of the modern metropolis. Within this affective structure, repulsion is not merely one of the constituent emotions underlying modern experience; it is the specific affective force that makes the phenomenological chaos of modern experience endurable. "We are saved by antipathy," Simmel writes, "which is the latent adumbration of actual antagonism since it brings about the sort of distanciation and deflection without which this type of life could not be carried out at all." Disgust becomes, for Simmel, the baseline affective experience of sociality, a means of asserting and defending the boundaries of the self that is a fundamental precondition of being put in relation to others. "What appears here directly as dissociation," he writes, "is in reality only one of the elementary forms of socialization."[69]

While Simmel begins by describing the centrality of "inner" repulsion specifically to urban social life as it is organized under modern industrial capitalism, he takes a universalizing turn in referring to the emotion as an "elementary form of socialization." In the former case we are given a particularized historical explanation, whereas in the latter, a formal and anthropological one. The discussion itself pivots at just this moment, and Simmel goes on to suggest that the modern disposition of "reserve with its concealed overtone of aversion . . . has roots in one of the great developmental tendencies of social life as a whole," and that repulsion is involved in provoking the seemingly improbable emergence of individuality out of narrow and clannishly defended social groups. The key for us is to observe how the switch in registers serves to embed disgust even deeper into the framework of social analysis; within the space of a page, it is elevated from its role as a prominent subjective feature of the modern urban habitus to a tectonic role as the element driving change in "the most elementary stage of social organization." *Plus ça change*: the more salient disgust appeared to be to Simmel's view of contemporary social relations, the more he sought to understand it always to have been there separating people out as individuals while binding them together in groups, already busily at work on the primal scene.

Simmel's thoughts on repulsion likely derived in part from his careful readings of Marx, although Marx's discussion of alienation in the *Grundrisse* would have been unknown to Simmel. Marx and Simmel both deemed disgust the medium through which antagonism enters into the social domain and lends its dynamism to social relationships; both were ambivalent too about whether this repulsion-alienation-antagonism is a subjective phenomenon or a nonsubjective force that is rather a prerequisite of social relations. Lurking in the backdrop of each of these complex formulations, however, is Engels's reflexive repulsion—the naturalized disgust of the bourgeois spectator in revolt against the sight of an unwanted social reality. The perceived naturalness and animality of disgust, its unwanted reflexive and instinctual character, are what make it available in the first place as a kind of drive or force within sociological discourse. Similarly, it is this putatively reflexive naturalness that allowed thinkers like Marx and Freud to see in disgust a conceptual template for other forms of unwanted externalization and repudiation, whether in the former's discussion of alienated labor or in the latter's early description of repression. In both cases, the alleged organic character of disgust provides the structure for the social-theoretical concept, just as its putative reflexivity makes it possible to see this emotion as a drive. Across a wide range of historical contexts and in a variety of theoretical idioms, the equation of disgust with a superseded, primitive, and yet nevertheless compulsory nature remains reliably constant, its allegedly primal quality consistently taken for fact.

It remains for us to ask what kind of a fact this is, and what kind of knowledge a sociology rooted in this constellation of received ideas about disgust can produce. For it is by no means clear how to sustain the idea that disgust is outside or prior to history and culture, an invariant, vestigial hangover from a primal past, when to the contrary we have seen its variable rise to the fore of social theory over the course of the nineteenth century. To chart disgust's course from Engels to Marx and on through Simmel is to follow its increasing centrality in the discourse of social analysis, whether as the affective face of a historically specific form of modern alienation or the name for the negative force binding all people together. And this rise of disgust depended on accepting the equation of the emotion with a surpassed human nature as though it were fact. What could hardly have been meant as much more than a rhetorical convention rooted in uninterrogated beliefs about the grammar of sensation in Engels came to be inscribed as a core tenet of sociological and social theoretical discourse. No matter which strain of fin-de-siècle social theory we follow, we come up against this fact of disgust, and the ersatz objectivity it has been marshaled to legitimate.

In this light, the problem of disgust begins to look like a condensation of the basic problem of determining the composition of social-scientific knowledge, as it related to the thorny distinction between objective fact and subjective value, separated, as Weber put it, only by an "often hair-thin line." The proximity of fact and value in the sociological domain gave the field its unique character and presented it with its own unique epistemological risks, Weber thought, because he believed that all social phenomena depended on the prior positing of an underlying value that allowed them to become sensible and recognizable as phenomena in the first place. "The *objective* validity of all empirical knowledge rests, and rests exclusively," he wrote, "upon the fact that the given reality is ordered according to categories that are in a specific sense *subjective*, in that they form the *precondition* of our knowledge, and that are based upon the presupposition of the *value* of that truth which empirical knowledge alone is able to give us."[70] The task that Weber sees falling to the social sciences is to explore these meeting points where the acts of valuation that are the precondition for knowledge of the social world allow for the production of knowledge itself. The function of disgust in the emergence of the modern social sciences represents precisely one of these hinges between value and fact, but one which in certain contexts has also been invested in the surreptitious disavowal of its own rootedness in subjective feeling. For with the unwanted fact of repulsion, the fact is constituted by the very strength of its empirical, sensory appeal; the fact that it is unwanted is the container that houses the fact that it is real. Hence it was through the fulfilment of the structure of unwanted feeling that nineteenth-century and fin-de-siècle sociological discourse destabilized its attempt at disciplinary self-definition.

Yet we can also see how the role of repulsion in Marx's thought as a template for social theoretical concepts seems to bridge this gap between fact and feeling in an illuminating manner that is not quite so blinkered by the pattern of disavowal that has characterized the larger discursive life of the emotion. In setting out to derive the concept of alienation from a group of insights pertaining to the inherent productivity of the body and its unwanted sensations, Marx began an important and still-unresolved inquiry into the relationship between the social and historical formation of the subject, on the one hand, and the way that the subject's understanding of affective and sensory experience forms the basis of concepts that allow for knowledge of the social world, on the other. The experience of the body has a fundamental but not a foundational meaning; it is socially conditioned and yet also sets the terms for social engagement. This is why in Marx's thought repulsion serves as a template for the analysis of alienation but does not naturalize it. Repulsion in Marx is a generative rather than a received idea, even though his most direct articulations of disgust expressed so precisely the Victorian structure of unwanted feeling. Raymond Aron wrote that, for Marx, "interpretation is born of our contact with the object—an object which is not acknowledged passively, but which is simultaneously acknowledged and denied; the denial of the object being our expression of our desire for another human reality."[71] In the 1840s, disgust seemed to Marx to offer just such a medium for the denial of the unwanted fact, which was already the articulation of a yearning for another reality, though it is possible that today, following the long train of historical transformations we have been tracking, disgust may no longer be capable of sustaining such a complex form of political aspiration.

# PART III

# *The Disenchantment of Disgust*

# CHAPTER 5

# The Age of Obscenity

> The jury asked whether it was necessary to read all of them.
> The RECORDER.—They are charged in the indictment as being the substance and essence of the case. They are revolting to a degree, but they are charged in the indictment, and must be proved.
> A juryman.—But is it necessary to read them all?
> The SOLICITOR-GENERAL.—I hope you will understand that it is at least as unpleasant to me to read them as it is to you to listen to them. If you think . . . that these passages are obscene, I will stop reading them at once.
>
> —"Central Criminal Court, October 31," *Times* (London), November 1, 1888

> It is all right if it comes out of my anus as flatus or faeces, but it mustn't come out of my mouth as words.
>
> —Susan Isaacs, "The Nature and Function of Phantasy"

"Inflamed by strong liquors" one June day in 1663, Sir Charles Sedley climbed the balcony of London's infamous Cock Tavern and "putting down [his] breeches excrementiz'd in the street: which being done, Sedley stripped himself naked, and with eloquence preached blasphemy to the people"; one bystander reports Sedley "throwing down bottles (pist in) among the people in Covent Garden," almost sparking a riot. "And that being done," Samuel Pepys observed in his diary, "he took a glass of wine and washed his prick in it and then drank it off." For producing this bombastic mix of profanity, bodily emission, and disorderly conduct, Sedley was fined, briefly incarcerated, and bound to his good behavior for a year—a punishment to which Sedley "made answer that he thought he was the first man that paid for shitting."[1] Nor was he far off the mark: as a notable early indictment for the common-law offense of "obscene libel," Sedley's case would provide a precedent for the following three centuries of Anglo-American obscenity trials and commentary. It was not until 1857, however, that this unwholesome concoction of speech and conduct became a statutory offense, when the passage of Lord Campbell's Obscene Publications Act allowed for the seizure and destruction by police of the unspecified range of texts and images—from pornographic postcards to anti-Catholic pamphlets to Zola's *La Terre*—constituting the "abominable traffic in obscenity."[2]

Victorian obscenities did not have to rain down from a balcony or be accompanied by actual human waste to be actionable, yet the language of the law never abandoned the evocative vocabulary of pollution and excrement that Sedley's explosive tirade so neatly illustrated. Thus when mid-century legislators railed against the "mass of impure publications which was poured forth on London" and hoped that "the public might be relieved of these contaminations," or when nauseated book reviewers warned of "those dark corners where the amateurs of filth find garbage to their taste," they were using their words in a manner that was not quite literal, but something more than metaphorical.[3] Intimations of an inescapable overlap between the emetic, the erotic, and the emotive sculpted the language of Victorian obscenity law in concrete ways. Long before Judge John Woolsey ruled that *Ulysses* was *not* obscene because it was emetic rather than erotic, this splanchnic rhetoric of disgust determined how the law would grant recognition to obscenities and understand them to function, providing a rubric for establishing the unwanted contaminating agency of a given text or representation.

This chapter turns to the passage of the Obscene Publications Act in order to scrutinize the historical moment when the domain of the law came into contact with and absorbed certain aspects of the aesthetics of disgust. My argument goes beyond the easily supported claim that Victorian censorship overwhelmingly made its case in the language of visceral outrage and disgust, asking instead what it means that this unwanted affect was so intimately involved in the formalization of a legal-aesthetic category whose explicit function was to police the boundaries between speech, representation, and action, as each intersected in turn with the regulatory domains of sexuality and morality. I take for granted that even before literary critics and art historians began to be called out of the classroom and down to the courthouse to testify to literary merit and aesthetic value, obscenity law was already a hybrid formation, reliant on the application of aesthetic principles in an inappropriately punitive legal context. What, this chapter asks, did the law take from the aesthetic domain, and specifically from the aesthetics of disgust, in codifying the obscene as a statutory offense? How are we to understand the transfer of aesthetic conceptions of judgment and of the relationship of feeling to discourse into what would seem to be an incompatible juridical framework?

In raising such questions, I see the passage of the Obscene Publications Act as a formal historical marker of a legal-aesthetic epoch or episteme, stretching forward to include contemporary Anglo-American free speech discourse, in which claims about the force and affective power of language and images have been increasingly neutralized by the legal requirement to attach all actions to an individual person.[4] While this legal episteme did not begin with the passage of Lord Campbell's Act in 1857, the transfer of obscenity regulation from common law to a statutory act of Parliament nevertheless betokens an important moment in the slow transfer of recognition and power away from speech and representation and toward individuals within what would later come to be theorized as the marketplace of ideas. Thus I am suggesting that what is noteworthy about this long historical moment—the age of obscenity—is not the straightforward rise of liberal tolerance in the face of reactionary state censorship, which is a historically unmoored story that nonetheless continues to inform most narratives of modern literary censorship. Rather, I want to bring into view a more tectonic shift toward the rationalization of human agency within the very fields of the law where it is granted that harm is not caused by human actions.

Whereas the preceding chapters foregrounded the reflexivity of disgust and its propensity to marshal collective agreement, the particular feature of the emotion at issue in the formation of obscenity law is its alleged animism. By animism, I mean that which motivated Kant to refer to the *obtrusiveness* of the disgusting artwork, the conviction that something about the experience of the emotion disrupts the normal allocation of minimal agency to the field of inanimate objects. Far from inert, the disgusting thing's purported agency enables it not only to overpower the aesthetic subject, to leap down one's throat, but also to pollute and contaminate other objects and subjects alike. As W. J. T. Mitchell has observed, the offensive or disgusting image in particular is often seen to "possess a kind of vital, living character that makes it capable of feeling what is done to it. It is not merely a transparent medium for communicating a message but something like an animated, living thing, an object with feelings, intentions, desires, and agency."[5] It is worth observing that this understanding of disgust's agency-granting (or agency-recognizing) power has remained a constant since its aesthetic formulation two and a half centuries ago. Angyal's influential study from the 1940s, for instance, describes how "the meaning of the disgusting object often includes some animistic notions. It is not regarded as belonging to the class of inorganic matter but as something related to life, as something 'almost living' which has the tendency or is endowed with the capacity to sneak up on, and to penetrate, the body in some unnatural way."[6] More recently, Rozin and Fallon have given this animistic reasoning a specifically Victorian pedigree, citing the laws of sympathetic magic—similarity and contagion—as outlined by James Frazer in *The Golden Bough*, and which Frazer himself had considered "to be merely two different misapplications of the association of ideas."[7] This is significant not only because it reflects the far-reaching influence of the aesthetic conception of disgust into the domains of contemporary psychology, but also because we see how that conception accrued, along the way, ideas about the so-called primitive mind that were themselves artifacts of the age of obscenity.

In what follows, we will be tracking the precise ways in which this unique revolted animism entered into and structured the discourse of obscenity law. Turning first to the debates over the Obscene Publications Act and then to the text of its first significant application in the 1868 trial *Regina v. Hicklin*, I will show how this body of law drew on precedents that dealt with physical poisoning and public nuisance. In this regard, the law came to regulate obscenities within the same legal and rational frameworks that were deployed for other forms of unwanted consumption and forced ingestion. Underlying these parallels in regulatory apparatuses, we shall see, was the implicit notion that the obscenity possessed a kind of corrupting, miasmatic agency, a notion that represents an absorption of the aesthetic conception of the obtrusiveness of the disgusting, here in its specific entanglement with sexuality.[8]

Yet in addition to this close-up and detailed account, I also advance a broader historical claim that we ought to consider the law's grappling with the question of how to represent agency in the absence of human agents as a problematic strand of the already uneven and often contradictory secularization processes at play in nineteenth-century European society.[9] While our previous chapters have examined the role that disgust played within particular areas of rationalization—for instance, in the administration of urban space, or in the emergence of the social-scientific method—the case of obscenity law shifts our focus instead to the way that revulsion participated in the so-called disenchantment of the world by subjecting its unwanted animism first to the formalism of aesthetics, where it was acknowledged but excluded, and then to the positivism of the law, where it was banished in the name of individual freedom.[10]

The concept that best captures this unexpected intersection of disgust, sexuality, law, and secularization is *pollution*. Indeed, there is no point along the word's long and varied etymological trajectory—from its premodern connotations of the state of spiritual desecration and improper sexual ejaculation to its more recent senses of moral corruption and ultimately physical and environmental contamination—that is not explicitly invoked in the birth of Victorian obscenity law.[11] The development of obscenity as a category was affected in crucial ways by the question of how a text could be treated as a form of pollution. In the final sections of the chapter, we will pursue this idea into the fin-de-siècle literary domain, examining how the pollution model of obscenity arose in the context of Henry Vizetelly's trial for the translation and publication of Zola in 1888, as well as in Hardy's writings on iconoclasm in *Jude the Obscure*.

## Aspirations

Assailed as pollution and enshrined as expression, decried as harmful misconduct and safeguarded as protected speech, the modern obscenity sprouted up in the gulf between two irreconcilable conceptions of aesthetic objects and has remained rooted there ever since. At each step of the way, outraged campaigns for censorship that cast certain texts in terms of the morally corrupting influence of poisonous ingestion and airborne contamination have been met by rationalistic arguments advocating the freedom to speak one's mind within a marketplace of ideas, while championing the autonomy of the artist and the personal liberty to judge for oneself and to consume as one pleases. Long before the feminist critiques of pornography of the 1980s or the trials of *Ulysses* and *Lady Chatterley's Lover*, the parliamentary debate over the Obscene Publications Act already epitomized this unique incompatibility in the way that opposing camps conceptualized the problem of obscenity.

The legislative process began with Lord Campbell's panicked declaration to the House of Lords that "he had learned with horror and alarm that a sale of poison more deadly than prussic acid, strychnine, or arsenic—the sale of obscene publications and indecent books—was openly going on" in Holywell Street. Campbell's call to arms, however, was met immediately with no-less-outraged protestations that his proposal would expose the fruits of high culture to the prudishness of middlebrow taste.[12] In a lengthy speech, for example, Lord Lyndhurst foretold a future when Correggio and Ovid "may be committed to the bonfire," undifferentiated from the illicit materials Lord Campbell claimed to be after. This highly classed cultural anxiety soon took the shape of the more pointed and intellectually compelling definitional critique that has since haunted the problem of obscenity: "My noble and learned Friend's aim is to put down the sale of obscene books and prints," Lyndhurst objected. "But what is the interpretation which is to be put on the word 'obscene'? I can easily conceive that two men will come to entirely different conclusions as to its meaning."[13] As the response to Lord Campbell developed, it lost some of its class resentment, and was adapted to the purposes of a liberal universalism. What for some was a matter of regulating an acknowledged public nuisance was for others an epistemological problem of proper judgment and interpretation.

Historical accounts of Lord Campbell's comparison of smut to strychnine have tended to treat it simply as rhetorical excess designed to whip up moral urgency—even at the time, the *Saturday Review* derided it as "a twaddling antithesis between physical and moral poisons"—but this misses something precise and concretizing about the choice of language.[14] Lord Campbell first broached the subject during a parliamentary session concerning the regulation of the sale of potentially dangerous chemicals (including arsenic and strychnine) by pharmacists, and the beginnings of his crusade against obscenity are to be found in the parliamentary record under the heading "Sale of Poisons and Poisonous Publications." By situating obscenities alongside other controlled substances in a Victorian pharmacopeia, the rhetoric had a structuring or homologizing effect; the point of the comparison was not only to connect obscenity rhetorically to the dangers of overdose and abuse but also to determine what class of object obscenities would be in the eyes of the law, in the first place, and therefore to establish how they would be regulated. Moreover, questions of judgment and rule raised in the discussion of administering actually dangerous chemical substances anticipated, almost uncannily, those that would come to the fore in the ensuing debate over the sale of pornography in Holywell Street. "The line which separated poisons from medicines was extremely difficult to define," the Lord Chancellor cautioned, and even after a year of consultation with the medical community there was still disagreement over which particular medicines ought to be regulated by the law.[15]

This very question of where to draw the line between poison and cure proved to be central to the critique of Lord Campbell's act. Liberal members of both parliamentary houses vehemently opposed the bill, noting that it criminalized a certain class of objects but could offer no better classification of the kind of object it was formulated to categorically forbid than the now-boilerplate "I know it when I see it." Reacting against this perceived circularity, detractors framed the matter as a problem of judging where to place the limits of the obscene. "To pass the Bill in its present shape," the MP James White cautioned the House of Commons, "it would be imperatively necessary to insert an interpretation clause, or pass a special law to first define what was obscene." Without clear interpretive guidelines, others concurred, the law threatened to encroach upon deeper, more inviolable liberties that sat at the heart of the social order: "If they armed policemen . . . to break into private houses, under the pretence of searching for obscene books and prints, they instituted an inquisition, and began the race of despotism." Following this slippery-slope logic, the basic workings of a free society depended on opposing the bill. By "establishing a system of domiciliary visits most dangerous in principle and most injurious to private individuals," the Liberal Richard Monckton Milnes argued, the law would inflict more harm than it could ever prevent. In a clever rhetorical reversal, Monckton Milnes insisted that infringements of individual privacy and freedom were far greater cause for repugnance than raunchy pamphlets. "The Bill was a clumsy method of meeting the evil, one totally alien to the habits of this country," he concluded, "certain . . . to be disgustful to the English people." "Where were they to stop?" a chorus of critics meanwhile demanded, as the debate intensified, "They could lay down no rule."[16]

Significantly, Lord Campbell did not seek to draw any lines or lay down any classificatory rules that would introduce a test or standard for obscenity. To the contrary, he had openly maintained that the determination that a cultural object was obscene was not a question of interpretation but rather a self-evident matter of sense perception. "There was a broad and marked distinction between such pictures as the noble and learned Lord had so graphically described [i.e., Correggio and other old masters]," Lord Campbell maintained, "and the abominable prints which could only disgust him, which possessed no artistic merits, and which could only be regarded with aversion by every right-minded person."[17] There was no need to search around inside a text or a picture for the qualities that would distinguish it as decent or obscene; that an obscenity existed was argued to be as readily—and as viscerally—evidenced as any other pollution or poison, and therefore to be a just cause for legal action and heightened policing. In other words, Lord Campbell sought to enshrine disgust and collective aversion within the law as testaments to the harm of obscenity, in much the same way that overdosing on a medicine would produce an obvious harm written in the unmistakable language of physiological reaction.

If these differences in position have not proved to be easily resolvable, it is because they make their evidentiary demands in what appear to be incommensurable registers. The censorship position has always been ready to cast the offending object as the perpetrator of a form of harmful action that is registered affectively, whereas the argument against censorship tends to depend instead on the interpretation of psychological categories such as motive, intention, and belief, as well as on the ascription of aesthetic or political value to the formal attributes of objects that betoken those categories. Such differences in register are not likely to be resolved through rational argument, unless the argument itself explicitly addresses the question of when and how particular kinds of experience (sensory, perceptual, affective) are able to claim the immediate and self-evidentiary social status that Lord Campbell wanted to claim for disgust. In a similar vein, Frances Ferguson has argued that the analysis of pornography's rise in the eighteenth century ought to focus on the production of its "extreme perceptibility" as a form of action that does not demand interpretation. For Ferguson, that is, pornography can be productively understood as a type of utilitarian social structure, within which the evaluation of actions depends on the perception of apparently self-evident phenomena. Just as the ranking of student performance in Bentham's proposals for the panoptic schoolroom depended on "the indubitability of the sequence of the series of numbers used to count," Ferguson observes that pornography depends as well on producing "conviction about things it would seem strange to question" and on the conversion of "visibility into perspicuousness."[18] From this perspective, Ferguson observes, "I know it when I see it" seems less like a tautological shortcoming and more like the mission statement of the pornographic enterprise.

Ferguson's discussion of pornography as a form of perspicuous action allows us to see how Lord Campbell's claim for the self-evidence of obscenity sought to arrogate to the subjective experience of disgust something akin to the axiomatic nature of numerical sequence or the perception of relative speed or magnitude. Didn't the unwanted experience of being revolted tell one something as clear, obvious, and incontrovertible as watching one person outrun another in a race or outperform one's coworkers at a task? Even if people might disagree over what counted as obscene, wasn't the unwantedness of the fact of disgust sufficient evidence of a harm that warranted regulation?

Such arguments for disgust's perspicuity and incontrovertibility have long been central to conservative attempts to use the law to regulate morality, often in transparently bigoted ways, both within and beyond the realm of obscenity law. In modern Britain, as Nussbaum observes, one of the most influential of these arguments was Lord Devlin's 1959 lecture "The Enforcement of Morals," which argued that the disgust experienced by the average and presumptively homophobic "man on the Clapham omnibus" toward homosexuality ought to be understood as an indubitable expression of public morality.[19] I am arguing that the ascription of this self-evidentiary grammatical function to revulsion enters into various social discourses, such as the law, through the project of Enlightenment aesthetics, and that in the specific instance of the law the development of the obscene offered a compelling point of entry. We might say that obscenity law sought to take from aesthetic disgust a model of perspicuity that was neither seen nor smelt, but nonetheless felt, registered affectively in some unspecified manner.

Unlike the model of urgent collective agreement that the shared sensory revulsion of the Great Stink was able to marshal, however, obscenity law also took from the aesthetics of disgust the no-less-deeply felt need for interpretive conventions that would govern how to judge a given cultural object, even in the absence of a fixed concept that could ground those conventions. That is, the calls in Parliament for an "interpretation clause" and the anxiety that "they could lay down no rule" can be seen as responses to the problem internal to aesthetics that Kant formulated as our speaking in a universal voice when we make aesthetic judgments, even though there can be no rule that compels anyone to accept those judgments, which remain rooted in feeling. As it developed to regulate the sale and circulation of texts and images, obscenity law therefore replicated the general tension within aesthetics between the endlessly debatable and the self-evidently sensorial, with one side of the censorship debate insisting on the need for formalistic interpretive clarity and the other calling for the exclusion of disgust on the grounds of its contaminating obtrusiveness. Although the stakes of the argument had to do with deciding what the role of feeling would be in the operation of law, the argument rarely engaged in an open-minded manner with this important question. Nor, it should be added, did the question of why some people felt comfortable giving their disgust a self-evidentiary function, while others did not, enter into the dialogue. It thus remains for studies such as this one to ask in what register we are to understand this difference in the ways that people have understood the political claims of their disgust.

## "Modo Absit Periculum Pollutionis"

Despite the impassioned debate, the Obscene Publications Act passed through Parliament relatively unchecked, empowering police to seize allegedly obscene materials and destroy them after trial, and remaining in effect for just over a century, until its replacement in 1959. However, it was the act's first major interpretation in the 1868 trial *Regina v. Hicklin* that not only sought to cement the conceptual connection between obscenity and public nuisance but also had the most enduring effect on Anglo-American obscenity law. The case is principally remembered for yielding the "Hicklin Test," the first written standard for judging obscenity, which formed part of Chief

Justice Lord Alexander Cockburn's opinion: "And I think the test of obscenity is this, whether the tendency of the matter charged as obscenity is to deprave and corrupt those whose minds are open to such immoral influences, and into whose hands a publication of this sort may fall."[20] Generations of critics have assailed Cockburn's distressingly circular standards for measuring corruption and depravity, even as the brief dictum exerted an outsized influence on nearly all obscenity proceedings in Britain and the United States in the first half of the twentieth century. (When the philosopher Bernard Williams was tasked with leading the 1977 Commission on Obscenity and Film Censorship, it was because of "this famous test—the deprave and corrupt test," he averred, "that the law, in short, is a mess."[21]) However, while the trial's afterlife has revolved around this interpretive touchstone, Cockburn—like Lord Campbell before him—was in fact largely unconcerned with providing a rule for determining obscenity, as perhaps ought to have been obvious from the brevity of the passage in question. Instead, the ruling focused on the way that circulation of an obscenity as a form of pollution disrupted the relationship between intention and motive, which had been the central problem the case presented.[22]

A brief review of the case and its convoluted trajectory is illuminating. Henry Scott, a Wolverhampton metal broker, was arrested and prosecuted under the Obscene Publications Act for distributing copies of an anti-Catholic pamphlet, *The Confessional Unmasked: Showing the Depravity of the Romish Priesthood, the Iniquity of the Confessional, and the Questions put to Females in Confession*, which were seized in his house. Scott was neither the author nor the publisher of the pamphlet, which had already been circulating for some time; he had purchased the text from the Protestant Electoral Union, a group, of which he was a member, targeting "teachings and practices which are un-English, immoral, and blasphemous," according to the pamphlet's caustic introductory essay.[23] Scott was convicted under the act by the local justices of Wolverhampton (among them Benjamin Hicklin), but the ruling was overturned on appeal, where it was found that the circulation of the text was justified by Scott's moral intentions of exposing and unmasking rather than promoting obscenity. However, the case was then referred to the Queen's Bench, which was asked to review the new ruling; it was at this last stage of the trial that the appeal was overturned and Hicklin's original decision was upheld, with Cockburn issuing the opinion that the obscenity of the text subsumed Scott's intentions, overriding the condemnatory frame he and the pamphlet both sought to put around the illicit material contained within. "If the work be of an obscene character, it may be questioned whether intention has anything to do with the matter," Cockburn argued. "But, if intention is necessary, it must be inferred that the appellant intended the natural consequences of his act."[24]

I will return to this question of intention momentarily, but the pamphlet itself also merits a closer look than previous scholarship has afforded it. Sandwiched between the introduction and a scathing conclusion, which sought to contextualize the materials presented, *The Confessional Unmasked* consisted of excerpts, printed in both Latin and English, from ecclesiastical texts offering different judgments regarding whether and to what degree certain behaviors were sinful, and how such behaviors should be addressed by the priest in confession. While much of the pamphlet dealt with relatively tame questions such as when it is appropriate for a priest to lie, or whether the priest can be said to "know" what he has heard in the confessional (or if, properly speaking, only God knows), the material alleged to be obscene concerned whether specific sex acts, like anal and oral sex, constituted mortal sins under particular circumstances. For example:

> *Quaeritur I. An peccet mortaliter vir inchoando copulam in vase praepostero, ut postea in vase debito, eam consummet. . . .*
>
> It is asked, 1st, does a man sin mortally by commencing the act of copulation in the hinder vessel, that he may afterwards finish it in the proper vessel?[25]

I wish to draw attention to two aspects of this text and the bizarre mise-en-abyme in which it found itself. First, the ecclesiastical texts raised questions about sin that were not so distant from the questions of obscenity *The Confessional Unmasked* raised in excerpting them. The source text's purpose, like the act under which the pamphlet was seized and destroyed, was to police sexual conduct by making ever-sharper distinctions between what was moral and immoral, and by regulating public and private conduct. It was in this sense a kind of Catholic obscenity test avant la lettre, designed to root out and prohibit sinful sexual behaviors. If the pamphlet's quoted contents offended against Victorian moralism, it was not because there was any substantive disagreement about, for example, the inappropriateness of female orgasm to the Christian procreative mission (the subject of a subsequent question), but presumably because according to prevailing sensibility such sexual questions ought not to be raised, either in public or in the religious context, where they were likely to augment temptation. Part of what we are witnessing with *Regina v. Hicklin* is the rationalizing transfer of the management of sexuality away from the already legalistic sphere of Church doctrine to the juridical domain, in more or less the same way that Foucault described this migration into the psychiatric and sexological domains; the blasphemy that the Protestant Electoral Union sought to combat in the shape of litigious Catholicism was absorbed by the relative secularism offered by the obscene.[26]

Second, this moment of rationalization depended in complex ways on the partial disenchantment of the notion of pollution, a concept that had played an essential role in the material reproduced in *The Confessional Unmasked*. All the purportedly obscene passages excerpted concern what kinds of sex acts are acceptable between married couples *"modo absit periculum pollutionis,"* that is, "provided there be no danger of pollution" (which is to say, ejaculation not understood to be directly in the service of procreation). Indeed, whole passages are given over entirely to remarkably detailed deliberation about this topic,

> for instance, if it be done from behind, or when the parties are on their sides, or standing, or sitting, or when the husband lies underneath. This method of doing it is a *mortal sin*, if there should therefrom arise to either party a danger of pollution, or of losing the seed, a thing which often happens[27] when the act is performed standing, or sitting, or the husband lying underneath; but if that danger be sufficiently guarded against, it is not, in the common opinion of Divines, a mortal sin; yet it is one of the weightier sort of venial sins.[28]

This preoccupation with preventing the pollutant spillage of any sexual fluids has a long history going back even before Aquinas, whose excursus on the so-called nocturnal pollution in the *Summa Theologica* was a touchstone for the authors reproduced in the pamphlet. In the Christian tradition, sexuality was the locus classicus for this form of nonagential pollution because it represented the primeval disobedience of the flesh, an unruliness of which the wet dream was really only a particularly concise example. What interests us here is the way in which pollution offers a flexible model for conceiving of moral harm that is not fully attached to human agency. Even in the contrived sexual scenarios explored in the pamphlet, pollution is able to split the difference between motive and intent, such that the consequence of an action either overrides or retroactively comes to stand for the intention of an agent, however unwitting.

At the same time, this aspect of pollution also allows it to raise important questions about the spheres or publics within which the meaning of an action is recognized. As Mary Douglas observed, one of the primary structural functions of pollution is to indicate, through the registration of disorder, the

describe the public space into which Scott distributed his pamphlets. Henceforth, an obscenity functioned like a miasmatic disease in a crowded place, infecting children, renters, workers, bystanders, idlers, horses. You could be carrying it to the dumpster to dispose of it forever, but there was nevertheless still a legal responsibility for producing the public pollution along the way. Likewise, in a second case the justices drew upon, *Rex v. Dixon*, Justice Colin Blackburn derived the conception of unintended harm from the precedent of a baker who unwittingly poisoned a group of children with "bread that was unwholesome and deleterious": "although it was not shewn or suggested that he intended to make the children suffer, yet Lord Ellenborough held that . . . an indictment could be sustained, as he must be taken to intend the natural consequences of his act."[34] Like spoiled or carelessly prepared food, obscenities act automatically once they have been consumed, regardless of the intentions or foreknowledge of the people who distribute them; and like airborne miasmas, obscenities impose their unwanted consumption, contaminating obtrusively, corrupting indiscriminately, rendering insignificant the wills and aspirations of those with whom they come into contact in the context of a labile and vulnerable public sphere.

The adaptation of the theological conception of pollution to the rational proceduralism of the law represented a form of "enchantment enacted in the idiom of calculability," to borrow an apt phrase from Peter Coviello's illuminating discussion of nineteenth-century secularization.[35] The emergence of this pollutant conception of obscenity in *Regina v. Hicklin* would not be rendered more coherent according to the rational standards of the law by inserting an "interpretation clause" that helped to adjudicate between art or literature, on the one hand, and pornography or obscenity, on the other, though with few notable exceptions this interpretive problem has anchored nearly all objections to proposals for obscenity censorship. Yet rather than a lack of definitional clarity about the nature of obscenities, what we have seen so far is a set of rigorously articulated convictions about the precise ways in which they function and in which the harms they cause are registered, and about the causal register in which they circulate and the manner in which the law can in turn be harnessed to regulate them. There is an immense fracture in the psychosocial dynamics of the obscenity debate, and depending on which side of this gulf one stands, obscenity resembles a wildly different problem: what appears as animistic pollution absorbed into the law through the secularizing process of aesthetic rationalization from one cliff looks like the suppression of what ought to be protected speech and commerce from the other. From the liberal-aesthetic side, obscenity censorship represents an abrogation of personal liberties in the name of sexual prudishness, whereas from the side of the censors, the object represents a threatening assault on social space.

In order to understand the significance of obscenity in modern Anglo-American culture, both sides of the debate need to be grasped as working toward the same end of rationalizing and neutralizing the way that agency is distributed in the public sphere and afforded recognition by the institutions of the law. On the one hand then, at the intersection of an increasingly liberalized legal domain and a public sphere understood to be more autonomous from the state than from the market, the very push to produce a specifically statutory censorship law already represents the most significant step toward the dissolution of the pollution model that it sought to enshrine in the law. This is neither to say that the drive toward statutory censorship intended its own unraveling nor to impute a coherence of motivation to that drive that simply did not exist. Yet the fact is that, however unintended, the consequence of bringing the pollution model to the doorstep of the law, where it would be demanded that its internal mechanics conform to the formal rules and requirements of legalistic argumentation, was to render illegible the agency of the obscenity along with the claim for disgust's affective power to register sexual offense. Obscenity only begins to come into focus as a concept at this moment, as the effect of its simultaneous incompatibility with and embedding within the rationalizing drift of the law.

On the other hand, it is crucial that we see the liberal critique of censorship for its abrogation of individual rights of expression and consumption as in some sense fulfilling the need expressed by proponents of censorship to be rid of pollution. Paradoxically, this has come about because the liberal critique of censorship within the law has never openly confronted the pollution model—indeed, has rarely even recognized its persistence within the putatively rational domain of the law. Instead, critiques of obscenity censorship have been driven by avoidance and the disavowal of the need for this confrontation. Texts are not supposed to override our intentions as readers; aesthetic objects are not meant to be so autonomous that they threaten our liberty as subjects; even to acknowledge such power through legal prohibition is to cede too much rational ground. What has resembled the progressive weakening of repressive attitudes toward sex and the enlightened defense of free expression has also culminated in the abolition of a supererogatory obscene agency within the public sphere. The unassailable value that critics of censorship ascribe to works of art comes freighted with a neutralizing foreclosure of those same words' and objects' autonomy and power. In protecting authors, the law has deauthorized the text; in defending the artist, the work is defanged. In this regard, the price of being able to say what one likes and consume as one pleases—of being a subject—has been the death of the object.

## "But Is It Necessary to Read Them All?"

The year 1857 saw the passage of the Obscene Publications Act as well as, in Paris, the tail end of Flaubert's trial for *Madame Bovary* and the swift, day-long prosecution of Baudelaire's *Fleurs du mal*, but British proponents of censorship would have to wait three decades before a literary text would be successfully prosecuted under the act, when the recently founded National Vigilance Association was able to convince the government to indict Henry Vizetelly for the publication of his translations of Zola's novels.[36] The two trials that ensued form an important landmark in the history of obscenity law for a number of reasons, not least among them that they reflect the Victorian state's relative lack of concern with bringing charges against art-works and literary texts without outside instigation, even as it developed new techniques for policing sexuality, and even as nonstate actors fought to censor literary publications through other means. Thus while Annie Besant and Charles Bradlaugh had been tried, convicted, and jailed under Lord Campbell's act in 1877 for publishing a book on birth control, and while works like Algernon Charles Swinburne's 1866 *Poems and Ballads* and George Moore's 1883 *A Modern Lover* had invited outraged allegations of obscenity and prurience, no novels or poetry had been prosecuted before Vizetelly's 1888 publication of *La Terre*—including the inexpensive translations of Zola's oeuvre that Vizetelly himself had been selling by the thousands since the 1884 translation of *Nana*.

The Vizetelly trials were in many ways the prototype for the twentieth-century literary obscenity proceeding. Unlike many of his more famously vindicated heirs, however, Vizetelly was unsuccessful in his defense, and he was forced to expurgate some of the novels, was ultimately imprisoned after a second trial, and died soon after his release. What was prototypical about the trials was the way that they modeled a split between a critique of censorship offered in the name of an artistic expression that needed to be able to inspire repulsion, on one side, and a carefully choreographed outpouring of revolted outrage, on the other, but made little effort to try to bridge or comprehend that split. Both sides made arguments based on the centrality of disgust, that is, but it was as though they were talking about different emotions.

Making reference to Cockburn's definition of obscenity from *Regina v. Hicklin*, the prosecutor in the trial argued that "he did not believe there was ever collected between the covers of a book so much bestial obscenity as was found in the pages of [*La Terre*]," and that "there was not a passage which contained any literary genius or the expression of any elevated thought." To prove his case, he simply began to read aloud from the novel's more salacious passages, whereupon the jurors began to cry out in disgust:

> The jury asked whether it was necessary to read all of them.
>
> The RECORDER.—They are charged in the indictment as being the substance and essence of the case. They are revolting to a degree, but they are charged in the indictment, and must be proved.
>
> A juryman.—But is it necessary to read them all?
>
> The RECORDER.—The Solicitor-General will exercise his discretion.
>
> The SOLICITOR-GENERAL.—I hope you will understand that it is at least as unpleasant to me to read them as it is to you to listen to them. If you think . . . that these passages are obscene, I will stop reading them at once.

The prosecution relied on the self-evidence of disgust in order to obviate the need to make an evaluative interpretation of the work's literary merit or obscenity; the fact that it caused jurors to cry out in revolt was deemed sufficient in itself, in much the same way that Lord Campbell had argued it should three decades earlier. In the face of this compelling evidence of the senses, Vizetelly's counsel caved and convinced the publisher to plead guilty, averring that "there was no doubt that the work which formed the subject matter of the indictment contained passages which the jury had intimated were very disgusting and unpleasant even in the discharge of a public duty to have to listen to. He would remind his Lordship that these works were works of a great French author." ("A voluminous French author," the prosecution corrected. "A popular French author," the Recorder compromised. "Of an author who ranks high among the literary men of France," the defense conceded.) At which point the defense acknowledged the novel's obscenity, and Vizetelly offered to expurgate his Zola catalog and republish at his own expense.[37]

Vizetelly, for his part, had anticipated the argument over disgust, and printed up a pamphlet in which he insisted that the great works of the literary canon already "contain[ed] passages far more objectionable than any that can be picked out from the Zola translations issued by me," and included dozens of excerpts from classic literary texts that he thought would make clear this point.[38] Moreover, Vizetelly had already published in 1884 a preface to *L'Assommoir* by the Italian author Edmondo de Amicis arguing that disgust was the proper response to reading Zola but that "you must conquer the first feeling of repugnance; then, whatever may be the final judgment pronounced upon the writer, you are glad to have read his works, and you arrive at the conclusion that you ought to have read them . . . even if it bring with it an odour not altogether agreeable." De Amicis opens his essay by dramatizing this overcoming of disgust with an anecdote about watching a man reading a novel in a railway car:

> Suddenly, whilst I was trying to discover the title, he exclaimed "Oh! this is disgusting!" and put the volume in his valise in the most contemptuous manner. He remained for some moments lost in thought, then re-opened the valise, took up the book again, and began reading. He might have finished a couple of pages, when he suddenly burst out into a hearty laugh, and turning to his companion, said, "Ah! my dear friend, here is the most marvelous description of a wedding dinner!" Then he resumed his reading, showing plainly that he was enjoying it intensely. The book was the "Assommoir."[39]

Like Vizetelly's later defense, de Amicis's account of the affective experience of reading rehashes much of the discussion earlier in this book of the dynamic interplay between realism and repulsion: here, the initial shock of disgust is said to prompt a contemplation that not only is replaced by enjoyment but actually works to augment it. Disgust is in this sense thrown under the bus, subordinated to the more canonical aesthetic experiences of reflection and pleasure. Yet while such accounts tend to minimize the disruptive obtrusiveness of disgust recognized by aesthetics, they also betray a heightened sensitivity and attentiveness to the strong demands that the emotion makes upon the subject. Of all the potent emotions that reading Zola might awaken in a reader, disgust alone was felt to need preemptive framing in this way. It was less that readers needed to be forewarned about whatever they might find in the text, and more an anxiety that they needed to be trained in advance to understand their own affective experience of revulsion in new minimizing ways that ran counter to their emotional common sense. Undergirding this fin-de-siècle argument against literary censorship, then, one finds a complex normative demand concerning how people should recognize and comprehend their experience of their own emotions—disgust in particular—a demand whose poorly understood relationship to the ideal of free expression has continued to cause confusion in debates on the subject.[40]

Nussbaum's position on obscenity law represents the strongest and most sophisticated version of this normative claim about disgust, and I want to use it as a bridge back to our discussion of secularism and obscenity. To summarize, Nussbaum argues that the important social issues raised in thinking about pornography and obscenity have to do with harm, inequality, misogyny, and the representation of sexual subordination—issues that are not, she insists, aided by the appeal to disgust. Nussbaum sees the censorship of literary texts like *Ulysses* or *Lady Chatterley's Lover* for their alleged obscenity as an expression of a misogynistic society's deep-seated "loathing of its own animality" projected outward, which is the essence of what she argues is performed by the articulation of disgust. In such cases of literary obscenity, Nussbaum argues, there is no real offense to speak of enacted by the text, only the censor's misogyny dressed up as prudish disgust. Disgust, on this account, "does not adequately register the thought that a harm has occurred," but only confuses the matter by promoting subrational and superstitious modes of thinking as though they had the force of authentic reason.[41] Thus there is a powerful sense in which obscenity, for Nussbaum, simply does not hold together as a coherent legal-aesthetic category, because it is anchored in the provocation of disgust.

At the same time that she dismisses literary obscenity, Nussbaum takes seriously Catharine MacKinnon's and Andrea Dworkin's arguments from the 1980s and 1990s that pornography can constitute a kind of misogynistic discriminatory harm, against which women ought to have legal recourse. Here too, Nussbaum finds that disgust fails to help the matter. "We don't vomit at subordination and inequality, we get mad," she writes. "In short, disgust seems not quite the relevant emotion. It does not respond to harms that are alleged and well supported by the evidence." Just as Nussbaum argues that disgust registers no harm in cases of literary obscenity, she also asserts that in cases of pornographic representation, where there may be misogynistic discrimination that ought to be addressed by the law, the articulation of disgust only serves to distract from that harm. "Its focus on contamination and pollution appears inadequate and irrelevant to the salient issues of harm that typically confront us in cases involving sexist obscenity," she observes, adding that "its strong link to traditional misogyny makes it a slippery and double-edged way of (apparently) expressing feminist sentiments."[42]

Nussbaum offers compelling guidelines for legal policy, but the normative dimensions of her argument need to be looked at more carefully. She provides more than a simple and straightforward rationale for disgust's disqualification as a basis for legal judgment. Rather, she offers a prescriptive grammar of emotional experience, rooted firmly in a nineteenth-century Millian liberalism, that seeks to represent certain emotional reactions as appropriate ("relevant") and others as inappropriate ("inadequate and irrelevant") within a national context in which equality is guaranteed but not evenly distributed. "To violations of the equality of a fellow citizen," she writes in an Aristotelian vein, "the appropriate response is anger, not disgust." In Nussbaum's view, disgust is an inappropriate response first because it is itself a hierarchizing emotion which enacts subordination and therefore cannot be put into the service of promoting equality, and second, because it is irrational and super-stitious and therefore incompatible with modern rational operations such as the law. In this latter respect, especially, disgust has a kind of disqualifying function; you can (and almost certainly will) experience it, but relying on that experience to some degree invalidates your claim of access to the mod-ern social institutions of "advanced liberal democracies," whose standards for rationality disgust's pollution thinking fails to meet.[43]

There is a tacit historicism animating Nussbaum's argument that con-nects it back to the argument about how to read Zola properly. After the pub-lication of On Liberty in 1859 laid out a rational political framework formally conceptualizing social harm in utilitarian terms, she implies, the member-ship requirements of liberal society began to shift, slowly, and to place new demands on how people relate to the publicity of their emotions. Thus what Vizetelly and de Amicis intuitively argued about Victorian prudishness was not far off from the normative vision Nussbaum articulates with precision and clarity in her liberal-utilitarian idiom: that the harms that disgust refers to are ersatz, discounted harms, and reflect a mode of primitive thinking that is supposed to be increasingly unacceptable and disqualified under the new regime of "advanced liberal democracy," and so must be overcome. As I have argued throughout this book, however, because it seeks to reduce all motivation to the stark terms of pleasure seeking and pain avoidance, utilitarianism fails to offer a convincing account of how the exclusion of the irrationality of disgust can be distinguished from the exclusions articulated by disgust. The unacceptability of disgust is a recursive conceptual problem that has ensnared theorists of the emotion and of social harm more gener-ally at least since the late eighteenth century. Even Nussbaum's otherwise incisive analysis of the emotion stumbles over precisely this recursive feature of the exclusion of disgust. "While the law may rightly admit the relevance of indignation as a moral response appropriate to good citizens and based upon reasons that can be publicly shared," she asserts with repugnance, "it would do well to cast disgust onto the garbage heap where it would like to cast so many of us."[44]

Nussbaum's call for the invalidation of disgust as grounds for legal action also misses out on the scale of disgust's historical productivity. Through-out the nineteenth century, law, social science, urban planning, literature, biological and physiological research, and imperial management were all deeply enmeshed with the putatively irrational motivation of disgust; even if such irrationality looks like a social pathology or superstition, the sheer scope of its historical reach ought to suggest that it will not and likely cannot be argued away rationalistically within a utilitarian framework that seeks to invalidate it as a motive for socially recognizable action. We continue to dwell inside these domains and institutions, to shape our values according to pressures and contours that were established in part by the unstable preeminence of disgust's productive function.

One of the lessons that we can take from obscenity law, then, is that it represents yet another contested battleground in which proponents of liberal modernity sought to contribute to the production of the new secular habitus of emotional restraint that we encountered in the previous chapter in Spencer's and Durkheim's problematic accounts of the birth of social science. For Nussbaum the connection of obscenity's irrationality to secularism is explicit. "Even if some citizens in a liberal society continue to believe that sex is disgusting," she writes, "the presence of sexually explicit materials in society is no more harmful to them than the presence of texts defending a religion different from their own. They can simply avoid those materials."[45] Being disgusted and being outraged by conflicting religious views are thus rendered analogous in the modernizing structure, where the social world is imagined to be capacious enough to solve the problem of pollution. But this position rather flagrantly oversimplifies the thorny intersection where religious and cultural difference collides with the politics and regulation of representations. And it also downplays the complexity of what it would mean to change one's relationship either to one's affective experience or to one's religious beliefs, as though one could simply choose or decide to attach a different set of propositional values to one's disgust (even while it is deemed beyond the pale of rationality). Against this reduction of habitus to bad habit, I am arguing that what is at stake in the age of obscenity is not so much a matter of conflicting viewpoints as it is a more tectonic coordination between relational modes pertaining to different regimes of representation.[46]

This point is thrown into even starker relief when one considers the extent to which calls to censor Vizetelly's translations of Zola invoked Britain's imperial status as a means of exploiting racialized civilizational anxieties, as Deana Heath has discussed in detail. For instance, after railing against Vizetelly's immorality in an extensive speech on "corrupt literature" in the House of Commons on May 8, 1888, the MP Samuel Smith went on to exclaim that "in India, [I] was surprised to find on all the bookstalls an unlimited supply of French novels . . . [I] was told that the worst class of French novels were brought in tens of thousands, and were regarded as examples of European civilization." As Heath aptly puts it, Smith argued that in the case of Vizetelly's Zola, "the act of translation from French to English therefore served not only to 'pollute' and transform English—and to demonstrate the permeability and corruptibility of 'Englishness'—but to undermine the very role of English and Englishness in 'civilizing' Britain's colonial subjects."[47] In this context, we see how the question of disenchanting disgust, of overcoming and subduing it, and of transforming one's whole relationship to it, was far more thoroughly embedded in an imperialist framework than Nussbaum's secular, nationalist, and liberal-utilitarian account acknowledges. Indeed, if we follow Coviello in imagining that secularism has a body, we see not only that disgust represents a disruption within that body, but that legal obscenity emerges as a crucial—and contested—site for the regulation and exploitation of that disruption within the already unstable matrix of Victorian civilizational ideology.

## Jude the Obscene

The example of *Jude the Obscure* can help disentangle this complex web of conceptual and historical problems. The novel's reception alone offers an interesting case study of the ways in which late Victorian moral outrage over the alleged revolting obscenity of a literary work could entangle concerns over secularization with anxiety about modern sexual mores.[48] Most infamously, the bishop of Wakefield reported being "so disgusted with its insolence and indecency that I threw it into the fire," though the novel was derided as obscene by members of the literary establishment as well.[49] Margaret Oliphant concurred, asserting that "nothing so coarsely indecent as the whole history of Jude in his relations with his wife Arabella has ever been put in English print. . . . There may be books more disgusting . . . in those dark corners where the amateurs of filth find garbage to their taste; but not . . . from any Master's hand."[50]

Burned but not banned, the novel was not only a lightning rod for allegations of pollutant obscenity but also a searching meditation on the aesthetics of the obscene in ways that actually censored texts like *Lady Chatterley's Lover* and *La Terre* were not: a meditation on the looseness of the category as well as on its animating power, on its relationship to the sacred and the profane, and on the hypocrisy with which it was attributed to works of literature. Indeed the novel itself abounds with burned texts, scenes of vandalism and graffiti, and defamation; idols are smashed, graven images are defaced, and photographs are adored fetishistically and guiltily stroked and kissed like pornography when nobody is watching. Moreover, unlike other fin-de-siècle authors who came under fire for their obscenity, Hardy managed to be a fierce critic of Victorian censorship and Grundyism while also maintaining a deep fascination with the animistic censoring impulse to erase the aesthetic frame and to treat works as active offenses rather than inert documents that derived all their force from the expressivity of human authors. Counterintuitively, Hardy believed that what artworks and artifacts actually express is their relative autonomy from the very people who created them, a view that put him curiously athwart of most defenses of authorial expression. "Makers of things," he once observed in his *Poetical Matter* notebook, "e.g. painters, writers, builders, furniture makers, are present as ghosts before their works."[51]

A scene from *Jude the Obscure* exemplifies Hardy's nuanced unwillingness to disenchant our attachments to aesthetic objects. When we first meet Sue Bridehead, she is, according to Jude's evangelical aunt, "an artist or designer in some sort of ecclesiastical warehouse, which was a perfect seed-bed of idolatry."[52] Despite this employment, and before her ultimate conversion, Sue nonetheless claims the novel's most thoroughly demystified and demystifying modern attitude, denouncing Christminster as "a place full of fetichists and ghost-seers!" (185). In part following and in part disobeying this irreverent and irreligious streak in her personality, Sue early on in the novel buys two pagan figurines—one Venus, one Apollo—from a peddler selling "I-i-i-images" just outside the town. Knowing that her churchgoing landlady will condemn the purchase, but also because the figurines seem to exert a mysterious affective power over her, Sue's anxiety spikes immediately after buying the statues.

> She clasped them as treasures. . . . [But] when they were paid for . . . she began to be concerned as to what she would do with them. They seemed so very large now they were in her possession, and so very naked. Being of a nervous temperament she trembled at her enterprise. . . . After carrying them along a little way openly an idea came to her, and, pulling some huge burdock leaves . . . from the hedge, she wrapped up her burden. . . . But she was still in a trembling state, and she seemed almost to wish she had not bought the figures. (129–30)

Growing ever larger and more erotically charged as she approaches home, the eerily tumescent figurines convey a palpably obtrusive and almost obscene agency, which Sue experiences negatively, as a desire to get rid of or at least conceal them. "Her purchases were taken straight up to her own chamber, and she at once attempted to lock them in a box that was her very own property; but finding them too cumbersome she wrapped them in large sheets of brown paper, and stood them on the floor in a corner."[53] Unable to hide her suddenly outsized acquisitions, Sue tells Miss Fontover, her prying landlady, that they represent St. Peter and Mary Magdalene. But the lie is quickly exposed, and Fontover (whose last name anticipates her violent overflow of iconoclastic zeal) destroys the icons and evicts Sue. "She broke some statuary of mine," Sue reports. "She found it in my room, and though it was my property she threw it on the floor and stamped on it, because it was not according to her taste, and ground the arms and the head of one of the figures all to bits with her heel—a horrid thing!" (139).

The scene represents two conflicting attitudes toward offensive artworks, staged as a generational conflict over modern secularism and sexuality: Fontover's censorious iconoclasm, which registers the mere presence of the pagan statuary in her household as a pollution that needs to be destroyed and expelled; and Sue's defiantly agnostic attempt to disenchant the thrill of her own transgression and to subordinate existential matters of belief to aesthetic questions of "taste" and individualistic economic concerns about "property." Contrasting the two women's reactions, the scene questions whether physical acts of defacement made in the name of religious difference and intolerance can in fact be assimilated to a liberalizing discourse of taste and ownership. To be sure, the novel does not hide its antipathy toward the hypocritical and damaging pieties of late Victorian religious culture, which it is constantly lambasting. However, by first foregrounding Sue's affective reaction to the figurines—her heightened physical anxiety at their nudity and size, and her own preemptive censorship with the burdock leaf—the scene asks us to read Sue's demystification of Fontover's iconoclasm skeptically as well. The notion that what is expressed by their two incompatible attitudes is a difference in taste not only feels reductive but also reads as a post hoc disavowal of Sue's strong embodied reaction and her dim sense of the agency of the icons. As we saw as well in Nussbaum's discussion of disgust, Sue is at pains to invalidate the harm felt by her censorious landlady.

The split or incommensurability that Hardy represents in this scene cuts to the core of the questions of pollution and expression that have dogged our discussion of obscenity law. How, ultimately, are we to understand these seemingly irreconcilable differences in the way that people respond to the offenses that they attribute to representations? And perhaps more importantly, what would have to change in order for someone to adopt a new view of this matter (as Sue in fact does over the course of the novel)? That is, what would it take for someone who subscribed to the pollution model of obscenity to no longer feel that disgust and outrage ought to have any claim on the social world, or for someone with staunch liberal and civilizational views like Nussbaum's to be converted to a belief that the moral urgency of revulsion represents a legitimate form of harm in need of legal redress?

Looking back at the 2005 controversy that gripped Europe and the Arab world over the Danish publication of offensive cartoons of the Prophet Muhammad, Saba Mahmood has offered a compelling account of how to conceive of the differences between secular and religious modes of taking offense at images. In her discussion, Mahmood seeks to understand such differences in terms of the Aristotelian concept of *schesis*, a term defined as both "the manner in which a thing is related to something else" and "a temporary habit or state of the body." Thus for Mahmood, what was at stake in a case like that of the Danish cartoons was precisely the recognition of differences in the embodied "modality of relation" that pertain to secular and religious regimes of representation. By focusing on the meaning and content of offensive images and texts, liberal secular accounts of outrage tend to imagine that "religion is ultimately a matter of choice . . . is about belief in a set of propositions to which one gives one's assent." In contrast to this secular position, Mahmood wants to understand the religious *schesis* or habitus as "a bodily condition or temperament that undergirds a particular modality of relation" and in turn "binds the subject to the object of veneration."[54] From this perspective, belief cannot be reduced to propositional content, just as representations cannot be reduced to their interpretive meaning, since both belief and representation are experienced in a lived and embodied manner at an affective level that is integrated with the whole personality structure. On the one hand, then, Mahmood's astute analysis shows why controversies such as the one sparked by the Danish cartoons can feel so much like obdurate, unchangeable problems that simply will not be resolved by hashing out differences of opinion. Yet on the other hand, her analysis also raises important questions about how such differences at the level of habitus are acquired, accrete, and deepen over time, and about how a set of differences can come to seem intractable.

Mahmood's discussion of religious *schesis* points to the urgent need in debates over the power of representations and the freedom of expression to identify differences that are operative in registers that are themselves hard to describe, or that cut across familiar categories in ways that can be defamiliarizing and even alienating. For if we cannot locate the actual points of conflict and differentiation in a debate, then resolution is not likely to be in the cards. Disgust, singled out for its partially secularized propensity for animistic pollution thinking, is just such a point of conflict in the historical formation of the legal-aesthetic category of the obscene. Tracking how disgust has had to be tamed or unleashed in obscenity debates therefore allows us to identify the ways in which affect has functioned as a crucial register of differentiation, operating below the more familiar levels of cultural and civilizational difference that have nonetheless tended to organize arguments over censorship. In order to transition into the modern regime of speech, we have seen, it continues to be argued that people will have to overcome the way that they think about the way that they feel their disgust. But with few notable exceptions, the question of how and why different people come to have such incompatible relationships to their revulsion has remained unstudied in the context of censorship debates, as has the question of how and at what costs one might be reeducated with respect to how one lives out and understands the meaning of one's own emotions.

In the following, concluding chapter, we will see how disgust's involvement with these very matters of secularization and cultural difference played out during the Indian Rebellion of 1857–58. But first I turn to one more scene from *Jude the Obscure*. Midway through the novel, Hardy stages a book burning that captures something about these difficult questions. After a long kiss, Jude has realized that he cannot overcome his sexual passion for his cousin, even though she is now seemingly locked in a loveless marriage to his old schoolteacher Phillotson. Convincing himself not only that he has sinned but also that his unruly sex drive has caused Sue to turn on Phillotson, Jude comes to feel it would be hypocritical of him to maintain his "standing desire to become a prophet, however humble, to his struggling fellow-creatures, without any thought of personal gain." He thus decides to renounce not his beliefs but his aspirations to promulgate those beliefs and to allow them to shape his ambitions. And this leads him in turn to realize a need not merely to be done with the teachings of the church, but to destroy his relationship to those teachings, as they are embodied by his library.

> At dusk that evening he went into the garden and dug a shallow hole, to which he brought out all the theological and ethical works that he possessed, and had stored here. He knew that, in this country of true believers, most of them were not saleable at a much higher price than waste-paper value, and preferred to get rid of them in his own way, even if he should sacrifice a little money to the sentiment of thus destroying them. Lighting some loose pamphlets to begin with, he cut the volumes into pieces as well as he could, and with a three-pronged

fork shook them over the flames. They kindled, and lighted up the back of the house, the pigsty, and his own face, till they were more or less consumed. (250)

The image captures the swirl of contradictions that constitute the uneven secularism of a modern moment that has dragged on from Hardy's time. In order to understand the age of obscenity, Hardy's diabolical image makes us feel, we are going to need to understand how burning books on religion and ethics in a pigsty might come to feel like the most pious or ethical thing to do; or why a novelist might seem to be expressing sympathies with book burning at all, within a novel that would itself come to be publicly denounced and burned by a bishop; or how a sexual relation between two people might come to feel mediated by and even to depend on the existence and affective power of texts and images, the presence of which might themselves come to feel a burden or obtrusion.

What is most striking about the role of disgust in the age of obscenity is that it has come to seem necessary to be surpassed or overcome in this manner, even though it has retained its self-evidentiary and perspicuous character. While we might achieve a rationalistic consensus about what the role of subjective emotions ought to be in the law, when we seek to ground that consensus normatively in the affective grammar of our social world we find wild unevenness and stark contrasts rather than collective agreement; and if we seek instead to draw on the modern history of the law as a storehouse of rational precedent, what we find instead is the law's dependency on the animism of disgust in its project of secularizing aesthetic pollution. Thus while we might characterize our age as one in which differences about the power of speech and representations have come to seem intractable, we might just as easily describe it as one in which our most difficult and volatile of subjective experiences are invertible, in which disgust might flip one way or the other depending on principles that we have yet fully to understand.

# Conclusion
## Horizons of Expectoration

Open a British newspaper from any day between the spring of 1857 and the close of 1859, and you will find that at least two or three articles, whose topics do not manifestly concern one another, nonetheless share a common language of disgust. Keep reading, and you will find that this shared rhetoric is not merely coincidental, but in fact a highly conventionalized discourse of unwanted feeling; it includes a set of unquestioned racialized presumptions about the primal and the primitive, as well as a recursive tendency to ascribe to the articulation of disgust itself an undesirable and uncivilized character and so, as we have seen, a tendency to mop up after itself. This discourse of disgust was not merely a characteristic feature of Victorian society's sense of its own civilization, but a productive force motivating social transformation; not merely an idiom for demanding or decrying change, but a medium of such changes in its own right. Describing this productivity has entailed tracking down the minute, counterintuitive ways that the regulation of and appeal to unwanted emotion were installed at the heart of historical processes that have been most insistently described in terms of rationality and rationalization.

But rather than detailing this theoretical complexity within the discourse of disgust once again, I want to take half a step back and refocus our attention instead on the emotion's complex and unpredictable itinerary across domains. Pursuing the Victorian structure of unwanted feeling has led us from the realms of politics and law to the natural and social sciences, from critiques of literary realism to debates over manuring practices, and from the physiology of the stomach to the disorders of the stock market. While disgust did not play precisely the same role in the transformation of each of these domains, the appeal to the emotion nonetheless proved to be a highly flexible discursive activity. It made available its calculability in one context, its unwantedness in another; offered its reflexivity in a third scenario and its pollution thinking in a fourth. What had at first seemed disconnected stories on facing newspaper pages—a financial collapse, a sewage crisis, the passage of a censorship law, an anticolonial uprising—turn out to meet in the paper's gutter.

This capacity to lump together disparate social phenomena has surely proved to be one of disgust's historical strengths. For one, it allows forms of unexpected connection and sites of shared preoccupation to become legible without imposing too strict an organizational or conceptual coherence on the resulting heterogeneous mass. There is no "grand narrative" of disgust, no single interpretation of the emotion or its history that could impose meaning and confer value on the whole constellation of unwanted social phenomena I have been describing. There are, however, the stories that have been told about disgust—of unwanted and surpassed primitivity, threatening contagion, repudiated immanence, and so on—and the circulation and deployment of those stories came to organize knowledge and structure social experience in particular ways that have yet to be fully examined, either by historians of emotion or by theorists of the nineteenth century. There is, in other words, a particular drift or directionality to the history of the conceptualization of disgust. And it is this discursive current, in which the emotion has long been caught up, that gave disgust its special charge within the more sweeping narrative matrices of civilizational ideology and rationalization that have concerned thinkers ranging from Weber and Elias to Foucault and Poovey.

Yet if there has been notable consistency in the conceptualization of disgust—from Kant's third *Critique* down to contemporary emotion psychology—the combined weight of this history of conceptualization has also in turn changed the emotion, limiting its possibilities for signification and use. Certain meanings are no longer very plausibly or very easily attached to disgust—Darwin's sense of the singularly capacious openness of the vomiting body, for instance—while others, such as Nussbaum's normative insistence on the emotion's unique subrationality, have been so naturalized through their repeated invocation that they come prepackaged in most conceptions of disgust, whether you like it or not. To write the history of disgust, or of emotions in general, is in this sense to alternate between two distinct modes of narrative retrieval, each with its own archives and its own particular set of aims, protocols, and aspirations. There are in the history of disgust moments of foreclosed possibility, on the one hand, when the emotion seemed to offer up an emergent or unusual set of meanings whose social uses remained to be seen—moments when even the act of naming the emotion threatens to rigidify some more diffuse affective configuration that, as Williams defined the structure of feeling, rests just on "the very edge of semantic availability."[1] And on the other hand, writing the history of disgust entails attending to the significant moments of the emotion's incorporation into dominant cultural formations, when disgust seems doomed only to express again and again modernity's most sedimented ideological banalities about what it means to possess a stomach or to be a body, to be cut off from one's reasons for disliking something or to register one's differences from someone.

Such considerations point us back toward general questions about the universalization of emotion and its formalization over the course of the nineteenth century as an object of scientific study that would henceforth be shared by psychologists and anthropologists alike. I have tried deliberately to resist fixing disgust within these disciplinary formations, while also trying to show how a unique set of contradictions ascribed to the emotion helped to transform and in some cases even to generate those formations themselves. Yet in resisting just such a bounded, disciplined conception of disgust, I have run into a number of crucial methodological problems that can help to point the way forward for future studies in the history of emotions. What is the specific perspective from which disgust appears as disgust in the historical materials I have assembled—appears, that is, as a discursive object in possession of enough conceptual as well as historical coherence to merit such a sustained analysis? What does such an analysis make visible, and what does it occlude? Attending to such questions has involved not only addressing the boundary-crossing, generative character of disgust, but reconsidering the incoherence of the ideology of civilization as well.

Foucault directs his attention to a closely related set of methodological questions in *The Archaeology of Knowledge*. When confronted with a set of themes or conceptual presumptions that carry across a wide array of disciplinary domains and social phenomena, and which persist over a long period of time, Foucault cautions against "seek[ing] in the existence of these themes the principles of the individualization of a discourse." Instead, Foucault suggests a model of historical analysis that pursues conceptual themes that fall outside specific discursive formations. The aim of such an analysis, he writes, is that "of arousing opposed strategies, of giving way to irreconcilable interests, of making it possible, with a particular set of concepts, to play different games. . . . Rather than seeking the permanence of themes, images, and opinions through time, rather than retracing the dialectic of their conflicts in order to individualize groups of statements, could one not rather mark out the dispersion of the points of choice, and define prior to any option, to any thematic preference, a field of strategic possibilities?"[2] Foucault here describes a method that is more oriented toward dissolving its historical object than retrieving or reconstituting it. This operation has been indispensable to my own articulation of the history of disgust, insofar as the goal of "making it possible, with a particular set of concepts, to play different games" concisely captures what I see as one horizon of possibility for writing about affect and emotion. Because subjective emotional experience and the forms of expression it prompts are constitutively interpretive, writing about emotions is an inherently normative enterprise. Saying what an emotion is or has been, or how it works, represents a form of contribution to the overall variety of meanings and values that can be plausibly attached to it at a given historical moment—whether that contribution is additive, restrictive, or representative of some other kind of mutation of the emotional discourse.

Before even approaching the question of the politics of the study of emotion, I would argue that the ambition to push the limits of (rather than foreclose) what gets counted as part of an emotion's repertoire of tendencies and uses should be a methodological given for any historiography of emotion that seeks to learn something new from its object. One cannot simply set out in search of an emotion, not least because in writing about it one changes—or restricts—what it can be made to mean. Moreover, one has to exert effort in order not to merely recapitulate what the emotion has already been tasked with meaning as a consequence of its historical development, a development that in the case of all the putatively universal affects is routed through the mid-nineteenth-century civilizational contexts I have described. Failing to recognize the normative aspect of writing the history of the emotions will therefore quickly turn even the most well-meaning visit to an emotion's past into its tacit colonization by the interests of the present. By contrast, Foucault suggests that pursuing this open-ended methodological strategy of expanding our sense of how much one can do with a particular category of emotional discourse risks pushing the object of analysis beyond the normative limits of what the emotion is understood to be at a given historical moment, or in a given cultural context. There is something inherently contradictory in the ambition to write the history of a single emotion that resists the tendency toward "the individualization of a discourse."

Foucault's methodological statements from *The Archaeology of Knowledge* (and my extension of them to the history of emotion) sit in tension with the more somber analysis of power relations that characterizes his later genealogical work on discipline and sexuality. In those works, the emphasis falls on the narrowing of the "field of strategic possibilities" across which one might trace the history of a set of concepts or themes. The emergence of sexuality as a discourse of biopolitical governance is not a methodological premise for Foucault, but rather something more akin to a historical finding. The set of historical developments he called modern sexuality is made apparent through the arousal of "opposed strategies," that is, by playing new games with an old set of concepts, such as repression, emancipation, and sexuality, power and perversion. But these discoveries that Foucault made later in his career very concretely detail the ways in which the operations of power, through the new nineteenth-century institutions of knowledge production, function as limitations on the different meanings that could accrue to sexuality, and especially to ideals of sexual liberation, even as the scenes of sexuality's articulation proliferated. Counterintuitively, the methodological impulse to dissolve the historical object and thereby to open it up to new avenues of interpretation and understanding led Foucault to the historical realization of the way that the ambitions of knowledge production, since the seventeenth century, had turned what may have seemed a field of possibility into a truncated scene of regulation and semantic control. Even if Foucault never quite returned us to the more linear narrative of progressive rationalization that Weber had critiqued earlier in the twentieth century, he described what I have been calling a drift, a discursive current in whose undertow the modern discourses of sexuality and punishment were caught up.

These methodological considerations can help sharpen the analysis of disgust's historical entanglement with the civilizational ideology of the nineteenth century. The relationship between disgust and civilization, that is, follows a tendency similar to my description of Foucault's work, according to which a commitment to methodological openness nonetheless leads to the examination of a historical process of circumscription and constraint. For if the discourse of disgust entered into a whole series of new domains, it is also true that the appeal to disgust always sat in some vexed relationship to the civilizing logic of British imperialism and the race thinking that propped it up. We need only briefly recall Hebert Spencer's racialized logic of emotional restraint or Jane Eyre's projection of her disgust beyond the boundary of the nation-state to register the extent to which the discourses of disgust and civilization have seemed to walk hand in hand throughout the Victorian period. In each chapter of this book, we have seen how the imperial project and its racial ideology have intersected with the structure of unwanted feeling, sometimes augmenting, sometimes underwriting its claims. From this angle, the history of civilization and the history of disgust are not merely two strands of nineteenth-century history that overlap considerably, but rather two mutually constituting perspectives on the European nineteenth century and its arrogation to itself of modernity and dominance. This relationship is structurally ambiguous. Sometimes disgust appears as a relatively stable form of rhetorical operation, a trope deployed within the framework of the civilizing project; at others, it appears instead as a discursive framework of its own, necessary for the concept of civilization to lay claim to its own provisional ideological coherence.

We can visualize this complex relationship by returning to the newspaper I invoked above. For if disgust was a common thread that ran through what otherwise appeared as disconnected stories on facing pages, almost the same thing can be said about the anticolonial uprising that spread across northern India for roughly eighteen months beginning in May 1857. As a crisis that struck right at the heart of British imperial arrogance, the Indian Rebellion served as a yardstick for the other forms of civilizational crisis that took place in the years after it began. Such comparisons were far more deliberate than the deployment of the language of disgust; they took place on a partially semantic level, inviting comparison, while disgust functioned in a more subterranean rhetorical register, serving to establish self-evidence. For instance, here is Lord Campbell, one last time, reporting back to the House of Lords after the passage of the Obscene Publications Act that the "siege of Holywell Street might be compared to the siege of Delhi. The place was not taken in a day, but repeated assaults were necessary, and at last he was told, it was now in the quiet possession of the law, for the shops where these abominations were found had been shut up, and the rest of the houses were now conducted in a manner free from exception."[3] Such invocations of the rebellion were not arbitrary, but rather reflected the extent to which the series of political, economic, and cultural crises that closed out the 1850s were generally viewed from the perspective of a civilizational ideology that took the maintenance of the British Empire as its foundation.[4] It is of course not surprising that the rebellion absorbed the civilizational anxieties of the moment, considering its significance as a turning point in the history of British colonial rule in India, as well as the news of the conflict's violent excesses that soon flooded the periodical press. Foremost among the outcomes of the rebellion was the transfer of India's colonial administration from the East India Company to the Crown, and the eventual dismantling of the company and its vast private army following the Government of India Act of August 1858.

But it is not so easy to discern the precise relationship of disgust to the civilizational crisis of the rebellion. To be sure, many scholars of the British Empire, such as Deana Heath and Tanya Agathocleous, have observed that sanitary hygiene and obscenity regulation were both deployed as techniques of colonial administration over the second half of the nineteenth century. In these discussions, the "sanitary idea" is seen to be exported to the colonies and unleashed upon the colonized as part of a broader regulatory regime.[5] Yet what was carried abroad and exported, in these cases, was not exactly a rationalized principle of bureaucratic management but rather a powerful form of pollution thinking that adapted the discourse of disgust to bureaucratic ends. Likewise, although the Indian Rebellion served as a measure of civilizational crisis, that crisis can be situated within the context of the Victorian structure of unwanted feeling no less than the events for which it was offered as a standard of comparison. Thus when we read that the "hot fortnight [of the Great Stink] did for the sanitary administration of the Metropolis what the Bengal mutinies did for the administration of India," it is not at all clear which term in the analogy should be granted priority.[6]

## The Bureaucracy of Colonial Pollution

While the full history of the rebellion lies beyond the scope of my discussion, what interests me is the overdetermined role that defilement, pollution thinking, and a specifically oral disgust played in the events that precipitated the military conflict and that continue to structure the historiography of the event.[7] As is both well known and well documented, these issues of pollution and disgust came to the fore when the East India Company sought to introduce the new Enfield rifle, which among other technological innovations included a paper cartridge that came pre-lubricated on one end in order to make loading the weapon easier. Soldiers would have to bite open the cartridge, before inserting the greased end down the barrel. The problem arose when a rumor began to circulate alleging that the grease on the cartridges was made from pig fat and cow tallow, and so represented a form of pollution to the predominantly Muslim and high-caste Hindu soldiers employed by the company. Importantly, neither East India Company officials nor latter-day historians have been able to confirm or conclusively deny that pig or cow fat had been used; the cartridges were greased with the fat of some animal, but the company could not say which kind.[8]

The perceived threats of defilement and of losing caste posed by contact with—let alone ingestion of—the cartridge grease fed an already pervasive anxiety among the soldiers that the company had for a variety of reasons long wanted to convert them to Christianity. This caused many Indian soldiers to refuse the new rifles, and these heightened tensions soon led to acts of insubordination at various locations, including several military buildings being burnt down. This escalation of resistance came to a head with the outright mutiny at Meerut, when Indian soldiers killed their British officers and marched for Delhi, where they sought to rally the aging Mughal emperor to their cause. At this point, mutiny spread throughout the East India Company, while at the same time rebellion against the British erupted in various different arenas across northern India and was carried out by a variety of actors not connected to the company and its professional army.

The role of disgust and the fear of contamination in the events that precipitated the rebellion has not escaped notice. In a study that shares many important coordinates with my own, Parama Roy has argued that "the events of 1857 in particular laid bare the ways in which the body in its moments of appetite, disgust, pollution, and purification was key to grasping the psycho-political arrangements of the colonial order." She continues, "Bread, grease, contaminated food supplies, bazaar gossip, and rumor were not the picayune details of a historically consequential event, but the very grammar—affective, symbolic, material, and political—of that history. This is true, I suggest, not just of the Hindus, Muslims, and other Indians who experienced appetites, incorporations, and aversions as the quotidian facts of colonial rule, but of Anglo-Indians as well. For Indians and Anglo-Indians alike, the experience of the Mutiny was routed through some fundamental questions of somatic and affective integrity."[9] For Roy, the instigating role of the greased cartridges reflects the centrality of disgust and especially pollution thinking on the colonial scene in general. Roy aptly points out that most scholarship on the rebellion—and there is a lot of it—has failed to adequately theorize the significance of the greased cartridges, tending to treat the matter instead as emblematic of the broader confrontation between the modern techno-rationality of British rule, in the form of the new rifle, and the premodern religiosity of the caste system, with its elaborate rules governing pollution.

Roy's argument is in keeping with other critical accounts of the failure of colonial and imperial historiography more generally to recognize the significance of affective experience to colonial administration. Ann Laura Stoler, for instance, has argued that "much of colonial studies . . . has worked from the shared assumption that the mastery of reason, rationality, and the exaggerated claims made for Enlightenment principles have been at the political foundation of nineteenth- and early twentieth-century colonial regimes, and should be at the center of critical histories of them." In contrast with such Weberian accounts, Stoler argues—in a formulation that ought to resonate with the argument I have been making throughout this book—"that affective knowledge was at the core of political rationality."[10] Thus for Stoler, like Roy, it is not so much that one must attend to the quotidian details of affective experience in order to recover what was devalued or denigrated under colonial rule, but rather that the processes of rationalization and domination traditionally understood as the drivers of nineteenth-century imperialism were not only concerned with but were themselves written in the languages of affective experience.

A page from Sir John Kaye's account of the events of the Indian Rebellion can help concretize this complex theoretical point. First published in three volumes beginning in 1864 as *A History of the Sepoy War in India, 1857–1858*, Kaye's detailed chronicle of the conflict was subsequently edited and expanded by George Bruce Malleson in 1890, when it ballooned to six hefty tomes. Once an officer himself in the Bengal Artillery, Kaye became the first head of the powerful Political and Secret Department of the newly-founded India Office in 1858, succeeding John Stuart Mill after the transfer of the East India Company's colonial authority to the British government.[11] In this sense, his history not only is written from the perspective of the colonizer but also represents in essence an "official" ideological accounting of the event, produced from a position of bureaucratic authority and in light of the author's privileged access to state and company secrets. Kaye devotes an entire chapter to the "story of the greased cartridges" and the subsequent "spread of evil tidings." I quote at length to give a sense of the texture of Kaye's prose, and in particular the way in which it presents not only an account of events, but an account of the logic of disgust and defilement.

> Now, it happened that, one day in January, a low-caste Lascar, or magazine-man, meeting a high-caste Sipáhi in the Cantonment, asked him for a drink of water from his lotah. The Brahman at once replied with an objection on the score of caste, and was tauntingly told that caste was nothing, that high-caste and low-caste would soon be all the same, as cartridges smeared with beef-fat and hog's-lard were being made for the Sipáhis at the depots, and would soon be in general use throughout the army.
>
> The Brahman carried this story to his comrades, and it was soon known to every Sipáhi at the depot. A shudder ran through the Lines. Each man to whom the story was told caught the great fear from his neighbour, and trembled at the thought of the pollution that lay before him. The contamination was to be brought to his very lips; it was not merely to be touched, it was to be eaten and absorbed into his very

being. It was so terrible a thing, that, if the most malignant enemies of the British Government had sat in conclave for years, and brought an excess of devilish ingenuity to bear upon the invention of a scheme framed with the design of alarming the Sipáhi mind from one end of India to the other, they could not have devised a lie better suited to the purpose. . . . It required no explanation. It needed no ingenious gloss to make the full force of the thing itself patent to the multitude. It was not a suggestion, an inference, a probability; but a demonstrative fact, so complete in its naked truth, that no exaggeration could have helped it. Like the case of the leathern head-dresses, which had convulsed Southern India half a century before, it appealed to the strongest feelings both of the Mahammadan and the Hindu; but though similar in kind, it was incomparably more offensive in degree; more insulting, more appalling, more disgusting.[12]

More than merely cataloging events, Kaye here writes from the perspective of someone equipped with a firsthand and pseudo-anthropological knowledge, with all its presumptions and allegations about how the primitive logic of pollution and contamination is said to work: "The contamination was to be brought to his very lips; it was not merely to be touched, it was to be eaten and absorbed into his very being." Beyond the immediate menace of oral ingestion, Kaye also moves outward. What is most important, he implies, is to describe the collective unfolding of the fear of pollution as though it were a form of pollution itself. In this social register, as Roy has observed, building on related work by Ranajit Guha and Homi K. Bhabha, pollution spreads as rumor, which without explanation is alleged to follow the rules of contagion, and can even be described in the language of revulsion.[13] "A shudder ran through the Lines," as Kaye puts it. "Each man . . . caught the fear from his neighbour, and trembled at the thought of the pollution that lay before him."

The passage is striking for the careful and detailed manner in which it elaborates what might be called a bureaucratic knowledge of the other's disgust. Not only does it unpack a detailed logic of pollution, which it nonetheless ascribes indiscriminately to both Hindu and Muslim soldiers, but it also acknowledges how that logic operates as a communicative activity that spreads fear and disgust throughout the army. Even more significant, however, is Kaye's pointed observation that "the most malignant enemies of the British Government" could not have devised a more effective plan for sowing unrest among the company's soldiers. For this reflection implies a different order of knowledge, one that is not merely rooted in the careful observation of another culture's rules of contamination. Instead, it suggests a top-down understanding of how the social organization entailed by such rules of contamination can be used and manipulated, a knowledge of how the discourse of disgust can be deployed rationalistically within a political framework that sets itself outside of the rules of the game. Thus Kaye writes that, while of course the British would not have wanted to spread this rumor themselves, the discursive knowledge of pollution was nonetheless available for exploitation and control. From this perspective, we can see that disgust was understood administratively not only as a cause for the uprising but reserved as a technology of counterinsurgency as well.

Yet the extent to which this discursive knowledge of pollution was rooted in a knowledge of the complex systems regulating contamination and purity in Islam and Hinduism needs to be questioned. This is not to say that the British were ignorant of such protocols; to the contrary, many Indian soldiers believed with good reason that the British knew more than enough to defile them, and moreover that the latter sought to forcibly convert the entire army in order to remove dietary prohibitions, thus facilitating overseas military campaigns. "That's just it," Kaye reports one Hindu soldier saying. "You want us all to eat what you like that we may be stronger, and go everywhere."[14] The soldiers were in this sense alert to the fact that they had to protect their disgust from the British, who were from this vantage point armed with a power that was ambiguously the power to defile and the power to overcome and supplant the logic of defilement. This knowledge that defilement via forced or surreptitious ingestion of contaminated foods would constitute a form of visceral subjectification was thus to a degree held in common by both British and Indians, and it was precisely the shared knowledge of this power that underwrote the urgency with which soldiers rebelled against the threat of the greased cartridges.

Nevertheless, the pollution knowledge the British possessed should be understood first and foremost as an articulation of their own distinct conception of disgust, brought into forcible contact with the differing models of contamination relevant to Muslims and Hindus living in nineteenth-century colonial India. Note how readily Kaye ascribes to the threat of unwanted ingestion precisely the same self-evidentiary character that we have been tracking in various other domains: "It required no explanation. It needed no ingenious gloss to make the full force of the thing itself patent to the multitude. It was not a suggestion, an inference, a probability; but a demonstrative fact, so complete in its naked truth, that no exaggeration could have helped it." This is, to reiterate, the bureaucratic knowledge of the other's disgust, but it is also an exemplary articulation of the Victorian structure of unwanted feeling. It offers a minutely detailed account of the way that revulsion disrupts the normal circuits of explanation and causation, rendering feeling into unwanted but indubitable fact. It takes for granted that there can be no argument, no skepticism, and no mistaking the import of an event that is "incomparably more offensive . . . more insulting, more appalling, more disgusting" than anything else one could dream up. The disgusting is the limit of the self-evidence of the senses. Moreover, it is the tipping point, a threshold beyond which it becomes impossible not to act; whereas unrest and rumors of forcible conversion had been swirling around at least since the Vellore Mutiny of 1807, Kaye writes, only with the imminent threat of oral defilement did decisive, violent revolt become a foregone conclusion. We might just as easily be describing the collective agreement commandeered by disgust during the hot weeks of the Great Stink.

The stakes and significance of this point need to be made especially clear, as they will bring us to the close of my argument. Roy has asserted that "Indians and Anglo-Indians *shared* a gestural repertoire, both oral and somatic, during the Mutiny. For the Anglo-Indians as for the Indians, the colonizer-colonized encounter, and indeed the experience of the Mutiny, was understood in significant ways through tropes of orality and of bodily purity and pollution; they were bound by unexpected forms of somatic, especially alimentary duplication." Her emphasis falls not merely on shared affective experiences of pollution, but on a shared discourse, the system of tropes through which those experiences were articulated. In the horrifically violent counterinsurgency that followed the uprising, she observes, the British resorted to forms of enforced ingestion and defilement far more brutal than those to which the Indian soldiers had feared from the outset they would be subjected, and which made specific use of the bureaucratic knowledge of the technology of pollution. This included forcing captives to eat pork and beef, and even to lick up human blood, before executing them, as well as the desecration of corpses in manners that reflected a detailed familiarity with prohibited burial practices. With these brutalities in mind, Roy describes the counterinsurgency as having "fully and inventively incorporated indigenous ideas about ingestion and contamination; its tactics seem driven by the desire to bear out, retrospectively, the logic of profanation and force-feeding in the bone dust and cartridge stories."[15]

According to Roy's line of argumentation, the extraordinary violence of the British and their exploitation of the knowledge of pollution reflects their identification with Hindu and Muslim religiosity and their incorporation of an "indigenous" Indian logic of contamination. However, I want to question precisely this assumption that the British necessarily absorbed a model of pollution thinking that was principally native or indigenous, an assumption that is a conceptual relative of Freud's characterization of the contents of the unconscious as an "aboriginal population of the mind."[16] Despite the complexity and criticality of Roy's account, I believe that she winds up preserving in this particular instance a conventional story of the Victorian colonial encounter as a drama of primal ingestion that is inimical to the overall thrust of her argument. It has the unwanted consequence of making pollution thinking seem foreign or exterior to British imperialism, even though we know to the contrary that it was at this very same historical moment a major engine of British culture. In lieu of the psychoanalytic principle of identification that Roy asserts allowed the British to absorb the logic of contamination, I would therefore propose instead a humbler principle of family resemblance. Rather than needing to imagine a scene of incorporation, we can see that the British were able to administer and to exploit as knowledge the two hierarchical discourses of contamination they encountered because these discourses already to some limited degree bore a likeness to their own culture's structure of unwanted feeling. The British did not need to leave home in 1857 in order to encounter the discourse of disgust and its tropological system; it was something that was continually expulsed, projected outward and onto an ever-widening frame of reference, even as it was already fueled by a long tradition of Enlightenment race thinking and prior imperial encounter.

Ranajit Guha's influential analysis of the rapid "transmission" of the rebellion across northern India can help to clarify this important theoretical distinction. In his landmark *Elementary Aspects of Peasant Insurgency in Colonial India*, Guha argues that the British tended to understand the way peasant rebellions in India spread according to a model of "contagion" and simultaneity that bordered on conspiracy theory or paranoid fantasy. "While the peasants regard rebellion as a form of collective enterprise," he writes, "their enemies describe it and deal with it as a contagion": "'Contagion': the word occurs so often and so persistently in official and pro-landlord accounts of agrarian uprisings . . . that it has acquired almost the status of a convention, that is, of a stereotyped figure of consciousness among those least likely to sympathize with disturbances of this kind. . . . In colonial India the authorities acknowledged its power in no uncertain terms. The spread of the sepoy and peasant rebellions of 1857–8 was often described as a function of contagion and infection in official statements." Guha goes on to provide numerous examples—"Revolt is contagious," one source baldly asserts—but we have already seen precisely this discursive tendency at work in Kaye's account of how "a shudder ran through the Lines [as] each man to whom the story was told caught the great fear from his neighbour, and trembled at the thought of the pollution that lay before him." The spread of information about pollution is itself patterned after a form of contamination and contagion. As Guha concisely sums it up, "A rebellion—any rebellion—is, in the eyes of its adversaries, a disease."[17]

Let us sit a bit longer with this analysis. Guha observes that the logic of contamination that the British claimed to see at work in the spread of rumor and rebellion during 1857 was in fact "a stereotyped figure of consciousness" that reflected their own interests. "Contagion" here refers to a colonial discourse, and not just a figure of speech. Closely related to the discourse of Victorian disgust, it is a structured set of conventions, used not merely to describe but to order and to control social and political action, and to legitimate the use of violence. Moreover, although the discourse of contagion presumes the "irrationality" of rebellious colonial subjects, in Guha's terms, the rules governing that presumption belong to the colonizer, not to the colonized; it is an imperial irrationality. This is a crucial distinction. In Roy's interpretation, the logic of contamination and disgust arose from a complex scene of incorporation. In stark contrast to this, Guha goes on to observe that "it is not difficult to see how this idea [of contagion] has its source in the psychosis of a dominant social group confronted suddenly by a revolt of those whose loyalty had been taken for granted." In Guha's analysis, contagion is in fact a projection, not an empirical observation or a discourse internalized and appropriated during the revolt. The contagion model is imposed—"psychotically"—as an attempt to make sense of the unwanted reality of revolt. However, this projection is not wholly arbitrary or hallucinatory. "There is perhaps an element of truth in this fantasy of 'preconcertation,' as Gramsci calls it," Guha continues. "It reflects an intuitive recognition of an organizing principle behind what looks like the world being turned upside down. . . . What the pillars of society fail to grasp is that the organizing principle lies in nothing other than their own dominance."[18]

In this dense and remarkable passage, Guha argues that the imagination of the rapid spread of rebellion as a form of simultaneously erupting primitive contagion is in fact nothing more than how the British perceived the rejection of the structure of their own domination. Contagion, that is, is the shape taken by the psychotic projection of colonial power faced with the unacceptable fact of its own repudiation. Guha thus identifies a fundamental misrecognition at work throughout this archive, in which projection and expulsion are taken for incorporation and ingestion. This line of argumentation is extraordinarily suggestive for thinking about how the British brought with them a discourse of disgust that they then appeared to discover already at work in Indian society as a primitive logic of contamination. For again, what Guha allows one to see is that in this instance disgust does not name something primitive, primal, or somehow aboriginal, but rather something technological, cunning, and calculable, but nonetheless involuntary, grounded in fantasy and feeling, and above all distorting. As in Marx's analysis of alienation as repulsion, disgust here is an affective grid that is involuntarily projected—spit out or thrown up—over the terrain of social experience, ordering it by distorting it.

Disgust therefore names a historically specific form of power relation, in which the rejection of domination is disavowed and then reimagined as a conflict between the savage and the civilized. Rather than the story of the identificatory encounter with the primitive, then, we see the drama of the British exportation of disgust, of the emotion's deployment as a technique of counterinsurgency that preys on two other historically entwined discourses of contamination and defilement. More precisely, we see disgust's motivating role in the violent effort, undertaken in the name of civilization, to superimpose a grammar of affective and sensory legibility, and so a form of life, over an ever-expanding terrain.

## Putting Matters Back in Place

Guha's discussion of contagion can help us to see our way through the methodological problem outlined at the beginning of this chapter. That problem arose out of the entanglement of the emotional discourse of disgust with the more nakedly ideological discourse of civilization. If each of those discourses can appear to claim a kind of priority over the other, it becomes difficult to know where the history and theory of disgust begin and end. If we follow Guha's assertion that the logic of contagion ought to be understood as the projection of a British set of "convention[s] pertinent to their own culture and rooted in their own history," then the civilizational ideology appears to derive its relative stability and coherence from the discourse of disgust.[19] Yet we have also seen, again and again, that the discourse of disgust derives its own relative coherence—slight as it may at times seem—from an imperial frame of reference and a racialized logic of the primitive. However, I would hesitate to describe this relationship as an aporia or paradox. Quite the contrary, it is characterized by its intense productivity, in terms of knowledge production as well as more evidently concrete, material forms of social transformation. We might instead visualize the entanglement of disgust and civilization as an unwieldy but therefore volatile edifice that is formed by the instability of these two discursive structures. As the two collapse under the weight of their mutually constitutive incoherencies, they fall into one another, achieving the lopsided ideological equilibrium whose outsized effects on the history of the last century and a half I have only been able to gesture toward.

This problematic in turn points us back toward the overarching question about the universality of disgust and of the Darwinian basic emotions paradigm in general that I raised in the opening pages of this book. Is disgust universal, or was its universality an outcome of its particularity, which is to say, of its violent imposition as a technology of imperial domination, its expulsion beyond the national frame? We need only briefly revisit the opening scene of coerced ingestion, taken from one of Darwin's sources, to observe the difficulties posed by these questions. To recall, what appeared as disgust in that passage was a refusal to drink Castor oil. "I have seen disgust thus strongly pronounced," the letter from John Scott reads, "frequently both in administering medicines to natives and in observing Hindoos of high caste coming contact in proximity [sic] to a defiling object."[20] Similar to Guha's analysis of contagion, disgust here names the rejection of a form of colonial domination, which from the ideological perspective of civilization takes shape as a chain of conflicts between the secular and the superstitious, the scientific and the irrational, and the deliberate and the reflexive. In a local register, Scott too grants himself access to the colonial administrator's supply of the bureaucratic knowledge of disgust. It is from this perspective— according to which rebellion appears as involuntary disease—that disgust comes to be understood as an unruly emotion that must be disciplined and overcome.

These questions about the universality of affect and emotion have recaptured the attention of contemporary psychological discourse, but in a restricted and largely defanged and dehistoricized form that fails to consider the vexed historical contexts that first made the emotions available for scientific research. Proponents of the Darwin-derived basic emotions paradigm continue to insist on the cross-cultural legibility of emotion expressions, as well as on their biologically hardwired and physiologically stereotyped character. Against this view, Lisa Feldman Barrett has sought to upset the essentialism of the universalizing paradigm, arguing that emotions are culturally constructed frameworks that help us to organize and to interpret physiological experiences that may not possess a unique "fingerprint" that repeats with every experience of the emotion. Rather than seeking a fixed set of unique physiological changes that constitute a single emotion and therefore make it available for scientific study, Barrett proposes that we see emotions "as a group of highly variable instances that are tied to specific situations" and are linked by a principle of family resemblance rather than one of identity.[21] Overall, she suggests, an emotion is best understood as a heterogeneous composite, pieced together out of the culturally informed interpretations of sensory experiences.

This theory entails that the study of emotions must in turn be the study of the patterns and paradigms according to which people have interpreted their affective experiences—a line of inquiry that lies principally outside disciplinary psychology and brain science. Pushed to its limit, however, Barrett's position regarding the social construction of emotions also has a destabilizing effect on the historiography of emotions. For if we jettison the idea that emotions are universal or refer to fixed physiological experiences, then it becomes difficult to separate the task of identifying their socially meaningful expression throughout history from the normative process of deciding what counts as an instance of a particular emotion and what does not. But beyond this normative dimension, the problem is not merely that emotions are constructed out of fundamentally interpretive cultural materials, but that different domains of social life—including the scientific discourse of emotion itself—are constructed, torn down, or preserved, in part thanks to the discursive work of emotion. Emotions may be constantly changing under the pressures of social, political, and economic transformations, but those latter changes would not take place without the pressure and force exerted by the appeal to emotion.[22]

One of the principal endeavors of this book has been to confront precisely this difficulty head on. I have sought not only to illuminate the complex character of the emotion of disgust, but to chart its historical course through diverse domains that were in turn changed through their contact with the emotion. The labile nature of disgust has demanded a historicist methodology that can represent the emotion's lack of fixity and coherence as it changes over time, even as I have tried to show that certain lines of continuity run through the discourse of disgust from the Enlightenment to the present. More to the point, disgust also uniquely illuminates the normative dimension of writing the history of emotions. As we have seen, the identification of disgust has been so thoroughly entangled with the normative enterprise of excluding the emotion that the articulation of disgust has often been treated as something disgusting in its own right—a structure epitomized by the act of vomiting.

This recursive dynamic, according to which disgust and the disgusting collapse into each other, presides over the question of the emotion's universality. In returning to the questions with which we opened, I also want to revisit a familiar text. In *The Civilizing Process*, Norbert Elias tracked the evolution of social attitudes toward spitting, as the prudent advice of the Middle Ages and early modern period—"Do not spit on the table"; "Do not spit into the basin when you wash your hands, but beside it"; "You should not refrain from spitting, and it is very ill-mannered to swallow what should be spat. This can nauseate others"—gave way to the austere histrionics of the late 1850s. "Spitting is at all times a disgusting habit," *The Habits of Good Society* proclaims, "I need say nothing more than—never indulge in it. Besides being coarse and atrocious, *it is very bad for the health*."[23] "In the pews of the churches," Ralph Waldo Emerson wrote in a similar but more philosophical vein, in his 1860 *Conduct of Life*, "little placards plead with the worshipper against the fury of expectoration."[24] For his part, Elias thought that "the modification in the manner of spitting, and finally the more or less complete elimination of the need for it, is a good example of the malleability of the psychic economy of humans."[25] Yet at the same historical moment that Elias notes the revolted elimination of spitting (along with the eventual abandonment of the spittoon from the bourgeois household), Darwin would declare that spitting and the opening of the mouth "as if to let an offensive morsel drop out" were the paradigmatic expression of disgust. The moment of the emotion's interdiction coincides with its universalization; the expression of disgust becomes disgusting as disgust become universal.

In the twentieth century, as discussed in chapter 1, Freud would further elevate the spitting out of an unwanted object to the primal scene of subject formation in his 1925 essay "Negation." The origins of the faculty of judgment, Freud postulated, lie in an originary instinctual expression of distaste that is constitutive of subjectivity. "Expressed in the language of the oldest—the oral—instinctual impulses," he writes, "the judgment is: 'I should like to eat this,' or 'I should like to spit this out.'" "Judgment devours and expels its objects," Jacqueline Rose paraphrases. "It derives from an orality which in turn becomes a metaphor for judgment itself."[26] This formulation, with its own roots in Kantian aesthetic disgust, would go on to influence not only Melanie Klein's development of the object relations paradigm but also, as Menninghaus has described in detail, Julia Kristeva's theory of abjection. The latter is itself a singularly important touchstone in the theoretical career of modern disgust, and readers familiar with Kristeva's work will, I hope, have noticed its resonance with and influence on my own thinking about disgust. "I expel *myself*," Kristeva memorably writes, "I spit *myself* out, I abject *myself* within the same motion through which 'I' claim to establish *myself*."[27] But I also want to suggest that one ought to experience a kind of historical and theoretical whiplash, in moving from Elias's quotidian examples of gradually accumulating cultural prohibitions to these conceptual meditations on the timelessness of the negative written in the universalizing idiom of structuralist thought. We move from the daily drama of manners to the forbiddingly operatic staging of the primal—each presenting itself as a scene from the lowly theater of the gaping mouth. On the one hand, do not spit on the table; throw out your spittoon; quit spitting outright. "On the other hand," Bataille writes, "affirming that the universe resembles nothing and is only *formless* amounts to saying that the universe is something like a spider or spit."[28]

Any one of these quotations could serve as the basis for a chapter of its own, but my aim in presenting them as a cluster at the close of my argument is simply to gesture once again toward the preeminent role that disgust came to take on in the modern theoretical imagination. As disgust came to claim a commonsense status as a universalizable as well as a structural phenomenon in twentieth-century thought, it became ever more important to seek the historical contexts out of which this theoretical common sense arose. For in the case of each of these examples, the presumption is that disgust sits in some relationship to an idea of structure that is no longer subject to meaningful historical variation, as it was for instance in Elias's account of the spittoon. Fixity, rather than malleability and flux, comes to the fore.

This idea—that disgust necessarily raises the question of a transhistorical structure—was most fully elaborated and lucidly articulated by Mary Douglas in her anthropological study *Purity and Danger* (1966), a book that Kristeva drew on extensively in presenting her own psychoanalytic theory of abjection. Douglas sought to distill from the comparative study of religious prohibitions and taboos a fundamental insight into the way that filth and the unclean are structural positions that sit in necessary relation to the organizational systems that order and give symbolic meaning to social life. "Dirt offends against order," Douglas writes. "Eliminating it is not a negative movement, but a positive effort to organise the environment. . . . In chasing dirt, in papering, decorating, tidying we are not governed by anxiety to escape disease, but are positively re-ordering our environment, making it conform to an idea. There is nothing fearful or unreasoning in our dirt-avoidance: it is a creative movement, an attempt to relate form to function, to make unity of experience."[29]

One way to understand my analysis in this chapter and in the book as a whole is as an attempt to reconstruct the historical conditions under which dirt became available as an object of social-scientific inquiry. When and how did filth become legible as one side of a structural relationship whose other term is a social-scientific concept of "unity of experience"—whether that concept is named culture, society, the nation, and so on? I have tried to answer that question by showing that the conditions under which eliminating filth comes to seem like a form of "positively re-ordering our environment, making it conform to an idea," are deeply interwoven with the civilizing projects of nineteenth-century European culture. The presumptions of universalizing theories of disgust and emotion may have been dislodged from their historical context as they entered into the twentieth century, but the connections are never too far off.

To make her case, Douglas drew on a tremendous wealth of religious and ethnographic sources from a vast range of historical periods, including the Hindu caste system and the food prohibitions of Islam and Judaism, as well as the abundant Victorian anthropological literature on the topic of "excremental magic." However, Douglas famously found that, at bottom, her argument rested on "the old definition of dirt as matter out of place."[30] It is, in a sense, the cornerstone of her argument, as well as an integral piece of Kristeva's theory of abjection. But what is the provenance of this nugget of folk wisdom that props up the social-scientific framework that in turn lies behind the psychoanalytic theory?

Douglas, who treats the definition as a commonplace or aphorism, once erroneously attributed it to a Lord Chesterfield. In fact, what she most likely had in mind was a toast that Lord Palmerston, then home secretary and soon to be the first Liberal prime minister, delivered to the meeting of the Royal Agricultural Society in July 1852.[31] In the toast, Palmerston proposes that scientific progress will soon bring to an end Britain's dependency on Peruvian guano, ushering in a period of bounty, in which Britain's agricultural needs will be supplied by the extraordinary fertility of its own human waste. "Now, gentlemen, I have heard a definition of dirt," he declares to an assembly hall full of agricultural chemists.

> I have heard it said that dirt is nothing but a thing in a wrong place. ["Hear," and laughter]. Now, the dirt of our towns precisely corresponds with that definition. ["Hear"]. The dirt of our towns ought to be put upon our fields, and if there could be such a reciprocal community of interest between the country and the towns—that the country should purify the towns, and the towns should fertilize the country [laughter]—I am much disposed to think the British farmer would care less than he does, though he still might care something, about Peruvian guano [Hear, hear, and cheers].[32]

Though Palmerston already grants an aphoristic character to the phrase, it would come to be associated with him in the following years, before the personal connection was severed and the phrase entered into the general lexicon of twentieth-century theory. In 1883, for instance, Thomas Hardy would write, in his essay "The Dorsetshire Labourer," that "it is not at all uncommon to find among the workfolk philosophers who recognise, as clearly as Lord Palmerston did, that dirt is only matter in the wrong place"; by 1908, Freud would quote the phrase without attribution, but nevertheless in English—"Dirt is matter in the wrong place"—in his controversial analysis of cleanliness and anality.[33] Reversing this trajectory and putting the words back into Palmerston's mouth allows us to reattach the discursive knowledge of filth and defilement to the domain of Victorian liberal imperialism, tethering the twentieth-century tradition of theorizing disgust to the enduring legacies of the nineteenth-century ideology of civilization.

Imploring the assembled scientific minds to set aside their distaste at the idea of feeding Britain on its own excrement, Palmerston frames the matter as one of imperial necessity. Your disgust is an impediment to economic, scientific, and geopolitical—which is to say civilizational—progress, he inveighs, going on to suggest an extended comparison of the Peruvian monopoly of the guano trade to British heteronomy under ancient Roman rule. Of course, the guano trade made some Britons extraordinarily wealthy—most notably, as the popular song went, William Gibbs, who "made his dibs / selling the turds / of foreign birds"—while at the same time the industry rapidly became a motivating force in the continued development and maintenance of a global reserve of coerced labor. Estimates suggest, for instance, that between the 1840s and the decline of the industry in the 1870s, Peru's guano pits and coastal sugar plantations alone were responsible for the exploitation of at least one hundred thousand Chinese laborers.[34] Palmerston's speech seems drawn toward the invocation of this scene of capitalist exploitation when, insisting that the Romans "could boast nothing to compare with railroads which multiply the communications of this country," he then goes on to quote Alexander Pope on Rome's "Imperial wonders rais'd on Nations Spoil'd, / Where, mix'd with Slaves, the groaning Martyrs toil'd." Here too, one thinks of Emerson, writing in *The Conduct of Life* of the various races of humankind that "have a great deal of guano in their destiny."[35]

It is from this civilizational context that the structural principle that dirt is matter out of place emerges. Ultimately, Palmerston's speech builds toward a familiar point. The overcoming of disgust toward your own excreta will be a source of knowledge, he finally suggests—you must open your minds and your mouths—following a logic that is indeed the direct forebear to the researches of Freud, Elias, Bataille, Klein, Douglas, and Kristeva, among others. However, it is not simply abstract, theoretical knowledge that is the endpoint of this alchemical passage, but the administrative knowledge of disgust—"the contamination was to be brought to his very lips; it was not merely to be touched, it was to be eaten and absorbed into his very being"—and, beyond that, the civilizational rule that such knowledge alone can facilitate. "I therefore recommend you, gentlemen," Palmerston concludes, "to ponder the maxim that 'knowledge is power'"—because for civilization, he might have added, the pursuit of power is beyond question; from the gallery: "Hear, hear, and cheers."

# NOTES

## Introduction

1. Darwin reproduced the survey in the introduction to *Expression*, 26–27. He sent slightly different versions of the survey to different contacts, many of which have been tracked down. Freeman and Gautrey, "Charles Darwin's *Queries*."

2. Darwin, *Expression*, 17. Darwin's views on race have garnered considerable attention. Of particular relevance to my discussion here, as well as in the third chapter (on Darwin) and the fifth chapter (on the self-evidentiary character of obscenity) is Irene Tucker's *The Moment of Racial Sight*. See especially the chapter "Observing Selection: Charles Darwin and the Emergence of the Racial Sign."

3. Darwin incorporated several of Scott's responses into the text of *Expression*. John Scott to Darwin, May 4, 1868, letter no. 6160, Darwin Correspondence Project, https://www.darwinproject.ac.uk/letter/DCP-LETT-6160.xml. The stereotype that non-Europeans are naturally prone to conceal their emotions recurs throughout the responses Darwin received. "The habitual endeavour of the maori," another correspondent writes, "is to conceal the workings of internal feeling." Or again: "It must not be forgotten that the Chinese face has the skin tightly drawn over it and is not nearly so capable of expression as the skin of European faces." Julius von Haast to Darwin, December 4, 1867, letter no. 5705, Darwin Correspondence Project, https://www.darwinproject.ac.uk/letter/?docId=letters/DCP-LETT-5705.xml;query=5705; Robert Swinhoe to Darwin, August 4, 1868, letter no. 6303, Darwin Correspondence Project, https://www.darwinproject.ac.uk/letter/?docId=letters/DCP-LETT-6303.xml;query=6303.

4. Mill, "Civilization," 120. I return to the ambiguities inherent to the civilization concept later in the introduction.

5. Darwin, *Expression*, 27.

6. Darwin, 238.

7. John Scott to Darwin, May 4, 1868, letter no. 6160, Darwin Correspondence Project, https://www.darwinproject.ac.uk/letter/DCP-LETT-6160.xml.

8. Rozin, Haidt, and McCauley, "Body and Soul Emotion," 429.

9. I do not strictly differentiate in this book between the terminological languages of affect, emotion, and feeling. In writing a historical account of disgust that takes into account its active role in shaping various domains and discourses related to the history of affect theory, it has seemed conceptually unwise to make a sharp terminological distinction between disgust as a diffuse form of sensory intensification and disgust as a more concretely defined emotional state. Thus for Darwin and Tomkins after him, disgust is a basic emotion, one of the allegedly universal affects; for others in the Deleuzian tradition, however, disgust points towards a diffuse, nonsemantic model of

affectivity, because smells are (following an Enlightenment hierarchy of the senses) considered to be the least semantically organized sensations. Winfried Menninghaus, following Kant, nominates disgust as a "strong sensation [*Empfindung*]," suggesting that the experience of revulsion itself carries the charge of an irreducible physical experience separate from discursive activity (Menninghaus, *Disgust*, 1). This is to say nothing of Jean-Paul Sartre's nausea, in which the irreducibility of physical experience seems less easily disarticulated from the activity of discourse and more akin to something like a structure of feeling. In general, I do my best to follow the rationale that Rei Terada lays out in *Feeling in Theory*: "Emotion terms overlap in ordinary language," Terada writes;

> battling the vagueness, philosophers have developed the distinctions between them. Inevitably, emotion words are inflected variously by different writers. I try to steer a middle course between imposing a single vocabulary on all discussions of texts and giving up on terminological distinctions altogether. The terms seem to me to differ most valuably in connotation, and I've tried to preserve their shades of meaning. Some of those shades are as follows: by *emotion* we usually mean a psychological, at least minimally interpretive experience whose physiological aspect is *affect*. *Feeling* is a capacious terms that connotes both physiological sensations (affects) and psychological states (emotions) . . . I use [feeling] when it seems fruitful to emphasize the common ground of the physiological and the psychological. (4)

10.  I take my methodological cues from the foundational work in historical social theory by Michel Foucault (on sexuality), Norbert Elias (on the civilizing process), and Mary Poovey (on historical epistemology), as well as from the important work in the history of sensation by Alain Corbin (on smell). My work has also been influenced to a lesser degree by scholarship within the disciplinary subfield of "the history of emotions," in particular by sharpening my own position against those of William Reddy and Barbara Rosenwein (I engage with Rosenwein's critique of Elias below). Reddy's influential conception of the "emotive" as a special kind of linguistic utterance that has a particular effect for its speaker has been especially useful, although I would also stress that the articulation and conceptualization of emotions also produce changes in the range of social meanings that are available to a form of emotion expression at any given historical moment. Writing the history of an emotion, that is, is a normative enterprise that can itself contribute to the discursive meaning of that emotion. Thus emotions are in my view less stable than Reddy considers them to be. Moreover, I believe that in framing his intervention as a polemic against "contructionism," Reddy mischaracterizes some of the important historical findings of thinkers like Foucault and Elias. Take, for instance, Reddy's general claim that "if we conceive of community conventions as stipulating styles of emotional control that exploit the capacity of emotives to shape emotions, then . . . emotional control is the real site of the exercise of power." "Against Constructionism," 335. I find it difficult to distinguish this useful formulation from Elias's landmark account of the role of affective molding in mediating between subject formation and the configuration of state power. Nor, I would argue, are Foucault's concepts of biopower and biopolitics too far off—though Reddy never engages with these concepts. For useful overviews of the field, also see Plamper, *History of Emotions*; Frevert, *Emotions in History*.

11. Rozin and Fallon, "Perspective on Disgust," 23. Among Rozin's other publications, see Rozin, Millman, and Nemeroff, "Laws of Sympathetic Magic"; Rozin, Haidt, and Fincher, "From Oral to Moral"; Chapman et al., "In Bad Taste."

12. Tomkins, *Affect Imagery Consciousness*, 357.

13. Tomkins, *Affect Imagery Consciousness*, 357.

14. Wicker et al., "Both of Us Disgusted," 661; Herz, *That's Disgusting*, 64; Kelly, *Yuck!*, 52; Curtis, *Don't Look*, 6; Angyal, "Disgust and Related Aversions," 411.

15. A landmark work in the history of sensation, Corbin's *The Foul and the Fragrant* sought to capture precisely this tension between the denigration of the sense of smell and its ubiquity in the social discourse of the nineteenth century. "The men and women of the nineteenth century muffled history with the clamorings of their desire," Corbin writes. "Meanwhile, however, other dialogues were taking place at a more fundamental level; heavy, animal scents and fleeting perfumes spoke of repulsion and disgust, sympathy and seduction. Despite Lucien Febvre's injunctions, historians have neglected these documents of the senses. The sense of smell was discredited. According to Buffon, it was the sense of animality. Kant excluded it from aesthetics. Physiologists later regarded it as a simple residue of evolution. Freud assigned it to anality. Thus discourse on odors was interdicted" (229).

16. Morris, "Art under Plutocracy," 64–65.

17. Williams's remains one the most perceptive and challenging English-language accounts of the entanglements of "civilization" with the already bifurcated concept of "culture." One of the underlying theoretical aims of this book is to bring Williams's account into proximity with Norbert Elias's treatment of the *Kultur*/*Zivilisation* antithesis in German language and history, and the *civilisation*/*civilité* pairing in French. Williams, *Marxism and Literature*, 15–16; Starobinski, "The Word *Civilization*," 31. Starobinski builds on an important 1930 study by Febvre, "*Civilisation*: Evolution of a Word and a Group of Ideas." For a more recent assessment of the concept and its historical development, see Bowden, *Empire of Civilization*.

18. Marx, *Economic and Philosophic Manuscripts*, 116–17.

19. Berlant, "Epistemology of State Emotion," 51. Also see Berlant, "Subject of True Feeling."

20. Hadley, *Living Liberalism*, 64–65. Also see Poovey, *Making a Social Body*. More than just an influence on my thinking, Poovey's articulation of the "historical epistemology" of the Victorian period is necessary, conceptually speaking, to my own attempt to describe the development of a historical affective formation or habitus of Victorian disgust.

21. Barnes, "Confronting Sensory Crisis," 105.

22. Owing to the topical nature of the chapters, I engage with a wide range of critical sources throughout this book, from specialists in particular (and often peculiar) historical subfields to aesthetic, literary, social, and legal theorists, as well as cultural histories of the period with focuses adjacent to my own. However, there is a core group of scholars of the Victorian period engaging questions of filth and disgust whose work has enabled my own. Among these works, William A. Cohen and Ryan Johnson's edited volume *Filth: Dirt, Disgust, and Modern Life* stands out for having brought many of these scholars together under the same cover. Of those authors, I have learned from and drawn on the following works in particular: Allen, *Cleansing the City*; Barnes, *Great Stink of Paris*; Cleere, *Sanitary Arts*; Trotter, *Cooking with Mud*.

To this list should be added Rosemarie Ashton's *One Hot Summer*. Although it was published late in my own process of writing this book, my work has been enriched (and emboldened) by Ashton's willingness to see in the microhistorical frame of the Great Stink a common thread uniting various other domains of Victorian cultural experience.

23. Engels, *Condition*, 36–37.

24. Swift, *Gulliver's Travels*, 167–68.

25. Lessing, *Laocoön*, 162, 161, 164.

26. Menninghaus, *Disgust*, 25–101. Menninghaus's intellectual history of disgust is an invaluable resource for thinking through the complexities of disgust's changing role over the last 250 years. Nonetheless, his claims about the impossibility of a social history of disgust are untenable and do not hold up to scrutiny. Carolyn Korsmeyer also extensively analyzes the role of disgust within the traditional aesthetic enterprise, but from a formalist rather than an intellectual-historical perspective in *Savoring Disgust*. Finally, my own thinking on disgust has been greatly influenced by the final chapter on the emotion in Sianne Ngai's *Ugly Feelings*, as well as by Ngai's subsequent writings on aesthetic theory in *Our Aesthetic Categories* and *Theory of the Gimmick*.

27. Lessing, *Laocoön*, 160.

28. My thinking here and in the next chapter on disgust's destabilization of the fact/value distinction is indebted to Rei Terada's compelling analysis of "Western culture's association of phenomenality with a discourse of satisfaction and dissatisfaction." *Looking Away*, 9. Of particular interest are the aspects of Terada's argument that deal with the intersection of the philosophical fact/value problem with "human beings' resistance to the mere recognition of unwelcome facts" (5).

29. For an in-depth treatment of Victorian attempts to extend this aspect of the aesthetic project and to turn it into a form of scientific, rather than confused, knowledge, see Morgan, *Outward Mind*.

30. Rancière observes that "for Baumgarten the term 'aesthetics' in fact does not designate a theory of art but rather the domain of sensible knowledge, the clear but nonetheless 'confused' or indistinct knowledge that can be contrasted with the clear and distinct knowledge of logic." Rancière, *Aesthetic Unconscious*, 5.

31. Arendt had intended to publish a third volume of *The Life of the Mind* specifically devoted to the faculty of judgment, adding to two other volumes on willing and thinking. After her death, her notes for a course on Kantian aesthetics were published as the *Lectures on Kant's Political Philosophy*, alongside some of her other writings on judgment.

32. The works in this growing field of political theory that have been most useful to me in developing my own argument have been Zerilli, *Democratic Theory of Judgment*, especially the chapter "The Turn to Affect and the Problem of Judgment: Making Political Sense of the Nonconceptual"; Rancière, *Politics of Aesthetics* and *Aesthetic Unconscious*; Panagia, *Political Life of Sensation*; and Nikolas Kompridis's edited volume, *The Aesthetic Turn in Political Thought*.

33. Rancière, *Politics of Aesthetics*, 12.

34. Bourdieu, *Distinction*, 488. See especially the postscript, "Towards a 'Vulgar' Critique of 'Pure' Critiques," in which Bourdieu elaborates this account of disgust as "the paradoxical experience of enjoyment extorted by violence, an enjoyment which arouses horror."

35. See, in particular, Menninghaus, "The Psychoanalysis of Stinking," in *Disgust*, 183–226.

36. While I am relatively uninterested in thinking of psychoanalysis as a body of theory that can be "applied" to the study of disgust in Victorian cultural phenomena, the fact remains that our study of the social transformations disgust motivated throughout the nineteenth century bears directly on the conceptual and discursive crystallizations in fin-de-siècle culture that gave rise to psychoanalysis and its institutions. In other words, one of the secondary endeavors of this book is to begin to historicize what has long appeared to theorists of the nineteenth century as the applicability of psychoanalytic theory to the cultural terrain of the period. On the idea that nineteenth-century culture helps to explain psychoanalysis without being fully explained by it, see Rancière, *Aesthetic Unconscious*. For examples of the tendency to deploy psychoanalytic concepts as tools to explain the cultural operations of nineteenth-century disgust, especially within a strain of theoretically sophisticated 1980s historicism, see Stallybrass and White, *Politics and Poetics of Transgression*, and Herbert, "Rat Worship," as well as Herbert's treatment of Mayhew in *Culture and Anomie*. For my own discussion of Herbert and Stallybrass and of the need to reconsider the relationship between history and method, see Samalin, "Plumbing."

37. Freud to Wilhelm Fliess, November 14, 1897, in Masson, *Letters*, 280.

38. Freud, *Five Lectures*, 48.

39. Freud, "Negation," 237.

40. Notably, Frazer himself remarks in *The Golden Bough* that "the two great principles [of sympathetic magic] turn out to be merely two different misapplications of the association of ideas" (12). For contemporary adaptations of Frazer, see, among other publications, Rozin, Millman, and Nemeroff, "Laws of Sympathetic Magic." Other works tend to cite Rozin in their treatment of disgust's logic of contamination, rather than presenting new ways of explaining the phenomenon. See, for instance, Herz, *That's Disgusting*.

41. For Nussbaum's sustained engagement with Rozin's work, see "The Cognitive Content of Disgust," in *Hiding from Humanity*, 87–93.

42. Elias, "The Social Constraint towards Self-Constraint," in *Civilizing*, 365–78.

43. See especially Rosenwein's pointed critique of Elias's "grand synthesis," in which she targets inaccuracies in his use of historical sources as well as his dependency on what she argues is an outdated psychoanalytical or "hydraulic model" of emotion and drive, in *Emotional Communities*, 7–20; also see Plamper, *History of Emotions*, 49–53. For Rosenwein's more fully developed theory of the history of emotions, see her *Generations of Feeling*. As an outsider to medieval studies, I find Rosenwein's strong repudiation of Elias ultimately to be more revisionary than damning, and at certain points to veer toward a mischaracterization of psychoanalytic theory that seems out of step with the nuance of her book on the whole. What I believe Rosenwein does help to identify, though, is the difficulty that Elias encounters in distinguishing at a theoretical level between the affective and the restrained, an antithesis that is itself an artifact of Victorian social-scientific presumptions about so-called primitive culture. Elias would continue to explore this problematic throughout his career, for instance in his important 1956 essay "Problems of Involvement and Detachment." Once that distinction is reassessed critically, the problem of treating medieval subjects as overly impulsive and emotional and moderns as rational and affectless also fades out of view

or is at least mitigated. However, unlike Rosenwein, I am inclined to read Elias as largely responsible for undermining the distinction between rationality and emotion, rather than reinforcing it.

44. Elias, *Civilizing*, 86.

45. Elias, *Civilizing*, 135.

46. Social theorists and historians of sociology have over the years begun to draw out the compelling resemblances between Foucault and Elias, including the discovery that Foucault had undertaken (but never published) a translation of Elias's late work *The Loneliness of the Dying*. See, among others, Paulle and Emirbayer, "Beneath Rationalization," and Smith, "Comparing Elias and Foucault," as well as a special section of *Foucault Studies* 8 (2010) devoted to comparing the two thinkers. In making the compelling case that "the terrain of disgust is . . . aesthetics or dietetics, not ethics or religion," Benedict Robinson has also noted points of contact between Foucault's notion of "care of the self" and Elias's conception of the civilizational habitus. See his fascinating article "Disgust c. 1600," 555.

47. Foucault, "Nietzsche, Genealogy, History," 153.

48. Elias, *Civilizing*, 135.

49. *Habits*, 100, 117.

50. *Habits*, 28; quoted in Elias, *Civilizing*, 85. For a more properly Foucauldian moment in the manual, see the instructions for carving a rabbit, which repeat the memorable execution scene with which *Discipline and Punish* opens: "You may perhaps master a *Rabbit*, because he may be treated like Damien, who was broken on the wheel, by removing the legs and shoulders with a sharp-pointed knife, and then breaking his back in three or four pieces by pressing the knife across it and pushing the body up against it with the fork." *Habits*, 227. Cf. Foucault, *Discipline*, 1.

51. Ruskin, "Storm-Cloud," 39.

52. Forster, *Howards End*, 245.

## 1. The Odor of Things

1. "The Thames," *Daily Telegraph*, 2; "State of the Thames," *Daily Telegraph*, 5; "Panic in a Committee Room," 3. I note in passing the casual anti-Semitism of the description of Disraeli's clenched nose—the only nose belonging to an actual individual that I encountered among hundreds of metaphorical and allegorical appeals to the public's nostrils in the archive of the stink. Cf. Theodor Adorno's and Max Horkheimer's important treatment of the sense of smell in their analysis of anti-Semitism: "In the ambiguous partialities of the sense of smell," they write, "the old nostalgia for what is lower lives on, the longing for immediate union with surrounding nature, with earth and slime. . . . In civilization, therefore, smell is regarded as a disgrace, a sign of the lower social orders, lesser races, and baser animals." *Dialectic of Enlightenment*, 151.

2. *Times* (London), July 29, 1858.

3. Law, *Fluids*, 53–54.

4. Weber, *Economy and Society*, 975. The passage forms the core of Weber's discussion of the role of bureaucracy within the overall process of the rationalization of modern European society. "The more complicated and specialized modern culture becomes," Weber goes on, "the more its external supporting apparatus demands the

personally detached and strictly objective *expert*, in lieu of the lord of older social structures who was moved by personal sympathy and favor, by grace and gratitude." Thus, Weber here describes a polarity between the personal, subjective, emotional, and irrational, on the one hand, and the depersonalized, specialized, and calculable, on the other—a polarity which is radically destabilized by the depersonalizing, calculable role of disgust in the rationalization process. Cf. Weber, "Science as Vocation," 12–13. In *Victorian Literature and the Victorian State*, Lauren Goodlad returns to this passage several times, arguing that Britain's liberal attachment to notions of character allowed it to develop a system of modern governance that was not organized around this antinomy of the bureaucratically calculable and the emotional. "Indeed, Britain is Weber's cardinal example," she writes, "of a country where 'calculable' rationality was achieved by nonbureaucratic means" (23). In other words, Goodlad preserves Weber's dualistic schema but suggests that liberalism offered British society a form of sympathetic subjectivity that could mesh unproblematically with the economic and political demands of the modern liberal-capitalist state without producing the need for a massive and fully rationalized state bureaucracy. Nevertheless, she points to the need to shift our focus from the rationalization of the state administrative apparatus to a more nuanced account of the rationalization of the liberal subject's affective *habitus*, a task that has been advanced significantly by Hadley's discussion of "embodied abstraction" throughout *Living Liberalism*. My contribution to this ongoing dialogue is to foreground the way in which the rationalization of social space and the rationalization of the *habitus* both transpired through the affective medium of revulsion, a fact that I believe destabilizes Weber's dualistic schema more profoundly than Goodlad acknowledges.

5. Freud, "Negation," 239. My thinking concerning the element of fantasy (of absence) that is performed by disgust has been influenced by André Green's writings on "the work of the negative." In particular, I draw here on his highly suggestive discussion of the role of negativity in the development of D. W. Winnicott's conception of the transitional object. "It is the bad object that never goes away," Green writes, *"And the bad thing, whether present or absent, is negative anyway in two ways: as bad and as non-existent.* The judgement of attribution and the judgement of existence coincide. The bad thing has to be there, and if it is not, it is this absence equated with void and emptiness that becomes real, more real than the existing objects that are around." Green, "Intuition of the Negative," 92–93.

6. Berlant, "Subject of True Feeling," 58.

7. Of course, many invocations of disgust focus their outrage on modernity and civilization themselves, including the passage from Morris discussed at length in the previous chapter. In those cases, one does encounter something like the call to return civilization to its "utopian odor." I discuss this tension at greater length in the third chapter, in my analysis of humanity's "primal scene" as a genre of imagining civilizational progress. For a more recent example of an invocation of a backward- rather than forward-looking disgust, see the conservative philosopher Leon Kass's sentimental argument against cloning in "Wisdom of Repugnance."

8. Menninghaus, *Disgust*, 3. Here as elsewhere, my work is indebted to Menninghaus, even as I reject his assumptions about the inability to locate a history of disgust beyond its intellectual history. What is perhaps most unsustainable in his reduction of the history of disgust to its various philosophical and psychoanalytic theorizations is

the premise that any intellectual or conceptual history could be fully isolated from the social-historical contexts in which theoretical concepts are formulated and deployed, and which are in fact shaped by those concepts. This is most obvious, perhaps, in the psychoanalytic material—whose theoretical significance Menninghaus nonetheless deftly explores—since it is impossible to imagine the accumulation of psychoanalytic material separate from the specific social contexts out of which it was culled (clinical observation and dialogue, anthropological studies, studies of literature and mythology, etc.). Indeed, against Menninghaus, one can argue that a case study such as Freud's "Notes upon a Case of Obsessional Neurosis" itself forms part of a "cultural" rather than a purely philosophical archive of disgust; though they are often overlooked, the cultural sources of psychoanalytic knowledge are always present on the surface of the Freudian text.

9. "The Thames," *Lancet*, 41.

10. "The Thames," *Daily Telegraph*, 2.

11. The full, memorable quotation is: "All smell is, if it be intense, immediate acute disease; and eventually we may say that, by depressing the system and rendering it susceptible to the action of other causes, *all* smell is disease." Quoted in Finer, *Life and Times*, 298.

12. Poovey, *Making a Social Body*, 130.

13. Chadwick, *Report*, 372.

14. I draw here on Christopher Hamlin's analysis of Chadwick's techno-rationality. "In the trinity of technologies making up the 'sanitary idea,' sewerage was primary." Hamlin, *Public Health*, 239.

15. Allen, *Cleansing the City*, 30.

16. Quoted in Halliday, *Great Stink*, 46.

17. Chadwick to Lord Francis Egerton, October 1, 1845, quoted in Finer, *Life and Times*, 222.

18. Mayhew, *London Labour*, 161.

19. "Dirty Cleanliness," 7.

20. Zola, *La terre*, 357–58.

21. Sloterdijk, *Globes*, 321–33.

22. Spencer, *Social Statics*, 374. Also quoted in Allen, *Cleansing the City*, 39–40.

23. Spencer, *Social Statics*, 394.

24. Spencer, 383.

25. Hamlin, *Public Health*, 255.

26. "The Thames," *Lancet*, 41.

27. "State of the Thames," *Times* (London), 6.

28. "What a Pity," 9.

29. "Pestilential State of the Thames," 535.

30. "What a Pity," 9.

31. "Old Father Thames," 8.

32. "Proceedings," 4.

33. 151 Parl. Deb. H.C. (3d. ser.) (1858) cols. 421–47.

34. 150 Parl. Deb. H.C. (3d. ser.) (1858) cols. 2113–14.

35. 151 Parl. Deb. H.C. (3d. ser.) (1858) cols. 421–47.

36. 151 Parl. Deb. H.C. (3d. ser.) (1858) col. 388.

37. 151 Parl. Deb. H.C. (3d. ser.) (1858) cols. 27–40.

38. 151 Parl. Deb. H.C. (3d. ser.) (1858) cols. 874–77.

39. 151 Parl. Deb. H.C. (3d. ser.) (1858) cols. 1509–10.

40. "Old Father Thames," 8.

41. "State of the River Thames," *Morning Chronicle*, 14.

42. "Debate of Monday Evening," 9.

43. "Report upon the State of the Thames," 44.

44. Snow, "Drainage and Water," 191. In a tragic twist of fate, Snow died, at age forty-five, on June 16, 1858, just at the beginning of the crisis, after suffering a stroke the previous week; his prediction that if the Thames were to be cleansed it would be for aesthetic rather than scientific reasons was largely borne out.

45. Snow's response in this regard anticipates the attitude prevailing during the Parisian stink of 1880, when, as Corbin writes, "the Pasteurian revolution made a reappraisal of the old sensitivities and tolerances necessary" (*Foul and Fragrant*, 223).

46. Law, *Fluids*; Cleere, *Sanitary Arts*.

47. Cooper, *Characteristics*, 36.

48. Lessing, *Laocoön*, 240.

49. Gigante, *Taste*, 50.

50. Williams, *Marxism and Literature*, 151–57.

51. Arendt, *Kant's Political Philosophy*, 67. "As a social animal," Gigante observes, echoing Arendt, "man doesn't just eat: he dines." *Taste*, 5.

52. Hume, *Essays*, 234.

53. Quoted in Menninghaus, *Disgust*, 38.

54. Lessing, *Laocoön*, 154.

55. Kant, *Critique of Judgment*, 12–18.

56. Kant, 15.

57. Kant, 36.

58. Kant, 36.

59. Arendt, *Kant's Political Philosophy*, 72. Also see Brenkman, "The Ordeal of Universalism," in *Cultural Contradictions*, 71–77; Zerilli, "We Feel Our Freedom."

60. Kant, *Critique of Judgment*, 106–7.

61. Menninghaus, *Disgust*, 104.

62. Here I draw on Silvan Tomkins's evocative description of the dynamics of projection and objectification at play in his account of the experience of disgust. "The disgustingness of the object of disgust is partly the affect which is referred to the object like an envelope of slime. Even when the self becomes the object of disgust, there is a minimum of self-consciousness of the self as subject." Tomkins, *Affect Imagery Consciousness*, 360.

63. Sloterdijk, *Globes*, 332–33; Ricoeur, "The Symbolism of Evil Interpreted," in *Conflict of Interpretations*, 269–380. In a closely related vein, Benedict Robinson has tracked the evolution of medieval conceptions of aversions such as *odium* and *abominatio*, as they gradually transformed into the early modern conception of disgust and, eventually, into the emotion's Enlightenment aesthetic iteration. "Disgust c.1600," 554-55.

64. Halliday, *Great Stink*, 100.

65. For an illuminating discussion of the architectural complexity and reception of the pumping stations, see Dobraszczyk, *London's Sewers*, 45.

66. "Opening of the Main Drainage," 5.

67. "Opening of the Great Main Drains," 4.
68. "Main Drainage System," 5.
69. "This Morning's Ceremony," 11.
70. "Opening of the Main Drainage," 5 (emphasis added).
71. "Opening of the Main Drainage," 5.
72. Jephson, *Sanitary Evolution*, 2.
73. Johnson, *Ghost Map*, 255.
74. Masson, *Letters*, 280. Cf. Freud, *Civilization*, 54–55.
75. Here I build on Poovey's important and closely related analysis of the relationship between the sanitary idea, the disaggregation of the social sciences, and what she calls the "production of abstract space." "The nineteenth-century institutionalization of separate social sciences owes as much to the naturalization of abstract space," she writes, "as does the physical reordering of London (the building of the Embankment, the laying of surface and underground rails, the hygienic reform of urban neighborhoods like St. Giles)." *Making a Social Body*, 25.
76. Freud, *Civilization*, 100.
77. Benjamin, *Arcades*, 391.
78. Benjamin, 389.
79. Benjamin, 392.

## 2. Realism and Repulsion

1. Dickens, *Little Dorrit*, 218, 44. Dickens is clear that Arthur sees the clean waters of the Thames at Twickenham as flowing ineluctably into the cloaca of London, referring to Arthur's "own associations of the troubled river running beneath the bridge with the same river higher up . . . so many miles an hour the peaceful flowing of the stream, here the rushes, there the lilies, nothing uncertain or unquiet" (281). For a definitive discussion of the function of insensibility within the tradition of the British novel, see Wendy Anne Lee's *Failures of Feeling*.
2. The most important reading of Swift's suite of "excremental poems" remains Norman O. Brown's "studies in anality," in *Life against Death*. Jed Esty has made the compelling case that Swift's scatological invective needs to be read in light of his ambivalent critique of British rule in Ireland, and that Swift thus "stands as a distant precursor to the excremental writers of postcolonial Africa and Ireland." I return to this argument in the conclusion to this book. Esty, "Excremental Postcolonialism," 28. For the critical tradition dealing with Swift, see Huxley, *Do What You Will*; Greene, "On Swift's 'Scatological Poems'"; Gilmore, "Comedy of Swift's Scatological Poems." For the connection between Swift's and Dickens's scatological tendencies, see Steig, "Dickens's Excremental Vision"; Lougy, "Filth"; Davis, *The Flint and the Flame*; and Sedgwick's important reading of *Our Mutual Friend* in *Between Men*, 161–79.
3. Trotter, *Cooking with Mud*, 31.
4. Bakhtin, *Rabelais*, 24.
5. Jameson, *Antinomies of Realism*, 35–38.
6. Brontë, *Jane Eyre*, 306.
7. My thinking about disgust's adversarial relationship to knowledge owes much to Eve Kosofsky Sedgwick's writings about Silvan Tomkins's theory of negative affect. More specifically, in her influential account of paranoid reading,

Sedgwick asserts that paranoid knowledge has a "practice of disavowing its affective motive and force and masquerading as the very stuff of truth." I adapt this formulation to my discussion of disgust in various places throughout this book. Sedgwick, *Touching Feeling*, 138.

8. Nussbaum, *Hiding from Humanity*, 102, 117. As will become clear in my chapter on obscenity censorship, while I agree with Nussbaum's more limited normative position that disgust ought not play a significant role in the functioning of the law, I believe her distinction between the irrational and the rational is difficult to maintain. Perhaps more significantly, the approach taken by this book would suggest that Nussbaum's idea of "re-creating our entire relationship to the bodily" in the name of the civilizing process needs to be situated more explicitly in the context of its nineteenth-century history—especially, as I argue in the concluding chapter, the history of Victorian imperialism.

9. Brontë, *Jane Eyre*, 312.

10. Brontë, 331.

11. Brontë, 385.

12. Rabelais, *Gargantua*, 257.

13. Robinson, "Disgust c. 1600," 568.

14. Swift, *Gulliver's Travels*, 50.

15. "Cassinus and Peter," in Swift, *Essential Writings*, 620.

16. Dickens, *Little Dorrit*, 398.

17. For a related argument, see Samalin, "Dickens, Disinterestedness," 229–30.

18. Moretti, *Bourgeois*, 109, 112.

19. Williams, "Social Criticism in Dickens," 224.

20. Dickens, *Little Dorrit*, 500–501.

21. Dickens, 267.

22. Bakhtin, *Dialogic Imagination*, 293.

23. Baudelaire, *Oeuvres posthumes*, 20.

24. Morris, "Art under Plutocracy," 64.

25. Quoted in Lessing, *Laocoön*, 153–54.

26. Ruskin, *Fiction—Fair and Foul*, 269.

27. Morris, "Art under Plutocracy," 65.

28. Lukács, "Narrate or Describe?," 127.

29. Lukács, 134.

30. Auerbach, *Mimesis*, 504.

31. Auerbach, 505.

32. See, for instance, McKeon's brief account of the emergence of the aesthetic: "The belief in the autonomous aesthetic could gain ascendancy only when the coarser and more material vestiges of empirical thought . . . had been ejected by the body of knowledge which in modern thought is designated as the last and lonely refuge of transcendent spirit, the sphere of artistic experience" (*Origins of the English Novel*, 120). Critical accounts of the function of negativity, refusal, and disavowal within nineteenth-century literature also bear directly on this question. See, for instance, Ablow, *Victorian Pain*; Terada, *Looking Away*.

33. For the canonical association of narrative with desire and, by extension, psychoanalytic drive per se, see, across a variety of different registers, Armstrong, *Desire and Domestic Fiction*; Brooks, *Reading for the Plot*; Edelman, *No Future*; Girard,

*Deceit, Desire, and the Novel*; and Sedgwick, *Between Men*. For an important counterargument rooted in the tradition of British object relations psychoanalysis, see Christoff, *Novel Relations*. For book-length accounts of nineteenth-century letters and the philosophical, physiological, and psychological discourses of sympathy, see, among many others, Ablow, *Marriage of Minds*; Chandler, *Archaeology of Sympathy*; Greiner, *Sympathetic Realism*.

34. In a related vein, Ablow argues that negative sensory and affective experiences such as pain and aversion represent "something like a condition of existence—something that brings us together at least as much as it separates us." *Victorian Pain*, 140.

35. There are no fewer than fifteen instances of this phrase and its cognates throughout the novel, among them, Gissing, *Nether World*, 26, 27, 41, 54, 58, 79, 215, 218, 275.

36. Orwell, "George Gissing," 55.

37. Hardy, *Jude*, 54–55.

38. Woolf, *Waves*, 224.

39. Proust, *Remembrance*, 231.

40. Sedgwick, *Weather in Proust*, 13. For two other influential discussions of the image of the glass jars dipped into the river, see De Man, *Allegories of Reading*, 70–71, and Benjamin, "The Image of Proust," in *Illuminations*, 204–5.

41. Hardy, *Jude*, 59, 118–19, 419. More literally, Hardy might also have conceived of Jude as suffering from an occupational hazard variously known at the time as "stonemason's lung," "grinder's asthma," or "stone-cutter's disease" (now, *silicosis*), the material particulate of the dank university and church stones from which he makes his livelihood lodged in his respiratory tract. Plant, *Pollutants*, 274.

42. Christoff, *Novel Relations*, 82. Although Christoff's *Novel Relations* was published too late for me to engage substantively with it here, I am lucky to have been in conversation with her while writing this book. My thinking about the figure of the container/contents in literary texts as well as psychoanalytic theory is greatly indebted to her and to Sedgwick.

43. Jameson, *Antinomies*, 33, 61, 50.

44. Jameson, 34; Rancière, "Auerbach," 236.

45. Elias, *Civilizing*, 472.

46. My thinking on this point is informed by and indebted to Joshua Wilner's work on internalization in Romantic poetry and psychoanalytic thought, *Feeding on Infinity*. Wilner observes that, in both these paradigms, to internalize can mean either to bring something into the self from without or to keep something internal that seeks to get out (2–6). Wilner's work has helped me to perceive a similar (but inverted) confusion in the discourse of disgust.

## 3. Darwin's Vomit

1. Darwin to Caroline Darwin, May 1838, letter no. 411, Darwin Correspondence Project, https://www.darwinproject.ac.uk/letter/DCP-LETT-411.xml.

2. Reprinted in Colp, *Darwin's Illness*, 187–257.

3. Dickens, *Christmas Carol*, 52. We might compare Dickens's parodic treatment here to William Hazlitt's more earnest discussion in "On Depth and Superficiality" of

the bearing of digestion on perception. "Suppose a man to labour under an habitual indigestion," he writes. "Does it not oppress the very sun in the sky, beat down all his powers of enjoyment, and imprison all his faculties in a living tomb? Yet he perhaps long laboured under this disease, and felt its withering effects before he was aware of the cause. It was not the less real on this account; nor did it interfere the less with the sincerity of his other pleasures." *Collected Works*, 354. I am grateful to Tristram Wolff for this reference.

4. On this particular point as well as in my overall approach to Darwin's work, I am indebted to Elizabeth Grosz's *Becoming Undone*.

5. Curtis, *Don't Look*, 6; Wicker et al., "Both of Us Disgusted," 661. The full passage bears a striking resemblance to Darwin's observation, though the authors do not seem to have drawn on it: "This 'primitive' mechanism may protect monkeys and young infants from the food poisoning described in the Introduction, even before the evolution/development of sophisticated cognitive skills." See also Ruth Leys's critique of Wicker's study in her "Both of Us Disgusted."

6. The nineteenth century saw radical alterations in the way that the primal and the primitive were theorized in relation to the social and the civilized, with many of the central innovations emanating out of Victorian Britain. Historians of anthropology, in particular, such as George Stocking and Adam Kuper, have mapped out the important ways in which ideas of primitive mind, emotion, and sociality, which were foundational to the social sciences, were influenced and transformed in the wake of Darwin's revolutionary work. Stocking is especially sensitive to the complex ways in which evolutionary theory rendered "problematic [the] relation of biological and social theory" for Victorian debates over the origins of culture and species alike. *Victorian Anthropology*, 145. Thus the decade after the publication of *On the Origin of Species* saw the rapid-fire publication of a trove of significant works that straddled the social and biological sciences, while advancing their claims through the language of the primitive, among them Thomas Huxley's *Man's Place in Nature* (1863); John Lubbock's *Pre-Historic Times* (1865) and *The Origin of Civilisation and the Primitive Condition of Man* (1870); Edward Tylor's *Researches into the Early History of Mankind and the Development of Civilization* (1865) and his landmark *Primitive Culture* (1871); Herbert Spencer's *Principles of Biology* (1864), followed by the equally important *Principles of Psychology* (1870) and *Principles of Sociology* (1874); as well as, of course, Darwin's own *The Descent of Man, and Selection in Relation to Sex* (1871). It was a period of extreme intellectual ferment, in which biology and social science developed through a shared set of scientific and ideological assumptions about the primitive and its thorny claims to priority.

7. Darwin, *Expression*, 236–37. I have added the enumerations for clarity; all subsequent citations to this book in this chapter are parenthetical.

8. See, among others, Ahmed, *Cultural Politics*; Leys, "Both of Us Disgusted"; McGinn, *Meaning of Disgust*; Miller, *Anatomy of Disgust*; Probyn, *Carnal Appetites*; Trotter, *English Novel*. For a more extended discussion of Darwin's experiences in Tierra del Fuego and of the ideas he formed about "savagery," see Duncan, "Darwin and the Savages."

9. Miller, *Anatomy of Disgust*, 3; Ahmed, *Cultural Politics*, 82–84.

10. Rozin and Fallon, "Perspective on Disgust," 30.

11. Sartre, *Being and Nothingness*, 774; Ahmed, *Cultural Politics*, 84.

12. Kolnai, *On Disgust*, 38, 78.

13. Ahmed, *Cultural Politics*, 82. Also see Ngai, *Ugly Feelings*, 335.

14. Take as a paradigmatic example of this tendency the following lines from *The Anatomy of Disgust*: "I need not spell out just how contaminating, how disgusting, the anus is," writes Miller. "It is the essence of lowness, of untouchability, and so it must be hemmed in with prohibitions" (100). In the passage I am quoting from, Miller is not promoting this normative perspective, so much as inhabiting it as part of his extended critical analysis of the mechanics of the emotion. Citing a range of theorists from Freud to Leo Bersani, he has, we might say, a demystified view of the emotion, one that need not fall prey to the prejudicial and irrational purposes for which it often is mobilized. And yet even though these examples from Ahmed and Miller are both written with a critical distance from the content of disgust, their account of its meaning and significance is nevertheless structured by the morphology of the emotion.

15. This absence of the disgusting from Darwin's theory of disgust is not due to a want of material gathered throughout his career. "At night I experienced an attack, & it deserves no less a name," he wrote in his *Beagle* diary, "of the Benchuca, the great black bug of the Pampas. It is most disgusting to feel soft wingless insects, about an inch long, crawling over one's body; before sucking they are quite thin, but afterwards round & bloated with blood, & in this state they are easily squashed." *Beagle Diary*, 315. Some of Darwin's medical biographers have speculated that he may have contracted Chaga's disease from these beetles, which could explain his cycles of vomiting.

16. Darwin to Joseph Dalton Hooker, February 20, 1864, letter no. 4412, Darwin Correspondence Project, https://www.darwinproject.ac.uk/letter/DCP-LETT-4412.xml.

17. As Daniel M. Gross has persuasively argued, such images reveal the sophisticated rhetorical complexity animating Darwin's understanding of what it meant to describe, or better yet to produce, an emotion as a scientific object. See especially "Defending the Humanities with Charles Darwin's *The Expression of the Emotions in Man and Animals*," in Gross, *Uncomfortable Situations*, 28–51. For a fascinating discussion focused on Darwin's relationship to photography and to his photographers, see Prodger, *Darwin's Camera*.

18. Darwin to Hooker, January 27, 1864, letter no. 4398, Darwin Correspondence Project, https://www.darwinproject.ac.uk/letter/DCP-LETT-4398.xml; Darwin to Hooker, December 5, 1863, quoted in Browne, "I Could Have Retched All Night," 244.

19. Darwin to Hooker, May 29, 1854, letter no. 1575, Darwin Correspondence Project, https://www.darwinproject.ac.uk/letter/DCP-LETT-1575.xml.

20. Wilson, *Gut Feminism*, 58.

21. Darwin to Hooker, January 25, 1864, letter no. 4397, Darwin Correspondence Project, https://www.darwinproject.ac.uk/letter/DCP-LETT-4397.xml.

22. Hillman, *Shakespeare's Entrails*, 15.

23. Wells, *Thomas Nashe: Selected Works*, 163.

24. In a related vein, Michael Schoenfeldt writes that in the early modern period "diet and digestion were seen to affect not just mood and mental capacity, but even the ineffable realms of the soul" ("Fables of the Belly," 253). "The stomach, then," he continues, "can be seen to have played a central role in the development of

political individuation and the articulation of devotional inwardness in early modern England. . . . The early modern stomach was a primal site for the exercise of ethical discrimination and moral virtue" (257).

25. Harvey, *Works*, 431. For an illuminating discussion of Harvey and Charleton on the "sensation without sense," especially as it relates to contemporary discussions of affect, see Harrison, "Personhood and Impersonal Feeling." I am grateful to Harrison as well for his profound intellectual generosity over the course of many personal conversations.

26. This was no less true for those early modern physiologists who believed that digestion was a chemical process than it was for the mechanistic school of Descartes. Paracelsus, for example, as Antonio Clericuzio has observed, imagined the stomach to contain a metaphorical "alchemist" who would distinguish what was toxic from what was nutritious, even when the senses could not detect the poison. "Chemical and Mechanical Theories," 331.

27. Charleton, *Natural History of Nutrition*, 120–21.

28. Charleton, 122–23.

29. Harrison, "Personhood and Impersonal Feeling," 228.

30. On this topic, see C. Riley Snorton's discussion of the American gynecologist J. Marion Sims's disturbing experimentation on enslaved women in *Black on Both Sides*.

31. Beaumont, *Experiments and Observations*, 11.

32. Beaumont, 29.

33. Beaumont, 3.

34. Beaumont, 10.

35. Rozin and Fallon, "Perspective on Disgust," 26.

36. "Extimacy," in Skelton, *Edinburgh International Encyclopaedia of Psychoanalysis*, 155. The connection to the uncanny is especially pertinent here, as the extimate nature of Beaumont's relationship to St. Martin's stomach leads to a new mechanistic understanding of digestion as a form of "animal automatism."

37. "Other physiologists have attempted to effect the same end by experiments performed upon lower animals," Beaumont's editor writes, but in such cases the cost of knowledge is offset by "the cruelty inseparable from the performance of such experiments," while "the pain which the animal suffers necessarily disturbs the regularity of the function under examination, and . . . vitiates the results." *Experiments and Observations*, viii.

38. For extensive evidence of the ways in which physiological knowledge of digestion was literally produced through the vivisection of the canine stomach, one need only turn to Starling's textbook, *Elements of Human Physiology*: "Hence if the stomach of a dog be cut out, and the lower end of the œsophagus sewn to the upper end of the duodenum, it is found that considerable quantities of fat pass undigested through the alimentary canal, since the connective tissue binding fat-cells together can no longer be dissolved by the stomachless dog" (229).

39. Miller, *History of the Stomach*, 64. Miller's meticulously researched book was published during the year in which I wrote the first draft of what would become this chapter, and I remain very grateful for his provocative argument as well as for the trove of primary sources his work has made available. (Not to be confused with *William* Ian Miller, whose *Anatomy of Disgust* I discuss earlier in this chapter.)

40. Descartes, *Discourse on Method*, 31. Also see Descartes's "Fourth Objection":

Still, so as not to pass over the topic in complete silence, I'll say the thing that it is most important to say, namely: in our bodies and those of the brutes, no movements can occur without the presence of all the organs or instruments that would enable the same movements to be produced in a machine. . . . Many of the motions occurring inside us don't depend in any way on the mind: heartbeat, digestion, nutrition, breathing when we are asleep, and also such waking actions as walking, singing and the like when we do them without thinking about them. When someone falls, and holds out his hands so as to protect his head, he isn't instructed by reason to do this. Rather, the sight of the impending fall reaches the brain and sends the animal spirits into the nerves in the manner needed to produce this movement of the man's hands, without any mental volition, just as it would be produced in a machine. (quoted in Huxley, "Animal Automatism," 198)

41. Huxley, "Animal Automatism," 205.

42. Huxley, 206–7.

43. "We feel sorry because we cry," James writes in a memorable passage, "angry because we strike, afraid because we tremble, and not that we cry, strike, or tremble, because we are sorry, angry, or fearful, as the case may be." "What Is an Emotion," 190. Also see Greenwood, "Huxley and Epiphenomenalism."

44. Taylor, "Locating the Victorian Unconscious"; Matus, "Victorian Framings of the Mind."

45. Stephen, "Thoughts of an Outsider," 476. Also quoted in Mayer, "Expression," 404–5. Browning's antivivisection poem, "Tray," offers a strong account of how the scientific drive toward the conceptual understanding of reflexive and instinctual behavior seemed to Victorians to be inextricably bound up with the willful performance of cruelty and the infliction of violence. Browning, *Poetic and Dramatic Works*, 142.

46. Quoted in Miller, *History of the Stomach*, 19, 22. The former quote is from an 1838 article in the *Dublin Journal of Medical Science*, the latter from the eminent physician James Johnson's "An Essay on Indigestion" (1827).

47. Miller, *History of the Stomach*, 26.

48. Parsons, *Anti-Bacchus*, 29. Also cited by Miller, *History of the Stomach*, 37.

49. Brunton, *On Disorders of Digestion*, 62–64. Mentioned in Miller, *History of the Stomach*, 35.

50. James Dickson to Darwin, December 14, 1872, letter no. 8680, Darwin Correspondence Project, https://www.darwinproject.ac.uk/letter/DCP-LETT-8680.xml. "One of my Father's male servants, a strong, healthy Scotch lad of about 18 years of age, possessed this power in an extraordinary degree," the letter reads.

I never saw him "throw up" (our lowland Scotch phrase for *vomit*, and the action in question) food because it disagreed with him, but I have seen him do it many times for our amusement. I have given him many a pocketful of fruit on the condition that he would "throw up" a portion of it. It was always done with apparent ease, and he assured us it caused him no pain or uneasiness—his only objection being that of parting with the food. On one occasion he was with us in a search for wild raspberries; and, while I was telling the other boys of this singular powe⟨r of his⟩ he joined us. We were standing on a bridge, and I remember distinctly that the very moment I asked him to do it before my companions, he bent down toward the ledge and performed it. It was done instantaneously; and I believe he could do it at any moment after eating. This youth, therefore, assuredly possessed the power of voluntarily rejecting food.

51. Séglas and Bourneville, "Du Mérycisme," 255. An important psychopathologist in his own right, Séglas was an assistant to and close collaborator with Charcot. Along with Jules Cotard, another member of Charcot's circle, Séglas helped produce the clinical description of the so-called *délires de negation*, in which patients would imagine their bodies to be emptied of blood or organs, or that certain parts of their bodies were simply gone—the original modern diagnosis of the body without organs about which Artaud and after him Deleuze would write. In addition to Charcot's direct influence on Freud (who arrived at the Salpêtrière Hospital in 1885), Séglas, Cotard, and their colleagues were all major influences on Lacan's early work, and indeed Lacan draws on the notion of *délires de negation* in his analysis of Freud's "Wolf Man" case study. Part of my interest here is in showing the actual proximity between Darwin's thoughts about disgust and vomiting and the psychoanalytic paradigm that would to some degree build on, and to some degree supplant them. For a related discussion of the impact of Darwin's writings and ideas on the development of psychoanalytic theory, see Rowlinson, "Foreign Bodies" and Ritvo, "Darwin's Influence on Freud."

52. Quoted in Einhorn, *Rumination*, 20.

53. Wilson, *Gut Feminism*, 58.

54. Rousseau, *Political Writings*, 10, 4, 19.

55. Kant, "Conjectures," 221, 227.

56. Menninghaus rightfully objects that Darwin fails to provide a basis on which our progenitors could ground their decisions to vomit up the foods they believed to disagree with them, a kind of primeval standard of taste. "How such classifications of certain foods . . . might have emerged," he writes, "and what function they might have served, Darwin has left entirely unanswered." We might say that for Menninghaus, in a sense, Darwin's evolutionary account of disgust is insufficiently Darwinian; it lacks conceptual economy and fails to live up to an implied functionalist expectation. "Not surprisingly, therefore," Menninghaus concludes with bravado, "[Darwin's] narrative of disgust's evolution has not found any followers to date; indeed, in psychology, it has been deemed hardly worth the effort of a commentary" (*Disgust*, 184). Although Menninghaus is correct to observe that Darwin's account provides no standard for these primeval judgments, his objection nonetheless reflects the overwhelming conceptual pressure to theorize the primal scene exclusively within the dualistic framework of an instinct-reason binary, in which the difference between the instinctual and the functional is arbitrarily collapsed. Moreover, against Menninghaus's historical claim about Darwin's lack of followers, this chapter has sketched the influence of Darwin's discussion of disgust and rumination on the subsequent development of psychoanalytic thought, Ferenczian and Lacanian strains in particular.

57. Darwin, *Origin*, 181. Also see Notebook N, "Instincts are unerring: no," in Darwin, *Metaphysics*, 85.

58. Darwin, *Origin*, 155.

59. Frederickson, *Ploy of Instinct*, 21.

60. Locke, *Essay Concerning Human Understanding*, 94–95.

61. Hume, *Treatise of Human Nature*, 176, 179.

62. For a full account of Hume's theory of reason as an instinct in the soul, see Richards, *Darwin and the Emergence*, 105–10. In this section, I draw on and largely accept Richards's authoritative account of the development of the instinct concept within the British tradition, from Locke to the natural theologians of the early nineteenth century.

63. Quoted in Richards, "Instinct and Intelligence," 216.

64. Hume, *Treatise of Human Nature*, 179.

65. Richards, *Darwin and the Emergence*, 93.

66. Darwin, *Metaphysics*, 14.

67. Darwin, *Origin*, 156.

68. Darwin, *Descent*, 38.

69. Curtis, *Don't Look*, x.

70. Curtis, 60–61, 52. Throughout the book, Curtis writes of disgust as though it articulated its demands in colloquial language. However, she does acknowledge in a footnote that this is simply a useful shorthand: "Technically what is happening is that some aspect of the neurology of the brain causes an animal to bias its choices towards one course of action rather than another" (119n8). Yet this equivocation about the personification of emotion is, I believe, a much larger methodological problem than Curtis is willing to deal with, at least in this book. For she at once raises and fails to address the question of the scale or level of articulation at which an emotion becomes legible as an object of study. Thus on the one hand, it is certainly unscientific to personify disgust as speaking in a voice, and on the other hand, if Curtis were to write only about neurological reactions, without recourse to the chunkier cultural dimensions of the emotion, one might not recognize her book as being about disgust. Yet what this means is that there may not be a science "behind" revulsion in the way that Curtis wants there to be. Rather, affect and emotion become available at certain intersections of scientific and cultural forms of knowledge.

71. Kant, "Conjectures," 223. Kant recognized that the philosophical enterprise of deducing the origins of the species from the present was bound to be speculative— "no more than a pleasure trip," as he puts it (221). Nonetheless, he also saw that it was precisely this element of fantasy under scrutiny that gave the genre its critical force and imaginative purchase as a means of trying to organize the composition of the subject along a diachronic or narrative axis. We might see in this conjectural genre, that is, a blueprint for Nietzsche's genealogical project, and after him Freud's and Foucault's as well. It is also worth noting in this context that Kant's account of the Fall rather closely resembles the serpent's false account, related to Eve, of what happened when he ate the forbidden fruit, in Milton's *Paradise Lost* (see the epigram to this chapter). Thus there is a case to be made that Kant here naturalizes the Fall by reading it, in a sense, as Satan (or as Satan persuades Eve to imagine it), and therefore that this rather diabolical account itself has exerted an important organizing influence over later speculative genealogies of the origins of humankind, the famous long footnote in *Civilization and Its Discontents* in particular.

72. Kant, "Conjectures," 224.

73. Kant, "Conjectures," 233.

74. Darwin, *Descent*, 55. Here and throughout I am drawing on the section on language in *Descent*, 53–62. For a comprehensive account of Darwin's theory of a musical protolanguage in particular, and of linguistic evolution in general, see Fitch, "Biology and Evolution of Music"; Fitch, *Evolution of Language*. For an overview of Darwin's composite theory of language evolution, and an account of how it relates to contemporary twenty-first century theories, see section 4 in particular.

75. Darwin, *Descent*, 56.

76. Foucault, *Order of Things*, 280.

77. Williams, *Marxism and Literature*, 25. For an in-depth account of this encounter, see Ahmed, *Archaeology of Babel*.

78. Foucault, *Order of Things*, 288.

79. Darwin, *Descent*, 56.

80. Foucault, *Order of Things*, 286.

81. Darwin, *Descent*, 56; Müller, *Lectures on the Science of Language*, 358. Also see Dowling, "Victorian Oxford," 160–78. In the chapter on disgust in *Expression*, Darwin refers his readers in a footnote back to precisely the subsection of Wedgwood's essay that was the target of Müller's derision. Titled "Pooh!," this text by Wedgwood precedes Darwin in arguing that "the attitude of dislike and rejection is typified by signs of spitting out an unsavoury morsel," the foremost of which is, he insists, across a great variety of cultures, the bilabial stop: "The sound of spitting is represented indifferently with an initial *p*, as in Maori *puhwa*, to spit out; Lat. Spuere, to spit; *respuere* (to spit back), to reject with disdain; *despuere*, to reject with disgust or disdain." *Dictionary*, xlv. Müller, by contrast, argued that such interjections formed part of a "layer of words which may be called purely *emotional*," and which could be distinguished scientifically from the roots of words, which are "the signs of general concepts" and therefore available only to humans. Müller's objections to Darwin's linguistic theories revolved in large part around "this distinction between *rational* and *emotional* language," which "enables us to see clearly in what sense man and beast may be said to share the gift of language in common, and in what sense it would be wrong to say so" ("Lectures on Mr. Darwin's Philosophy of Language," 676–77).

82. Müller, *Lectures on the Science of Language*, 354.

83. Müller, *Science of Thought*, 171. Fitch asserts that Müller's idiosyncratic blend of anti-Darwinian Christianity with the new science of language "played a role in creating the historical chasm between linguistics and biology which is only being bridged today." *Evolution of Language*, 394.

84. Alter, "Darwin and the Linguists"; for a full treatment of the relationship of Darwinian thought to nineteenth-century linguistics, see Alter, *Darwinism and the Linguistic Image*. To complicate Alter's view, see Richards, "Linguistic Creation of Man."

85. Darwin, *Descent*, 57.

86. I am largely following Raymond Williams's distinction between originary and constitutive conceptions of human linguistic capacity: "It is precisely the sense of language as an *indissoluble* element of human self-creation that gives any acceptable meaning to its description as 'constitutive.' To make it *precede* all other connected activities is to claim something quite different" (*Marxism and Literature*, 29).

For a riveting and thought-provoking discussion of the interplay between Darwin's thinking on the origins of language and his shifting perspectives on race, see Winter, "Darwin's Saussure." Here too, see Irene Tucker's discussion of the perspicacity of the racial signifier in her chapter on Darwin in *Moment of Racial Sight*, especially 186–99.

87.  Tomasello, *Origins*, 11. Heavily influenced by Wittgenstein, Tomasello's fascinating discussion also offers an alternative conception of semiotic or symbolic naturalness that is illuminating in the context of Darwin's genealogy of disgust: "It is also important . . . that the human use of pointing and pantomiming—as the successors to ape gestures after things became cooperative—are 'natural' in a way that 'arbitrary' linguistic conventions are not. Specifically, pointing is based on humans' natural tendency to follow the gaze direction of others to external targets, and pantomiming is based on humans' natural tendency to interpret the actions of others intentionally. This naturalness makes these gestures good candidates as an intermediate step between ape communication and arbitrary linguistic conventions" (9). Strikingly, what Tomasello implies is "natural" in the natural sign is not its semantic meaning, but rather the social expectation of its interpretation. The development of language, this line of argumentation insists, is partly the outcome of biological adaptation to a social world in which one must expect to be addressed by others.

88.  Winter, "Darwin's Saussure," 144.

89.  If this seems an obvious feature of most emotion expressions, it has nevertheless not been widely accepted as a starting point for thinking about disgust. Indeed, in terms of its communicative complexity, Darwin's "I wouldn't eat that if I were you" blows most dyadic accounts of disgust out of the water. Most philosophical literature on disgust recognizes the emotion as *at most* presupposing an unwieldy dyadic relationship, which tends, almost invariably, to dissolve into a convoluted solipsism. The philosopher Colin McGinn, for example, has argued that "the intention of disgust is reflexive in a way," asserting that "in disgust, consciousness seeks to avoid a state of itself—namely, perception of the eliciting stimulus." For this line of thinking, the presumption of the instinctivity of disgust leads toward this insistence on the human as a kind of emotionally contorted monad—a *homo clausus* who has sprung a leak. McGinn, *Meaning of Disgust*, 11.

90.  In his critique of the Kantian paradigm of disgust (excerpted as one of the epigraphs to this chapter), Jacques Derrida expresses a kind of anxiety that a philosophical study of revulsion which focused on "the process of vomiting" rather than the "vomit itself" would run the risk of tacitly endorsing a fantasy of self-sovereignty in the form of the belief that one could make oneself vomit. This dream, of course, is precisely the focus of this chapter, and I see Darwin's entertaining the possibility of voluntary vomiting as disrupting rather than abetting an Enlightenment vision of subjectivity as self-mastery. The discrepancy between Derrida's deconstructive/Kantian approach to the question of vomiting and Darwin's genealogical account is actually what gives Darwin his critical purchase in thinking through the issue. Derrida, "Economimesis," 23–25.

91.  Menninghaus, *Disgust*, 184.

92.  As Bruno Latour put it, "Sorting out the kernels of science from the chaff of ideology became the task for generations of well-meaning modernizers. In the

[natural-cultural] hybrids of the first Enlightenment thinkers, the second group too often saw an unacceptable blend that needed to be purified by carefully separating the part that belonged to things themselves and the part that could be attributed to the functioning of the economy, the unconscious, language, or symbols." *Never Been Modern*, 35–36.

93. Proverbs 26:11 (King James Version).

## 4. The Masses Are Revolting

1. Bataille, "Attraction and Repulsion I–II," in *College of Sociology*, 106, 114.
2. Simmel, "Metropolis and Mental Life," 331.
3. Simmel, *Conflict*, 21.
4. Weber, *City*, 77.
5. Weber, *Economy and Society*, 387.
6. In tracking these shifts in the relationship of alienation and disgust, it is useful to outline a loose constellation of psychosocial concepts and terms in German and English whose deployment and coordination is a major through-line of this chapter. Already, for instance, we have seen how Simmel depends on the German words *Aversion*, *Fremdheit* (strangeness), and *Abstoßung* (repulsion). The latter term, in particular, represents an important hinge between the affective sense of disgust and a more neutral sense of rejection and repudiation. I believe Simmel inherited this language of repulsion from Marx, who throughout his career strove to coordinate the sense of alienation as estrangement (*Entfremdung*) with a distinct conception of alienation as the exploitation and more specifically the expropriation of labor, which he often described as involving an extractive process of repulsion (*Abstoßung*). The affectively neutral sense of repulsion as a negative physical force needs to be kept in relationship with the more emotionally charged sense of repulsion as disgust that informed protosociological accounts of the city, such as Engels's sense—discussed at length below—that there is something "disgusting [*Widerlich*]" about the alienation of London's masses. Simmel's identification of disgust and aversion (*Aversion*) as important social drives might be seen as an attempt to mediate between this emotionally heated sense of disgust and the more abstract sense of repulsion. Casting a wider net, this whole constellation of terms can be expanded to include the psychological and psychoanalytic sense of alienation as repression, as being cut off from a whole side of oneself, which Freud had defined early on as an experience of mental disgust. In this light, an important overlap comes into view between the constellation of sociological terms designating repulsion and alienation and a related chain of psychoanalytic terms for defense mechanisms, including repression (*Verdrängung*), negation (*Verneinung*), disavowal (*Verleugnung*), and repudiation/foreclosure (*Verwerfung*), each of which Freud in one way or another links to a concept of repulsion. Finally, as I discuss at the end of this chapter, Freud's development of the concept of repression was also deeply influenced by nineteenth-century British sociological and anthropological thought, including the work of Herbert Spencer and his argument that emotional "restraint" was a signal achievement of modern European civilization. Synthesizing many of these different social theoretical traditions, Elias would identify disgust, shame, and repugnance as the forces of restraint that constituted this so-called civilizing process.

7. I have found the following accounts of the rise of sociology to be particularly useful in thinking about the specific problem that emotion posed to method: Lepenies, *Between Literature and Science*; Levine, *Visions of the Sociological Tradition*; Heilbron, *Rise of Social Theory*; Halsey, *History of Sociology in Britain*; Goldman, *Science, Reform, and Politics*; Porter, *Rise of Statistical Thinking*.

8. Durkheim, *Rules*, 39–40.

9. Lepenies, *Between Literature and Science*, 7.

10. Durkheim, *Rules*, 40.

11. Engels, *Condition*, 36–37.

12. As Susan Faye Cannon has put it, statistics developed out of "an intricate dovetailing of inherited, ideological, moral, socioeconomic, intellectual and personal factors," including "a heritage from the Enlightenment . . . a realization that great social changes were taking place that no one understood as a whole . . . a conclusion that social reform was needed but could not be justified without evidence . . . a desire to refute Ricardo and a general dissatisfaction with the deductive school of social theorists." *Science in Culture*, 240–44. Also see Goldman, "Origins of British 'Social Science,'" 591.

13. Martineau, *Illustrations of Political Economy*, xiii, xviii.

14. Quoted in Humpherys, *Henry Mayhew*, 89.

15. Engels, *Condition*, 36.

16. Carlyle, *Two Note Books*, 210–11.

17. Engels, *Condition*, 36–37.

18. The German phrase "das ganze tolle Treiben" conveys a much different sense than the English translation here. "Fabric," in particular, loses the sense of the buzzing turmoil of economic activity that the German conveys. I am grateful to Florian Klinger for his help with the German here and throughout this chapter.

19. Engels, *Outlines of a Critique of Political Economy* (1844), quoted in Marcus, *Engels*, 111. Marcus's discussion of Carlyle's influence on Engels remains one of the most nuanced treatments of the matter.

20. Engels, *Condition*, 40.

21. Marx, "Eighteenth Brumaire," in Marx and Engels, *Collected Works* 11: 149. Marx's repulsion toward the lumpenproletariat can be compared to later characterizations of the mob or crowd as primal and atavistic. However, what Marx finds grotesque about these heterogeneous lower rungs of society is precisely their disorganized character, their inability to coalesce around a consciousness of their economic conditions, whereas what Le Bon and others decried in the crowd was precisely its swarm-like unity of purpose. For a fascinating discussion of Marx's conception of the lumpenproletariat, and of some of Marx's thinking about attraction and repulsion more generally, see Denning, "Wageless Life."

22. Marx, *Economic and Philosophic Manuscripts*, 74–75.

23. Marx, 74–75.

24. On this point and on Marx's theory of alienation in general, see Ollman, *Alienation*. Of particular interest here is Ollman's discussion of Marx's conceptions of the animal, the human, and the species (131–52). For a definitive account of the biopolitical discourse of human animality in Marx and Engels's early writings, as well as in the Victorian literature of social observation more broadly, see Steinlight, "Political Animals: The Victorian City, Demography, and the Politics of Creaturely Life," in *Populating the Novel*, 74–106.

25. Marx, *Economic and Philosophic Manuscripts*, 75.

26. Marx, 116–17.

27. Compare too Morris's assertion that "every little market-town seizes the opportunity to imitate, as far as it can, the majesty of the hell of London and Manchester," with the continuation of Marx's invective: "The Irishman no longer knows any need now but the need to *eat*, and indeed only the need to eat *potatoes*—and *scabby potatoes* at that, the worst kind of potatoes. But in each of their industrial towns England and France have already a *little* Ireland." Marx, 117. The point here is about the rational, replicable character of the industrial city and its degradations, but the criticism itself is no less replicable and structured. Or, yet again, we might imagine Carlyle gulping down Marx's scabby Irish potatoes as preparation for his own racist pumpkins in the *Occasional Discourse on the Negro Question* (1849).

28. Ruskin, "Storm-Cloud," 39.

29. Marx, *Capital*, 341.

30. Marx, *Contribution*, 20.

31. Marx, *Grundrisse*, 92.

32. See Negri, *Marx beyond Marx*, especially the chapter "The Method of the Antagonistic Tendency" (41–58), from which I have taken the title for this section of the chapter.

33. Marx, *Contribution*, 21.

34. For historical accounts of the 1857 revulsion, see Shakinovsky, "1857 Financial Crisis"; Fabian, "Speculation on Distress"; Kindleberger and Aliber, *Manias, Panics and Crashes*.

35. For discussions of the importance of the revulsion to the development of the *Grundrisse*, as well as of the significance of Marx's journalistic output during these years, see Krätke, "First World Economic Crisis"; Krätke, "Marx's 'Books of Crisis'"; Musto, "Marx's Life." Also see Bologna, "Money and Crisis."

36. Marx and Engels, *Collected Works*, 40: 74. In November 1857, at the height of the crisis, Marx declared to Engels that even "though my own financial distress may be dire indeed, never, since 1849, have I felt so cosy as during this outbreak." Marx and Engels, *Collected Works*, 40: 199.

37. Kindleberger and Aliber, *Manias, Panics and Crashes*, 81, 177–78; Fabian, "Speculation on Distress," 137.

38. Evans, *History of the Financial Crisis*, 121.

39. Quoted in Fabian, "Speculation on Distress," 138.

40. Marx, "British Revulsion," New York *Tribune*, November 27, 1858, reprinted in Marx and Engels, *Collected Works*, 15: 387.

41. Marx, "British Commerce and Finance," New York *Tribune*, October 4, 1858, reprinted in Marx, *Dispatches*, 200–204.

42. Marx, 201.

43. Negri, *Marx beyond Marx*, 4. Emphasis in original.

44. The *Oxford English Dictionary* cites this example from William Lewis's 1778 pharmaceutical tract, *The New Dispensatory*: "Sydenham assures us, that among all the substances which occasion a derivation or revulsion from the head, none operate more powerfully than garlick applied to the soles of the feet." "revulsion, n.". OED Online. December 2020. Oxford University Press. https://www-oed-com.proxy.uchicago.edu/view/Entry/164997?redirectedFrom=revulsion (accessed December 30, 2020).

45. Walley, *Financial Revulsion of 1857*, 5–6.

46. Marx, *Contribution*, 21.

47. Here and throughout, my discussion of Marx's *Grundrisse* and of the transition in Marx's thought from the language of alienation to that of exploitation is informed by Moishe Postone's influential analysis in *Time, Labor, and Social Domination*. See especially Postone's account of the alienation-exploitation relationship (30–36).

48. Marx, *Grundrisse*, 453.

49. Marx, 454.

50. Marx, 454.

51. Sianne Ngai's fascinating discussion of what she calls the "visceral abstractions" of Marx's later writings was published too late for me to incorporate fully into my discussion of Marx's conception of repulsion, but I understand myself to be posing a very similar question to Ngai when she asks, "What is the reason for using an image that makes a specifically capitalist abstraction . . . sound confusingly *like* simple physiological human labor?" "Visceral Abstractions," in *Theory of the Gimmick*, 186.

52. As Gareth Stedman Jones has observed, Marx's dissertation had in fact delved deeply into the topic of physical repulsion—at the level of the atom—in the philosophical theories of Democritus and Epicurus. Unlike Epicurus, Marx accused Democritus of having seen "in repulsion only the material side, the fragmentation, the change, and not the ideal side, according to which all relation to something else is negated and motion is established as self-determination." Quoted in Jones, *Greatness and Illusion*, 81.

53. Negri, *Marx beyond Marx*, 55–58.

54. Denning ("Wageless Life," 18) refers us to an important corner of *Capital* in which Marx describes how the "greater attraction of workers by capital is accompanied by their greater repulsion" (783). A few pages earlier, Marx also notes that the "fragmentation of the total social capital into many individual capitals, or the repulsion of its fractions by each other, is counteracted by their attraction" (777). Significantly, Marx here uses the German word *Repulsion* (along with *Attraktion*), as opposed to the term *Abstoßen*, which he uses throughout the *Grundrisse*. These passages are in this sense good examples of the decreasing emphasis on the affective connotations of repulsion, and Marx's general movement toward thinking of repulsion in terms of a more impersonal physical law.

55. Marx, *Grundrisse*, 93–94.

56. Marx, 661.

57. Simmel, *Conflict*, 17.

58. Marx, *Grundrisse*, 661.

59. Spencer, *Principles of Sociology*, 450–51; "The Social Organism" was originally published in the *Westminster Review* in 1860 and reprinted in Spencer, *Essays Scientific, Political and Speculative*.

60. Elias, *Civilizing*, 86.

61. Arendt, "Race-Thinking before Racism," in *Origins*, 183–84.

62. Spencer, *Principles of Sociology*, 71.

63. Spencer, *Study of Sociology*, 144.

64. For example, Spencer, *Principles of Sociology*, 63.

65. Spencer, 58.

66. Weber, *Protestant Ethic*, 121; Freud, *Civilization*, 110.

67. Durkheim, *On Suicide*, 413.

68. Freud, *Five Lectures*, 48.

69. Simmel, "The Metropolis and Mental Life," 331–32. Marcus refers to this passage in Simmel in the midst of his own extensive treatment of Engels's depiction of London, which he also compares to Dickens and Wordsworth. The comparison is significant but, for the most part, allusive rather than substantive. Regarding Simmel's point that "dissociation is in reality one of the elementary forms of association," Marcus writes: "One feels that this last clause, true enough as far as it goes, ought to have about three further dialectical turns appended to it" (*Engels*, 154–55).

70. Weber, "'Objectivity' of Knowledge," 137.

71. Aron, *Main Currents*, 192.

## 5. The Age of Obscenity

1. Ironically, this account of the obscenity was itself expurgated in earlier published versions of Pepys's diaries. Robertson, *Obscenity*, 21; Pepys, *Diary*, 209; Craig, *Suppressed Books*, 24.

2. 146 Parl. Deb. (3d ser.) (1857) col. 327.

3. 146 Parl. Deb. (3d ser.) (1857) col. 866; Margaret Oliphant, "The Anti-Marriage League," a review of *Jude the Obscure* in *Blackwood's Magazine*, January 1896, reprinted in Cox, *Critical Heritage*, 257.

4. My thinking about obscenity and action is deeply indebted to both Frances Ferguson's and Catharine MacKinnon's writings on pornography. Ferguson's account of the simultaneous rise of pornography and of utilitarian social structures, and of the related developments in tort law, is especially important to my argument. Ferguson, *Pornography, the Theory*, especially chapters 1 and 2; MacKinnon, *Only Words*.

5. Mitchell, *What Do Pictures Want?*, 127. See also Mitchell's influential essay "The Rhetoric of Iconoclasm: Marxism, Ideology, and Fetishism," in *Iconology*, 160–208.

6. Angyal, "Disgust and Related Aversions," 397.

7. Frazer, *Golden Bough*, 12. According to the law of contagion, Rozin and Fallon explain, disgusting objects contaminate everything they touch; while according to the law of similarity, anything resembling a disgusting object—including its representation—will also provoke disgust. Rozin and Fallon, "Perspective on Disgust," 30.

8. The "obscene" libel with which Charles Sedley was charged was a vague new offense arising out of older and better-defined transgressions such as seditious and blasphemous libel, which treated certain uses of language as conduct antagonizing either the sovereign or the sacred. As Lynn Hunt has noted, most seventeenth-century texts that might today be termed obscene or pornographic for their erotic content were also socially critical in nature, couching political and religious critique alike in sexually explicit writing and illustration. The focus on obscene words as actionable content derived most directly from these libel laws, which protected the integrity of specific institutions. At the same time, more nebulous common-law transgressions, including outraging the public decency, the conspiracy to corrupt public morals, and keeping a disorderly house, while not typically deployed to police representations,

offered a potent vocabulary of social depravity and corruption that entered into the ambit of the obscene. In lieu of the better-defined institutional spheres of Church and Crown or State, these misdemeanors operated within the less circumscribed realms of decency and moral hygiene. Combining these two strands of offense, obscene libel thus provided a new way of understanding certain uses of language as conduct against, or nuisances within, an emergent public sphere or social domain. Hunt, *Invention of Pornography*, 9–48; Robertson, *Obscenity* and Craig, *Suppressed Books*. For a related argument about the historical rise of pornography as a narrowing of sexuality to focus on the representation of genital sex acts, see Lubey, "Making Pornography, 1749–1968."

9. My thinking here is indebted to Peter Coviello's lucid anatomy of the discourses of secularism and secularization in the opening "Axiomatic" section of *Make Yourself Gods*, 23–47. In particular, Coviello's insistence that secularism is "a normative project" that, moreover, "has a body" helps us to see what is on the line in the disciplining of disgust that forms the heart of the liberal rejoinders to statutory obscenity regulation (29, 33).

10. For an incisive discussion of the specific problems that the analysis of sexuality poses to the Weberian "disenchantment" thesis, see Scott, *Sex and Secularism*, 66–69.

11. Per the *Oxford English Dictionary*, the dominant meaning of pollution follows a path of increasing secularization, moving from the spiritual realm to the naturalized world of environmental pollution and physical contamination:

1. Desecration of that which is sacred; the condition of being desecrated. *rare after 17th cent.*
2. Ejaculation of semen without sexual intercourse, *esp.* a nocturnal emission (*cf. nocturnal pollution, n.*)
3. a. Spiritual or moral impurity or corruption. Sometimes also with an implication of physical impurity conveyed by bodily contact.
   b. Physical impurity or contamination; (now) *esp.* the presence in or introduction into the environment (esp. as a result of human activity) of harmful or poisonous substances, or excessive levels of light, noise, organic waste, etc.

"pollution, n.". OED Online. December 2020. Oxford University Press. https://www-oed-com /view/Entry/146992?redirected from=pollution.

For accounts of how the law has relied on conceptions of pollution in its treatment of pornography and obscenity, see Benjamin, "Possessing Pollution"; Nagle, "Idea of Pollution"; Nagle, "Pornography as Pollution." The most thought-provoking account of pollution in the humanities and social sciences more generally remains Mary Douglas's *Purity and Danger*.

12. 145 Parl. Deb. (3d ser.) (1857) cols. 102–4.

13. 146 Parl. Deb. (3d ser.) (1857) cols. 327–28.

14. The full quotation reads, "Here is Lord Campbell apparently making, for the first time, the discovery that there is such a place as Holywell-street, and cackling like an old hen, and clucking out his information in the House of Lords, seemingly for the sake of a twaddling antithesis between physical and moral poisons." *Saturday Review*, May 16, 1857, 447. For an informative account of the Obscene Publications Act as an example of "moral panic," see Roberts, "Morals, Art, and the Law."

15. 145 Parl. Deb. (3d ser.) (1857) col. 103.

16. 147 Parl. Deb. H.C. (3d ser.) (1857) cols. 1475–84.

17. 146 Parl. Deb. (3d ser.) (1857) cols. 327–28.

18. Ferguson, *Pornography, the Theory*, xiv, 20, 21.

19. Devlin, *Enforcement of Morals*, 15. "Nothing should be punished by the law that does not lie beyond the limits of tolerance," Devlin writes.

> It is not nearly enough to say that a majority dislike a practice; there must be a real feeling of reprobation. Those who are dissatisfied with the present law on homosexuality often say that the opponents of reform are swayed simply by disgust. If that were so it would be wrong, but I do not think one can ignore disgust if it is deeply felt and not manufactured. Its presence is a good indication that the bounds of toleration are being reached. Not everything is to be tolerated. No society can do without intolerance, indignation, and disgust; they are the forces behind the moral law, and indeed it can be argued that if they or something like them are not present the feelings of society cannot be weighty enough to deprive the individual of freedom of choice. (17)

For a liberal rejoinder, see Nussbaum, *Hiding from Humanity*, 72–87. In particular, Nussbaum sees conservative arguments like Devlin's, which seek to use disgust as a means of justifying bigotry, as emblems of disgust's inadequacy as an emotional basis for the law.

20. *Regina v. Hicklin*, 3 L.R. Q.B.D. (1868), 360. Simon Stern has observed that by the time of the *Hicklin* ruling in 1868 there already existed a considerable body of common-law rulings taking into account the "harmful tendencies of obscene publications," as well as a long-standing legal tradition of considering the particular susceptibilities of the "young person" in this context. Cockburn almost certainly had such precedents in mind. For an especially illuminating example of this prehistory to *Hicklin*, see the 1791 Old Bailey trial of John Ryal, who was convicted for selling texts said to "inflam[e] passions in the young and tender mind, to an immoderate extent, when reason is not a match for them." "The tendency of such a publication to corrupt the morals of both sexes," the verdict reads, "is too manifest and too enormous to require any demonstration." *Old Bailey Proceedings Online* (www.oldbaileyonline.org, version 8.0, January 1, 2021), February 16, 1791, trial of John Ryal (t143). I am grateful to Stern for providing me with a trove of such cases. Stern, "Defining Obscenity before *Hicklin*."

21. Williams, *Obscenity and Film Censorship*, 20.

22. Hunter, Saunders, and Williamson note that neither Cockburn's ruling nor Blackburn's concurring opinion was concerned with providing a robust or even coherent definition of the obscene, and my reading of the Hicklin case is indebted to their account. However, they overstate the case when they argue that "in assuming such a lacuna [i.e., the lack of a coherent definition], historians of obscenity must be suspected of anachronism." As we have seen, the passage of Lord Campbell's act was nearly stymied by Liberal MPs who did in fact see the lack of an "interpretation clause" as a damning conceptual shortcoming of the law. The challenge lies in theorizing how and why these two attitudes toward the obscene coexisted in nineteenth-century culture, as well as in the present. Hunter, Saunders, and Williamson, *On Pornography*, 71. Also see Gillers, "Tendency to Deprave and Corrupt."

23. *Confessional Unmasked*, iii.

24. *Hicklin*, 3 L.R. Q.B.D. (1868), 368.

25. *Confessional Unmasked*, 58. For an illuminating and wide-ranging discussion of the pamphlet's publication history and its eventual deployment by the Protestant Electoral Union, see Mullin, "Unmasking *The Confessional Unmasked*," 491–94. Of particular note is Mullin's discussion of the "disreputable" activities undertaken by the group.

26. In thinking about the uneven temporalities of secularization, it is worth noting that the ecclesiastical sources excerpted and singled out by the pamphlet are precisely those cited by Foucault in the first volume of *The History of Sexuality* as having slowly begun to fall out of use following the Council of Trent in the sixteenth century. Foucault, *Sexuality*, 18–20.

27. Here the authors of the pamphlet inserted an outraged footnote, which captures some of the tinny pathos of their scandalization: "*Often happens!* How did he know! There is nothing done, it appears, that can escape the knowledge of the priest; he knows the secrets of young and old: he can tell the real father of every child in the parish—nay, the very attitude in which each was begotten, and the words with which each embrace was given! And yet, in this very sentence, these *prurient inquisitors* are called 'Divines.'" *Confessional Unmasked*, 56.

28. *Confessional Unmasked*, 56.

29. See especially Douglas, "Primitive Worlds," in *Purity and Danger*, 91–116.

30. The case is *Riley v. 1987 Station Wagon*, 650 N.W.2d 441, 443 (Minn. 2002). Gillers, "A Tendency to Deprave and Corrupt," 226–27.

31. Ferguson, *Pornography*, 67. The English law of torts transformed significantly during the middle decades of the nineteenth century. Most relevant to our discussion, only a few months after the final *Hicklin* ruling, the case of *Rylands v. Fletcher* was decided in the House of Lords, establishing strict liability as a controversial new branch of tort law. Under strict liability law, a person could now be held responsible for damages under certain circumstances even in the absence of intention or tortious negligence. Notably, Justice Colin Blackburn had issued the ruling in *Rylands* when it came before the Court of the Exchequer in 1866, and his language and thinking there clearly anticipate his position in *Hicklin* that Scott "must be taken to intend the natural consequences of his act." *Hicklin*, 3 L.R. Q.B.D. (1868), 376.

32. *Hicklin*, 3 L.R. Q.B.D. (1868), 368.

33. "The King *against* Vantandillo" (1815), in Maule and Selwyn, *Reports of Cases*, 73–75.

34. *Hicklin*, 3 L.R. Q.B.D. (1868), 376.

35. Coviello, *Make Yourselves Gods*, 31. Coviello here builds on the work of John Lardas Modern, who suggestively writes, "Disenchantment was not the vanquishing of ghosts. Rather, it was the matter of calculating them." Quoted in Coviello, *Make Yourselves Gods*, 252n21.

36. Deana Heath has made the compelling case that Vizetelly's trial in the late 1880s represented a turning point in the history of obscenity regulation, a moment when the link forged by the passage of the 1857 act between "obscenity, governmentality and empire" was realized in the new project of "imperial hygiene." I explore this link in the following chapter. Heath, *Purifying Empire*, 65. For an informative account of Vizetelly's publishing enterprises before and during the trials, see Korey, *Vizetelly & Compan(ies)*.

37. All excerpts from the trial are as reported in "Central Criminal Court, October 31," *Times* (London), November 1, 1888, 13. The column makes clear that the prosecution had argued that were the press to reproduce the obscenities aired throughout the proceedings they would be liable to indictment as well. For a slightly longer transcript, see the National Vigilance Association's pro-censorship pamphlet, *Pernicious Literature*, 16–19.

38. The argument, which is familiar from our earlier discussion of realism, was not especially well-organized: great literature was disgusting, he seemed to be saying, but "unclean, as distinguished from obscene, tendencies" were not enough to warrant censorship; to the contrary, a novelist like Zola promoted morality by rendering in lurid detail the consequences of vice and corruption, whereas the works of the past (and especially of antiquity) were truly prurient; it was not literature that was prurient, however, but the hypocrisy of the censors themselves, who "can gloat over the filthiest Divorce cases, while pretending to be greatly shocked at M. Zola's bluntness." Vizetelly, *Extracts*, 2, 3. Vizetelly's position is close to Moore's, who published his *Literature at Nurse, or Circulating Morals* with Vizetelly in 1885.

39. De Amicis, "Notes upon the 'Assommoir,'" v. See also Leckie's discussion of this preface in "'A Preface Is Written to the Public,'" 452–53. Zola remained a kind of benchmark in the literature of disgust even in the twentieth century. Thus Sartre could write that "those who easily stomach a Zola novel like *The Earth* are sickened when they open an existential novel" in *Existentialism Is a Humanism*, 19.

40. In a related vein, Tanya Agathocleous has argued that British colonial law in particular mobilized the censorship apparatus in order to mark "the difference between legitimate and criminal affect" and in so doing "to sanitize the imperial public sphere." "Criticism on Trial," 437.

41. Nussbaum, *Hiding from Humanity*, 143.

42. Nussbaum, 143–44.

43. Nussbaum, 143, 146.

44. Nussbaum, 75.

45. Nussbaum, 139.

46. Here and below I will be drawing on Saba Mahmood's essay "Religious Reason and Secular Affect: An Incommensurable Divide?" In particular, my own thinking has been influenced by Mahmood's argument that religious beliefs ought to be understood as nonpropositional and rooted in what she refers to as a *schesis* or habitus that describes a complex set of embodied relationships. For a different perspective on the imbrication of obscenity regulation with questions about the religious prohibition of images, see Adler, "First Amendment." Adler in turn draws on Mitchell's writings on iconoclasm, which have greatly influenced my own thinking. Also see Latour, "A Few Steps," and Taussig, *Defacement*.

47. 325 Parl. Deb. (3d ser.) (1888), col. 1713. Heath also quotes from Smith's long parliamentary performance in her illuminating account of Vizetelly's trial, "Imperial Hygiene and the Regulation of the Obscene," in *Purifying Empire*, especially 66–68.

48. Joss Marsh makes a compelling argument for reading *Jude the Obscure* in the context of late nineteenth-century blasphemy cases. I am heavily indebted to her reading and hope to have shown that the emergence of the obscene as a legal-aesthetic category absorbs many of the energies of the blasphemous that Marsh describes as part of a broader process of secularization. *Word Crimes*, 269–328.

49. Quoted in Hardy, *Life and Work*, 294.

50. Quoted in Cox, *Critical Heritage*, 257.

51. Dalziel and Millgate, *Hardy's Poetical Matter*, 15. Cf. Mitchell, *What Do Pictures Want?*, 127: "Images are sometimes treated as pseudopersons—not merely as sentient creatures that can feel pain and pleasure but as responsible and responsive social beings. Images of this sort seem to look back at us, to speak to us, even to be capable of suffering harm or of magically transmitting harm when violence is done to them."

52. Hardy, *Jude*, 122. Subsequent parenthetical citations are to this edition.

53. Their tumescence bears a family resemblance to Jacques Derrida's discussion of the "colossal" in his reading of Kant's third *Critique*: "One would say, by reason of its almost excessive size, that it was obscene." *Truth in Painting*, 125.

54. Mahmood, "Religious Reason and Secular Affect," 76, 81, 74.


## Conclusion

1. Williams, *Marxism and Literature*, 134.

2. Foucault, *Archaeology*, 36–37.

3. 148 Parl. Deb. (3d ser.) (1857), cols. 226–27.

4. Even Marx's writing on the financial revulsion was thoroughly entangled with the series of articles he wrote simultaneously on the uprising in India. Tracking both events in the New York *Tribune* with his characteristic precision, Marx's journalism from the autumn of 1857 and the winter of 1858 alternates between an analysis of the global financial system and detailed accounts of the military vulnerabilities of the British Empire. His coverage of the two ongoing crises dovetails most completely in an article concerning the effects on the already reeling London stock exchange of the massive loan Parliament had authorized to service the East India Company's debts incurred during the ongoing conflict. "The Approaching Indian Loan," in Marx and Engels, *Collected Works* 15: 443–46.

5. Heath, in *Purifying Empire*, offers the most extensive discussion of how the invention of obscenity was put to work as a discourse of moral hygiene and a technique of colonial governmentality in late nineteenth-century India and Australia. On this topic, also see Agathocleous, "Criticism on Trial" and Sigel, *Governing Pleasures*. For discussions of public health and the sanitary idea in the imperial context, see Bashford, *Imperial Hygiene*; Arnold, *Colonizing the Body*; and especially, in this context, Anderson, "Excremental Colonialism."

6. "Debate of Monday Evening," 9.

7. The rebellion is by far the most voluminously documented and well-studied event dealt with in this book, and it is unnecessary to provide a full bibliography for the purposes of my discussion. Among the primary sources I have consulted, the most useful for my discussion were Metcalfe, *Two Native Narratives*; Qureshi, *Qaisar-ut-Tawarikh of Kamal-ud-din Haidar*; Roberts, *Letters Written during the Indian Mutiny*; Farooqi, *Besieged*; Bush, *Warner Letters*. Among the Victorian and contemporary histories of the events, I have consulted Kaye's and Malleson's multivolume *History of the Indian Mutiny*; Pati, *1857 Rebellion*; Wagner, *Great Fear of 1857*; Dalrymple, *Last Mughal*; Chaghatai, *1857 in the Muslim Historiography*. My thinking about the event has

also been greatly influenced by Nathan Hensley's treatment of the violence of the British counterinsurgency that is woven throughout his *Forms of Empire: The Poetics of Victorian Sovereignty*.

8. Wagner reports that the army's inspector general of ordnance, "stated that 'he was told that the composition was that which the regulations prescribed, and that the tallow might or might not have contained the fat of cows and other animals.'" *Great Fear of 1857*, 30.

9. Roy, *Alimentary Tracts*, 32–33. The whole first chapter, "Disgust: Food, Filth, and Anglo-Indian Flesh in 1857" has been extremely helpful in clarifying my own thoughts about the rebellion, and rather than articulating a disagreement with Roy, my argument seeks to extend hers. My book was already in production when Anjuli Fatima Raza Kolb's *Epidemic Empire* was published, but I have nonetheless tried to incorporate some of her incisive and comprehensive analysis of the rhetoric of contagion in the archive of the Rebellion.

10. Stoler, *Archival Grain*, 57–58. Stoler goes on to characterize this strain of colonial studies as Weberian in a reductive sense. "Viewed in this frame," Stoler elaborates,

> colonial states would seem to conform to a Weberian model of rationally minded, bureaucratically driven states, outfitted with a permanent and assured income to maintain them, buttressed by accredited knowledge and scientific persuasion, and backed by a monopoly of weaponed force. Similarly, they have been treated as contained if not containable experimental terrains for efficient scientific management and rational social policy, "laboratories of modernity," information-hungry machines that neither emergent European states nor capitalist enterprises in Europe could yet realize or afford. In either account, it is the conceit of reason and the celebration of rationality on which imperial authority has been seen to rest—and eventually to fail and fall. (98)

My earlier discussion of Foucault in this chapter is also indebted to Stoler's writings on the *History of Sexuality*, especially "A Colonial Reading of Foucault: Bourgeois Bodies and Racial Selves," in *Carnal Knowledge*, 140–61. More recently, Chris Taylor has made the compelling case for understanding the British Empire's rational-economical turn away from the West Indies through the affective-rhetorical framework of the "neglect" articulated by West Indian writers. Like Stoler, Taylor sees affective experience as constitutive of the "at times eye-droopingly boring changes in the politico-economic fabric of the British Empire," rather than simply supplementing or sitting alongside it. Taylor, *Empire of Neglect*, 1–2.

11. Rapson, E. J., and Roger T. Stearn. "Kaye, Sir John William (1814–1876), military historian." *Oxford Dictionary of National Biography*. Sep. 23, 2004. https://www.oxford dnb.com/view/10.1093/ref:odnb/9780198614128.001.0001/odnb-9780198614128-e-15201.

12. Kaye and Malleson, *History of the Indian Mutiny*, 359–61.

13. In a highly suggestive passage, Sloterdijk observes "the kinship, not only etymological, between smells [*Gerüche*] and rumors [*Gerüchte*]. The rumor is the spoken smell," he writes. "Rumor is as infectious and rapid as ill will." *Globes*, 330.

14. Kaye and Malleson, *History of the Indian Mutiny*, 435.

15. Roy, *Alimentary Tracts*, 50, 70–71. The "bone dust" story refers to another rumor that the British had surreptitiously introduced ground bones into the flour and salt sold at markets.

16. Freud, "Unconscious," 195. Once again I take my cue from Stoler's important "colonial reading of Foucault," in which she observes that "in colonial studies the carnal is often suspended as a precultural instinct, given and unexplained. Such analyses often proceed, *not* from a Foucauldian premise that sexual cravings are a social construct and sex a nineteenth-century invention, but from an implicitly Freudian (and imperial) one." *Carnal Knowledge*, 156.

17. Guha, *Elementary Aspects*, 220–21. For a related discussion of Guha's analysis, also see Bhabha, "By Bread Alone: Signs of Violence in the Mid-Nineteenth Century," in *Location of Culture*, 283–302. For a sustained discussion of contagion in the literary and historical documentation of 1857–58 and throughout colonial discourse more generally see Kolb, *Epidemic Empire*, 38–54.

18. Guha, *Elementary Aspects*, 225. Guha goes on to elaborate the semiotic dimensions of the colonial discourse of contagion in great detail, in a discussion of the circulation of chapati prior to the initial uprising of 1857. Significantly, he argues that the perception of contagion depends on the "misreading of a *symbol* as an *index*. . . . The colonial administrators and British writers close to them were not familiar with the rule by which the symbol of the circulating chapati could be identified. Some of them therefore sought to extract its meaning in terms of a convention pertinent to their own culture and rooted in their own history, and ended up identifying it as the index of a preconcerted design to destroy the Raj." *Elementary Aspects*, 240–41. Once again, Guha describes as projection what is often analyzed in terms of incorporation. The misrecognition of symbol for index, too, resonates with the aesthetic conception of the disgusting artwork as obtruding.

19. Guha, 225.

20. John Scott to Darwin, May 4, 1868, letter no. 6160, Darwin Correspondence Project, https://www.darwinproject.ac.uk/letter/DCP-LETT-6160.xml.

21. Barrett, *How Emotions Are Made*, 23.

22. I adapt this formulation from Elias, who observes that "the formation of feelings of shame and revulsion and advances in the threshold of repugnance are both at once natural and historical processes. These forms of feeling are manifestations of human nature under specific social conditions, and they react in their turn on the socio-historical process as one of its elements." *Civilizing*, 135.

23. Elias, *Civilizing*, 129–30; *Habits*, 256.

24. Emerson, "Behavior," in *Conduct of Life*, 153.

25. Elias, *Civilizing*, 135.

26. Freud, "Negation," 237. Rose, "Negativity in Klein," 136.

27. Kristeva, *Powers of Horror*, 3. In the Kleinian tradition, as Rose discusses in great detail, the focus on oral expulsion has less to do with subject formation per se than with the corporeal basis of symbolization.

28. Bataille, "Formless," in *Visions of Excess*, 31.

29. Douglas, *Purity and Danger*, 2–3. For Kristeva's engagement with Douglas, see "The Fundamental Work of Mary Douglas" in *Powers of Horror*, 65–67.

30. Douglas, 36.

31. The citation was tracked down by Douglas's biographer and literary executor, Richard Fardon, in "Citations Out of Place."

32. Reprinted in "Great Annual Dinner," 137–38.

33. Hardy, "Dorsetshire Labourer," 257; Freud, "Character and Anal Erotism," 172–73. Also quoted in Fardon, "Citations Out of Place," 26. One might reasonably speculate that Hardy could have come across Palmerston's speech in the paper, either in preparation for writing the essay, or as part of his extensive reading in archival news sources; Freud—reputed to have been an avid reader of Hardy's novels—might in his turn have picked the phrase up from reading "The Dorsetshire Labourer."

34. Matthew, *House of Gibbs*; Hu-Dehart, *Coolies*, 92.

35. Emerson, *Conduct of Life*, 15. For a discussion of this disturbing passage in light of Emerson's race thinking more generally, see Cadava, "Guano of History"; Goffe, "Guano in Their Destiny."

# BIBLIOGRAPHY

Ablow, Rachel. *The Marriage of Minds: Reading Sympathy in the Victorian Marriage Plot.* Stanford, CA: Stanford University Press, 2007.

Ablow, Rachel. *Victorian Pain.* Princeton, NJ: Princeton University Press, 2017.

Adler, Amy. "The First Amendment and the Second Commandment." *New York Law School Law Review* 57 (2012/13): 42–58.

Adorno, Theodor, and Max Horkheimer. *Dialectic of Enlightenment: Philosophical Fragments.* Stanford, CA: Stanford University Press, 2002.

Agathocleous, Tanya. "Criticism on Trial: Colonizing Affect in the Late-Victorian Empire." *Victorian Studies* 60, no. 3 (2018): 434–60.

Ahmed, Sara. *The Cultural Politics of Emotion.* Edinburgh: Edinburgh University Press, 2004.

Ahmed, Siraj. *The Archaeology of Babel: The Colonial Foundation of the Humanities.* Stanford, CA: Stanford University Press, 2017.

Allen, Michelle. *Cleansing the City: Sanitary Geographies in Victorian London.* Athens: Ohio University Press, 2008.

Alter, Stephen G. "Darwin and the Linguists: The Coevolution of Mind and Language." *Studies in History and Philosophy of Biological and Biomedical Sciences* 38 (2007): 573–84.

Alter, Stephen G. *Darwinism and the Linguistic Image: Language, Race, and Natural Theology in the Nineteenth Century.* Baltimore: Johns Hopkins University Press, 1999.

Anderson, Warwick. "Excremental Colonialism: Public Health and the Poetics of Pollution." *Critical Inquiry* 21 (Spring 1995): 640–69.

Angyal, A. "Disgust and Related Aversions." *Journal of Abnormal and Social Psychology* 36, no. 3 (1941): 393–412.

Arendt, Hannah. *Lectures on Kant's Political Philosophy.* Chicago: University of Chicago Press, 1982.

Arendt, Hannah. *The Origins of Totalitarianism.* New York: Meridian, 1962.

Armstrong, Nancy. *Desire and Domestic Fiction: A Political History of the Novel.* New York: Oxford University Press, 1982.

Arnold, David. *Colonizing the Body: State Medicine and Epidemic Disease in Nineteenth-Century India.* New Delhi: Oxford University Press, 1993.

Aron, Raymond. *Main Currents in Sociological Thought.* New York: Doubleday Anchor, 1968.

Ashton, Rosemarie. *One Hot Summer: Dickens, Darwin, Disraeli, and the Great Stink of 1858.* New Haven, CT: Yale University Press, 2017.

Auerbach, Eric. *Mimesis: The Representation of Reality in Western Literature.* Princeton, NJ: Princeton University Press, 1991.

Bakhtin, Mikhail. *The Dialogic Imagination*. Austin: University of Texas Press, 1981.

Bakhtin, Mikhail. *Rabelais and His World*. Bloomington: Indiana University Press, 1983.

Barnes, David S. "Confronting Sensory Crisis: The Great Stinks of London and Paris." In Cohen and Johnson, *Filth*, 103–32.

Barnes, David S. *The Great Stink of Paris and the Nineteenth-Century Struggle against Filth and Germs*. Baltimore: Johns Hopkins University Press, 2006.

Barrett, Lisa Feldman. *How Emotions Are Made: The Secret Life of the Brain*. New York: Houghton Mifflin, 2017.

Bashford, Alison. *Imperial Hygiene: A Critical History of Colonialism, Nationalism and Public Health*. New York: Palgrave, 2003.

Bataille, Georges. *The College of Sociology*. Edited by Dennis Hollier. Minneapolis: University of Minnesota Press, 1988.

Bataille, Georges. *Visions of Excess: Selected Writings, 1927–1939*. Edited by Allen Stoekl. Minneapolis: University of Minnesota Press, 1985.

Baudelaire, Charles. *Oeuvres posthumes*. Paris: Société du Mercure de France, 1908.

Beaumont, William. *Experiments and Observations on the Gastric Juice and the Physiology of Digestion*. Edinburgh: MacLachlan & Stewart, 1838.

Benjamin, Matthew. "Possessing Pollution." *New York University Review of Law and Social Change* 31 (2007): 733–72.

Benjamin, Walter. *The Arcades Project*. Cambridge, MA: Harvard University Press, 2002.

Benjamin, Walter. *Illuminations*. New York: Schocken Books, 1969.

Berlant, Lauren. "The Epistemology of State Emotion." In *Dissent in Dangerous Times*, edited by Austin Sarat, 46–78. Ann Arbor: University of Michigan Press, 2008.

Berlant, Lauren. "The Subject of True Feeling." In *Cultural Pluralism, Identity Politics, and the Law*, edited by Austin Sarat and Thomas R. Kearns, 49–84. Ann Arbor: University of Michigan Press, 1999.

Bhabha, Homi K. *The Location of Culture*. New York: Routledge, 1994.

Bologna, Sergio. "Money and Crisis: Marx as Correspondent of the New York *Daily Tribune*, 1856–57, Parts I–II." *Common Sense* 13–14 (1993): 29–53, 63–88.

Bourdieu, Pierre. *Distinction: A Social Critique of the Judgment of Taste*. Cambridge, MA: Harvard University Press, 1984.

Bowden, Brett. *The Empire of Civilization: The Evolution of an Imperial Idea*. Chicago: University of Chicago Press, 2009.

Brenkman, John. *The Cultural Contradictions of Democracy: Political Thought since September 11*. Princeton, NJ: Princeton University Press, 2007.

*A Brief Popular Account of All the Financial Panics and Commercial Revulsions in the United States, from 1690 to 1857, with a More Particular History of the Two Great Revulsions of 1837 and 1857 by Members of the New-York Press*. New York: J. C. Haney, 1857.

Brontë, Charlotte. *Jane Eyre*. New York: Norton, 2001.

Brooks, Peter. *Reading for the Plot: Design and Intention in Narrative*. Cambridge, MA: Harvard University Press, 1992.

Brown, Norman O. *Life against Death: The Psychoanalytical Meaning of History*. Middletown, CT: Wesleyan University Press, 1959.

Browne, Janet. "I Could Have Retched All Night: Charles Darwin and His Body." In *Science Incarnate: Historical Embodiments of Natural Knowledge*, edited by Steven Shapin, 240–87. Chicago: University of Chicago Press, 1998.

Browning, Robert. *The Poetic and Dramatic Works of Robert Browning*. Cambridge, MA: Riverside Press, 1887.

Brunton, Thomas Lauder. *On Disorders of Digestion, Their Consequences and Treatment*. London: Macmillan, 1886.

Bush, June, ed. *The Warner Letters: The Experiences of Two English Brothers during the Indian Rebellion of 1857–1859*. New Delhi: Rupa, 2008.

Cadava, Eduardo. "The Guano of History." In *The Other Emerson*, edited by Branka Arsić and Cary Wolfe, 101–30. Minneapolis: University of Minnesota Press, 2010.

Cannon, Susan Faye. *Science in Culture: The Early Victorian Period*. New York: Dawson, 1978.

Carlyle, Thomas. *Two Note Books of Thomas Carlyle*. New York: Grolier Club, 1898.

"Central Criminal Court, October 31," *Times* (London), November 1, 1888.

Chadwick, Edwin. *Report to Her Majesty's Secretary of State for the Home Department, from the Poor Law Commissioners, on an Inquiry into the Sanitary Conditions of the Labouring Population of Great Britain*. London: Clowes and Son, 1842.

Chaghatai, M. Ikram, ed. *1857 in the Muslim Historiography*. Lahore: Sang-E-Meel, 2007.

Chandler, James. *An Archaeology of Sympathy: The Sentimental Mode in Literature and Cinema*. Chicago: University of Chicago Press, 2013.

Chapman, H. A., D. A. Kim, J. M. Susskind, and A. K. Anderson. "In Bad Taste: Evidence for the Oral Origins of Moral Disgust." *Science* 323 (February 27, 2009):1222–26.

Charleton, Walter. *The Natural History of Nutrition*. London: Henry Herringman, 1659.

Christoff, Alicia Mireles. *Novel Relations: Victorian Fiction and British Psychoanalysis*. Princeton, NJ: Princeton University Press, 2019.

Cleere, Eileen. *The Sanitary Arts: Aesthetic Culture and the Victorian Cleanliness Campaigns*. Columbus: Ohio State University Press, 2014.

Clericuzio, Antonio. "Chemical and Mechanical Theories of Digestion in Early Modern Medicine." *Studies in History and Philosophy of Biological and Biomedical Sciences* 43 (2012): 329–37.

Cohen, William A., and Ryan Johnson, eds. *Filth: Dirt, Disgust, and Modern Life*. Minneapolis: University of Minnesota Press, 2005.

Colp, Ralph. *Darwin's Illness*. Gainesville: University Press of Florida, 2008.

*The Confessional Unmasked: Showing the Depravity of the Romish Priesthood, the Iniquity of the Confessional, and the Questions put to Females in Confession*. London: Protestant Electoral Union, 1867.

Cooper, Anthony Ashley. *Characteristics of Men, Manners, Opinions, and Times*. New York: Cambridge University Press, 1999.

Corbin, Alain. *The Foul and the Fragrant: Odor and the French Social Imagination*. Cambridge, MA: Harvard University Press, 1986.

Coviello, Peter. *Make Yourself Gods: Mormons and the Unfinished Business of American Secularism*. Chicago: University of Chicago Press, 2019.

Cox, Reginald, ed. *Thomas Hardy: The Critical Heritage*. New York: Barnes and Noble, 1970.

Craig, Alec. *Suppressed Books: A History of the Conception of Literary Obscenity*. New York: World, 1966.

Crook, Tom. *Governing Systems: Modernity and the Making of Public Health in England, 1830–1910*. Los Angeles: University of California Press, 2016.

Curtis, Valerie. *Don't Look, Don't Touch, Don't Eat: The Science behind Revulsion*. Chicago: University of Chicago Press, 2013.

Dalrymple, William. *The Last Mughal: The Fall of Delhi, 1857*. New York: Vintage Books, 2007.

Dalziel, Pamela, and Michael Millgate, eds. *Thomas Hardy's Poetical Matter Notebook*. New York: Oxford University Press, 2009.

Darwin, Charles. *Charles Darwin's Beagle Diary*. Edited by R. D. Keynes. New York: Cambridge University Press, 1988.

Darwin, Charles. *The Descent of Man and Selection in Relation to Sex*. Princeton, NJ: Princeton University Press, 1981.

Darwin, Charles. *The Expression of the Emotions in Man and Animals*. New York: Penguin, 2009.

Darwin, Charles. *Metaphysics, Materialism, and the Evolution of Mind: Early Writings of Charles Darwin*. Edited by Paul Barrett. Chicago: University of Chicago Press, 1980.

Darwin, Charles. *On the Origin of Species by Natural Selection*. New York: Oxford University Press, 2008.

Darwin Correspondence Project. University of Cambridge. https://www.darwin project.ac.uk.

Davis, Earle. *The Flint and the Flame: The Artistry of Charles Dickens*. Columbia: University of Missouri Press, 1963.

"The Debate of Monday Evening." *Times* (London), July 21, 1858.

De Amicis, Edmondo. "Notes Upon the 'Assommoir.'" In *The 'Assommoir' (The Prelude to 'Nana'): A Realistic Novel* by Émile Zola, v–xiii. London: Vizetelly, 1884.

De Man, Paul. *Allegories of Reading*. New Haven, CT: Yale University Press, 1979.

Denning, Michael. "Wageless Life." *New Left Review* 66 (November/December 2010): 79–97.

Derrida, Jacques. "Economimesis." *Diacritics* 11, no. 2 (Summer 1981): 3–25.

Derrida, Jacques. *The Truth in Painting*. Chicago: University of Chicago Press, 1987.

Descartes, René. *Discourse on Method*. Indianapolis: Hackett, 1998.

Devlin, Patrick. *The Enforcement of Morals*. London: Oxford University Press, 1965.

Dickens, Charles. *A Christmas Carol*. Peterborough: Broadview Press, 2003.

Dickens, Charles. *Little Dorrit*. New York: Penguin Books, 2003.

"Dirty Cleanliness." *Times* (London), August 18, 1858.

Dobraszczyk, Paul. *London's Sewers*. London: Bloomsbury, 2014.

Douglas, Mary. *Purity and Danger: An Analysis of the Concepts of Pollution and Taboo*. New York: Routledge, 2008.

Dowling, Linda. "Victorian Oxford and the Science of Language." *PMLA* 97, no. 2 (1982): 160–78.

Duncan, Ian. "Darwin and the Savages." *Yale Journal of Criticism* 4, no. 2 (Spring, 1991): 13–45.

Durkheim, Émile. *The Rules of Sociological Method*. New York: Simon and Schuster, 2014.

Durkheim, Émile. *On Suicide*. New York: Penguin, 2006.

Edelman, Lee. *No Future: Queer Theory and the Death Drive*. Durham, NC: Duke University Press, 2004.

Einhorn, Max. *Rumination in Man*. New York: Trow's Printing and Bookbinding, 1890.

Elias, Norbert. *The Civilizing Process: Sociogenetic and Psychogenetic Investigations*. Rev. ed. Oxford: Blackwell, 2000.

Elias, Norbert. *The Loneliness of the Dying*. New York: Continuum Books, 1985.

Elias, Norbert. "Problems of Involvement and Detachment." *British Journal of Sociology* 7, no. 3 (September 1956): 226–52.

Emerson, Ralph Waldo. *The Conduct of Life*. London: Smith, Elder, 1860.

Engels, Friedrich. *The Condition of the Working Class in England*. New York: Oxford University Press, 1993.

Esty, Jed. "Excremental Postcolonialism." *Contemporary Literature* 40, no. 1 (1999): 22–59.

Evans, D. Morier. *The History of the Financial Crisis, 1857–58 and the Stock Exchange Panic of 1859*. London: Groombridge and Sons, 1859.

Fabian, Ann. "Speculation on Distress: The Popular Discourse of the Panics of 1837 and 1857." *Yale Journal of Criticism* 3, no. 1 (Fall 1989): 127–42.

Fardon, Richard. "Citations Out of Place." *Anthropology Today* 29, no. 1 (February 2013): 25–27.

Farooqi, Mahmood, ed. *Besieged: Voices from Delhi 1857*. New York: Penguin, 2010.

Febvre, Lucien. "*Civilisation*: Evolution of a Word and a Group of Ideas." In *A New Kind of History: From the Writings of Lucien Febvre*, edited by Peter Burke, 219–57. New York: Harper, 1973.

Ferguson, Frances. *Pornography, the Theory: What Utilitarianism Did to Action*. Chicago: University of Chicago Press, 2004.

Finer, S. E. *The Life and Times of Sir Edwin Chadwick*. London: Methuen, 1952.

Fitch, W. Tecumseh. "The Biology and Evolution of Music: A Comparative Perspective." *Cognition* 100 (2006): 173–215.

Fitch, W. Tecumseh. *The Evolution of Language*. New York: Cambridge University Press, 2010.

Forster, E. M. *Howards End*. New York: Knopf, 1921.

Foucault, Michel. *The Archaeology of Knowledge*. New York: Pantheon Books, 1972.

Foucault, Michel. *Discipline and Punish*. New York: Vintage Books, 1995.

Foucault, Michel. *The History of Sexuality*. Vol. 1, *An Introduction*. New York: Vintage Books, 1990.

Foucault, Michel. "Nietzsche, Genealogy, History." In *Language, Counter-Memory, Practice: Selected Essays and Interviews*, edited by D. F. Bouchard, 139–64. Ithaca, NY: Cornell University Press, 1977.

Foucault, Michel. *The Order of Things*. New York: Random House, 1973.

Frazer, James. *The Golden Bough: A Study in Magic and Religion*. New York: Macmillan, 1923.

Frederickson, Kathleen. *The Ploy of Instinct: Victorian Sciences of Nature and Sexuality in Liberal Governance*. New York: Fordham University Press, 2014.

Freeman, R. B., and P. J. Gautrey. "Charles Darwin's *Queries about Expression*." *Bulletin of the British Museum of Natural History (Historical Series)* 4, no. 3 (1972): 205–19.

Freud, Sigmund. "Character and Anal Erotism." In *The Standard Edition of the Complete Works of Sigmund Freud*, Vol. 9, edited by James Strachey, 167–75. London: Vintage Classics, 2001.

Freud, Sigmund. *Civilization and Its Discontents*. New York: Norton, 2010.

Freud, Sigmund. *Five Lectures on Psycho-Analysis*. New York: Norton, 1989.

Freud, Sigmund. "Negation." In *The Standard Edition of the Complete Works of Sigmund Freud*, Vol. 19, edited by James Strachey, 235–41. London: Vintage Classics, 2001.

Freud, Sigmund. "Notes upon a Case of Obsessional Neurosis." In *Three Case Histories*, edited by Philip Rieff, 1–81. New York: Touchstone Books, 1996.

Freud, Sigmund. "The Unconscious." In *The Standard Edition of the Complete Psychological Works of Sigmund Freud*, Vol. 13, edited by James Strachey, 159–219. London: Vintage Books, 2001.

Frevert, Ute. *Emotions in History: Lost and Found*. New York: Central European Press, 2011.

Gigante, Denise. *Taste: A Literary History*. New Haven, CT: Yale University Press, 2005.

Gillers, Stephen. "A Tendency to Deprave and Corrupt: The Transformation of American Obscenity Law from Hicklin to *Ulysses* II." *Washington University Law Review* 85, no. 2 (2007): 215–96.

Gilmore, Thomas B. "The Comedy of Swift's Scatological Poems." *PMLA* 91, no. 1 (January 1976): 33–43.

Girard, René. *Deceit, Desire, and the Novel*. Baltimore: Johns Hopkins University Press, 1976.

Gissing, George. *The Nether World*. New York: Oxford University Press, 1998.

Goffe, Tao Leigh. "'Guano in Their Destiny': Race, Geology, and a Philosophy of Indenture." *Amerasia Journal* 45, no. 1 (2019): 27–49.

Goldman, Lawrence. "The Origins of British 'Social Science': Political Economy, Natural Science and Statistics, 1830–1835." *Historical Journal* 26 (September 1983): 587–616.

Goldman, Lawrence. *Science, Reform, and Politics in Victorian Britain: The Social Science Association 1857–1886*. New York: Cambridge University Press, 2004.

Goodlad, Lauren. *Victorian Literature and the Victorian State*. Baltimore: Johns Hopkins University Press, 2003.

"The Great Annual Dinner." *Farmer's Magazine*, August 1852: 134–140.

Green, André. "The Intuition of the Negative in *Playing and Reality*." In *André Green at the Squiggle Foundation*, edited by Jan Abram, 85–106. London: Karnac, 2016.

Greene, Donald. "On Swift's 'Scatological Poems.'" *Sewanee Review* 75, no. 4 (Autumn 1967): 672–89.

Greenwood, John. "Whistles, Bells, and Cogs in Machines: Thomas Huxley and Epiphenomenalism." *Journal of the History of the Behavioral Sciences* 46, no. 3 (Summer 2010): 276–99.

Greiner, Rae. *Sympathetic Realism in Nineteenth-Century British Fiction*. Baltimore: Johns Hopkins University Press, 2012.

Gross, Daniel M. *Uncomfortable Situations: Emotion between Science and the Humanities*. Chicago: University of Chicago Press, 2017.

Grosz, Elizabeth. *Becoming Undone: Darwinian Reflections on Life, Politics, and Art*. Durham, NC: Duke University Press, 2011.

Guha, Ranajit. *Elementary Aspects of Peasant Insurgency in Colonial India*. Durham, NC: Duke University Press, 1999.

*The Habits of Good Society: A Handbook of Etiquette for Ladies and Gentlemen*. London: James Hogg and Sons, 1859.

Hadley, Elaine. *Living Liberalism: Practical Citizenship in Mid-Victorian Britain*. Chicago: University of Chicago Press, 2010.

Halliday, Stephen. *The Great Stink: Sir Joseph Bazalgette and the Cleansing of the Victorian Metropolis*. London: History Press, 2001.

Halsey, A. H. *A History of Sociology in Britain*. New York: Oxford University Press, 2004.

Hamlin, Christopher. *Public Health and Social Justice in the Age of Chadwick*. New York: Cambridge University Press, 1998.

Hardy, Thomas. "The Dorsetshire Labourer." *Longman's Magazine*, July 1, 1883: 252–69.

Hardy, Thomas. *Jude the Obscure*. Peterborough: Broadview Press, 2004.

Hardy, Thomas. *The Life and Work of Thomas Hardy*. Edited by Michael Millgate. Athens: University of Georgia Press, 1985.

Harrison, Timothy M. "Personhood and Impersonal Feeling in Montaigne's 'De l'excertation.'" *Modern Philology* 114, no. 2 (November 2016): 219–42.

Harvey, William. *The Works of William Harvey*. London: Sydenham Society, 1847.

Hazlitt, William. *The Collected Works of William Hazlitt*. Vol. 7. New York: McClure, Philips, 1903.

Heath, Deana. *Purifying Empire: Obscenity and the Politics of Moral Regulation in Britain, India and Australia*. New York: Cambridge University Press, 2010.

Heilbron, Johan. *The Rise of Social Theory*. Minneapolis: University of Minnesota Press, 1995.

Hensley, Nathan. *Forms of Empire: The Poetics of Victorian Sovereignty*. New York: Oxford University Press, 2016.

Herbert, Christopher. *Culture and Anomie: Ethnographic Imagination in the Nineteenth Century*. Chicago: University of Chicago Press, 1991.

Herbert, Christopher. "Rat Worship and Taboo in Mayhew's London." *Representations* 23 (Summer 1988): 1–24.

Herz, Rachel. *That's Disgusting: Unraveling the Mysteries of Repulsion*. New York: Norton, 2012.

Hillman, David. *Shakespeare's Entrails*. New York: Palgrave Macmillan, 2007.

Hu-Dehart, Evelyn. "Coolies, Shopkeepers, Pioneers: The Chinese of Mexico and Peru (1849–1930)." *Amerasia Journal* 15, no. 2 (1989): 91–116.

Hume, David. *Essays: Moral, Political and Literary*. Indianapolis: Liberty Fund, 1985.

Hume, David. *A Treatise of Human Nature*. London: Clarendon Press, 1896.

Humpherys, Anne. *Henry Mayhew*. Boston: Twayne, 1984.

Hunt, Lynn, ed. *The Invention of Pornography: Obscenity and the Origins of Modernity.* New York: Zone Books, 1996.

Hunter, Ian, David Saunders, and Dugald Williamson. *On Pornography: Literature, Sexuality and Obscenity Law.* New York: St. Martin's Press, 1993.

Huxley, Aldous. *Do What You Will.* London: Chatto and Windus, 1929.

Huxley, Thomas. "Animal Automatism." In *Selected Works of Thomas Huxley,* 194–208. New York: John B. Alden, 1886.

James, William. "What Is an Emotion?" *Mind* 9, no. 34 (April 1894): 188–205.

Jameson, Frederic. *The Antinomies of Realism.* New York: Verso, 2015.

Jephson, Henry. *The Sanitary Evolution of London.* London: T. Fisher Unwin, 1907.

Johnson, Steven. *The Ghost Map: The Story of London's Most Terrifying Epidemic and How It Changed Science, Cities, and the Modern World.* New York: Penguin, 2006.

Jones, Gareth Stedman. *Karl Marx: Greatness and Illusion.* Cambridge, MA: Harvard University Press, 2016.

Kant, Immanuel. "Conjectures on the Beginning of Human History." In *Kant: Political Writings,* edited by Hans Reiss, 221–34. New York: Cambridge University Press, 1991.

Kant, Immanuel. *Critique of Judgment.* New York: Barnes and Noble, 2005.

Kass, Leon. "The Wisdom of Repugnance." *New Republic,* June 2, 1997: 17–26.

Kaye, John, and George Bruce Malleson. *History of the Indian Mutiny of 1857–8,* Vol. 1. London: Longmans, Green, 1898.

Kelly, Daniel. *Yuck! The Nature and Moral Significance of Disgust.* Cambridge: MIT Press, 2011.

Kindleberger, Charles P., and Robert Z. Aliber. *Manias, Panics and Crashes: A History of Financial Crises.* New York: Palgrave, 2005.

Kolb, Anjuli Fatima Raza. *Epidemic Empire: Colonialism, Contagion, and Terror, 1817–2020.* Chicago: University of Chicago Press, 2021.

Kolnai, Aurel. *On Disgust.* Translated by Carolyn Korsmeyer and Barry Smith. Chicago: Open Court Press, 2004.

Kompridis, Nikolas, ed. *The Aesthetic Turn in Political Thought.* New York: Bloomsbury, 2014.

Korey, Marie Elena, and Richard Landon, eds. *Vizetelly & Compan(ies): A Complex Tale of Victorian Printing and Publishing.* Toronto: University of Toronto Press, 2003.

Korsmeyer, Carolyn. *Savoring Disgust: The Fair and the Foul in Aesthetics.* New York: Oxford University Press, 2011.

Krätke, Michael R. "The First World Economic Crisis: Marx as an Economic Journalist." In Musto, *Essays,* 162–68.

Krätke, Michael R. "Marx's 'Books of Crisis' of 1857–8." In Musto, *Essays,* 169–76.

Kristeva, Julia. *Powers of Horror.* New York: Columbia University Press, 1982.

Kuper, Adam. *The Idea of Primitive Society.* New York: Routledge, 1988.

Latour, Bruno. "A Few Steps toward an Anthropology of the Iconoclastic Gesture." *Science in Context* 10 (1997): 63–83.

Latour, Bruno. *We Have Never Been Modern.* Cambridge, MA: Harvard University Press, 1993.

Law, Jules. *The Social Life of Fluids: Blood, Milk, and Water in the Victorian Novel.* Ithaca, NY: Cornell University Press, 2010.

Leckie, Barbara. "'A Preface Is Written to the Public': Print Censorship, Novel Prefaces, and the Construction of a New Reading Public in Late-Victorian England." *Victorian Literature and Culture* 37 (2009): 447–62.

Lee, Wendy Anne. *Failures of Feeling: Insensibility and the Novel.* Stanford, CA: Stanford University Press, 2019.

Lepenies, Wolf. *Between Literature and Science: The Rise of Sociology.* New York: Cambridge University Press, 1992.

Lessing, G. E. *Laocoön: An Essay upon the Limits of Painting and Poetry.* Boston: Little, Brown, 1910.

Levine, Donald N. *Visions of the Sociological Tradition.* Chicago: University of Chicago Press, 1995.

Leys, Ruth. "Both of Us Disgusted in *My* Insula: Mirror Neuron Theory and Emotional Empathy." In *Science and Emotions after 1945,* edited by Frank Biess and Daniel M. Gross, 67–95. Chicago: University of Chicago Press, 2014.

Locke, John. *An Essay Concerning Human Understanding.* New York: Oxford University Press, 2008.

Lougy, Robert E. "Filth, Liminality, and Abjection in Charles Dickens's *Bleak House.*" *ELH* 69, no. 2 (Summer 2002): 473–500.

Lubey, Kathleen. "Making Pornography, 1749–1968: The History of *The History of the Human Heart.*" *ELH* 82, no. 3 (Fall 2015): 897–935.

Lukács, György. "Narrate or Describe?" In *Writer and Critic and Other Essays,* edited by Arthur Kahn, 110–48. New York: Merlin Press, 1970.

"The Main Drainage System." *Morning Post,* April 5, 1865.

MacKinnon, Catharine. *Only Words.* Cambridge, MA: Harvard University Press, 1993.

Mahmood, Saba. "Religious Reason and Secular Affect: An Incommensurable Divide?" In *Is Critique Secular? Blasphemy, Injury, and Free Speech,* by Talal Asad, Wendy Brown, Judith Butler, and Saba Mahmood, 58–94. New York: Fordham University Press, 2013.

Marcus, Steven. *Engels, Manchester, and the Working Class.* New York: Vintage Books, 1974.

Marsh, Joss. *Word Crimes: Blasphemy, Culture, and Literature in Nineteenth-Century England.* Chicago: University of Chicago Press, 1998.

Martineau, Harriet. *Illustrations of Political Economy.* Vol. 1. London: Charles Fox, 1834.

Marx, Karl. *Capital.* Vol 1. New York: Vintage, 1977.

Marx, Karl. *A Contribution to the Critique of Political Economy.* New York: International, 1989.

Marx, Karl. *Dispatches for the New York* Tribune: *Selected Journalism of Karl Marx.* New York: Penguin, 2007.

Marx, Karl. *Economic and Philosophic Manuscripts of 1844.* Amherst, NY: Prometheus Books, 1988.

Marx, Karl. *Grundrisse: Foundations of the Critique of Political Economy.* New York: Penguin, 1993.

Marx, Karl, and Friedrich Engels. *Marx and Engels Collected Works.* 50 vols. London: Lawrence and Wishart, 1975–2004.

Masson, Jeffrey Moussaieff, ed. *The Complete Letters of Sigmund Freud to Wilhelm Fliess, 1897–1904.* Cambridge, MA: Harvard University Press, 1985.

Matthew, W. M. *The House of Gibbs and the Peruvian Guano Monopoly*. London: Royal Historical Society, 1981.

Matus, Jill. "Victorian Framings of the Mind: Recent Work on Mid-Nineteenth Century Theories of the Unconscious, Memory, and Emotion." *Literature Compass* 4, no. 4 (2007): 1257–75.

Maule, George, and William Selwyn. *Reports of Cases Argued and Determined in the Court of King's Bench*. London: A. Strahan, 1817.

Mayer, Jed. "The Expression of Emotions in Man and Laboratory Animals." *Victorian Studies* 50, no. 3 (Spring 2008): 399–417.

Mayhew, Henry. *London Labour and the London Poor*. Vol. 2. London: Frank Cass, 1967.

McGinn, Colin. *The Meaning of Disgust*. New York: Oxford University Press, 2011.

McKeon, Michael. *The Origins of the English Novel, 1600–1740*. Baltimore: Johns Hopkins University Press, 2002.

Menninghaus, Winfried. *Disgust: Theory and History of a Strong Sensation*. Albany: State University of New York Press, 2003.

Metcalfe, Charles Theophilus, trans. *Two Native Narratives of the Mutiny in Delhi*. Westminster: Archibald Constable, 1898.

Mill, John Stuart. "Civilization." In *Collected Works of John Stuart Mill*, Vol. 18, edited by J. M. Robson, 117–49. Toronto: University of Toronto Press, 1977.

Miller, Ian. *A Modern History of the Stomach*. New York: Routledge, 2016.

Miller, William Ian. *The Anatomy of Disgust*. Cambridge, MA: Harvard University Press, 1999.

Mitchell, W. J. T. *Iconology: Image, Text, Ideology*. Chicago: University of Chicago Press, 1986.

Mitchell, W. J. T. *What Do Pictures Want? The Lives and Loves of Images*. Chicago: University of Chicago Press, 2004.

Moore, George. *Literature at Nurse, or Circulating Morals*. London: Vizetelly, 1885.

Moretti, Franco. *The Bourgeois: Between History and Literature*. New York: Verso, 2013.

Morgan, Benjamin. *The Outward Mind: Materialist Aesthetics in Victorian Science and Literature*. Chicago: University of Chicago Press, 2017.

Morris, William. "Art under Plutocracy." In *Political Writings of William Morris*, edited by A. L. Morton. New York: International, 1979.

Müller, Max. "Lectures on Mr. Darwin's Philosophy of Language (II)." *Fraser's Magazine*, June 1873: 659–78.

Müller, Max. *Lectures on the Science of Language*. New York: Scribner, 1862.

Müller, Max. *The Science of Thought*. New York: Scribner, 1887.

Mullin, Katherine. "Unmasking *The Confessional Unmasked*: The 1868 Hicklin Test and the Toleration of Obscenity." *ELH* 85, no. 2 (Summer 2018): 471–99.

Musto, Marcello, ed. *Essays on Marx's Grundrisse*. New York: Routledge, 2008.

Musto, Marcello. "Marx's Life at the Time of the *Grundrisse*: Biographical Notes on 1857–8." In Musto, *Essays*, 149–61.

Nagle, John C. "The Idea of Pollution." *UC Davis Law Review* 43 (November 2009): 1–78.

Nagle, John C. "Pornography as Pollution." *Maryland Law Review* 70 (2011): 939–84.

Negri, Antonio. *Marx beyond Marx*. Brooklyn, NY: Autonomedia, 1991.

Ngai, Sianne. *Our Aesthetic Categories: Zany, Cute, Interesting*. Cambridge, MA: Harvard University Press, 2012.

Ngai, Sianne. *Theory of the Gimmick: Aesthetic Judgment and Capitalist Form*. Cambridge, MA: Harvard University Press, 2020.

Ngai, Sianne. *Ugly Feelings*. Cambridge, MA: Harvard University Press, 2005.

Nussbaum, Martha. *Hiding from Humanity: Shame, Disgust, and the Law*. Princeton, NJ: Princeton University Press, 2004.

"Old Father Thames," *Times* (London), June 17, 1858.

Ollman, Bertell. *Alienation: Marx's Conception of Man in Capitalist Society*. New York: Cambridge University Press, 1976.

"Opening of the Great Main Drains." *Sheffield Daily Telegraph*, April 5, 1865.

"Opening of the Main Drainage by the Prince of Wales." *Daily Telegraph*, April 5, 1865.

Orwell, George. "George Gissing." In *Collected Articles on George Gissing*, edited by Pierre Coustillas, 50–57. New York: Barnes and Noble, 1968.

Panagia, Davide. *The Political Life of Sensation*. Durham, NC: Duke University Press, 2009.

"Panic in a Committee Room." *Daily Telegraph*, July 2, 1858.

Parsons, Benjamin. *Anti-Bacchus: An Essay on the Crimes, Diseases, and Other Evils Connected with the Use of Intoxicating Drinks*. London: John Snow, 1840.

Pati, Biswamoy, ed. *The 1857 Rebellion*. New Delhi: Oxford University Press, 2010.

Paulle, Bowen, and Mustafa Emirbayer. "Beneath Rationalization: Foucault, Elias, and the Body." *European Journal of Social Theory* 19 (2016): 39–56.

Pepys, Samuel. *The Diary of Samuel Pepys*. Vol. 4, *1663*, edited by Robert Latham and William Matthews. Berkeley: University of California Press, 2000.

*Pernicious Literature: Debate in the House of Commons; Trial and Conviction for the Sale of Zola's Novels, with the Opinions of the Press*. London: National Vigilance Association, 1889.

"The Pestilential State of the Thames." *British Medical Journal* s4-1, no. 79 (3 July 1858): 535.

Plamper, Jan. *The History of Emotions*. New York: Oxford University Press, 2015.

Plant, Jane A., ed. *Pollutants, Human Health, and the Environment*. Hoboken, NJ: John Wiley and Sons, 2012.

Poovey, Mary. *Making a Social Body: British Cultural Formation 1830–1864*. Chicago: University of Chicago Press, 1994.

Porter, Theodore M. *The Rise of Statistical Thinking, 1820–1900*. Princeton, NJ: Princeton University Press, 1986.

Postone, Moishe. *Time, Labor, and Social Domination*. New York: Cambridge University Press, 1993.

Probyn, Elspeth. *Carnal Appetites*. New York: Routledge, 2000.

"Proceedings." *Daily Telegraph*, June 30, 1858.

Prodger, Philip. *Darwin's Camera: Art and Photography in the Theory of Evolution*. New York: Oxford University Press, 2009.

Proust, Marcel. *The Remembrance of Things Past*. Translated by C. K. Scott Moncrieff. New York: Henry Holt, 1922.

Qureshi, Hamid Afaq, trans. *Qaisar-ut-Tawarikh of Kamal-ud-din Haidar*. Lucknow: New Royal Book Company, 2008.

Rabelais, François. *Gargantua and Pantagruel.* Translated by M. A. Screech. New York: Penguin, 2006.

Rancière, Jacques. *The Aesthetic Unconscious.* New York: Polity, 2009.

Rancière, Jacques. "Auerbach and the Contradictions of Realism." *Critical Inquiry* 44 (Winter 2018): 227–41.

Rancière, Jacques. *The Politics of Aesthetics: The Distribution of the Sensible.* New York: Continuum Books, 2004.

Reddy, William. "Against Constructionism: The Historical Ethnography of Emotions." *Current Anthropology* 38, no. 3 (June 1997): 327–51.

Reddy, William. *The Navigation of Feeling: A Framework for the History of Emotions.* New York: Cambridge University Press, 2004.

"Report upon the Present Condition of the Thames." *Lancet*, July 10, 1858.

Richards, Robert J. *Darwin and the Emergence of Evolutionary Theories of Mind and Behavior.* Chicago: University of Chicago Press, 1989.

Richards, Robert J. "Instinct and Intelligence in British Natural Theology: Some Contributions to Darwin's Theory of the Evolution of Behavior." *Journal of the History of Biology* 14, no. 2 (Fall 1981): 193–230.

Richards, Robert J. "The Linguistic Creation of Man: Charles Darwin, August Schleicher, Ernst Haeckel, and the Missing Link in Nineteenth-Century Evolutionary Theory." In *Experimenting in Tongues: Studies in Science and Language*, edited by Matthias Doerres, 22–48. Stanford, CA: Stanford University Press, 2002.

Ricoeur, Paul. *The Conflict of Interpretations.* Evanston, IL: Northwestern University Press, 1974.

Ritvo, Lucille B. *Darwin's Influence on Freud: A Tale of Two Sciences.* New Haven: Yale University Press, 1990.

Roberts, Fred. *Letters Written during the Indian Mutiny.* New Delhi: LAL, 1979.

Roberts, M. J. D. "Morals, Art, and the Law: The Passing of the Obscene Publications Act, 1857." *Victorian Studies* 28, no. 4 (Summer, 1985): 609–29.

Robertson, Geoffrey. *Obscenity: An Account of Censorship Laws and Their Enforcement in England and Wales.* London: Weidenfield, 1979.

Robinson, Benedict. "Disgust c. 1600." *ELH* 81, no. 2 (Summer 2014): 553–83.

Rose, Jacqueline. "Negativity in the Work of Melanie Klein." In *Reading Melanie Klein*, edited by John Phillips and Lyndsey Stonebridge, 123–56. New York: Routledge, 2005.

Rosenwein, Barbara. *Emotional Communities in the Early Middle Ages.* Ithaca, NY: Cornell University Press, 2006.

Rosenwein, Barbara. *Generations of Feeling: A History of Emotions 600–1700.* New York: Cambridge University Press, 2016.

Rousseau, Jean-Jacques. *Rousseau's Political Writings.* Edited by Alan Ritter. New York: Norton, 1988.

Rowlinson, Matthew. "Foreign Bodies; or, How Did Darwin Invent the Symptom?" *Victorian Studies* 52, no. 4 (Summer 2010): 535–59.

Roy, Parama. *Alimentary Tracts: Appetites, Aversions, and the Postcolonial.* Durham, NC: Duke University Press, 2010.

Rozin, Paul, and April Fallon. "A Perspective on Disgust." *Psychological Review* 94, no. 1 (1987): 23–41.

Rozin, Paul, J. Haidt, and C. R. McCauley. "Disgust: The Body and Soul Emotion." In *Handbook of Cognition and Emotion*, edited by T. Dalgleish and M. J. Power, 429–45. New York: John Wiley & Sons, 1999.

Rozin, Paul, Jonathan Haidt, and Katrina Fincher. "From Oral to Moral." *Science* 323 (February 27, 2009): 1179–80.

Rozin, Paul, Linda Millman, and Carol Nemeroff. "Operation of the Laws of Sympathetic Magic in Disgust and Other Domains." *Journal of Personality and Social Psychology* 50 (1986): 703–12.

Ruskin, John. "Fiction—Fair and Foul." In *The Works of John Ruskin*, Vol. 34, edited by Edward Tyas Cook and Alexander Wedderburn, 265–397. New York: Cambridge University Press, 2009.

Ruskin, John. "The Storm-Cloud of the Nineteenth Century." In *The Works of John Ruskin*, Vol. 34, edited by Edward Tyas Cook and Alexander Wedderburn, 5–84. New York: Cambridge University Press, 2009.

Samalin, Zachary. "Dickens, Disinterestedness, and the Poetics of Clouded Judgment." *Dickens Studies Annual* 45 (2014): 229–45.

Samalin, Zachary. "Plumbing the Depths, Scouring the Surface: Henry Mayhew's Scavenger Hermeneutics." *New Literary History* 48 (Spring 2017): 387–410.

Sartre, Jean-Paul. *Being and Nothingness*. New York: Washington Square Press, 1992.

Sartre, Jean-Paul. *Existentialism Is a Humanism*. New Haven, CT: Yale University Press, 2007.

Schoenfeldt, Michael. "Fables of the Belly in Early Modern England." In *The Body in Parts: Fantasies of Corporeality in Early Modern Europe*, edited by David Hillman and Carla Mazzio, 243–61. New York: Routledge, 1997.

Scott, Joan Wallach. *Sex and Secularism*. Princeton, NJ: Princeton University Press, 2017.

Sedgwick, Eve Kosofsky. *Between Men: English Literature and Male Homosocial Desire*. New York: Columbia University Press, 1985.

Sedgwick, Eve Kosofsky. *Touching Feeling: Affect, Pedagogy, Performativity*. Durham, NC: Duke University Press, 2003.

Sedgwick, Eve Kosofsky. *The Weather in Proust*. Durham, NC: Duke University Press, 2011.

Séglas, Jules, and Désiré-Magloire Bourneville. "Du Mérycisme III." *Archives de Neurologie*, Tome VI (1883): 246–61.

Shaftesbury, Earl of. *See* Cooper, Anthony Ashley.

Shakinovsky, Lynn. "The 1857 Financial Crisis and the Suspension of the Bank Act." *BRANCH: Britain, Representation, and Nineteenth-Century History*. Edited by Dino Franco Felluga. Published March 2015. http://www.branchcollective.org/?ps_articles=lynn-shakinovsky-the-1857-financial-crisis-and-the-suspension-of-the-1844-bank-act.

Sigel, Lisa Z. *Governing Pleasures: Pornography and Social Change in England, 1815–1914*. New Brunswick, NJ: Rutgers University Press, 2002.

Simmel, Georg. *Conflict and the Web of Group Associations*. New York: Free Press, 1964.

Simmel, Georg. "The Metropolis and Mental Life." In *On Individuality and Social Forms*, edited by Donald N. Levine, 324–39. Chicago: University of Chicago Press, 1971.

Skelton, Ross, ed. *The Edinburgh International Encyclopaedia of Psychoanalysis*. Edinburgh: University of Edinburgh Press, 2006.

Sloterdijk, Peter. *Globes: Macrospherology*. Los Angeles: Semiotext(e), 2014.

Smith, Dennis. "'The Civilizing Process' and 'The History of Sexuality': Comparing Norbert Elias and Michel Foucault." *Theory and Society* 28 (1999): 79–100.

Snorton, C. Riley. *Black on Both Sides: A Racial History of Trans Identity*. Minneapolis: University of Minnesota Press, 2017.

Snow, John. "Drainage and Water Supply in Connexion with the Public Health." *Medical Times and Gazette*, February 13, 1858.

Spencer, Herbert. *Essays Scientific, Political, and Speculative*. New York: Appleton, 1916.

Spencer, Herbert. *The Principles of Sociology*. Vol. 1. New York: Appleton, 1906.

Spencer, Herbert. *Social Statics*. London: John Chapman, 1851.

Spencer, *The Study of Sociology*. New York: Appleton, 1901.

Stallybrass, Peter, and Allon White. *The Politics and Poetics of Transgression*. Ithaca, NY: Cornell University Press, 1986.

Starling, Ernest Henry. *Elements of Human Physiology*. London: Churchill, 1892.

Starobinski, Jean. "The Word *Civilization*." In *Blessings in Disguise; or, the Morality of Evil*, 1–35. Cambridge, MA: Harvard University Press, 1993.

"State of the River Thames." *Morning Chronicle*, June 21, 1858.

"State of the Thames." *Daily Telegraph*, June 18, 1858.

"The State of the Thames," *Times* (London), June 21, 1858.

Steig, Michael. "Dickens's Excremental Vision." *Victorian Studies* 13, no. 1 (March 1970): 339–54.

Steinlight, Emily. *Populating the Novel: Literary Form and the Politics of Surplus Life*. Ithaca, NY: Cornell University Press, 2018.

Stephen, Leslie. "Thoughts of an Outsider: The Ethics of Vivisection." *Cornhill Magazine*, April 1876: 468–78.

Stern, Simon. "Defining Obscenity before *Hicklin*: Corrupting Texts in the Seventeenth and Eighteenth Centuries." In *Literature on Trial*, edited by Sylvia Sasse and Matthias Meindl. Berlin: Matthes & Seitz, 2021.

Stocking, George. *Victorian Anthropology*. New York: Free Press, 1987.

Stoler, Ann Laura. *Along the Archival Grain: Epistemic Anxieties and Colonial Common Sense*. Princeton, NJ: Princeton University Press, 2009.

Stoler, Ann Laura. *Carnal Knowledge and Imperial Power*. Berkeley: University of California Press, 2002.

Swift, Jonathan. *The Essential Writings of Jonathan Swift*. Edited by Ian Higgins and Claude Rawson. New York: Norton, 2009.

Swift, Jonathan. *Gulliver's Travels*. New York: Oxford University Press, 2005.

Taussig, Michael. *Defacement*. Stanford, CA: Stanford University Press, 1999.

Taylor, Christopher. *Empire of Neglect: The West Indies in the Wake of British Liberalism*. Durham, NC: Duke University Press, 2018.

Taylor, Jenny Bourne. "Locating the Victorian Unconscious." In *Writing and Victorianism*, edited by J. B. Bullen, 137–79. London: Longman, 1998.

Terada, Rei. *Feeling in Theory: Emotion after the Death of the Subject*. Cambridge, MA: Harvard University Press, 2001.

Terada, Rei. *Looking Away: Phenomenality and Dissatisfaction, Kant to Adorno*. Cambridge, MA: Harvard University Press, 2009.

"The Thames." *Daily Telegraph*, June 28, 1858.

"The Thames." *Lancet*, July 10, 1858.

"This Morning's Ceremony." *Times* (London), April 4, 1865.

Tomasello, Michael. *Origins of Human Communication*. Cambridge, MA: MIT Press, 2008.

Tomkins, Silvan. *Affect Imagery Consciousness*. New York: Springer, 2008.

Trotter, David. *Cooking with Mud: The Idea of Mess in Nineteenth-Century Art and Fiction*. New York: Oxford University Press, 2000.

Trotter, David. *The English Novel in History 1895–1920*. New York: Routledge, 1993.

Trotter, David. "The New Historicism and the Psychopathology of Everyday Life." In Cohen and Johnson, *Filth*, 30–50.

Tucker, Irene. *The Moment of Racial Sight: A History*. Chicago: University of Chicago Press, 2012.

Vizetelly, Henry. *Extracts Principally from English Classics: Showing that the Legal Suppression of M. Zola's Novels Would Logically Involve the Bowdlerizing of Some of the Great Works of English Literature*. London: Henry Vizetelly, 1888.

Wagner, Kim. *The Great Fear of 1857: Rumors, Conspiracies, and the Making of the Indian Uprising*. Oxford: Peter Lang, 2010.

Walley, Samuel Hurd. *The Financial Revulsion of 1857, an Address*. Boston: American Statistical Association, 1858.

Weber, Max. *The City*. New York: Free Press, 1958.

Weber, Max. *Economy and Society: An Outline of Interpretive Sociology*. Berkeley: University of California Press, 1978.

Weber, Max. "The 'Objectivity' of Knowledge in Social Science and Social Policy." In *Max Weber: Collected Methodological Writings*, edited by Hans Henrik Bruun and Sam Whimster, 100–138. New York: Routledge, 2012.

Weber, Max. *The Protestant Ethic and the "Spirit" of Capitalism and Other Writings*. New York: Penguin, 2002.

Weber, Max. "Science as Vocation." In *The Vocation Lectures*, edited by David Owen and Tracy B. Strong, 1–31. Indianapolis: Hackett, 2004.

Wedgewood, Hensleigh. *A Dictionary of English Etymology*. London: Trubner, 1872.

Wells, Stanley, ed. *Thomas Nashe: Selected Works*. New York: Routledge, 2015.

"What a Pity." *Times* (London), June 18, 1858.

Wicker, Bruno, Christian Keysers, Jane Plailly, Jean-Pierre Royet, Vittorio Gallese, and Giacamo Rizzolatti. "Both of Us Disgusted in *My* Insula: The Common Neural Basis of Seeing and Feeling Disgust." *Neuron* 40 (October 2003): 655–64.

Williams, Bernard. *Obscenity and Film Censorship*. New York: Cambridge University Press, 1981.

Williams, Raymond. *Marxism and Literature*. New York: Oxford University Press, 1977.

Williams, Raymond. "Social Criticism in Dickens: Some Problems of Method and Approach." *Critical Quarterly* 6 (1964): 214–27.

Wilner, Joshua. *Feeding on Infinity: Readings in the Romantic Rhetoric of Internalization*. Baltimore: Johns Hopkins University Press, 2000.

Wilson, Elizabeth A. *Gut Feminism*. Durham, NC: Duke University Press, 2015.

Winter, Sarah. "Darwin's Saussure: Biosemiotics and Race in *Expression*." *Representations* 107, no. 1 (Summer 2009): 128–61.

Woolf, Virginia. *The Waves*. New York: Harvest Books, 1978.

Zerilli, Linda M. G. *A Democratic Theory of Judgment*. Chicago: University of Chicago Press, 2016.

Zerilli, Linda M. G. "'We Feel Our Freedom': Imagination and Judgment in the Thought of Hannah Arendt." In Kompridis, *Aesthetic Turn*, 29–60.

Zola, Emile. *The Soil*. London: Vizetelly, 1888.

# Index

abstraction, abstract space, 272n75; and alienation, 196–97; embodied, 16–17, 268n4; and the human/animal gap, 154, 186–87; of political economy, 170, 178; visceral, 286n51

Addison, Joseph, on proper conduct as corporeal, 61. *See also* body, the; etiquette

Adorno, Theodor, on anti-Semitism and sense of smell, 268n1

aesthetics, 62, 273n32; as broad category, 25, 40, 60, 87, 266n30; and disgust, 6, 21–26, 40, 58–70, 83–85, 100, 106–7, 124, 129, 214–40, 271m44; and judgment, 58–70; and obscenity law, 214–40; and politics, 24–25; vs. the social, 106–7, 171; and taste, 52, 61–70; and valuation, 14, 61–70

affect, affective knowledge, 248–49, 293n10; affective life, 29–30, 99; autonomy of, 89, 108, 114–17, 122; and temporality, 115. *See also* emotion; expression, affective/emotional; restraint

Agathocleous, Tanya, on colonial hygiene and obscenity law, 247, 291n40. *See also* colonialism; imperialism; obscenity law; sanitation / sanitary reform

agency, 146; of the artwork, 68; and disgust, 90–91, 135–36, 215; distribution of, 228; lack of, 141, 160, 184; of the stomach, 136–39, 148–49; of vomiting, 135–39; without human agents, 214–16, 224–25, 236–37. *See also* animism; intent

Ahmed, Sara, on disgust and contamination, 128–29

alienation, 172–73, 176–87, 190–91, 196–97, 200–201, 204, 206–9, 255, 283n6. *See also* Marx, Karl

Allen, Michelle, 78–79; on sanitary reform, 46, 49. *See also* centralization; sanitation / sanitary reform; sewage

Alter, Stephen G., 165

Angyal, András, on the animism of the disgusting object, 215; on disgust and primitivity, 10

animism, 215–16, 227–28, 236–40, 292n51. *See also* agency; intent; obscenity law

antagonism, as binding agent, 195, 199; and contagion, 194–95; social, 98, 184, 191, 194–95; and vomiting, 197

anti-Semitism, and sense of smell, 268n1

Aquinas, Saint Thomas, on "nocturnal pollution," 224. *See also* body, the, and dreams; obscenity law; religious belief

Arendt, Hannah, 40, 65–67; on imperialism (and racism), 202; on Kant's third *Critique*, 24, 65–66

Aron, Raymond, on Marx's conception of the desire for another reality, 209

atmospheric, the, 12–14, 33; and the self, 112–14. *See also* miasma

atomization, of social relations, 179–80

Auerbach, Eric, 19; on disgust and naturalist literature, 88, 106–9. *See also* realism; Zola, Émile

autocoprophagia, 46, 48, 59, 261–62. *See also* Great Stink, the; ingestion; shit

automatism, 145–46, 148–49. *See also* digestion

autonomy, of the aesthetic, 23–24, 63, 273n32; of affect, 89, 108, 114–17, 122; of artworks, 126, 228, 236; of the body, 6, 136, 149, 151–52; of decision-making, 60; domestic, 49; of the high from the low, 62; and the social, 190, 228; of the subject, 90, 151, 159–60, 217

Babbage, Charles, 177. *See also* statistics

Bakhtin, Mikhail, on the corporality of the novel, 109; on disgust in realist literature, 88–89, 95; on novelistic "heteroglossia," 99. *See also* realism

Balzac, Honoré de, 102; *Le Pére Goriot*, 114